OPENING OPPORTUNITIES FOR DISADVANTAGED LEARNERS

A. Harry Passow, editor

Teachers College Press
Teachers College, Columbia University
New York, New York

Library of Congress Catalog Card Number: 72–178197

Manufactured in the United States of America

CONTENTS

FOREWORD

Since 1962, an Annual Work Conference on Urban Education has been held each summer at Teachers College, Columbia University. The purpose of these conferences, as set forth at the first one, has been "to examine the many dimensions of education in depressed urban areas and to develop sound guiding principles for program planners in city school systems." *Education in Depressed Areas* (Teachers College Press, 1963) contained the thirteen working papers plus two additional papers shared by the participants at the first work conference. The contributors to that volume were asked to address their manuscripts to major theoretical and empirical considerations and, where possible, to confront participants and readers with implications for educational planning. Two other volumes, *Developing Programs for the Educationally Disadvantaged* (Teachers College Press, 1968) and *Reaching the Disadvantaged Learner* (Teachers College Press, 1970), have presented papers and reports from subsequent work conferences, providing guidance for policy and practice while indicating problems and shortcomings in present efforts to provide more relevant and appropriate education in urban settings.

The articles which follow were first presented at the Seventh and Eighth Annual Work Conferences on Urban Education at Teachers College, Columbia University. They include critiques and analyses of existing programs; reviews of research and development activities at various education levels, from preschool through college; descriptions of alternative educational systems; and some predictions of what is ahead in urban education. While it is still difficult to be overly optimistic about the state of education in urban schools, the articles do indicate that opportunities for disadvantaged learners are being opened. In the past decade, we have learned more about effects of the total social milieu on educational opportunity. We have begun to understand the interaction of various factors in creating conditions for educational opportunity. We now realize that the educative process cannot be conceived in terms of the classroom and the school but must be thought of in a broader community setting. Educational objectives which are limited to traditional skills of literacy or computation are far too restricted in terms of present-day needs of America's urban disadvantaged. It is these ideas of expanded opportunities which are discussed in the articles to follow.

I am grateful to the Anti-Defamation League of B'nai Brith for a grant which made possible the preparation of three of the papers included herein.

A. Harry Passow
Teachers College, Columbia University

March 1971

OPENING OPPORTUNITIES FOR DISADVANTAGED LEARNERS

URBAN EDUCATION IN THE 1970's

A. Harry Passow

A. Harry Passow reviews developments of the past decade as the basis for looking ahead at urban education in the 1970's. Despite a very considerable investment of effort and money, "the nation's schools continue to operate in a vortex of segregation, alienation, and declining achievement" and the so-called "urban crisis" continues to become more intense in all of its dimensions. Whatever indicators and criteria are applied, urban schools, and, more specifically the inner-city units of large city systems, are clearly not serving the children of the poor and of racial and ethnic minority groups. A number of reports—notably the Coleman Report, the Report of the U.S. Commission on Civil Rights, the Kerner Commission Report, and the HEW Urban Education Task Force—have examined the state of urban education and set forth recommendations for change.

Calls for "quality education" and for "equality of educational opportunity" by various groups have forced more meaningful definitions of these concepts and analysis of the factors affecting their attainment. Questions of equality and inequality in educational process inputs and outcomes are being examined more intelligently than in the past with research insights being substituted for some of the rhetoric of the past.

Passow discusses what he calls "a rich and growing body of literature on cognitive and affective development differences among various racial, ethnic, and socioeconomic groups; on family structure, life styles, and child rearing patterns as these affect educational processes; on language development and linguistic differences; and on other behavioral characteristics of individuals and groups." This research and experimentation has been the basis for new treatment and program intervention strategies, sometimes explicit, more often implicit. No single theory or model explains performance of disadvantaged children nor is it likely that one will emerge. Yet, hopefully, theoretical models can provide better direction for program planners and decision-makers at all levels.

Program evaluations leave much to be desired. Few compensatory projects have been designed, Passow observes, with the necessary sophistication to produce findings as to what apects of the treatment or program resulted in change, if any. He points to the fact that a major obstacle is that we are diagnosing problems and their causes while prescribing solutions and moving to action because society demands change and improvement. Various strategies and models for urban education reform and change are set forth and discussed.

Since the early 1960's hundreds of programs for the disadvantaged have emerged. These can be characterized and catalogued in a variety of ways—by target population, by nature of treatment, by nature of services, by basic intent of strategy, by focus of diagnosis and prescriptive activities, and by source of funding. Some programs are specific and limited while others are global and comprehensive; most tend to be additive rather than aimed at fundamental reform. Some twenty-one general patterns of strategies and programs are discussed to indicate the range and diversity of activities aimed at some aspect of the urban education problem.

Passow sees almost every aspect of the educational process being modified and adapted to open educational opportunities and improve the quality of urban education. The major recommendation of the HEW Urban Task Force was for legislation "designed to fund the planning, development, and implementation of a comprehensive master plan to meet the specific, long-range broadly conceived educational needs of inner-city areas." (p. 44) It may be that the crisis in urban education may indeed stimulate total rethinking about the educative process—the goals, the means, the resources, the strategies, the relationships. Certainly, education will no longer be considered as consisting of activities in a classroom or even a school as presently conceived. The entire community will become the site for education of future urban populations so that the whole process—programs, personnel, facilities, resources, relationships, and delivery systems—will need to be redesigned.

A. Harry Passow is Professor of Education and Chairman of the Department of Curriculum and Teaching at Teachers College, Columbia University.

URBAN EDUCATION IN THE 1970's*

A. Harry Passow

What is ahead for urban education in the 1970's? What will be the future of the ghetto and the slum in American cities, and how will this affect and be affected by education? In what ways will education for urban populations—particularly the increasing portion designated as the "disadvantaged"—be reshaped, and will changes result in substantial opening of opportunities for individuals from these groups? These are hard questions about which to speculate, especially in the light of events of the past decade.

In the early 1960's, as the civil rights movement and the war on poverty gathered momentum and as the post-Sputnik concern for skilled manpower highlighted the inadequate development of talent among minority groups, Congress was on the threshold of new social legislation and one could be optimistic, despite the apparent complexities of the problems. A summer 1962 conference concerned with education in depressed areas concluded on this note: "The outlook is hopeful in the forces which are being mobilized to dissect and resolve this wasteful, destructive problem of displaced citizens in a rejecting and ignoring homeland" (Passow, 1963, p. 351).

Since then, having spent billions of dollars on compensatory education, initiated thousands of projects (each with its own clever acronym title), completed hundreds of studies of uneven significance and even more disparate quality, entered numerous judicial decisions and rulings, experienced dozens of riots and disorders, and generated whole new agencies and educational institutions, the nation's urban schools continue to operate in a vortex of segregation, alienation, and declining achievement.

Despite a considerable amount of rhetoric and numerous studies and reports, what has been called the "urban crisis" grows more intense in all its dimensions. The Kerner Commission, probing for the causes of civil disorders, pointed to the interactions of a variety of factors—economics, politics, health, welfare, education, justice, security—and warned: "None of us can escape the consequences of the continuing economic and social decay of the central city and the

*This chapter also appears as the opening article in *Urban Education in the 1970's*, edited by A. Harry Passow (New York: Teachers College Press, 1971), pp. 1–45.

closely related problem of rural poverty" (National Advisory Commission on Civil Disorders, 1968, p. 410). The Commission saw a continued movement toward two societies—one essentially white in the suburbs, small cities, and outlying districts, and the other largely nonwhite, located in the central cities—and declared that "we are well on the way to just such a divided nation."

While the concentration of the poor and the nonwhite populations continues in central cities, Downs (1968) asserts that "not one single significant program of any federal, state, or local government is aimed at altering this tendency or is likely to have the unintended effect of doing so" (p. 1333). Preliminary data from the 1970 national census indicate that the greatest population growth has been in suburbia, with the segregation of the poor and minority groups becoming even more intense in central cities. Black and other nonwhite migration to suburbia does appear to be increasing at a rate which seems to be exceeding earlier projections. An analysis by Birch (1970) noted that the consequences of these population shifts "on the inner suburbs and, eventually, on the outer suburbs, may be quite dramatic. Already inner suburb densities are approaching those of central cities, and increasingly this density growth is attributable to the poor and the Blacks" (p. 36).

The American city faces a fourfold dilemma: fewer tax dollars available as middle-income taxpayers move out and property values, business, and commerce decline; more tax dollars needed for essential public services and facilities and for meeting the basic needs of low-income groups; increasing costs of goods and services, resulting in dwindling tax dollars buying less; and increasing dissatisfactions with services provided, as needs, expectations, and living standards increase (National Advisory Commission on Civil Disorders, 1968, p. 399). While it is possible to cite improvements in many aspects of urban life and development, the imperative needs call for far greater investments of our intellectual and financial resources. In the current crisis, education is part of the problem as well as part of the solution. Aside from the role of schools in developing "brainpower" and all that is entailed in those endeavors, education represents the means for creating the commitments and attitudes needed to grapple with the problems as well as the promise of our urban centers.

Urban Education in Trouble

Surveys of large city school systems continue to document the failures of the inner-city schools, confirming that they are, as the situation in Washington, D.C., was characterized, "in deep and probably worsening trouble." The District of Columbia Schools report, noting that the same findings would undoubtedly obtain in most large city systems, observed:

> Applying the usual criteria of scholastic achievement as measured by holding power of the school, by college-going and further education, by post-secondary school employment status, by performance on Armed Forces induction tests, the District schools do not measure up well. Like most school systems, the District has no measures on the extent to which schools are helping students attain other educational objectives, for there are no data on self-concepts, ego-development, values, attitudes, aspirations, citizenship and other "non-academic" but important aspects of personal growth. However, the inability of large numbers of children to reverse the spiral of futility and break out of the poverty-stricken ghettos suggests that the schools are no more successful in attaining these goals than they are in the more traditional objectives. (Passow, 1967, p. 2)

The HEW Urban Education Task Force cited as indicators of the challenge facing urban schools such facts as student unrest on secondary school and college campuses, groups seeking community control of neighborhood schools, teacher strikes, voter rejection of bond issues, court suits, lack of priority for education evidenced by state and local governments, and a sharp increase in alternative plans for schooling. Most important, however, is the conviction of large numbers of minority ethnic and racial groups that "they have been short-changed by their fellow American citizens—the white majority—who largely control the social, economic, political and educational institutions of our nation" (HEW Urban Education Task Force, 1970, p. 5).

After presenting "evidence which indicates the enormity of the failure of the urban public schools to educate the poor in the past and the present," Harvey Pressman (1966) argued that those concerned with educating the urban poor "cannot realistically rely on the public schools to do more than a disappointingly small fraction of the job at hand" (p. 62). And gloomy observers such as Jonathan Kozol (1970) warned: "An ominous cloud hangs over the major cities of America: It is the danger that our ghetto schools, having long ceased to educate children entrusted to their care, will shortly cease to function altogether" (p. 28).

The Kerner Commission pointed to the failure of the ghetto schools to provide the kind and quality of education which would help overcome the effects of discrimination and deprivation as one of the festering sources of resentment and grievance in black communities, contributing to increasing conflict and disruption. Moreover, the "bleak record of public education for ghetto children is growing worse. In the critical skills—verbal and reading ability—Negro students fall farther behind whites with each year of school completed" (National Advisory Commission on Civil Disorders, 1968, p. 425).

Assessing the nation's response to the Kerner Commission Report one year later, the staffs of Urban America, Inc., and the Urban Coalition (1970) concluded that "the indictment of failure passed on education in the slums and ghettos is just as valid and even more familiar" (p. 33). However, the staffs felt that the ferment begun by the so-called Coleman Report (*Equality of Educational Opportunity*, 1966) and the Commission on Civil Rights study (*Racial Isolation in the Public Schools*, 1967) and accelerated by the Kerner Commission Report had "increased to the point where it is rocking—in some instances, even toppling—the educational establishment."

The massive Coleman Report, 737 pages plus a 548-page supplemental appendix, represented the U.S. Commissioner of Education's compliance with the provision of the Civil Rights Act of 1964 for a survey on the "lack of availability of equal educational opportunities for individuals by reason of race, religion, or national origin in public educational institutions at all levels . . ." (U.S. Office of Education, 1966, p. iii). The Coleman Report yielded a rather bleak picture of widespread segregation of both students and staffs, of scholastic attainment of black students substantially below that of white students, and of achievement disparities becoming progressively greater with each year of schooling.

The "companion report" by the U.S. Commission on Civil Rights, *Racial Isolation in the Public Schools*, involved some further analyses of data presented in the Coleman Report, some special studies for the Commission, and assessments of the effectiveness of a number of compensatory education programs in large cities. The Commission reported that in the metropolitan areas where two-thirds of the black and white populations now live, school segregation was even more severe than for the nation as a whole: "In 15 large metropolitan areas in 1960, 79 per cent of the nonwhite public school enrollment was in the central cities, while 68 per cent of the white enrollment was suburban" (U.S. Commission on Civil Rights, 1967, p. 3).

The Commission on Civil Rights rejected "number of years of schooling" as a meaningful measure of educational attainment. Coleman data on verbal ability and reading achievement indicated that "by the time 12th grade is reached, the average white student performs at or slightly below the 12th-grade level, but the average Negro student performs below the 9th-grade level. Thus years of school completed has an entirely different meaning for Negroes and whites" (p. 14). Moreover, while acknowledging that the 1950's had brought some economic progress to the black population in absolute terms (i.e., higher income levels, greater college-going rate, increased entrance to the professions and more skilled jobs), the relative change with respect either to whites or to more affluent blacks was small. Most blacks, the Commission concluded, are still have-not Americans: "The closer the promise of equality seems to come, the further it slips away. In every American city today, most Negroes inhabit a world largely isolated from the affluence and mobility of mainstream America" (p. 15). With some exception for the Oriental population, much the same picture could be detailed for other minority groups—the Puerto Ricans, the Mexican-Americans, the American Indians—and all poor groups, including whites. Socioeconomic differences in scholastic performance have been consistently significant. In 1968, it was estimated that twice as many whites were below the poverty level as nonwhites —17.4 million as compared to 8.0 million (U.S. Bureau of the Census, 1969). Income level alone does not take into account discriminatory practices. Consequently, "poverty" takes on different meanings for different populations; to be poor and a member of a nonwhite group can have different consequences from being poor and white.

Schools and the educational delivery systems are part and parcel of the urban crisis—both a consequence and a contributing factor. The HEW Urban Education Task Force pointed out that the problems facing urban schools are not entirely new and have actually existed for a considerable period of time. What is different now is the surfacing of these problems nationally and the recognition of their complexities and severity, including: "the steadily dwindling financial resources; the persistence of racism; the rising expectations of impoverished urban residents; and the interrelatedness of *all* the problems to poverty" (HEW Urban Education Task Force, 1970, p. 5).

Quality and Equality

The increasingly active and militant demands for schools to upgrade the achievement levels of inner-city pupils and prepare them more adequately for life in an urban technical society have been expressed in the calls for "quality education" and "equality of educational opportunity." Neither phrase has been clearly defined, but discussions have served a useful function in highlighting existing ambiguities and resulting conflicts in educational practice. *Quality education* is defined by some groups as "the kind of education provided the white middle-class suburban child" and measured by standardized tests of achievement and admissions gained to colleges and universities. Others see such a goal as too limited and describe quality in terms of "maximization of human potential," maintaining that the kind of education presently provided even the majority child is totally inadequate and inappropriate.

Conceptions of the meaning of *equality of educational opportunity* are equally varied, ranging from equality with respect to various school and community inputs to equal educational outcomes. The mandate to assess "the lack of equality of educational opportunity" among racial and other minority groups required that Coleman and his staff define equality and inequality. He has observed:

> The original concept could be examined by determining the degree to which all children in a locality had access to the same schools and the same curriculum, free of charge. The existence of diverse secondary curricula appropriate to different futures could be assessed relatively easily. But the very assignment of a child to a specific curriculum implies acceptance of the concept of equality which takes futures as given. And the introduction of the new interpretations, equality as measured by results of schooling and equality defined by racial integration, confounded the issue even further. (Coleman, 1969, p. 18)

In a memorandum to his staff which determined the design of the survey, Coleman set forth five "types of inequality" defined in terms of: (1) differences in *community inputs* to the school (e.g., per-pupil expenditures, facilities, teacher quality, etc.); (2) *racial composition* of the school, on the basis of the 1954 Supreme Court decision that segregated schooling was inherently inferior; (3) differences in *various intangible characteristics* of the school and other factors related to community inputs to the school (e.g., teachers' expectations, level of student interest in learning, teacher morale, etc.); (4) differences in educational outcomes for students with equal backgrounds and abilities (i.e., unequal results given similar inputs); and (5) differences in educational consequences for individuals with unequal backgrounds and abilities (i.e., equal results given different individual inputs). The Coleman study focused primarily on the fourth type of inequality, on the basis that the findings might best be translated into policies which could improve the effects of schooling—that is, determine those elements that are effective for learning (Coleman, 1969, pp. 18–19).

Among the controversial findings from the Coleman survey was one stressing the significance of the social context, in contrast to school services and resources, in determining achievement. The survey reported that differences in majority black and majority white school characteristics which had been considered significant—e.g., per-pupil expenditures, physical facilities, teacher preparation expressed as years of training, etc.—were not nearly as large as had been expected.

In fact, regional differences were much greater than differences between majority black and majority white schools. Because the school service variables explained only a small part of the pupil performance variances, Coleman concluded:

> Taking all these results together, one implication stands above all: That schools bring little influence to bear upon a child's achievement that is independent of his background and general social context; and that this very lack of independent effect means that the inequalities imposed upon children by their home, neighborhood, and peer environment are carried along to become the inequalities with which they confront adult life at the end of school. For equality of educational opportunity through schools must imply a strong effect of schools that is independent of the child's social environment, and that strong independent effect is not present in American schools. (U.S. Office of Education, 1966, p. 325)

The Coleman study did find differences among ethnic groups in their apparent sensitivity to the effect of some school factors, such as the quality of teachers and the availability of enriched programs. Generally, school factors appeared to be strongest for black schools in the South. In addition, a pupil-attitude factor which appeared to have a particularly strong relationship to achievement—stronger than all school factors—was the extent to which the individual pupil felt he had some control over his own destiny. While minority pupils tended to have far less conviction than whites that they could affect their own environments and futures, when they did have such a belief, their achievement was higher than that of whites who lacked it. Furthermore, for black students, the environmental-control variable appeared to be related to the proportion of whites in the school—the blacks in schools with a higher proportion of whites had a greater sense of control. What the origins of strong feelings of fate or environmental control are is quite unclear—whether the conviction is a cause or consequence, and how the school influences it.

The Coleman Report raised many questions for policy makers and program planners. For example, Guthrie has pointed out that since the publication of the Coleman Report,

> the belief has become increasingly pervasive that patterns of academic performance are immutably molded by social and economic conditions outside the school. If incorrect, and if allowed to persist unexamined and unchallenged, this belief could have wildly disabling consequences. It is not at all difficult to foresee how it could become self-fulfilling; administrators and teachers believing that their school and schoolroom actions make no difference might begin to behave accordingly. Conversely, if the assertion is correct but allowed to pass unheeded, the prospect of pouring even more billions of local, State, and Federal dollars down an ineffective rathole labeled "schools" is equally unsettling. (Guthrie, 1970, p. 25)

A reanalysis of the Coleman data by the Office of Education, tempering somewhat the flat assertion in the original report, has suggested that the influence of the school on achievement cannot be separated from that of the student's social background and vice versa: "In conclusion, it may be stated that the schools are indeed important. It is equally clear, however, that their influence is bound up with that of the student's social background" (U.S. Office of Education, 1970, p. xiv). On the basis of a review of nineteen studies, Guthrie (1970) reported that he was "impressed with the amount and consistency of evidence supporting the effectiveness of school services in influencing the academic performance of pupils" (p. 46). While expressing the hope that the time would come when it would be possible to determine which school service components have greatest impact and in what proportion, he nevertheless concluded, "there can be little doubt that schools do make a difference."

The Commission on Civil Rights interprets the Coleman findings as supporting school desegregation—both racial and socioeconomic—since they show a strong relationship between family economic and educational background and the child's achievement and attitudes: "Regardless of his own family background, an individual student achieves better in schools where most of his fellows are from advantaged backgrounds than in schools where most of his fellow students are from disadvantaged backgrounds" (U.S. Commission on Civil Rights, 1967, p. 203). However, some analysts accept the Coleman findings on the extent of segregation and academic retardation but question the causal relationships between segregation and retardation.

The then U.S. Commissioner of Education James E. Allen viewed "opportunities for learning" as encompassing much more than school buildings and specially trained, qualified teachers:

> "Opportunity for learning" means, to me, a community where fathers are employed and where children can learn through their fathers about the dignity of man. It means a community where the population of rats does not exceed the population of children, and where children can learn the values of a healthy society. It means a community of clean streets, of playgrounds, of uncrowded homes, where children can learn the value of living in a free country and the importance of keeping it free. And finally, it means a community free of fear, where children can learn to love life and their fellow man. (Allen, 1969, p. 81)

The policy implications of the Coleman and Commission on Civil Rights reports point to the effect of the interaction of family, neighborhood, and school on the academic and affective growth of children and the need to improve these environments. But the questions concerning equality and inequality in educational process inputs and outcomes are now being more intelligently examined.

Research and Development

Poor scholastic performance of disadvantaged populations has been so amply documented that few challenge the accuracy of such reports. The past decade has witnessed an outpouring of research and experimentation and the initiation of a vast array of programs and projects. Most of this research, Gordon (1970a) notes, can be divided into two broad classifications—studies of the performance characteristics of disadvantaged groups, and descriptions and superficial assessments of programs presumably designed to provide for the disadvantaged. Much of the research tends to focus on "deficits" of disadvantaged populations, or "differences" between them and more advantaged populations, with such deviations "used to account for the observed dysfunctions in educational performance among members" of the former group (Gordon, 1970a, pp. 1–2).

There is a rich and growing body of literature on cognitive and affective development differences among various racial, ethnic, and socioeconomic groups; on family structure, life styles, and child-rearing patterns as these affect educational processes; on language development and linguistic differences; and on other behavioral characteristics of individuals and groups. Whereas many studies focus on social and cultural factors affecting educational achievement, there is increasing attention to the health of the disadvantaged child as a factor contributing to scholastic failure. Reviewing a variety of studies, H. G. Birch (1967) concluded that "a serious consideration of available health information leaves little doubt that children who are economically and socially disadvantaged and in an ethnic group exposed to discrimination, are exposed to massively excessive risks for maldevelopment" (pp. 30–31). Social class and the socialization processes have been widely studied with respect to behavioral correlates, especially of young children (Zigler, 1970). A variety of studies have focused on the effects of segregation and desegregation on minority group performance (Weinberg, 1970). Research has also shed some light on the effects of organizational and grouping practices, teacher expectations, curricular options, instructional materials, neighborhood setting, and similar factors on achievement of disadvantaged students.

Some research and experimentation has stimulated new treatment programs and intervention strategies—for example, the mushrooming of preschool and early childhood programs—in which the relation of program to theory and research has been somewhat tenuous. Gordon has observed that:

treatments tended to emerge from special biases or dominant models in the field, with either the fact of intervention or the magnitude of interventions receiving more attention than the specific nature or quality of interventions. This tendency may account for the fact that much of the research referable to treatment and programs is characterized by superficial description of program or practice and general evaluation of impact. (Gordon, 1970a, p. 8)

Most program proposals, almost by necessity, contain some implicit, if not explicit, indication of the hypotheses or theoretical bases underlying the proposed intervention or treatment. For example, if experiential differentials and deprivations in infancy are perceived as accounting for minority group youngsters entering classrooms ill-prepared to cope with the demands of the school, then early childhood programs should be designed to compensate for such deficiencies. If language development impedes transition from concrete to abstract modes of thought, then programs should provide linguistic experiences which will nurture such growth. If child-rearing patterns and maternal teaching styles affect cognitive growth, then parent education programs should develop different skills and behaviors. But even research which does provide the kinds of analyses which contribute to building theory and understanding behavior often reports equivocal findings which open debate rather than provide guidelines for the practitioner. Consequently, there are several "theories," or explanations, or models set forth to explain inferior scholastic attainment and intellectual functioning of poor children—none of which is completely satisfying. Nor is it likely that *a* theory will emerge, although it is hoped that theoretical models will provide better guidance for program planners and decision makers. The cafeteria-eclectic approach which presently prevails leaves much to be desired.

Some of the ambiguities plaguing the program planner and practitioner are illustrated by an analysis of early childhood research by the Baratzes. In a review of "the interventionist literature with particular emphasis on the role of social pathology in interpreting the behavior of the ghetto mother," Baratz and Baratz (1970) conclude that much of the research represents "the predominant ethnocentric view of the Negro community by social science [which] produces a distorted image of the life patterns of that community" (p. 30). They contend that intervention programs which aim at changing the child's home environment, altering the child-rearing patterns of black families, and improving the child's language and cognitive skills "are, at best, unrealistic in terms of current linguistic and anthropological data and, at worst, ethnocentric and racist." The Baratzes reject interpretations of research which support either the social pathology or genetic inferiority models and set forth instead a cultural difference model based on the assumption "that the behavior of Negroes is not pathological but can be explained within a coherent, distinct, American-Negro culture which represents a synthesis of African culture in contact with American European culture from the time of slavery to the present day" (p. 45). Thus, they argue that intervention programs are needed but that these should deal with the materials and processes of the school rather than with the children being served in such programs. They also point out that interpretations of research are often subject to the socio-political convictions of the researcher.

Gordon (1970b) has observed that "in contrast to the rather well-designed and detailed research into the characteristics of disadvantaged groups, the description and evaluation of educational programs and practices for these children have generally been superficial" (p. 8). He suggests that such research can be grouped into four categories: (1) studies of large-scale projects such as Head Start, Title I of the Elementary and Secondary Education Act (ESEA), and Upward Bound; (2) studies of specific projects and services in schools, such as curricular innovations, remedial reading programs, and tutoring groups; (3) studies of administrative and organizational changes, such as desegregation, flexible grouping, pupil-teacher ratios; and (4) studies of attitudinal and skill changes in school personnel, focusing on teacher expectations and role models (pp. 8–12).

Evaluation of various kinds of programs, from preschool through college, compensatory and remedial, has not indicated uniform or considerable "success." On the basis of its comprehensive review of compensatory programs, the U.S. Commission on Civil Rights (1967) concluded that such efforts had not produced lasting effects in improving student achievement, probably "because they have attempted to solve problems that stem, in large part, from racial and social class isolation in schools which themselves are isolated by race and social class" (p. 205).

A study of Title I ESEA programs in thirty-nine cities at the end of the second year indicated that concentrated remedial help could raise the level of pupil achievement but that such programs were extremely costly in terms of teachers, space, specialists, and materials—resources which tend to be particularly scarce in the central cities. The costs per student were often almost prohibitive (U.S. Office of Education, 1968). The Fourth Annual Report of the National Advisory Council on the Education of Disadvantaged Children observed:

> It has long been clear that the mere addition of people, equipment, and special services does not by itself constitute compensatory education; success in making up for the educational deprivation which stems from poverty requires a strategy for blending these resources in an integrated program that strikes at both roots and consequences of disadvantage. The

details of this strategy, however, have by no means been clear. (National Advisory Council on the Education of Disadvantaged Children, 1969, p. 3)

All Title I ESEA proposals require an evaluation component; yet, in the view of the Advisory Council, the combination of insufficient experience with compensatory programs and the wide variation in the kind and quality of evaluative data collected has prevented any overall nationwide evaluation of such efforts and made it difficult to identify elements which contribute to any successes. The Advisory Council observes rather ambiguously: "What is clear is that among the thousands of different programs and approaches labeled as compensatory education, some efforts are paying off and others are not" (p. 3). The Council's report included details concerning 21 programs (screened from 1,000 of the more than 20,000 ESEA programs) which the American Institute for Research (AIR) had found to have produced "significant achievement gains in language and numerical skills." The successful programs were compared by the AIR with unsuccessful ones to ascertain what distinguished the two. The AIR identified two requirements: to establish clear goals and specific academic objectives and to concentrate attention and resources on these objectives.

A different kind of assessment of Title I ESEA was prepared by the Washington Research Project and the NAACP, two organizations whose concern is with the rights of the poor. Their report focused on how Title I ESEA is administered, the money spent, and the consequences for poor children. They did not attempt to study the educational value or impact of specific programs of compensatory education. The review found that in school systems across the country, Title I:

—has not reached eligible children in many instances;
—has not been concentrated on those most in need, so that there is reasonable promise of success;
—has purchased hardware at the expense of instructional programs;
—has not been used to meet the most serious educational needs of school children; and
—has not been used in a manner that involves parents and communities in carrying out Title I projects. (Washington Research Project and NAACP Legal Defense and Educational Fund, Inc., 1969, pp. i–ii)

This review of the administration of Title I funds at the local, state, and federal levels raised serious questions about whether the pessimistic evaluations of compensatory programs were due to mismanagement and misapplication of funds rather than to the nature of the programs themselves. The report reinforced observations made earlier that compensatory education had not failed—rather, it had never really been tried as yet.

Even studies of nationwide programs such as Head Start have been rather restricted in scope or results. The Westinghouse–Ohio University National Evaluation of Head Start (Cicirelli et al., 1969) reported that: summer programs alone produced neither cognitive nor affective gains which persisted through the early elementary grades; year-round programs had marginal effects on cognitive development which persisted in the early grades but had little influence on affective development; programs appeared to be most effective in mainly black centers of scattered cities; Head Start children seemed still to be below norms on achievement and psycholinguistic tests but approached norms on readiness tests; and parents approved and participated in Head Start activities (Smith and Bissell, 1970, pp. 51–52).

The Westinghouse–Ohio University evaluation was not the first study of Head Start, but the timing and the nature of the release of the findings resulted in a widespread impression that such programs were of very limited value and such efforts were generally futile. Smith and Bissell (1970) reanalyzed some of the data and indicated that findings were far more positive. However, the Westinghouse–Ohio University researchers rejected most of the reanalysis and defended their own procedures and findings (Cicirelli, Evans, and Schiller, 1970).

Evaluative and research studies of such nationwide projects as Upward Bound (intended to help underachieving low-income students prepare for higher education) and the Neighborhood Youth Corps (intended to prevent youth from dropping out of high school and to assist those who do) have provided insights into the nature of the populations served as well as some of the consequences of the program activities (Office of Economic Opportunity, 1970; U.S. Department of Labor, 1970). In general, project evaluations consist of pre- and post-treatment testing, usually of reading, mathematics, and general intelligence. Few efforts have been made to assess affective growth. Few compensatory projects have been designed with sufficient sophistication to provide insights about what aspects of the treatment or program produced a change, if any. The vast majority of evaluation efforts have simply attempted to determine whether there has been an "improvement" in basic skills and intellectual ability after a period of time. Most school-based projects are primarily interested in program development—providing what it is hoped will be more appropriate experiences—and not in research to determine what inputs account for change. The fact that it is in the area of preschool and early childhood education that the best designed research is taking place may be due, in part, to the fact that such programs function outside the ongoing school framework and controlled experimentation is feasible.

Discussing the complexities in assessing compensatory education,

McDill, McDill, and Sprehe (1969) point to three general problems: (1) difficulties in determining program effectiveness because the critical variables are either unknown or cannot be measured adequately—for example, are changes due to treatment or maturational effects or both, and to what extent? (2) difficulties in separating the effects of interaction of various socializing agencies, since learning takes place in a variety of settings in and out of the school; and (3) technical difficulties due to the shortage of rigorous measuring instruments even when the criterion and predictor variables are known. Along with these general problems, compensatory program evaluators face such recurring problems as: pressures for immediate as opposed to long-term, carefully planned evaluation; vagueness of criteria and the setting of objectives which are politically sound but operationally impossible; alteration of treatment before adequate evaluation; scarcity of such resources as money and skills, which mitigates against replicability; and difficulties in initiating and maintaining treatment and non-treatment populations (McDill, McDill, and Sprehe, 1969, pp. 7–13). Underlying all of these is the fact that "in compensatory programs, we are still trying to diagnose the problems and their causes while simultaneously applying remedies. Society insists on finding a workable solution even before we understand the mechanism by which the solution works" (p. 66).

Strategies and Models for Urban Programs

A continuum of six basic strategies for reforming urban schools has been set forth by Fantini and Young (1970): (1) *compensatory education*—attempts to overcome shortcomings in learners and to raise their achievement levels; (2) *desegregation*—designed to improve educational achievement and human relationships through a better racial and socioeconomic mix; (3) *model subsystems*—development of experimental units to improve staff training, curriculum, methodologies, and school-community relations and have such units serve as demonstration and dissemination bases for the rest of the system; (4) *parallel systems*—establishment of private schools, often operated by non-profit companies, which presumably would be free of public school bureaucracies and be more responsive to ghetto educational needs; (5) *total system reform*—aimed at providing new leadership and structural changes and increasing efficiency of the existing system; and (6) *new systems development*—conceptualization of an educational system for a new community or a newly designated area, independent of the rest of the system (pp. 13–20).

A somewhat different analysis of alternative models for transforming the institutional structure of inner-city schools has been set forth by Janowitz (1969): (1) the *mental health model* assumes that slum family resources are so limited and the values so different from those of the school that the school itself must intervene to insure that the needs and services required by each child are made available, becoming responsible for the total social space of the child even if this means becoming a residential institution; (2) the *early education model* assumes that if the school is unable to become a residential institution then it can at least intervene during the critical years of infancy and early childhood; (3) the *specialization model* involves the introduction on a piecemeal basis of new techniques, programs, specialists, and administrative procedures—each of which may appear valid—so that the teaching process is broken up into more and more specialized roles performed by specialists and resource personnel; and (4) the *aggregation model* stresses the need for maintaining and strengthening the teacher's role as central manager of a classroom which is essentially a social system, and involving other personnel and resources as needed (pp. 35–60). Each of these models has different implications for such aspects as "classroom management; the use of the new media; teacher education and career lines; authority and decentralization; pupil composition; school-community relations" (p. 60).

Miller and Roby (1969) believe that the various strategies for improving educational performance of poor and minority group children can be subsumed into five categories: (1) *changing the student and his family*—aiming at "'compensatory socialization' in which the deficiencies of the educational environment provided by low-income family life would be made up later"; (2) *changing the school*—aiming at bringing about changes in the teachers, administrators, curriculum, materials, services, etc., rather than focusing on the deficiencies of the learners; (3) *increasing resources and changing their distribution*—increasing the level of funding and also altering the integration; (4) *changing the student composition*—providing for greater socioeconomic and racial balance; and (5) *changing control of the schools*—decentralizing administrative arrangements for schools and providing for greater community control and involvement in decision-making. Miller and Roby contend that our limited understanding of how to bring about changes at the micro-level of education (teaching of reading or teachers' attitudes, for example) results in efforts at alteration at the macro-level: "Hopefully, when we have accomplished change at the macro-level—change in the organizational context, changes across urban-suburban lines in student composition, changes in the distribution of educational and economic resources, and the development of alternatives to education for economic self-improvement—we will be able to function at the micro-level" (p. 29). However, it can be argued that many programs are simply projects at a micro-level with no basic conceptual model involved.

A U. S. Office of Education publication titled *Profiles in Quality Education* (1968), which is typical of program description literature, contains information on "150 outstanding Title I projects . . . designated by State Title I Coordinators as worth emulating." No data are provided to support the introductory statement that each of these programs "provides valuable assistance to the low-income children it serves" (p. iv). The projects have a variety of foci and include examples of "work-study programs, health services, remedial programs, English-as-a-second-language activities, college preparatory classes, teacher training, . . . programs that concentrate on early childhood education, the dropout, the vocational student." The various projects encompass all aspects of the educational process, with most restricted to some facet of the problem and only a few designed to be comprehensive.

Most such programs, particularly those at the secondary school level, are aimed at upgrading academic achievement in standard subjects. A comprehensive study of student objectives of compensatory programs for adolescents by Harrison (1969) involved gleaning stated or implied goals from 432 documents. Harrison identified 689 distinct, operational objectives which could be cataloged by behavior (cognitive or affective) and by referent (specific school subject, general academic achievement, social development, or career development) and found that primary emphasis (75 per cent of all objectives) was on academic achievement, with little or no concern for social or career development. This stress on academic achievement at the expense of the development of other behaviors was essentially the same as for the more advantaged youth and represented a rigidity in school structure that requires "all students to adapt to the system of expectations, rather than changing the system and its expectations to adapt to the contemporaneous need of the students" (p. 13).

To reverse present trends and to move toward the provision of full equality of educational opportunity, the Kerner Commission recommended the pursuit of four "basic strategies," and provided suggested programs for each:

1. *Increasing efforts to eliminate de facto segregation*—increased financial aid to school systems seeking to eliminate segregation within the system itself or in cooperation with neighboring systems; establishment of major educational magnet schools to draw racially and socioeconomically mixed populations and provide special curricula and specialized educational programs; establishment of

supplemental education centers to provide racially integrated educational experiences for white and black students.

2. *Improving the quality of teaching in ghetto schools*—year-round education for disadvantaged students; establishment of early childhood programs designed to overcome effects of disadvantaged environment, involving parents and the home as well as the child; provision of extra incentives for highly qualified teachers in ghetto schools; reduction in maximum class size; curricular recognition of the history, culture, and contribution of minority groups; individualized instruction; intensive concentration on basic verbal skills; and development of new patterns of education for students who do not fit into traditional forms.
3. *Improving community-school relations*—elimination of obstacles to community participation in the educational process; opening schools for a variety of community service functions; use of local residents as teacher aides and tutors; increasing the accountability of schools to the community.
4. *Expanding opportunities for higher and vocational education*—expansion of Upward Bound Program; removal of financial barriers to higher education; emphasis on part-time cooperative education and work-study programs through use of released time; elimination of barrier to full participation in vocational education programs; increased training to meet the critical need for more workers in professional, semi-professional, and technical fields. (National Advisory Commission on Civil Disorders, 1968, pp. 438–455)

The Kerner Commission suggests no priorities for these four "strategies." It could well be that education in the ghetto is in such a state that any of the suggested programs has some potential payoff. In fact, examples of each of these suggested programs can already be found in operation in some urban school systems. In a critique of operating compensatory programs, Gordon and Wilkerson observed:

> For all their variety of means, the programs have generally suffered from one fundamental difficulty—they are based on sentiment rather than fact. . . . The great majority of the programs are simply an attempt to "do something" about these problems. Their stated aims are usually couched in unarguable generalities. . . . The urge to do something has been so compelling that many of the programs have been designed without grounding in any systematic study of ways and means. (Gordon and Wilkerson, 1966, p. 158)

What is needed, Gordon and Wilkerson argue, is not simply a filling in of gaps so that disadvantaged children can be reached by existing practices, but rather an inquiry of a different kind: "What kind of educational experience is most appropriate to what these children need and to what our society is becoming?"

Urban Programs and Projects

The many urban education programs and projects can be characterized and cataloged in a variety of ways—by *target population* (preschool, elementary, higher education, adult, teacher, etc.); by *nature of treatment* (therapeutic, compensatory, remedial, enrichment, etc.); by *nature of services* (instructional, counseling, community development, health, etc.); by *focus of activities* (in school, family, community, industry, non-school agency, etc.); by *basic intent of strategy* (reform of system, redistribution of power, integration, reallocation of resources, etc.); by *focus of diagnosis and prescriptive activities* (learners, professionals, the educational system, society, etc.); and by *source of funding* (Office of Education, Office of Economic Opportunity, state, non-governmental, foundation, etc.). These catalog sets are not mutually exclusive, of course. Some efforts are limited and restricted (e.g., a Head Start class for 15 four-year-olds), while others are more global and comprehensive (e.g., an "open" high school or a model school subsystem). Most school programs tend to be additive rather than designed for fundamental reform. Some proposals deal with personnel changes, some with organization changes, and still others with affecting the relationships among various components of the educational enterprise—formal and informal, school and non-school.

Any listing of urban projects would be quite lengthy, as indicated by publications issued by the U.S. Office of Education and the ERIC Information Retrieval Center on the Disadvantaged at Teachers College, Columbia University. The general patterns of strategies and programs which follow provide an overview of the range and diversity of activities attacking some aspect of the urban education problem.

Infant Education and Intervention in Family Life

Efforts have been aimed at changing child-rearing styles through educational programs designed to alter interactions and relationships between parent (usually the mother) and child. Research has indicated that parent-child and familial interactions strongly influence intellectual and affective development of children. Programs of parental involvement range from helping the mother become an active teacher of her child, to altering the mother's language usage, to improving family stability. (See, for instance, Grotberg, 1969.)

Early Childhood Education

There has been an explosion in the number and variety of early childhood and preschool programs in the past half-dozen years, particularly with the inception of the Head Start programs. Preschool programs may consist of traditional nursery school activities or provide much more structured activities, such as a therapeutic curriculum in language, math, science, reading skills, and concept formation; an academically-oriented program in verbal skills and language training; a Montessori program; a diagnostically-based language curriculum; and a cultural enrichment program. By far the largest number of pupils are found under the Head Start canopy in programs which are intended primarily for the children of the poor. The nature and quality of Head Start and other early childhood programs vary considerably. Various public and private non-profit agencies are eligible for assistance in organizing Head Start activities for children beginning at age three.

Reading, Language, and Basic Skills Development

Because of the poor academic achievement of disadvantaged pupils, reading, language, and basic skills development programs have been the focus of many compensatory efforts. It has been estimated that in the early years of Title I ESEA, more than half of all the projects dealt directly with the improvement of reading through new curricula, methodologies, materials, personnel deployment, and "systems." New basal reader series and supplementary materials have been produced, including self-instructional programmed materials, reading aids, and mechanical devices. New technologies include language laboratories, talking typewriters, individualized teaching machine devices, and computer-aided instruction. Professionals and non-professionals have been used in a variety of teaching and tutoring situations. Various publishing and industrial groups have prepared new "systems" for teaching reading. Yet, reading disability and scholastic failure have become more, rather than less intense, and the incidence of functional illiteracy among urban disadvantaged populations grows.

Bilingual Education

For large numbers of pupils, English is not the mother tongue. Spanish is the first language of thousands of Puerto Rican, Chicano, and Cuban pupils in the East and Southwest. More than a half-million American Indian children speak one of the tribal languages. There is a large concentration of French-speaking children in Louisiana. In addition, there are many children in urban settings whose speech patterns and dialect are considered "non-standard" English. Past practice has been to provide instruction in English, to make every effort to teach the child to speak and read English, and to eliminate non-standard speech. Increasingly, programs have been developed to provide bilingual instruction based on the recognition that a reading program for disadvantaged children must take into consideration the children's spoken language. The question of non-standard dialects and their affect on communication is being reassessed. Many disadvantaged children communicate quite effectively in non-standard English, and efforts are being made to capitalize on this base rather than ignore its existence.

Curriculum Relevance

Responding to the argument that much of what is taught in today's schools is irrelevant for the student, efforts are being made to provide more meaningful and appropriate instruction. *Relevance* is a term which is still being defined and has many meanings. Generally, the indictment of irrelevant programs is based on the premise that "they have no relationship to the world the student knows outside school or to the roles he plays now or will later play in his adult life" (Fantini and Young, 1970, p. 50). Curriculum development efforts have involved students and parents, as well as professionals, in designing new courses and emphasizing different content within traditional subjects. For example, a high school English course may add black writers to the literature studied or a new course may be added dealing with black writers and their contributions to various kinds of literature. Or, the standard Problems of American Democracy course may be completely redesigned to grapple with the immediate manifestations of these problems—poverty, pollution, population, war, economic politics—rather than the more general aspects.

The concern with developing a black identity has resulted in reassessment of content in existing language, literature, and social studies courses as well as the development of new courses with titles such as: The Black Experience in America, African Studies, World Cultures, and Afro-American Art. There are similar curriculum development projects dealing with the heritage and condition of other racial and ethnic groups—the American Indian, the Mexican-American, and the Puerto Rican, for example. Sometimes such programs are designed for the minority group students alone, and, in other instances, the experiences are meant for all students. Some projects deal with the problems of cultural renewal and change, with questions of political, economic, and social power-redistribution, or with "cities in crisis."

The traditional educational goals, largely middle-class, majority-group oriented, have come under scrutiny as to their appropriateness and value. In the course of this reappraisal, all aspects of the instructional program are being reexamined for relevance. As a consequence, curriculum changes range from minor tinkering (e.g., substituting one novel for another) to major reconstruction (e.g., student-faculty operated schools). Such changes have meant different responses to the traditional curriculum questions, with students and parents participating more actively in program development. Building more relevant curricula is one of the reasons advanced for greater community control of schools.

Compensatory and Remedial Programs

Compensatory programs may involve a variety of provisions aimed at presumed defects or deficiencies in disadvantaged learners. Such programs may include remedial instruction designed to overcome poor performance, especially in the basic skills areas. Remedial programs range from supplying an itinerant specialist to comprehensive clinics and diagnostic-treatment centers. Techniques include more individualized treatment, extra instruction, special teaching materials, reading laboratories, language arts centers, and provisions for one-to-one or small group teaching. Such programs may focus on pupil attitudes and motivation as well as learning-how-to-learn skills. Compensatory programs may also include cultural enrichment opportunities, experiences designed to broaden the horizons of disadvantaged pupils. The New York City Higher Horizons Program, at one time, represented the prototype for many such programs, combining a variety of remedial and guidance services in school with a cultural enrichment program of museum, theater, concert, and field trips. Many preschool programs are designed to compensate for various experiential deprivations presumably suffered by disadvantaged learners.

Guidance and Counseling Programs

Guidance, psychological, and therapeutic services are provided in some projects for the disadvantaged. In some instances, the absence of personnel has been due to shortage of funds, and Title I ESEA has made it possible to add counselors. In other cases, intensive group therapy programs and concentrated clinical services for pupils with academic, social, and psychological difficulties have been provided. Social workers have been involved to bridge the gap between school and family, focusing on social rather than academic problems of learners. Parent involvement in counseling and therapy programs has been arranged.

Tutoring Programs

Individual and small-group tutoring programs with professionals, paraprofessionals, and volunteers based in school and non-school agencies (churches, settlement houses, and storefronts) have spread rapidly. The tutors range from middle and secondary school youth to college students to adults of all ages. In one of the earliest such programs, Mobilization for Youth's Homework Helper Program, high school youth were trained and paid to work with fifth- and sixth-graders, with the two-pronged goal of enhancing the self-image and academic achievement of the tutors as well as the scholastic attainment of the younger children. Tutoring programs may involve nothing more than reading to a disadvantaged child or may consist of a highly structured program in mathematics and language development. The tutoring programs often aim at providing a positive adult model and a one-to-one relationship to indicate that someone really cares enough about the disadvantaged child to devote time to him.

Testing and Measurement

Tests and testing procedures have been criticized for cultural and social class bias. The validity of standardized tests of intelligence and achievement used with minority group students has been seriously questioned. Minority group students are seen as handicapped by language difficulties in test-taking, by lack of experience with testing requirements, by inadequate understanding of the purposes of the tests, and by low motivation to succeed on such tests. Moreover, the testing procedures are viewed as a means by which black and other minority group students are "tracked" into inferior educational programs and effectively blocked from pursuing further education. Test scores and grading procedures affect both pupil and teacher expectations, often contributing to early dropout. Some efforts are being made to develop more effective diagnostic and prognostic procedures, to develop evaluation procedures which serve instructional rather than selection functions, to train staff members to interpret and use testing results more meaningfully, and to sensitize staff to the consequences of misuse of testing and grading procedures. The demands for accountability from various community groups have resulted in the search for evaluation and assessment procedures to determine the effectiveness of teachers and teaching and organizational arrangements.

School Organization

Programs in urban schools have involved a variety of organizational changes. These include such changes as extended school days, extended school years, and year-round school programs. Team teaching, non-graded programs, open classrooms, flexible schedules, and similar arrangements—first introduced in many instances in suburban schools—are being adapted to the urban school. Because tracking has become controversial, alternate flexible grouping arrangements are being made.

Instructional Materials and Resources

Concern with urban education has resulted in a flood of new materials, some of which are part of the general flow of multi-media instructional resources, but focused rather specifically on the real or perceived needs of central-city students. Publishers have broadened their production from white, middle-class oriented textbooks to a variety of resources, print and non-print. Varieties of multi-sensory materials have been developed, often packaged in kits, some of which are visual, some audio, often providing for "sound, touch, move, and make." There are units consisting of individualized self-instructional materials. Talking typewriters, teaching machines, and computer-aided devices have been adopted for use with disadvantaged children and adults. The production of materials for teaching reading has been especially prolific. (See Cohen, 1970.)

In addition, there has been a sharp increase in the availability of materials appropriate for disadvantaged and minority group children. Insofar as materials are concerned, appropriate may mean: (1) materials which are multi-racial, multi-ethnic, multi-social class—through the text or content, the illustrations, or both; (2) materials which are urban-oriented rather than suburban or rural, depicting life in the urban setting with its problems as well as its resources; (3) materials which present the historical and cultural contributions of various minority groups to the American story, attempting to correct the distortions of the past; (4) materials which try to develop an understanding of the pluralistic world which surrounds children and youth today, often through literary and social science materials; (5) materials which draw on the art, music, dance, drama, and cultural heritage of various groups and societies; and (6) materials which use the contemporary story of emerging nations to help pupils understand the story of America's emergence and quandaries (Passow, 1966b, p. 246). The output has been especially marked recently in the area of Black Studies materials, with resources for the study of other minority groups just beginning to emerge.

Vocational Education and Dropout Prevention and Return Programs

Since the dropout rate for the disadvantaged minority students is several times that of more advantaged white students, a number of school programs are aimed at preventing school dropouts or facilitating their return to an educational program of some kind. Numerous studies have been made and psychological, sociological, and economic as well as educational and other explanations have been advanced to explain early school withdrawal (Tannenbaum, 1966; Dentler and Warshauer, 1965). From time to time, various programs have been mounted to reduce school dropouts, ranging from advertising ("Stay in School") to comprehensive school programs restricted to students who have already left. Numerous work-study programs giving equal importance to work skills and basic skills have been organized. Usually some kind of vocational or technical education is central to such programs, with opportunities for work exploration, on-the-job training, and subsidized work experience. Some school systems have provided short-term work experience for unemployed dropouts and combined this with in-school instruction. In some instances, afternoon and evening schools are provided for high school students, who then combine work with study. Arrangements are made with industry and business for cooperative programs for vocational training. Other dropout prevention programs include: compensatory and remedial instruction; counseling and guidance; reduction of social distance between home and school through social and community workers; vocational preparation out of school; training and re-training by private industry (Tannenbaum, 1966, pp. 21–30).

The Vocational Education Act of 1963 and the amendments enacted in 1968 aimed at making vocational preparation an integral part of the educational process at the elementary and secondary school level, preparing all students for the world of work. The act emphasized development of programs "for equipping in-school youth, persons who have completed or left high school, and the disadvantaged and handicapped with job attitudes, knowledge, and skills. It was specifically oriented toward reaching those in the ghetto—the potential dropouts" (Venn, 1969, p. 4). The law authorized special programs for the disadvantaged and earmarked funds for this purpose. Vocational-technical programs are viewed as one of the vehicles for making curricula more relevant for urban youth. Thus far, the possibilities of new vocational programs have not been realized, but school systems are beginning to develop and test more meaningful approaches.

Finally, some of the alternative programs now operating are specifically designed to provide an option to the school experience from which the youth has withdrawn. Sometimes these options are designed to re-motivate the student to return to the regular secondary school; in other instances, the intent is to bypass the high school and provide other avenues to further education and training.

Urban School Staffing

Clearly, if any school factor makes a difference in academic performance, it appears to be the professional staff. Although far from conclusive, research data supports the notion that teacher attitudes and expectations are related to performance of the inner-city pupil. Surveys of literature on the disadvantaged often result in

a bleak montage of teachers and administrators who are blinded by their middle-class orientation; prejudiced toward all pupils from lower-class, racial, and ethnic minority groups; culturally shocked and either immobilized or punitive in the classroom; and groping for safer berths where success, in terms of academic achievement, is more likely. (Passow, 1966b, p. 104)

The NDEA National Institute for Advanced Study in Teaching Disadvantaged Youth "came to consider teacher education more and more as a whole, to attribute failures and inadequacies of education for the disadvantaged to defects in the education of teachers" (Smith, Cohen and Pearl, 1969, p. ix). Much the same criticisms are being made with respect to all professional personnel—administrators, counselors, and supervisors.

Numerous programs are aimed at recruitment, training, induction, retention, and continuing education of professional personnel at both the pre-service and in-service levels. Such programs have meant the beginning of major reform at teacher-preparing colleges and universities as well as in in-service programs in schools. It has meant new and different relationships between schools and institutions of higher education, as well as the entry of publishing and other commercial firms into the teacher training field. With the concern for developing differentiated staffing patterns has come a need for diverse modes of recruitment and preparation.

At the pre-service level, program revisions include: (1) early and continuous contact with children and adults in disadvantaged areas in a variety of school and non-school activities, ranging from tutoring, to supervising after-school activities, to observations, to intensive clinical teaching experience; (2) involvement of behavioral and social scientists, such as cultural anthropologists, political scientists, and social psychologists, who apply research and theory from their disciplines to the needs and problems of disadvantaged areas; (3) intensive involvement of successful school practitioners—teachers, principals, counselors, and others—in working with students and faculties in planning, supervising, and evaluating experiences; (4) provisions for working with non-school agencies and for becoming actively involved in ongoing anti-poverty and community development activities in order to understand better the problems and resources of ghetto life; (5) modification of college courses to make them more relevant to acquisition of insights, skills, and techniques needed for teaching in depressed areas; (6) provisions for examining and analyzing, and planning local program adaptations to known situations, current research, and experimentation being reported by other centers; and (7) provision of means for continuing relationships with college staff and resources beyond the initial induction period (Passow, 1966a, pp. 108–109).

Based on the twin assumptions that professional preparation has not provided the attitudes, insights, skills, and knowledge needed to work effectively in today's schools and that continuing education is a necessity for all professionals, numerous programs have been initiated involving schools, colleges, and other agencies. These programs may focus on: changing attitudes and increasing self-understanding; remedying deficiencies in earlier preparation; developing insights into new skills, techniques, and resources; preparing to specialize in some new area of education or service; preparing to work in a school with a changing population, such as one that is newly desegregated; developing skills needed for working in a differentiated staffing pattern; acquiring skills for working with paraprofessionals and volunteers; preparing to fill new instructional and non-instructional roles.

The high correlation of academic achievement with race, ethnic group, and social class has led to a number of studies attempting to understand and explain the causal factors. In recent years, a number of studies have focused on teacher expectations—the so-called Pygmalion effect and the "self-fulfilling prophecy"—and several studies have attempted to test the notion that the pupil's performance can be altered by changing teacher expectations (Rosenthal and Jacobson, 1968). Others have attempted to analyze the factors that are critical in determining teacher expectations (Rist, 1970). Although the phenomenon is not clearly understood, a number of projects at colleges and in schools are aimed at sensitizing teachers to the consequences of their attitudes and expectations on pupil performance.

Various programs often involve new staffing patterns. Sometimes funds are used simply to improve the pupil-teacher ratio in an effort to provide more one-to-one contacts between pupil and adult. In other instances, various "specialists" are added to the staff to work in the classroom, in a clinic or ancillary service, in the community, or in the home. New positions are being created, requiring different kinds of entry skills and preparation.

Auxiliary School Personnel

The recruitment, training, and use of auxiliary personnel—paraprofessionals, volunteers, and aides—have mushroomed in the past half-dozen years, particularly as federal funds have been made available through Office of Education, Office of Economic Opportunity, and Manpower Development and Training sources. Bowman and Klopf (1970) have cited four basic differences between present programs involving auxiliary personnel and earlier ones employing "teacher aides." These include: (1) emphasis on the right of all persons to essential human services coupled with the paucity of existing services; (2) shift from new entry-level jobs leading nowhere to the idea of a career ladder, with training available at each step; (3) emphasis on involvement of low-income workers as participants in the problem-solving process rather than as recipients of directions from professionals; and (4) a systematic approach involving role development, training, and institutionalization of such personnel as a stable and integral part of public service. Paraprofessionals and aides tend to come primarily from low-income minority groups. They help provide individualized attention to students, improve communication between disadvantaged students and middle-class teachers, and provide concerned-adult models. They extend their own understandings into child development and community involvement while, at the same time, they are gainfully employed on a career ladder. Thus, the use of low-income auxiliaries in disadvantaged areas could potentially yield positive pupil outcomes and have other socially valuable outcomes as well.

Low-income parents also may participate as volunteers in programs in which parent involvement is an integral element. Volunteers, on the other hand, often come from middle-income groups and provide somewhat different kinds of services to students and schools.

Post-Secondary and Higher Education

The percentage of minority group youth who go on for post-secondary and higher education has been but a small fraction of that of whites who pursue further education. As late as 1965, Coleman found that racial segregation in higher education was about as complete as it was in elementary and secondary schools. While college attendance is dependent on availability of financial resources, for nonwhites inadequate preparation for college and poor counseling have been equally important factors affecting attendance. Programs concerned with increasing participation of disadvantaged youth in higher education take a variety of forms. These include:

1. *High School Programs and Programs for Secondary School Youth*—Several large-city school systems have initiated programs which attempt to identify disadvantaged ninth-graders living in ghettos who appear to have potential for college work, and to arrange conditions which will improve their academic attainment and increase their motivation for higher education. Usually such programs involve intensive instruction in the basic subjects, smaller classes, additional counseling, cultural enrichment, and assurance of admission to local colleges and universities upon successful completion of the secondary school program. In some instances, financial assistance is included during high school and college years. Often colleges and universities cooperate in various aspects of such programs. The federally sponsored Upward Bound Program is aimed at secondary school youth, providing an intensive residential summer educational and counseling program at a college or boarding school plus an academic-year follow-up, de-

signed to motivate disadvantaged youth to prepare for college. Other programs involve college students tutoring high school students or university facilities being made available to secondary school youth in order to help orient them toward higher education.

2. *Admission to College*—It has been argued that college admissions procedures are stacked against disadvantaged youth, with the specific criticisms directed toward tests that are culturally unfair and alleged racism among admissions officers. A variety of procedures are being used by colleges and universities in efforts to increase the numbers of minority group youth who are admitted to college. These range from "open admissions" policies, to differential requirements, to substitution of nominations for test performance, to admission by lottery. While studies of prediction of success and selection of admittees abound, their inapplicability to minority group youth has resulted in testing alternative procedures to those conventionally employed.

3. *Transition to College for Disadvantaged Youth*—A variety of programs have been initiated to increase the probability of success for disadvantaged youth once admitted to college. These include: "summer-preadmissions programs, reduced course load, remedial courses, tutorial assistance, guidance and counselling, extended length of time to meet graduation requirements, and financial assistance" (Kendrick and Thomas, 1970, p. 167). Most of these programs are compensatory or remedial in nature, although there have been substantive curricular changes as well. Kendrick and Thomas (1970) concluded from the limited research available "that existing compensatory programs and practices have made little impact in eradicating the problems of disadvantaged college students, nor have the majority of colleges accepted this area as their role." However, as admissions procedures increase the number of disadvantaged youth who enter college with preparation that differs from the traditional patterns and standards, colleges and universities are forced to develop new and different instructional programs. Gordon (1969) has suggested that the immediate problem "is a radical distribution of labor in higher education, with the stronger institutions increasing their share of the responsibility for educating weaker students, and the smaller and weaker institutions serving more of the stronger students" (p. 10).

4. *Extension of Post-Secondary Opportunities*—Although colleges and universities have expanded their enrollments substantially, perhaps even greater growth has occurred in other areas of post-secondary education. Two-year community colleges in a number of states have made such institutions readily available to high school graduates on a full- or part-time basis, offering an opportunity to demonstrate one's capability for higher education. Technical and vocational schools at the post-secondary level are being developed in

some areas specifically to increase opportunities for disadvantaged youth.

5. *Open Enrollment*—Finally, most programs represent efforts to increase recruitment and attendance in the more or less traditional forms of higher education. Efforts at major reforms in higher education are as sparse as those at lower levels. There are those who see the increase in college-going of disadvantaged youth as a stimulus toward bringing about reform not only in programs of higher education but in the relationships between colleges and their surrounding communities.

Community School and Community Development

In an effort to extend education into the family and the neighborhood and to make the school an integral part of the area, some systems have attempted to develop "community schools." The concept is not a new one, although its genesis seems to have been in rural areas. The community school as defined by the New Haven Board of Education should function as: (1) an education center where children and adults have opportunities for study and learning; (2) a neighborhood center where persons of all ages may take part in a variety of recreational, cultural, leisure-time, and civic activities; (3) a center for community services where individuals and families may obtain health, counseling, legal aid, employment, and other services; and (4) a center for neighborhood and community life, a catalyst for uniting citizens in the study and solution of significant neighborhood problems (Twyman, 1970, p. 205). Variations of the community school concept are being developed and implemented in large cities, and the possibilities for reconceiving the role of the school in ghetto areas loom large. In some instances, issues of community control and accountability are being worked through in community school settings.

A more comprehensive approach is exemplified by Chicago's Woodlawn Development Project whose purpose is:

> To improve the quality of education in two inner-city *de facto* segregated schools through: a change in the social structure of the institutions which will include parents and children as participants; a comprehensive in-service education program and a substantial increase in human and material sources; all concerned and implemented within a collaboration structure involving the Chicago Public Schools, the Woodlawn Organization and the University of Chicago. (Congreve, 1969, p. 178)

The staff views this collaborative arrangement as having considerable potential for bringing about local reform in urban education. The tripartite arrangement enables each of the participating agencies to bring its strengths to bear on school and community development problems.

Desegregation and Integration

In its 1954 decision in *Brown v. Board of Education of Topeka*, the Supreme Court ruled that segregation compelled or expressly permitted by law was unconstitutional. The implementation of the ruling that *de jure* segregation was to be eliminated "with all deliberate speed" proved to be very slow, and it was not until the fall of 1970 that real desegregation began to take place. At that time, 543 school districts in the eleven Southern states were scheduled to take desegregation action, most under court ordered and approved plans. Whether implementation of these plans will in fact place the majority of Southern black children in desegregated school systems is yet to be determined. An equally, if not more, complex aspect of the problem is that of *de facto* segregation and racial isolation, both of which are most concentrated in the central cities. Residential segregation is particularly severe in the inner cities.

A variety of plans have been initiated to correct racial and ethnic imbalance (defined differently by state and locality, but generally meaning a high concentration of black, Puerto Rican, Chicano, or other minority group children and an absence or small proportion of white pupils). These plans for desegregation have been used in both *de jure* and *de facto* situations. They include:

1. Altering attendance areas or rezoning school catchment areas.
2. Open enrollment or voluntary transfer from schools with heavy concentrations of non-whites to schools where space is available.
3. Voluntary exchange, wherein white and non-white children are transferred on a one-to-one exchange.
4. Free-choice transfer, under which parents may enroll their children in any school where space is available.
5. Princeton Plan, or school pairing, under which school units and/or grade levels are combined to create larger attendance pools and achieve better racial balance.
6. Educational parks, which provide for a concentration of educational facilities serving school populations from a large attendance area or even the total pupil population of the system.
7. Supplementary centers and magnet schools representing specialized educational programs, which draw from all or many parts of the city.
8. Metropolitanization, involving voluntary cooperation and exchanges between inner-city and suburban schools or actual merger and consolidation of educational functions in a metropolitan area.
9. Site selection, wherein new schools are strategically placed with respect to housing patterns to provide for better balance.

Variations and combinations of these techniques for desegregating schools have been used with some success in smaller cities and suburbs, but racial isolation has, if anything, increased in inner cities, primarily because of socioeconomic and racial residential patterns. In many instances, it becomes necessary to transport children to achieve racial balance. Despite the fact that millions of school children are and have been transported by school buses each day, particularly in the rural and sparsely populated regions, a nationwide Gallup Poll taken in March 1970 disclosed that 86 per cent of those questioned opposed busing as a means of achieving school desegregation. The poll disclosed only small regional differences and very little difference between those who called themselves "liberal" and "conservative" (*The New York Times*, 1970a). Other studies indicate that resistance to desegregation is not limited to the white majority.

The educational consequences of desegregation have been mixed and inconclusive. Often a resegregation has taken place within the classrooms of desegregated schools through grouping and tracking procedures. Commenting on the "inconclusive evidence of a relation between ethnic integration and achievement," St. John observed:

> One good reason that there has been no adequate research to date on the effect of integration is that there have been no adequate real-life tests—no large-scale, long-run instances of top-quality schooling in segregated minority-group schools. Until our society tries such experiments, researchers will not be able to evaluate them. (St. John, 1970, p. 129)

The fact that substantial desegregation, let alone significant integration, has not been achieved in central cities, combined with growing ethnocentrism and nationalism, has resulted in proposals by some groups for separate school districts and systems (Day, 1969; Jencks, 1968). The Congress of Racial Equality (CORE), for instance, has pressed for legislation for a separate school district in New York's Harlem and in Mobile County, Alabama. In Mobile, CORE supported a plan for two districts—one predominantly white and the other predominantly black. Testifying before a Senate committee, a Mexican-American educator commented: "Integration of poor black with poor brown or even a few poor whites is not benefiting any group of this nation" (*The New York Times*, 1970b). The disenchantment of some minority groups with desegregation efforts is found in the drive for separatism and for community control.

Decentralization and Community Control

Large-scale educational bureaucracies, unresponsive to community needs, have been blamed in part for inferior education. The prime argument for decentralization is the belief that the educational program will be improved qualitatively to the extent that the school, parents, and community are brought into a more meaningful relationship with one another, with the community having a greater voice in educational decision-making. As a strategy for improving education for poor and minority groups, the rationale for decentralization and community control varies, from the conviction that parental involvement in determination of curriculum and selection of staff is essential, to the abandonment of faith in desegregation and compensatory programs, to the belief that separatism and isolation are the means by which power will be attained and quality provided.

A number of large city school systems have initiated various plans for decentralizing, some simply for administrative purposes and others to facilitate community involvement in control and decision-making. The domain within which control is exercised varies, but the key areas involve: hiring and firing of school personnel, determination of broad curriculum goals, selection of instructional materials, determination of nature and site of physical facilities, allocation of funds, and setting conditions of accountability. The issues concerning decentralization and community control are just being raised, sometimes through confrontation and struggle for power and sometimes through political processes. Gittell (1969) argues that community control of education is only one aspect of a more general movement: "Underlying the effort toward this goal is the desire to guarantee a meaningful redistribution of power in our cities. . . . The ends that they seek and the thrust of their actions may benefit the political system and the larger community as a whole" (p. 375).

Alternative Schools and School Systems

Arguing that urban schools have become instruments for blocking rather than facilitating economic mobility and for intensifying class distinctions, Clark (1969) has proposed six competitive systems. These include: state-supported regional schools, federal regional schools, college- and university-related open schools, industrial demonstration schools, labor union sponsored schools, and defense department schools.

> With strong, efficient, and demonstrably excellent parallel systems of public schools, organized and operated on a quasi-private level, and with quality control and professional accountability maintained and determined by Federal and State educational standards and supervision, it would be possible to bring back into public education a vitality and dynamism which are now clearly missing. . . . American educational health may be made possible through educational competition. (Clark, 1969, p. 186)

A number of proposals have been made for keeping the educational market free and installing competing systems. These involve providing parents with vouchers, enabling them to choose the kind and quality of education their children will receive. With the voucher, the parent could shop for better schooling, and competition would be fostered between public and private schools where the grants could be used. Some proposals call for differential grants, with large amounts going to poor children (Carr and Hayward, 1970). At least one version of "education by chit" is being tested in the field.

Another kind of competition has been proposed by Levin (1970), who advocates that decentralized, community controlled public schools should be provided lump-sum allocations which they could use to purchase appropriate services from industries, non-profit groups, universities, or any other source. The community school board, in conjunction with the professional staff, would work out relevant educational strategies and then solicit competitive bids from a variety of sources.

Still another proposal is that of Coleman (1967), who advocates publication of standardized test scores as a basis for interscholastic and intramural competition. Coleman suggests an open school with subject-specific choices—the student would spend part of the day at his home base but could take other courses outside the school, with payment of teachers based on results. He sees the focus on scholastic achievement increments as providing an incentive structure, as part of a competitive games approach.

The past few years have seen the establishment of alternative schools of another kind, schools specifically designed for youth who have dropped out of public high school: Chicago's CAM Academy and Harlem Preparatory School in New York. Both are private schools, supported by grants from foundations and industrial concerns, enrolling primarily dropouts and providing "a second chance" to prepare for a college career. Harlem Prep is ungraded, with a flexible, highly individualized curriculum which emphasizes pride in self, solidarity with one's peers, and commitment to success. Both schools have a deep commitment to the potential of the students despite their past records, and both believe that the school and its program must adjust to the student, not vice versa. In addition to Harlem Prep, a number of "street academies" have been established in storefronts in ghetto areas of New York, staffed by one or two teachers, a number of volunteers, and a street worker. The stress of the street academy is more on re-motivating students than on trying to attain specific academic objectives.

Even within the public school system, major reforms are being undertaken. Philadelphia's Parkway Project, or "School without Walls,"

Portland's Adams High School, and Newton, Massachusetts' Murray Road School represent totally flexible, informal, student-teacher planned programs, in which traditional subjects and requirements are dropped. These and other proposals represent a belief that urban schools are failing and can only be reformed by being faced with competition which they must meet if they are to survive.

Finally, arrangements are beginning to be made with business and industrial groups for what are known as "performance contracts." In Texarkana, Arkansas, for instance, the Dorsett Educational System was contracted to provide instruction in reading, math, and study skills for a minimum of 200 students from low-income families in grades 7 through 12. Presumably, Dorsett is paid on the basis of grade-level increases in reading and math, and the payments are subject to reduction if achievement gains are not made. Several other school systems are just initiating performance contracts with publishers of curriculum materials and producers of reading "systems," with payment usually based on achievement increment gains, although some contracts are for flat fees. In July 1970, the Office of Economic Opportunity granted $6.5 million dollars to six companies in 18 school districts to test the performance contract concept during the school year.

Federally Supported or Assisted Programs

Since the 1960's, a number of programs have been launched as a consequence of federal legislation. These range from the Pilot School Breakfast Program, in which preference is given to schools in low-income areas, to Title I of the Elementary and Secondary Education Act of 1965 in which "the Congress hereby declares it to be the policy of the United States to provide financial assistance . . . to local educational agencies serving areas with concentrations of children from low-income families. . . ." While not specifically aimed at urban schools, clearly the target populations of a good many federally-assisted programs are the populations of the central cities. Any consideration of urban programs must include federal programs, even though many of them operate outside the public school system. The Vocational Education Act of 1963, the Civil Rights Act of 1964, the Economic Opportunity Act of 1964, the Elementary and Secondary Education Act of 1965, and the Higher Education Act of 1965 are the major pieces of legislation. Each authorizes a variety of programs affecting urban education. Among the most significant are:

1. *Job Corps*—a program of basic education, skill training, and useful work experience for young men and women, ages 16 through 21. Job Corpsmen reside at training centers located at

national parks or forests or in or near urban areas. The centers are operated by public or private agencies, school and non-school.

2. *Neighborhood Youth Corps*—a program open to students from low-income families in grades 9 through 12, or in lower grades but of high school age. The three components are an in-school program of part-time work and on-the-job training; an out-of-school program of work experience and on-the-job training to encourage return of dropouts; and a summer work program.
3. *College Work-Study Programs and College Work-Study Grants*—a program which provides part-time employment and grants to students from low-income families. The Work-Study Program is designed to stimulate worthwhile work experience either on-campus, for the institution, or off-campus, with agencies involved in the Community Action Programs and other Economic Opportunity Act–supported activities.
4. *Upward Bound Program*—a pre-college program designed to motivate disadvantaged high school students to reach their academic potential and apply for college. A residential program, Upward Bound combines a six-to-eight week intensive educational and counseling experience in the summer with an academic year follow-up to consolidate summer gains.
5. *National Teacher Corps*—a program for teacher interns with supplementary teaching assignments and for work in home-school relations in areas where there are concentrations of disadvantaged students. The Teacher Corps teams are supervised by experienced teachers and continue their academic study at nearby institutions of higher education.
6. *Full Utilization of Educational Talent*—a program designed to encourage high school or college dropouts to reenter educational programs and to encourage able disadvantaged youth to enter and remain in college.
7. *New Careers Program*—a program for adults 22 years of age or older which provides work-training employment primarily in the fields of health, education, welfare, community development, and public safety. The program is designed to provide entry-level employment opportunities, improve prospects for advancement and continued employment, and create new career jobs in public service.
8. *Manpower Development and Training Programs*—various programs provide occupational training for unemployed and under-employed persons, including disadvantaged youth be-

tween 16 and 22 years of age. Basic education and occupational training, either in vocational schools or on-the-job, are provided, together with training allowances.

9. *Aid for Public School Desegregation*—a program designed to aid schools and school personnel in dealing with problems which arise from school desegregation by providing technical assistance, grants to school boards, and grants to teacher training institutions.

In addition to these education-specific programs, urban schools are affected by a variety of other federally-legislated activities dealing with health, community development, urban renewal, recreation, cultural facilities, transportation, and regional planning and rehabilitation.

Allocation of Educational Resources

It has been argued that "greater pupil needs, higher costs, municipal overburdens, and smaller resources to draw upon mean that the present system of financing schools places a city at a severe disadvantage relative to its suburbs" (Levin, 1970, p. 68). Moreover, as Cohen (1969) has pointed out, "there is no simple identity between dollars allocated among school districts and the equality of resources delivered to their students" (p. 123). Beyond the overall discrepancies in educational costs and available financial resources between city and suburb, it has been demonstrated that there are often sharp differences in the allocation of available resources to schools within a large city system, with schools in ghetto areas being shortchanged. In recent years, through court litigation and pressures for new legislation, there have been attempts to correct such inequalities on intrastate and intradistrict bases (Silard and White, 1970). In some cases, the action has been brought to insure that categorical aid is spent where the act intended it to be—e.g., ESEA Title I funds on disadvantaged populations—and that it be added to, not substituted for, general aid. A very different approach has been tried by some school districts which have established projects with substantial additional funding in depressed area schools. New York City's More Effective Schools Program is an example of a program in which a limited number of ghetto schools receive compensatory funds and resources, enabling a drastic increase in staffing and an improved pupil-teacher ratio.

In the Decade Ahead

Almost every aspect of the educational process is being modified and adapted through projects, programs, and "innovations," each aimed at improving the quality of urban education and opening educational opportunities. Most of these efforts represent changes intended to increase the effectiveness in attaining the traditional educational objectives of public schools—at a minimum, the attainment of basic literacy. Few projects aim at fundamental reappraisal of urban education, propose major reforms, or suggest new goals or delivery systems. Some programs could result in significant reform, but, generally, schools have been responsive to immediate crises, to the availability of funds, or to pressure from groups.

The Washington, D.C., schools may represent a prototype for what America's central-city schools have become. Since 1947, the pupil population of the District of Columbia Schools has changed from 46 per cent black to more than 93 per cent black. Scholastic achievement on standardized tests has fallen far below national means. A 1965 bulletin titled *Innovation in Education* included almost one hundred separate programs and projects, each aimed at improving instruction. As funds became available through ESEA and other federal legislation in 1965 and the years following, the number of programs and projects increased further. Since 1967, the District Board of Education has been presented with four major documents, each containing recommendations, proposals, and plans for changing the school system or a part thereof. The so-called Passow Report (*Toward Creating a Model Urban School System*) resulted from a large-scale comprehensive study of all aspects of education and schooling in the District and contained scores of recommendations regarding the total school system and its functioning in the nation's capital community (Passow, 1967). The *Anacostia Community School Project* proposal emerged from a month-long summer workshop and consisted of no fewer than twenty-five programs, ranging from total community participation in school decision-making to updating equipment in the ten schools in the Anacostia area, which contains about half of Washington's public housing (Anacostia Community Planning Council, 1968). The Fort Lincoln New Town proposal represented a case study in the development of an educational program for a completely new town to be built on a 335-acre site in northeast Washington (Fantini and Young, 1970). Finally, the so-called Clark Report (*A Possible Reality*) proposed focusing on the improvement of reading achievement through a Reading Mobilization Year, with a Reading Mobilization Team in each school and differentiated staffing and salaries based on teacher accountability (Clark, 1970). These four reports contain a wide range of proposals for confronting the educational crisis in the schools in the nation's capital.

The HEW Urban Education Task Force (1970) urged "that the problem of urban areas should be considered as the major priority of the Administration's domestic program in the 1970's. Within this priority, education—broadly conceived and with new constituencies involved—should become a first consideration" (p. 6). Recognizing a need for long-term comprehensive planning, the Task Force concluded that the urgency of the situation required proposals for immediate action as well. The report called for:

1. Money—significantly increased levels of funding far exceeding current appropriations and authorizations from the federal government.
2. Concept of urban education—expansion of the concept of the educative process to deal with the whole individual, "his health, his emotional well-being, his intellectual capacities, his future employment, his self-realization. . . ."
3. Master plan for urban education—development and implementation of master plans for education, each tailored to particular urban areas, dealing with causes and symptoms "within a framework of over-all urban problem-solving rather than education per se. . . ."
4. Institutional changes—deliberate sequencing of plans and steps leading to institutional changes, fundamental changes within the system itself.
5. Community determination—active participation in decision-making by community residents and students, including priorities for using funds, designing curriculum and program components, and employing and evaluating personnel.
6. Performance standards—clear statements of specific knowledges, attitudes, and skills students are expected to demonstrate and which can serve for personnel and school accountability.
7. Assessment—continuous assessment of all aspects of the educational program with regular feedback enabling immediate adjustments and modifications.
8. Racial and ethnic integration—integration should be a major element for all planning; separatism, local control, and a demand for a recognized identity are viewed as alternate channels to the ultimate goal of integration. (HEW Urban Education Task Force, 1970, pp. 6–7)

The major recommendation of the HEW Urban Education Task Force was for development of an Urban Education Act, "designed to fund the planning, development, and implementation of a comprehensive master plan to meet the specific, long-range broadly conceived educational needs of inner-city areas" (p. 44). If enacted, such legislation would only set in motion preparation of guidelines and criteria for potential grantees to develop their own local master plans. No model master plan for urban education is provided, but rather the report calls attention to the need for comprehensive consideration of education in the urban setting instead of the present fragmented project approach.

What the crisis in urban education has done is to stimulate a total rethinking of the educative process—the goals, the means, the resources, the strategies, the relationships. The "tinkering approach" having proved less than adequate, the "do something, try harder" stance having failed, we may now be ready for more comprehensive reforms based on sound research, theory, and experience. We have already been reminded that education is taking place in settings other than the classroom and that much learning consists of behavior to which the school has given little consideration. As one looks at the dilemmas the nation faces, one must ask to what extent adequate and appropriate education is being provided any group or set of individuals, advantaged or disadvantaged, majority or minority. Reform in education, like reform in society, of which the schools are a part, does not come easily, for there are constant struggles for power and prerogatives among individuals, groups, and agencies.

A master plan for urban education will necessarily deal with urban schooling in the broadest sense, with many components of the educative process at many different levels. There are not nor can there be panaceas in urban education; no single program or system or approach will resolve the problems of urban schools. Poverty, discrimination, racism, and other problems of our society have very deep roots. Full and equal employment opportunities, sound housing, political power, safety and security, adequate health and sanitation, and cultural satisfactions are part and parcel of the solution to urban educational problems, just as they are, in part, a consequence of good education. The school represents one component in the educative process in the community. It cannot remain isolated from the other components nor can it do the educative job alone. In some instances, the school may serve as the catalyst for other agencies to plan jointly their educative efforts; in other instances, the school has prime leadership responsibility.

There is no clear blueprint for urban education in the decade ahead, but a considerable reservoir of experiences and research, which, when combined with serious intent and fundamental commitment to build a better society for all, can provide the basis for more effective nurturing of human potential. What is needed now is a reassessment of the total educational process—programs, personnel, facilities, resources, relationships, and delivery systems—within the family, the community, and the school to ascertain where and how effective learning opportunities can be arranged. The entire community, not the locations we now call "school," must become the site for education of future urban populations.

A decade ago, educators were pressed by events to drop their defensive stances and face up to their responsibilities for educating all

Americans. Even then, the directions were well marked and the goals quite clear. Comprehensive planning for education, rather than fragmented proposals for schooling, is needed if America's public schools are to fulfill their responsibility to help build a richer urban society in which all individuals can "do their thing."

References

Allen, J. E., Jr. "Educational Problems of the Handicapped in the Inner City." Background Paper for the Conference on Problems of Education of Children in the Inner City. Washington, D.C.: President's Committee on Mental Retardation, 1969.

Anacostia Community Planning Council. *The Anacostia Community School Project.* Washington, D.C.: The Council, 1968.

Baratz, S. S. and J. C. Baratz. "Early Childhood Intervention: The Social Science Base of Institutional Racism," *Harvard Educational Review,* 40 (February 1970), 29–50.

Birch, D. L. *The Economic Future of City and Suburbs.* New York: Committee for Economic Development, 1970.

Birch, H. G. "Health and the Education of Socially Disadvantaged Children." Paper presented at the Conference on Bio-Social Factors in the Development and Learning of Disadvantaged Children. Syracuse University, 1967.

Bowman, G. W. and G. J. Klopf. "Auxiliary Personnel in Educational Programs for the Disadvantaged," in *Reaching the Disadvantaged Learner,* ed. A. H. Passow. New York: Teachers College Press, 1970. Pp. 337–360.

California State Department of Education. *Evaluation of ESEA Title I Projects of California Schools: Summary of Annual Report, 1966–67.* Sacramento: The Department, 1968.

Carr, R. A. and G. G. Hayward. "Education by Chit: An Examination of Voucher Proposals," *Education and Urban Society,* 2 (February 1970), 179–191.

Cicirelli, V. G. et al. *The Impact of Head Start: An Evaluation of the Effects of Head Start on Children's Cognitive and Affective Development.* Washington, D.C.: Office of Economic Opportunity, June 12, 1969.

Cicirelli, V. G., J. W. Evans, and J. S. Schiller. "The Impact of Head Start: A Reply to the Report Analysis," *Harvard Educational Review,* 40 (Winter 1970), 105–129.

Clark, K. B. "Alternative Public School Systems," in *Equal Educational Opportunity,* ed. Harvard Educational Review Editorial Board. Cambridge: Harvard University Press, 1969. Pp. 173–186.

——— and Staff of MARC. *A Possible Reality.* New York: Metropolitan Applied Research Center, Inc., 1970.

Cohen, D. "School Resources and Racial Equality," *Education and Urban Society,* 1 (February 1969), 121–138.

Cohen, S. Alan. *Teach Them All to Read: Theory, Methods, and Materials for Teaching the Disadvantaged.* New York: Random House, 1970.

Coleman, J. S. "Toward Open Schools," *Public Interest,* 9 (Fall 1967), 20–27.

———. "The Concept of Equality of Educational Opportunity," in *Equal Educational Opportunity,* ed. Harvard Educational Review Editorial Board. Cambridge: Harvard University Press, 1969. Pp. 9–24.

Congreve, W. J. "Collaborating for Urban Education in Chicago: The Woodlawn Development Project," *Education and Urban Society,* 1 (February 1969), 177–191.

Day, N. A. "The Case for All-Black Schools," in *Equal Educational Opportunity,* ed. Harvard Educational Review Editorial Board. Cambridge: Harvard University Press, 1969. Pp. 205–212.

Dentler, R. A. and M. E. Warshauer. *Big City Dropouts and Illiterates.* New York: Frederick A. Praeger, 1968.

Downs, A. "Alternative Futures for the American Ghetto." *Daedalus,* 97 (Fall 1968), 1331–1378.

Fantini, M. D. and M. A. Young. *Designing Education for Tomorrow's Cities.* New York: Holt, Rinehart & Winston, Inc., 1970.

Gittell, M. "Community Control of Education," in *The Politics of Urban Education,* ed. M. Gittell and A. G. Hevesi. New York: Frederick A. Praeger, 1969.

Gordon, E. W. "Higher Education and the Challenge of Universal Access to Post-Secondary Education," *IRCD Bulletin,* 5 (Winter 1969), 1–2, 10–11.

———. "Education for Socially Disadvantaged Children: Introduction," *Review of Educational Research,* 40 (February 1970), 1–12. (a)

———. *Significant Trends in the Education of the Disadvantaged.* New York: Eric-IRCD, Teachers College, Columbia University, 1970. (b)

——— and D. A. Wilkerson. *Compensatory Education for the Disadvantaged.* New York: College Entrance Examination Board, 1966.

Grotberg, E. (ed.). *Critical Issues in Research Related to Disadvantaged Children.* Princeton, N.J.: Educational Testing Service, 1969.

Guthrie, J. W. "A Survey of School Effectiveness Studies," in *Do Teachers Make a Difference?* Washington, D.C.: U.S. Government Printing Office, 1970. Pp. 25–54.

Harrison, F. I. *Objectives and Instruments for Evaluation of Compensatory Programs.* Washington, D.C.: Bureau of Research, U.S. Office of Education, 1969.

HEW Urban Education Task Force. *Urban School Crisis: The Problem and Solutions.* Washington, D.C.: National School Public Relations Association, 1970.

Horn, T. D. (ed.). *Reading for the Disadvantaged: Problems of Linguistically Different Learners.* New York: Harcourt, Brace & World, Inc., 1970.

Janowitz, M. *Institution Building in Urban Education.* New York: Russell Sage Foundation, 1969.

Jencks, C. "Private Schools for Black Children," *New York Times Magazine,* November 3, 1968, pp. 30, 132–139.

Kendrick, S. A. and C. L. Thomas. "Transition from School to College," *Review of Educational Research,* 40 (February 1970), 151–179.

Kozol, J. "In Roxbury, Way Out of a Fortress," *Think,* 36 (January-February 1970), 28–32.

Levin, H. M. "Why Ghetto Schools Fail," *Saturday Review,* 53 (March 21, 1970), 68–69, 81–82.

McDill, E. L., M. S. McDill, and J. T. Sprehe. *Strategies for Success in Compensatory Education.* Baltimore: The Johns Hopkins Press, 1969.

Miller, S. M. and P. Roby. "Educational Strategies and the Disadvantaged: An Overview." Paper presented at Seventh Annual Work Conference on Urban Education at Teachers College, Columbia University, June 1969.

National Advisory Commission on Civil Disorders. *Report of the National Advisory Commission on Civil Disorders.* New York: Bantam Books, 1968.

National Advisory Council on the Education of Disadvantaged Children. *Title I ESEA—A Review and a Forward Look.* Washington, D.C.: U.S. Government Printing Office, 1969.

New York Times. "Busing Is Opposed by 8-to-1 Margin, Gallop Poll Finds," April 5, 1970, p. 49. (a)

New York Times. "3-Man Panel Scores Education for Spanish-Speaking Students," August 19, 1970, p. 24. (b)

Office of Economic Opportunity. *Findings and Conclusions: An Evaluation of Upward Bound.* Washington, D.C.: Office of Economic Opportunity, 1970.

Passow, A. H. (ed.). *Education in Depressed Areas.* New York: Teachers College Press, 1963.

———. "Diminishing Teacher Prejudice," in *The Inner-City Classroom: Teacher Behaviors,* ed. R. D. Strom. Columbus: Charles E. Merrill, 1966. Pp. 93–109. (a)

———. Statement for the Ad Hoc Subcommittee on De Facto Segregation of the Committee on Education and Labor of the U.S. House of Representatives. Washington, D.C.: U.S. Government Printing Office, 1966. Pp. 244–247. (b)

———. "The Gifted and the Disadvantaged," in *Notes and Working Papers Concerning the Administration of Title III Programs.* Washington, D.C.: U.S. Government Printing Office, 1967. Pp. 215–229. (a)

———. *Toward Creating a Model Urban School System: A Study of The Washington, D.C. Schools.* New York: Teachers College, Columbia University, 1967. (b)

Pressman, H. "The Failure of the Public Schools," *Urban Education,* 2, 2 (1966), 61–81.

Rist, R. C. "Student Social Class and Teacher Expectations: The Self-fulfilling Prophecy in Ghetto Education," *Harvard Educational Review,* 40 (August 1970), 411–451.

Rosenthal, R. and L. Jacobson. *Pygmalion in the Classroom.* New York: Holt, Rinehart & Winston, 1968.

St. John, N. H. "Desegregation and Minority Group Performance," *Review of Educational Research,* 40 (February 1970), 111–134.

Silard, J. and S. White. "Intrastate Inequalities in Public Education: The Case for Judicial Relief under the Equal Protection Clause," *Wisconsin Law Review,* 7 (1970), 7–34.

Smith, B. O., S. B. Cohen, and A. Pearl. *Teachers for the Real World.* Washington, D.C.: American Association of Colleges for Teacher Education, 1969.

Smith, M. S. and J. S. Bissell. "Report Analysis: The Impact of Head Start," *Harvard Educational Review,* 40 (Winter 1970), 51–105.

Tannenbaum, A. J. *Dropout or Diploma.* New York: Teachers College Press, 1966.

Twyman, C. R. "The Community School in New Haven," in *Reaching the Disadvantaged Learner,* ed. A. H. Passow. New York: Teachers College Press, 1970. Pp. 203–218.

Urban America, Inc., and the Urban Coalition. *One Year Later: An Assessment of the Nation's Respone to the Crisis Described by the National Advisory Commission on Civil Disorders.* Washington, D.C.: Urban America, Inc. and the Urban Coalition, 1969.

U.S. Bureau of the Census. *Current Population Reports.* Washington, D.C.: The Bureau, August 1969.

U.S. Commission on Civil Rights. *Racial Isolation in the Public Schools.* Washington, D.C.: U.S. Government Printing Office, 1967.

U.S. Department of Labor. *The Neighborhood Youth Corps: A Review of Research.* Manpower Research Monograph No. 13. Washington, D.C.: U.S. Government Printing Office, 1970.

U.S. Office of Education. *Equality of Educational Opportunity.* Washington, D.C.: U.S. Government Printing Office, 1966.

———. *Title I Year II.* Washington, D.C.: U.S. Government Printing Office, 1968.

———. *Profiles in Equality Education.* Washington, D.C.: U.S. Government Printing Office, 1969.

———. *A Study of Our Nation's Schools.* Washington, D.C.: U.S. Government Printing Office, 1970.

Venn, G. "Vocational-Technical Education Needs and Programs for Urban

Schools." Paper presented at Seventh Work Conference on Urban Education, Teachers College, Columbia University, June 1969.

Washington Research Project and NAACP Legal Defense and Educational Fund, Inc. *Title I of ESEA: Is It Helping Poor Children?* Washington, D.C.: Washington Research Project, 1969.

Weinberg, M. *Desegregation Research: An Appraisal,* rev. ed. Bloomington, Ind.: Phi Delta Kappa, 1970.

Zigler, E. "Social Class and the Socialization Process," *Review of Educational Research,* 40 (February 1970), 87–110.

EDUCATIONAL STRATEGIES AND THE DISADVANTAGED: AN OVERVIEW

S. M. Miller
Pamela Roby

S. M. Miller and Pamela Roby examine various strategies designed to improve the educational performance of the children of the poor. Discussing what they call "a bewildering kaleidoscope of policy recommendations" of the past decade or so, Miller and Roby suggest that the various approaches can be placed in five categories: (a) changing the student and his family, (b) changing the school, (c) increasing resources and changing their distribution, (d) changing the student composition, and (e) changing control of the schools. Each of these approaches is discussed in terms of apparent strengths and weaknesses, although the general absence of evaluative data concerning success and failure of programs continues to amaze the authors.

Numerous programs have been shaped to remedy the presumed educational deficiencies of the low-income family but such compensatory education has produced rather uneven results. Whether the failure to produce dramatic results is due to the conceptual bases of these efforts or to the inadequate funding of such programs is unclear. One consequence, however, has been a move toward economic, rather than educational or psychological means of overcoming family-engendered educational difficulties. The limited success of compensatory education has led to the argument that it is the school as an institution which must be changed in rather important and basic ways. Here, the stress is on the internal changes in all aspects of the educational processes of the school rather than on deficiencies of the disadvantaged child. Changing the school has proved to be difficult, partly because of recalcitrant bureaucracies and partly because of the general complexities of the system itself. Program parallelism or alternate educational arrangements have been advocated and implemented in the hope that competition would lead to change. Some of the competitive alternatives are examined in terms of their potential value.

A third strategy argues for both increased educational expenditures and for more equitable allocation of such expenditures. Data suggest that per pupil expenditures in inner-city schools are substantially lower than in higher income and suburban schools. Miller and Roby point to the significance of Title I of the Elementary and Secondary Education Act which attempted to funnel increased federal money into schools with substantial numbers of low-income children, providing a differential increase in expenditures.

The fourth strategy involves social class integration and racial balance and is aimed at changing the composition of the student body as a means of increasing pupil achievement. Miller and Roby caution that integration (or separatism) should not be discussed only in terms of direct and immediate educational effects but also as a long-range policy of improved relationships among race and class groups which can only accrue through an integrated society. Unfortunately, they point out, the slow pace of desegregation combined with the growth of other goals, has led to demands, particularly in black communities, for separatism and control. This change in control of schools is analyzed by Miller and Roby as a fifth strategy. The arguments for and against decentralization and community control, arguments which are not restricted to educational processes, are examined.

Miller and Roby conclude that the major social policy implications of their analysis indicate a need for coupling educational strategies with economic and social strategies on experimental bases since the proper mix is still unknown. The authors argue that until education provided in public schools for low-income pupils is improved, alternatives to such schools for "making it" in the occupational world must be provided.

S. Michael Miller is Professor of Sociology and Education at New York University. Pamela Roby is Research Associate in the Department of Sociology at the same institution.

EDUCATIONAL STRATEGIES AND THE DISADVANTAGED: AN OVERVIEW

S. M. Miller
Pamela Roby

Education is frequently offered as the key to the economic and social advance of the poor, especially the black poor. We have argued elsewhere that education is a limited solution to problems of poverty and discrimination (Miller and Roby, 1969). Here we concentrate on the strategies for improving the educational performance of the children of the poor.

In the late 1950's and early 1960's, a bewildering kaleidscope of policy recommendations were offered, and some were tried. These strategies can, in our opinion, be subsumed under five categories:

1. changing the student and his family;
2. changing the school;
3. increasing resources and changing their distribution;
4. changing the student composition; and
5. changing control.

These categories do not have firm boundaries, but we believe that they make discussion of issues in educational policy easier. Some policies are in conflict; others converge at certain points. Some strategies are more desirable in one situation than another, and most are designed to serve non-educational as well as educational ends. The absence of data to attest to the success or failure of the different strategies is amazing in a society that prides itself on its computers and research.

Despite the national concern with education, prohibitive costs will prevent us from pursuing each strategy fully. We must choose either to emphasize some policies and to exclude others, or to develop a balance among them. To do so, we need to know from what range of possibilities we are making choices.

Strategy 1: Changing the Student and His Family

The psychological defeat that the Soviet Sputnik inflicted on the United States led to the demand that American education improve its concern with and teaching of science. No such spectacular event propelled attention to the children of the poor. Whereas little attention was paid to school dropouts in the early and mid-fifties, more and more interest developed in the late fifties and early sixties. The first programs designed to aid the children of low-income families were intended to overcome the purported limitations of slum life.

In September 1959, a New York City program alliteratively called "Higher Horizons" was introduced with great fanfare. Patterned after the Demonstration Guidance Project of Junior High School 43 in Manhattan, but reduced in substance, it was intended to expand the cultural awareness of children in 50 elementary and 13 junior high schools through music and art instruction as well as field trips to museums and other points of interest outside the narrow enclaves in which they lived. Supplementary program teachers and guidance counselors were introduced within the schools to help "rehabilitate" students.

Other innovations in the early programs included small-group and half-class instruction in reading, mathematics, and other curriculum areas; demonstration lessons by program teachers; and parent involvement through workshops, committees, and trips (Gordon and Wilkerson, 1966; Hillson, 1963; Landers, 1963). Early success was reported, and programs in other cities copied Higher Horizons. As the program spread, its per capita costs were reduced and the "Hawthorne effects" resulting from committed teachers being involved in an exciting experiment was lost (Wrightstone et al., 1964; Hechinger, 1966).

Nonetheless, these programs shaped the general style of the early educational efforts to deal with low-income children, stressing the child's inadequate preparation for school. Because his family had failed to provide an adequate educational environment, when he entered school he was already behind middle-class children in his ability to learn.

Compensatory education emerged as the widely heralded device to remedy the educational deficiencies of the low-income family. What was needed, it was believed, was "compensatory socialization." Some slight increases in educational expenditures and some programs, such as increased guidance, remedial reading, parent contact, summer school, or after-school programs, would make the difference. These programs were adopted in many cities, though more frequently in public relations releases than in practice (Gordon and Wilkerson, 1966; Silverman, 1965).

The effects of these programs is hard to measure since the data are so scarce. The general feeling of those close to the programs is that they did little to close the gap between the low-income and higher-income school children. Despite the lack of positive results, "watered-down" compensatory programs appeared to many to be a good bargain. After all, they were, as Albert Shanker (1969) points out, "relatively inexpensive: if we were to reduce class size from a maximum of thirty-five or forty to a maximum of ten, fifteen, or twenty, we would at least double the educational budget; if we hire a teacher after school for as much as $8 an hour to work with a group of children, we spend a comparatively small amount of money and gain public credit for keeping the school open longer."

The increasingly apparent difficulties of compensatory education led, in the mid-sixties, to programs to reach the low-income child before he began school. Some kindergarten and pre-kindergarten programs had been begun as part of compensatory education, but the big change was in the introduction of the Office of Economic Opportunity's Head Start program for younger children. The intention was to make the preschool experience not only a day-care operation, but more important, to give it educational content, so that it improved the performance of children once they entered the regular school.

Head Start was widely heralded as a success almost before it had begun (Kraff, 1965). It undoubtedly did secure some important gains —in highlighting health deficiencies of the children, in involving black parents in the schools of Mississippi and other states, in providing needed day-care services, and in spurring leaders of day-care programs to be interested in education as well as in providing an amenity for working mothers. But its success in improving the educational performance of the children is more doubtful. At first, the programs reported great increases in IQ and other measures of school-related performance, but these gains over similar children not in Head Start programs began to disappear when the Head Start children entered schools that did not build on their earlier experiences (Eisenberg and Conners, 1966; Wolff and Stein, 1966).

It is unclear, as in so many other programs, whether the difficulties of Head Start are due to poorly conducted and financed programs or to inadequate concepts. It is our impression that few would contend that an improvement in administration and funding of Head Start would make vital differences. A group of social scientists does argue that the cognitive damages of a deprived family situation are so great and continuing that attempting to remedy them at the age of four may be too late, for, as early as eighteen months, disadvantaged children start trailing their middle-class age-mates in tests of intelligence and language development (Edwards, 1968). If "the right experience" does not "come at the right time, the infant's potential to grasp certain cognitive skills" must remain forever unrealized. "Educational check-ups," they argue, "should be provided for babies and young children, similar to medical checkups" (Edwards, 1968, p. 69). Remedial attention should be provided for those whose cognitive development is not progressing on schedule (Pines, 1967b; Pines, 1968; Pines, 1967a). We think that the more compelling conclusion is that schools must adapt to the special experiences of Head Start children. The OEO has now initiated a Follow-Through program to support programs which do this.

Recently, some have argued against compensatory education on the basis that it is essentially an attempt to get poor families to act as though they were not poor, and actually had middle-class jobs, incomes, and experiences. Since such a scheme is unlikely to have great success, Rainwater (1967) and others suggest that educational improvement may be obtained indirectly by increasing the family incomes of low-income children through better jobs and improved income maintenance programs. With higher and more secure incomes, their families would give more beneficent and educational experiences to their children. This line of analysis, which moves toward economic, rather than educational or psychological ways of overcoming family-engendered educational difficulties, is very attractive. Yet we have hesitations about it since evidence shows that the connection between family income and educational level of children is not impressive. While higher family income is associated with higher levels of education of offspring, the education of parents is also very important. For example, the children of low-income families with parents who are well educated go farther in school than those from higher-income families with parents who did not graduate from high school. In 1960, 51 per cent of youths aged 16 to 21 whose fathers attended college and whose families had incomes of less than $5,000 were enrolled in, or had attended, college, as compared with 43 per cent of those whose family incomes were over $10,000, but whose fathers had not graduated from high school (U.S. Bureau of the Census, 1961). This fact lends support to such efforts as the "New Careers Movement," which is intended to increase adult skills and educational levels as well as earnings.

In addition to the "economic" critics of compensatory education, there are others who point out that there is little convincing evidence that compensatory socialization programs are highly effective. In view of such criticisms as well as the high cost of many programs, the search is on for other strategies to supplement or supplant compensatory education.

Strategy 2: Changing the School

The limited success of compensatory education has led to the argument that the school itself must be changed. Teachers must learn how to teach the disadvantaged child; administrators must be innovative; curriculum must be made more relevant to slum children; non-professional workers from the community must be introduced to ease the burdens of the teacher and bridge the gap between school and home; new kinds of teachers must be introduced through the Teachers Corps; and new technology must be adopted to meet the needs of slow learners. This strategy stresses the need for internal change in the school rather than the deficiencies of the disadvantaged child. The school must improve itself if it is to improve the performance of the child.

Strategy 2 represents an improvement over Strategy 1, for it does not assume that the schools are in fine shape and only need to adjust children to fit them more effectively. Rather, it recognizes that schools have to change in important and basic respects.

Changing schools is not easy. Recalcitrant bureaucracies are not easy to move—and large school systems have developed many ways of absorbing change without changing (Rogers, 1968). For example, Frank Riessman and other early supporters of educational aides saw them as agents of change in adapting schools to the needs of the disadvantaged child (Pearl and Riessman, 1965). So far, however, non-professionals have played a useful but limited role within the schools (Roby, 1968). Nor have schools of education changed rapidly enough to produce a new breed of teachers which can change the schools. Part of the problem is: who wants a new breed of teacher?

Mobilization for Youth (MFY) provides us with other illustrations of the difficulty involved in changing schools. In the early sixties, MFY decided to attempt to change schools in its neighborhood, rather than to create a parallel system, since existing schools would probably be around longer. When MFY wanted to try out new reading materials, the decision to work through the schools resulted in the attempt becoming entangled in the rigidities of the school bureaucracy. Back and forth, back and forth its staff went for months between Junior High School 71 and 110 Livingston Street, the Board of Education headquarters. Finally, MFY ended up by paying junior high youths a dollar an hour to try out the new reading materials at Mobilization's own headquarters.

The demonstration project was another device employed in the early sixties by comprehensive local planning projects to change schools and other agencies (Rein and Miller, 1965). The hope was that by introducing new practices and new personnel into the school on a small scale in the guise of a demonstration project testing new ideas, the host institution would be infected by the enthusiasm of the experimenters, and disturbed in its bureaucratic and encrusted ways by the evident accomplishment of new practices (Harris and Rein, 1967).

The general conclusion is that the educational bureaucracies triumphed over their innovative invaders (*The New York Times*, November 26, 1967). Demonstration projects failed to have much impact on basic educational practices. Increasingly, there is concern with the capacity of the basic service bureaucracies to cope with efforts to change them. Increasingly, too, there is the feeling that the rigidity, stubbornness, and traditionalism of these bureaucracies is a major factor in their low performance. As a result, many efforts for educational change are aimed at loosening up the bureaucracies.

The need is seen for increasing pressure on schools so as to cause them to change. Sometimes the pressure is linked with a specific remedial program. More often, the pressure is an effort to generate concern for a neglected disadvantaged population or to get schools to be more flexible in their practices.

With the rise in black militancy and expectation, parents and community groups have formed in some cities, independent of the old PTA's, and with much greater militancy. For example, in the mid-sixties in New York City, EQUALITY, an organization of Harlem parents and community leaders, was formed to push for integration of schools. Following the 1968 New York City teachers' strike, parents' groups which had organized to open the schools, began to press for deeper changes. Sometimes these pressure groups, which use traditional and non-traditional means of social protest, have been effective in getting a specific policy changed or in getting the educational bureaucracy to be more concerned with how one or another of its policies is going to be viewed by an activist group.

Another mode of change is non-political. It attempts to utilize "science" as a pressure. The emphasis is upon monitoring the performance of the school by collecting data on how well children are doing, and thus having an informational base on which to be able to criticize the schools and win support for change. After strenuous lobbying, an elite group of educators and citizens succeeded, in 1968, in getting Congress to pass a law which would provide national test data on schools. Although hedged with many restrictions, as a result of the strong counter-lobbying by school officials, the National Assessment Program will provide important data on the general performance of schools. The pressure on specific schools will not be great, however, because the data will be presented in such a way as to protect the identity of schools and cities. Nonetheless, the program is a step toward monitoring school performance and raising questions about the effectiveness of school practice. The absence of such basic information on school outputs is significant. The reluctance of schools to submit themselves to an objective appraisal of some aspects of their performance may indicate that such data could have a strong impact in the direction of change.

In the sixties, public education has been challenged to change through the development of a third tier of education, competing with, and in some instances replacing, public and parochial-private education. This is the federal-local, non-board of education style of education promoted through the Manpower Development and Training Act (MDTA) and the Economic Opportunity Act. These two acts have provided federal funds for educational programs to be conducted outside as well as inside the regular schools. Through Head Start, the OEO provided funds for both boards of education and non-educational organizations (e.g., churches) to develop educational programs for young children. The OEO and MDTA funds have also constructed a vocational education program, the administration and control of which is outside local school systems.

This third tier educational system is a new mold, mixing federal funds with very small local funds, federal guidelines with local programs and operations. This action not only serves to meet needs unmet by the local schools, but also places pressure on the schools to meet these needs. Many school boards have now begun to provide Head Start programs; others will clearly be doing so in the future. Although some OEO-sponsored innovations in the schools have been adopted on a more general basis, vocational education appears to be slow in adapting to a new clientele and new kinds of vocational objectives. The likelihood is that manpower training for youth will increasingly be conducted outside of vocational schools.

A few private efforts have similarly become institutionalized as parallel educational systems. For example, the Harlem street academies have developed into Harlem Prep, a full-fledged school sponsored by the Urban League, which is sending many of its students, most of whom are former dropouts or holders of "general diplomas," on to college (Bigart, 1968).

Parallel programs have had some impact in indicting traditional schools for failing in their obligations, but the changes have not been great. Consequently, it is felt that direct competition with the schools is needed, so that they will lose not only prestige, but funds. Instead of having public schools as the only educational alternative, Coleman (1967), Friedman (1955), Jencks (1965), and others (Clark, 1968; Erickson, 1968; Levine, 1968) suggest providing families with educational vouchers which could be tendered to a public school or a private school. The second form of competitive education which has been suggested recently is public financing of Catholic and black schools in addition to city schools (Sizer, 1969). The third scheme is for private firms to compete not only in selling textbooks to schools, but also in contracting for teams of teachers, pedagogical equipment, and whole educational programs.

With any form of competitive, publicly-supported education, teachers and schools would have to improve in order to keep their students, for their students would have an alternative, a choice such as is currently available only to families that can afford to send children to parochial or private schools. The spur of financial competition would force public schools to become more effective, or they would lose prestige as the more successful alternate schools won away their pupils. Consumers' choice would provide the market incentive now lacking in public education, which has a monopoly on the education of the poor.

The idea of competition is exciting. On a small scale it might work. But there is little likelihood of a large-scale move along these lines, since the cost of totally new plants would be enormous. Some have suggested, however, that as public schools fail to win students, the plants could be sold off to the more effective private schools, at discounts. Unfortunately, if this scheme is successful, it is likely that the better-educated will be able to sift through the competing claims of schools and engineer their children into the schools of greatest value, while the less-educated will not. The result would again be high-level and low-level education. A possible offset to this danger would be a counseling-advisory linking service which would help parents operate more effectively. Groups of parents might negotiate with a private school to see that their children received the kind of education that they desired. To assure a cross-section of all kinds of students, the independent school might be required to have diversity in its student population if it is to receive vouchers, or better still, a bonus for attaining a useful diversity.

Another version of the voucher system might also offset the danger of poor children being multiple losers: the poorest families would receive the most valuable vouchers. This scheme would make poor children financial assets to schools and might even provoke inter-school competition for low-income children. Total free-enterprise would not be tolerated; instead, as under the G.I. Bill, only accredited schools could cash vouchers, and accreditation would require fulfillment of certain standards, including admittance of children of any race, creed, or color. In addition to such safeguards, parents must be given some means—more reliable than gossip—with which to evaluate the strengths and weaknesses of various schools. Objective evaluation, such as the National Assessment Program, must be strengthened and extended if parents are to have the opportunity to make "rational choices."

Many obvious difficulties and potential abuses exist. But the idea of competitive educational systems is worth trying in several cities to see what impact it has. It would be an expensive experiment, for each independent school would be costly, and the experiment would have to run for several years for its possibilities and deficiencies to be understood (Pressman, 1967). We believe that it is too early to have confidence that a competing educational system can solve the problems of education of the disadvantaged. Nevertheless, it is an interesting device that deserves exploration.

Effecting changes in the school through demonstration projects, parallel educational programs, or competing school systems is expensive. Getting additional money for these purposes is made more difficult by the past experiences which show that gains in educational performance are not always rapid or stable. The Coleman Report (Coleman et al., 1966), for example, presents data which show that school facilities (but not teacher quality) have little effect on the performance of students in comparison with the effect of the child's fellow students in school. The Coleman findings show that school characteristics (school facilities, curriculums, and teachers) account for a greater fraction of the differences in achievement among minority than among majority children. For example, in the South, 20 per cent of the achievement of Negroes is associated with the schools they attend (and 80 per cent with the socioeconomic background of the students), whereas for whites the figure is put at 10 per cent. The qualities of teachers showed a stronger relationship to pupil achievement than did school facilities (instruction rooms, textbooks, cafeterias, etc.). The Coleman survey found no significant national differences in the educational attainment (as measured by years of school completed) of teachers in majority and minority schools. Negro students, however, were exposed less often than white students to teachers whose college major was in an academic subject—mathematics, science, literature—and Negro students were more likely than whites to have teachers with low verbal achievement levels (U.S. Commission on Civil Rights, 1967). Irwin Katz (1968) has theorized that some of the favorable effect on Negroes of attendance at predominantly white schools is due to less of the unrealistic self-devaluation and strong anxiety which research has shown are common features of Negro behavior in racially isolated institutions. The Coleman Report, in turn, can be criticized for its inadequate measures of school resources and inadequate control for students' social backgrounds, as well as statistical inadequacies and the magnitude of the non-response rate for some crucial items in the questionnaires, particularly those having to do with socioeconomic status (Bowles, 1968; Bowles and Levine, 1968; Pfautz, 1967; Dyer, 1968; Wilson, 1968).

It can still be argued that the technical, financial, and qualitative deficiencies of American education must be overcome if low-income children are to improve their educational and, therefore, their occupational prospects. The Coleman Report does not show high relations between many educational inputs and outputs because the quality of the inputs was low. Coleman was unable, for instance, to test the effect of small elementary school classes—of perhaps 10 or 15 children—because such classes do not exist in the public schools. Additional analysis of data from the Coleman survey which were not included in the Coleman Report also suggests that raising the quality of teaching resources devoted to the education of Negroes to the level of that currently devoted to whites would reduce the gap between Negro and white verbal achievement at grade 12 by approximately a quarter (Bowles, 1968). We believe that a change in school inputs, a change which disproportionately favors the poor, would make a difference.

The counter argument is, however, increasingly strong. It holds that the deficiencies of schools are not primarily technical or financial, but normative. That is, the difficulty lies not in what the school tries to do, but rather in what it wants to do. As Edgar Friedenberg and Paul Goodman have consistently argued, the source of school problems is that the purpose of schools is to socialize children, that is, to increase their acceptance of a peculiar society and to erode their spontaneous and emotive responses to their environments (Eddy, 1965; Friedenberg, 1959; Goodman, 1956). Thus, the issue becomes not a technical one of how to teach, but what it is that schools are designed to do. Technical improvements supported by financial increments will not resolve value choices concerning whether schools should prepare children for a sadly imperfect world, or whether they should develop children to become themselves.

Strategy 3: Increasing Resources and Changing Their Distribution

Whatever policies are undertaken for the reform and improvement of education, more money will be needed. Some argue that we do not know the value of any educational experiment because all have been under-financed. Others, who are more content with school know-how, assert that nothing is wrong with schools that money cannot fix. Their cry is for more resources to be devoted to education. The argument is persuasive. In 1966, we spent over $6 million more for the purchase and upkeep of cars than we did for education. The total personal consumption expenditure for user-operated transportation (including purchase, gasoline, repairs, tolls, insurance, and accessories) was $55.607 million in 1966, as compared with $48.8 million for education (public and non-public elementary, secondary, and higher education)

(U.S. Department of Commerce, 1967; U.S. Office of Education, 1967). A school which spends $569 annually per child (the national average per-pupil expenditure for 1966–1967), in classrooms with 30 students, has an hourly per-student expenditure of 50 cents, below the usual babysitting fee of $1.00 an hour (assuming they are in class 30 hours a week for 40 weeks).

Such data do make a case for increased educational expenditures. Although schools need more money, the nation's resources are limited and there is no assurance that more money guarantees higher educational performance. We doubt, for example, that the difference of over 40 per cent in educational expenditures between Illinois and New York schools is paralleled by superior educational performance in New York. After comparing inputs and outputs of Chicago public high schools, Burkhead summarized his findings as follows:

1. The socioeconomic variables (median family income) are of the greatest importance in determining differences in school outputs. The out-of-school variables are far more significant than the in-school variables.
2. Neither class size nor teacher man-years per student is important in producing different educational outcomes within the range of variation that exists in Chicago.
3. Some inputs are important for some outputs, but not for others. Newer buildings do reduce school dropouts, but new buildings have no influence on eleventh grade reading scores.
4. The experience of the teacher is important, particularly in its impact on reading scores. This is generally a more important determinant of outcomes than class size or the formal education of the teacher.
5. The size of the high school, within the range of Chicago school size, is not uniformly important as an educational variable.

In Atlanta, he found:

1. The major determinants of school performance are factors external to the school itself, such as family income and family housing conditions.
2. Current expenditures, as such, have very little influence on school outputs.
3. The ratio of faculty to students is of some importance in explaining tenth grade verbal scores. (Burkhead, Fox, and Holland, 1967).

Similarly, the Coleman study found, as noted earlier, that school facilities and curriculums account for relatively little of the difference between schools in pupil achievement.

The argument about resources moves in another direction. Not the level, but the distribution of expenditures, is important. The facts about the distribution of educational expenditures are disturbing. In

37 of the largest metropolitan areas, expenditures in central cities—where there are many children of low-income families—were $145 per pupil less than in the contiguous suburbs—where there are few children of low income (Burkhead, Fox, and Holland, 1967).

In state aid, suburban schools in 1962 received $17 more per pupil than did city schools. Campbell reports that in New York State's six metropolitan areas, during the school year 1966–67, the average difference between educational aid to the central cities and to the rest of the counties in which the central cities are located, was more than $100 per pupil (Campbell, 1969). Even more disconcerting is that the gap between the cities and the suburbs is growing: the 1962 difference did not exist in 1958, for then the two areas were spending the same amount. Even within large cities, better neighborhoods usually receive more per student than do low-income neighborhoods (Sexton, 1964). In Chicago, Burkhead found that the lower- and upper-income schools had more resources at their disposal than middle-income schools. In Atlanta, low-income schools were older and larger, and classes were larger than those in middle- and high-income areas (Burkhead et al., 1967).

Redistribution can most easily be obtained when educational expenditures are rising. New educational funds need to be distributed in favor of the poor. Because municipalities are having increasing difficulties obtaining adequate income through property taxes, sizeable increases in educational resources are most likely to come from the federal government. As industries continue to move outward, taxable assessed valuation—the source of local property taxes and school funds—has barely held its own, and has actually decreased in Baltimore (–11 per cent), Boston (–1 per cent), Buffalo (–1 per cent), Detroit (–2 per cent), and Cleveland (–3 per cent). Furthermore, non-educational expenditures constitute 68 per cent of total public expenditures in the central cities of the 37 largest metropolitan areas, as compared with 47 per cent in their contiguous suburbs (Campbell, 1969). It is, therefore, federal funds which must be distributed in such a way as to benefit the poor more than they benefit the non-poor. The Elementary and Secondary Education Act of 1965 was significant not only because it funneled federal money into local schools, but also because it tried to see that districts with many low-income children received the funds. It aimed at the *differential* increase in expenditures for the poor. To what extent such a shift has taken place is unclear, for cities have absorbed funds into general educational revenues and the ESEA funds are very small compared to local and state educational expenditures. Nonetheless, the intent is there, and carrying it out can be made more mandatory in the future.

It is easy, however, to find schools with high educational expenditures which fail to produce high achievers, and schools with low expenditures which do produce high achievers. Unfortunately, increasing educational expenditures does not insure the desired results. The crucial factor is how the funds are used. Nevertheless, expecting either traditional programs or innovational efforts to work without adequate funding is foolish. Before we accept the slogan that "money is not the answer," we ought, as Albert Shanker points out, to try the money approach, "just once."

Strategy 4: Changing the Student Composition

The 1954 Brown decision of the Supreme Court declared that separated facilities are inherently unequal. Integration was thus not only morally, but also pragmatically, necessary if Negro children were to have equal educational opportunity. Although school integration is attacked by many whites and blacks today, there has been evidence supporting the *educational* importance of integration. The Coleman Report (Coleman et al., 1966) and the Pettigrew Report (U.S. Commission on Civil Rights, 1967) conclude that students from low-income families do better in schools with children from higher-income families than they do in schools that are made up mainly of the children of the poor. Similarly, Negroes do better in integrated schools than in all-Negro schools. In further analysis of data from the Equality of Educational Opportunity survey, Armor found that Negro students in majority-white schools are more likely to have definite college plans than similar students in majority-Negro schools, regardless of the quality of their teachers (teacher quality was more closely related to student achievement than other school characteristics) (U.S. Commission on Civil Rights, 1967, Vol. II, pp. 143–164). At the same time, Wilson has found that the degree of racial integration of a school has no effect on the achievement of white students who attend middle-class schools (U.S. Commission on Civil Rights, 1967). However, the benefits of *social class* integration do not accrue to *low-income* children without a cost to middle-class children. Wilson has reported that "the achievement of white students who attended predominantly white elementary schools has been strongly affected by the social class composition of the school, *and* it is not racial integration per se, but social class integration—the better educational background and higher educational aspirations that are, on the average, found among white students—which accounts for the higher educational achievement of Negro students who attend predominantly white schools" (Coleman et al., 1966). However, it may be argued on purely practical grounds (and practical rather than humanitarian arguments will be the means by which most white, middle-class parents will be convinced of the merits of integration for *their* children) that the "cost" of social class integration to middle-class students in terms of educational achievement is offset by the benefits which they receive from an integrated education. Such benefits include the opportunity to learn how to relate to persons with different backgrounds—a skill which will be very important to students who, later in their lives, pursue careers (from sales to social work) which involve understanding low-income and minority group persons.

Nonetheless, it is clearly tunnel vision to discuss integration (or separatism) only in terms of direct and immediate educational effects. Integration is offered as educational policy because many feel that they desire an integrated society and that schools are an important step in bringing closer relationships among race and class groups. Broader and perhaps longer term national goals must be debated.

While many espouse integration as a goal, they find it difficult to envision how it can be accomplished in the short-run in big cities where Negro, Puerto Rican, and Mexican-American populations are the most rapidly growing, and whites are increasingly locating in suburbs. In Baltimore, for example, McDill et al. (1968) found that segregation within the city public school system accounts for only a small part of educational disadvantage, as compared with the important segregating influences of the city-suburban boundary and the private school system. One way of attempting to increase integration in these circumstances is to provide city-suburb schools with federal and state financial incentives to share facilities and students. Busing is another device that has been used to try to obtain a higher degree of class and race mixing. A third measure is to establish educational parks, major educational concentrations which all levels of students attend. For some reason, even though educational parks also require long-distance travel for many children, this model incurs less anger than busing children to individual schools.

These are devices to be used in the short run. In the long run, integration cannot take place on a substantial scale without broad economic and housing policies which reduce the accelerating rate of residential segregation and close the economic gap between black and white, poor and non-poor.

The doubts that we have cast on the firmness of the research data pointing to the gains of integration, and on the need for broad policies going beyond education if integration is to have long-run promise, do not speak against the desirability of integration as a goal and a means. As a goal, we think integration is desirable even if educational gains are not forthcoming. If it is to be pursued, then substantial financial and social commitments will have to be made. The call for integration, once high among the demands of Negro communities, has been overcome, in many black neighborhoods, by the cry for separatism. The following section discusses this new demand in the context of community control.

Strategy 5: Changing Control

As part of Strategy 1, many schools began to pay more attention than ever before to the parents of their disadvantaged children. Parents' meetings occurred more frequently; parents were invited into the schools; teachers were encouraged to visit the homes of their children; schools employed people to spend time in the communities and to inform parents of how they could help their children in school (Bloomberg and Kincaid, 1968). At the same time, in some big cities, new sponsorship of school boards took place. Elite groups which had had little connection with public schools began to be involved with them, and to be concerned about the education of the disadvantaged.

Education has become an increasingly important issue in black communities, and a hot political issue in cities as a whole. Separatism as a political and economic doctrine has grown. Coupled with dissatisfaction over the schools' failure to improve the educational performance of black children, there has been an increasing demand for "decentralization" (Haskins, 1969).

What "decentralization" means is now being defined. Many support it because of the inevitable bureaucratic rigidities of large-scale school systems. But what degree of control a neighborhood board should have is a very controversial issue, as seen, for instance, in the difficulties in New York City schools in the fall of 1968. For some, decentralization is thorough, and means control, with very limited functions left to the city-wide board; for others, decentralization is thin, an administrative device whereby neighborhood boards deal with only limited and very localistic issues.

The educational argument for thorough decentralization is that only with black domination can the children feel secure and be given a positive self-image conducive to learning, and the curriculum and teaching reshaped to benefit the children. The opponents argue that changing the control of schools does not guarantee a higher level of teacher performance. Offered in support of this argument is the conclusion that in New York City's decentralization districts little real innovation has taken place. Thorough decentralization is also attacked on the basis that it will prevent integration in schools and promote segregationist policies by some white neighborhood boards.

Decentralization proposals have a twofold purpose which has sometimes been ignored. One purpose is to shake up school bureaucracies and make schools more flexible and adaptive to neighborhood needs and concerns. The other is to satisfy a political demand by blacks for greater control over institutions which impinge upon them. For many, the short-run and long-run educational impacts of decentralization are secondary to the immediate gains in terms of community self-determination. They argue that in the long run, educational gains will also take place.

Conclusion

During the fifties and sixties, attempts to promote social mobility of the disadvantaged focused on education. Thousands of educational experiments with the intention of furthering the academic achievement or social development of low-income were conducted in the United States. We believe that three major social policy implications for the seventies may be drawn from our review of a sampling of the more interesting educational experiments: (1) in order to increase the educational attainment of low-income youth, we must couple educational strategies with economic and social strategies; (2) since we do not know the proper mix of educational, economic, and social strategies, we will need to be experimental; and (3) until the time when we are able to perfect education for low-income youth to the point where the educational sorting system operates as a true "meritocracy," we must provide alternative means of "making it" in the occupational world.

With Lee Rainwater (1967), we believe that significantly changing the student and his family requires changing their economic position. No educational strategy or set of educational strategies alone will significantly improve the educational attainment of low-income youth. Youth must be relieved of constant familial economic crises before all but the most exceptional can perform well in school. However, we must caution that improved family income is not a panacea for educational problems. Rather, it is a "necessary but not sufficient condition" for gains in school readiness. Educational changes are also required if low-income youth are to obtain success in school.

Although we know that educational resources must be both increased and redistributed (low-income youth are obviously not going to catch up as long as they are increasingly shortchanged in the distribution of educational monies), increasing resources by itself will not be enough. Changes in the control and operation of the school and in classroom teaching are also required. But we do not know what changes will lead to success. Therefore, our educational, social, and economic efforts must continue to be experimental.

In planning for continued experimentation during the seventies, we must face two certain realities: (1) we are never going to have enough money to pursue all, or even many, educational, economic, and social strategies; therefore, we need to discover what "mix" can accomplish most with our limited funds; and (2) we are never going to have enough *good* teachers—the ability to teach, like most other things, is distributed along a normal curve. The needs of not only education but all professional fields are expanding, and all will face a shortage of "good" people. We will, therefore, have to tailor our experimentation and planning to maximize the results which can be obtained from average and poor as well as outstanding professionals.

Although changing schools is still very difficult to do, we are learning how to create change through the monitoring of programs, through the introduction of competition among educational delivery units, through changing student composition, and through changing school control. Our great lack is deciding on the content of change—the educational curriculum.

Beyond curriculum content, the prospect of being experimental raises questions as to the fundamental purpose of the school. Some see the purpose as narrowly vocational; others see it as redistributive; others see it as one of social control; still others see it as one of social change. Most educational strategies have non-educational as well as educational ends. Integration, parent participation in educational decision-making, and the extension of student horizons are not merely instrumental means to higher achievement scores. Therefore, they cannot be judged solely on their educational merits. The ends of a socially integrated society, community rule or self-government, and students' social development must also be weighed.

Finally, and most important for thousands of young adults, we must stop punishing youth who drop out of school. *We* do not know how to meet their needs, and there is no justice in society's forever excluding them because of *our* lack of knowledge. The challenge of the next decade is not only to develop successful educational strategies for low-income youth, but also to construct alternatives to education for "making it" in our society.

Thus, the fact that we do not know how to make changes at the micro-level of education—how to significantly improve teachers' teaching of reading, how to improve teachers' attitudes toward low-income youth, or how to move low-income families to educationally motivate their youth—drives us to attempt changes at the macro-level of education. Hopefully, when we have accomplished change at the macro-level—changes in the organizational context, changes in student composition across urban-suburban lines, changes in the distribution of educational and economic resources, and alternatives to education for economic self-improvement—we will be able to function at the micro-level. During the seventies we must continue to strive for improvement at the micro-level of education, but our greatest efforts to create change will need to be aimed at the macro-level.

References

Bigart, H. "Harlem Prep Gives Dropouts a Door to College," *The New York Times,* May 8, 1968.

Bloomberg, W. and J. Kincaid. "Parent Participation: Practical Policy or Another Panacea?" *The Urban Review,* 2, 7 (June 1968), 5–11.

Bowles, S. "Towards Equality of Educational Opportunity," *Harvard Educational Review,* 38, 1 (Winter 1968), 89–99.

Bowles, S. and H. M. Levin. "The Determinants of Scholastic Achievement: An Appraisal of Some Recent Evidence," *The Journal of Human Resources,* 3, 1 (Winter 1968), 3–24.

Burkhead, J., T. G. Fox, and J. Holland. *Input and Output in Large-City High Schools.* Syracuse: Syracuse University Press, 1967.

Campbell, A. K. "Inequities of School Finance," *Saturday Review,* 52 (January 11, 1969), 44–48.

Centre for Educational Research and Innovation, Organization for Economic Cooperation and Development. Seminar on Educational Programs for Disadvantaged Populations. New York. January 14, 1969.

Clark, K. B. "Alternative Public School Systems," *Harvard Educational Review,* 38, 1 (Winter 1968), 100–113.

Coleman, J. S. "Toward Open Schools," *Public Interest,* 9 (Fall 1967), 20–27.

——— et al. *Equality of Educational Opportunity.* Washington, D.C.: U.S. Government Printing Office, 1966.

Dyer, H. S. "School Factors and Equal Educational Opportunities," *Harvard Educational Review,* 38, 1 (Winter 1968), 38–56.

Eddy, E. *Walk the White Line: A Profile of Urban Education.* New York: Doubleday and Co., 1965.

Edwards, E. P. "Kindergarten Is Too Late," *Saturday Review,* 51 (June 15, 1968), 68–70, 76–79.

Eisenberg, L. and C. K. Conners. "The Effects of Head Start on Developmental Processes." Paper presented at 1966 Joseph P. Kennedy, Jr., Foundation Scientific Symposium on Mental Health. Boston. April 1966.

Erickson, D. A. "Public Funds for Private Schools," *Saturday Review,* 61 (September 21, 1968), 68–70, 78.

Friedenberg, E. Z. *The Vanishing Adolescent.* Boston: Beacon Press, 1959.

Friedman, M. "The Role of Government in Education," in *Economics and and the Public Interest,* ed. R. A. Sold. New Brunswick, N.J.: Rutgers University Press, 1955.

Goodman, P. *Growing Up Absurd: Problems of Youth in an Organized Society.* New York: Vintage Books, 1956.

Gordon, E. W. and D. A. Wilkerson. *Compensatory Education for the Disadvantaged. Programs and Practices: Preschool through College.* New York: College Entrance Examination Board, 1966.

Harris, P. and M. Rein. *Dilemmas of Social Reform.* London: Routledge and Kegan Paul, 1967.

Haskins, K. W. "The Case for Local Control," *Saturday Review,* 52 (January 11, 1969), 52–54.

Hechinger, F. M. "Curtain for Higher Horizons," *The New York Times,* July 10, 1966.

Hillson, H. T. *The Demonstration Guidance Project: 1957–1962.* New York: Board of Education of the City of New York, May 1963.

Jencks, C. "Private Management for Public Schools," Memorandum No. 4. Washington: Institute for Policy Studies, October 1965.

Katz, I. "Academic Motivation and Equal Educational Opportunity," *Harvard Educational Review,* 38, 1 (Winter 1968), 57–65.

Kraff, I. "Are We Overselling the Pre-School Idea?," *Saturday Review,* 48 (December 18, 1965), 63.

Landers, J. *Higher Horizons Progress Report.* New York: Board of Education of the City of New York, January 1963.

Levin, H. M. "The Failure of the Public Schools and the Free Market Remedy," *The Urban Review,* 2, 7 (June 1968), 32–37.

McDill, M. S., A. L. Stinchcombe, and D. Walker. "Segregation and Educational Disadvantage: Estimates of the Influence of Different Segregatory Factors," *Sociology of Education,* 41 (Summer 1968), pp. 239–246.

Miller, S. M. and F. Riessman. *Social Class and Social Policy.* New York: Basic Books, 1968.

——— and P. Roby. "Education and Redistribution: The Limits of a Strategy," in *Racial Crisis in American Education,* ed. R. L. Greene. Chicago: Follett Publishing Co., 1969.

———. "Urban Change and Schools of Education," in J. A. Lauwerys and D. G. Scanlon, *The World Year Book of Education.* New York: Harcourt, Brace and World, 1970. Pp. 166–174.

New York City Bureau of Educational Research. *Evaluation of Higher Horizons Program for Underprivileged Children.* New York: Board of Education of the City of New York, CRP No. 1124, April 1965.

The New York Times. "New York University Experiment Fails to Upgrade Slum School," November 26, 1967, p. 83.

Pearl, A. and F. Riessman. *New Careers for the Poor.* New York: The Free Press, 1965.

Pfautz, H. W. "Review Symposium on the Coleman Report," *American Sociological Review,* 32 (June 1967), 481–483.

Pines, M. *Revolution in Learning—The Years From Birth to Six.* New York: Harper and Row, 1967. (a)

———. "Slum Children Must Make Up for Lost Time," *The New York Times Magazine,* October 15, 1967. (b)

———. "Someone to Mind the Baby," *The New York Times Magazine,* January 7, 1968.

Pressman, H. *New Schools for the Cities: Designs for Equality and Excellence.* Washington, D.C.: New Community Press, 1967.

Rainwater, L. "The Lessons of Pruitt-Igoo," *The Public Interest,* 8 (Summer 1967), 116–126.

Rein, M. and S. M. Miller. "The Demonstration as a Strategy of Change," in *Social Welfare Institutions: A Sociological Reader,* ed. M. Zald. New York: John Wiley and Sons, 1965.

Roby, P. "Educational Aides in Inner City Schools," *Integrated Education,* 6, 6 (November 1968), 47–56.

Rogers, D. *110 Livingston Street.* New York: Random House, 1968.

Sexton, P. C. *Education and Income.* New York: Viking Press, 1964.

Shanker, A. "What's Wrong with Compensatory Education?," *Saturday Review,* 52 (January 11, 1969), 56–61.

Silverman, S. B. "An Annotated Bibliography on Education and Cultural Deprivation," in Bloom, B. S., A. Davis, and R. Hess. *Compensatory Education.* New York: Holt, Rinehart and Winston, Inc., 1965. Pp. 67–173.

Sizer, T. R. "The Case for a Free Market," *Saturday Review,* 52 (January 11, 1969), 34–42, 93.

U.S. Bureau of the Census. *Current Population Reports.* No. 110, July 24, 1961.

U.S. Commission on Civil Rights. *Racial Isolation in the Public Schools.* Washington, D.C.: U.S. Government Printing Office, 1967.

U.S. Department of Commerce. *Survey of Current Business,* 47 (July 1967).

U.S. Office of Education. *Digest of Educational Statistics: 1967.* Washington, D.C.: U.S. Government Printing Office, 1967.

Wilson, A. B. "Educational Consequences of Segregation in a California Community," in Commission on Civil Rights, *Racial Isolation in the Public Schools,* Vol. 2. Washington, D.C.: U.S. Government Printing Office, 1967. Pp. 165–206.

———. "Social Class and Equal Educational Opportunity," *Harvard Educational Review,* 38 (Winter 1968), 77–84.

Wolff, M. and A. Stein. "Long Range Effect of Pre-Schooling on Reading

Achievement." New York: Ferkauf Graduate School of Education, Yeshiva University, 1966. Mimeographed.

———. "Six Months Later: A Comparison of Children Who Had Head Start, Summer 1965, with their Classmates in Kindergarten, 1966." New York: Ferkauf Graduate School of Education, Yeshiva University, 1966. Mimeographed.

Wrightstone, J. W. et al. *Evaluation of the Higher Horizon Program for Underprivilege Children.* New York: Board of Education of the City of New York, 1964.

A CRITIQUE OF THE CONCEPT "COMPENSATORY EDUCATION"

Basil B. Bernstein

Basil B. Bernstein critically examines the idea of compensatory education. He expresses some inability to comprehend the term itself, asking, "How we can talk about offering compensatory education to children who, in the first place, have as yet not been offered an adequate educational environment?" Citing English studies, Bernstein points to inadequate facilities, unstable teaching staffs, and oversized classes as contributing to an initially unsatisfactory educational environment for low-income children. Further, he maintains that the concept of compensatory education directs attention away from the internal organization and the educational context of the school and focuses it instead on presumed deficiencies in families and children. Thus, the concept acts as a distractor, focusing attention on the wrong deficiencies. What is needed is a curb on thinking in terms of compensation and far more attention to serious consideration of the conditions and contexts of the educational environment.

Bernstein indicates how his own research may have inadvertently contributed to the stress on subcultural and familial socialization while ignoring the conditions and contexts of learning in the school. The significant differences occur in the extent to which children use speech to generate universalistic meanings *as contrasted with* particularistic meanings, *the former not bound to a given context while the latter are severely context-bound. Thus, low-income children are not "linguistically deprived" or non-verbal but rather are oriented differently toward receiving and offering universalistic meanings in certain contexts. Thus, orientations toward meta-languages of control and innovation are not provided low-income children as part of their initial socialization. Bernstein clarifies the meaning of his terms "elaborated codes" and "restricted codes" as affecting access to universalistic meanings.*

Urging that we give attention to and practice the adage that the teacher should work with what the child can offer, Bernstein argues that introducing the child to the universalistic meanings of public forms of thought represents education, not compensatory education. Finally, the author suggests that we give more attention to what constitutes "sets of optimal learning environments."

Basil B. Bernstein is Professor in the Sociology of Education and Head of the Sociological Research Unit, University of London Institute of Education.

A CRITIQUE OF THE CONCEPT "COMPENSATORY EDUCATION"

Basil B. Bernstein

Since the late 1950's there has been a steady outpouring of papers and books in the U.S.A. which are concerned with the education of children of low social class whose *material* circumstances are inadequate, or with the education of black children of low social class whose *material* circumstances are chronically inadequate. An enormous research and educational bureaucracy developed in the U.S.A. financed by funds obtained from federal and state governments or private foundations. New educational categories were established —the culturally deprived, the linguistically deprived, the socially disadvantaged—and the notion of compensatory education was introduced as a means of changing the status of the children in those categories. Compensatory education emerged in the form of massive preschool introductory programs, large-scale research programs, such as those of Deutsch in the early 1960's, and a plethora of small-scale "intervention" or "enrichment" programs for preschool children or children in the first years of compulsory education. Very few sociologists were involved in these studies, since, until recently, education was a low-status area. Most studies were carried out by psychologists.

The focus of these studies was on the child in the family and on the classroom relationships between teacher and child. In the last two or three years, one has been able to detect a change in this focus. As a result of the movement toward integration and the opposite movement toward segregation (the latter a response to the wishes of the various Black Power groups), more studies of the *school* are now being made in the U.S.A.

Work in England has been almost limited to the effects of streaming. Rosenthal and Jacobson's study *Pygmalion in the Classroom* (1968) drew attention to the critical importance of the teacher's expectations for the child. In England, we have been aware of the educational problem since the writings of Sir Cyril Burt before World War II. His book, *The Backward Child,* is probably still the best descriptive study we have. After the war, a series of sociological surveys and public inquiries into education brought this educational problem into the arena of national debate, and so of social policy.

At the moment, in Wales there is a large research unit, financed by the Schools Council, concerned with compensatory education. Important research of a most significant kind is taking place in the University of Birmingham into the problems of the education of Commonwealth children. The Social Science Research Council and the Department of Education and Science have given £175,000, in part for the development of special preschool programs concerned to introduce children to compensatory education. One university Department of Education offers an advanced diploma in compensatory education. Colleges of Education also offer special courses under the same title. It might be worth a few lines to consider the assumptions underlying this work and the concepts which describe it, particularly as my own writings have sometimes been used (and more often abused) to highlight aspects of the general problems and dilemmas.

Assumptions Underlying Compensatory Education

To begin with I find the term "compensatory education" a curious one for a number of reasons. I do not understand how we can talk about offering compensatory education to children who, in the first place, have as yet not been offered an adequate educational environment (Central Advisory Commission for Education, 1963). The Newsom Report, *Half Our Future,* showed that 79 per cent of all secondary-modern schools in slum and problem areas were grossly inadequate materially, and that the holding power of these schools over the teachers was horrifyingly low. The same report also showed very clearly how the depression in the reading scores of these children compared with the scores of children who were at schools in areas which were neither problem nor slum. This does not conflict with the findings that, on the average, for the country as a whole, there has been an improvement in children's reading ability. The Plowden Report, *Children and Their Primary Schools* (Central Advisory Commission for Education, 1967), was rather more coy about all the above points, but we have little reason to believe that the situation is very much better for primary schools in similar areas.

Thus we offer a large number of children, both at the primary and secondary level, materially inadequate schools and unstable teaching staffs, and we further expect a small group of dedicated teachers to cope. The strain on these teachers inevitably produces fatigue and illness, and it is not uncommon in any week to find teachers having to deal with doubled-up classes of eighty children. We then wonder why the children display very early in their educational life a range of learning difficulties. At the same time, the organization of schools creates delicate overt and covert streaming arrangements which neatly lower the expectations and motivations of teachers and taught. A vicious spiral is set up with an all too determinate outcome. It would seem then that we have as yet failed to provide on the scale required a satisfactory *initial* educational environment.

The concept of compensatory education serves to direct attention away from the internal organization and the educational context of the school, and focus attention upon the families and children. "Compensatory education" implies that something is lacking in the family, and so in the child. As a result, the children are unable to benefit from schools. It follows then that the school has to "compensate" for the something which is missing in the family, and the children become little deficit systems. If only the parents were interested in the goodies we offer; if only they were like middle-class parents, then we could do our job. Once the problem is seen even implicitly in this way, then it becomes appropriate to coin the terms "cultural deprivation," "linguistic deprivation," et cetera. These labels then do their own sad work.

If children are labelled "culturally deprived," then it follows that the parents are inadequate and the spontaneous realizations of their culture, its images and symbolic representations, are of reduced value and significance. Teachers will have lower expectations of the children, which the children will undoubtedly fulfill. All that informs the child, that gives meaning and purpose to him outside of the school, ceases to be valid and accorded significance and opportunity for enhancement within the school. He has to orient toward a different structure of meaning, whether it is in the form of basal readers (Dick and Jane), in the form of language use and dialect, or in the patterns of social relationships. Alternatively, the meaning structure of the school is explained to the parents and imposed upon, rather than integrated within, the form and content of their world. A wedge is progressively driven between the child as a member of a family and community, and the child as a member of a school. Either way, the child and his parents are expected to drop their social identity, as well as their way of life and its symbolic representation, at the school gate. For, by definition, their culture is deprived, the parents inadequate in both the moral and skill orders they transmit. I do not mean by this that no satisfactory home-school relations can or do take place; I mean rather that the parents must be brought *within* the educational experience of the schoolchild by doing what they *can* do, and can do with *confidence*. There are many ways in which parents can help the child in his learning which are within the parents' sphere of competence. If this happens, then the parents can feel adequate and confident in relation to both the child *and* the school. This may mean that the *contents* of the learning in school should be drawn much more from the child's experience in his family and community.

Concept of Compensatory Education as a Distractor

Thus far, I have criticized the use of the concept of compensatory education because it distracts attention from the deficiencies in the school itself and focuses upon deficiencies within the community, family, and child. We can add to these two criticisms a third. The concept of compensatory education points to the overwhelming significance of the early years of the child's life in the shaping of his later development. Clearly, there is much evidence to support this view and the implication that we should create an extensive nursery school system. However, it would be foolhardy indeed to write off the post-seven-years-of-age educational experience as having little influence. Minimally, what is required initially is to consider the whole age period up to the conclusion of the primary stages as a unity. This would require considering our approach at any *one* age in the context of the *whole* of the primary stage. This implies a systematic, rather than a piecemeal, approach.

I am arguing here for taking as the unit, not a particular period in the life of the child (for example three to five years, or five to seven years), but rather a stage of education: the primary stage. We should see all we do in terms of the sequencing of learning, the development of sensitivities within the context of the primary stage. To accomplish this, the present social and educational division between infant and junior stages (five to seven and seven to eleven) must be weakened, as well as the insulation between primary and secondary stages (five to eleven and eleven to fifteen); and otherwise gains at any one age may well be vitiated by losses at a later age.

I suggest that we should stop thinking in terms of compensatory education and instead consider most seriously and systematically the conditions and contexts of the educational environment. The very form our research takes tends to confirm the beliefs underlying the organization, transmission, and evaluation of knowledge by the school. The research proceeds by assessing criteria of attainment that schools hold and then measures the competence of different social groups in reaching these criteria. We take one group of children whom we know beforehand possess attributes favorable to school achievement, and a second group of children whom we know beforehand lack these attributes. Then we evaluate one group in terms of what it lacks when compared with the other. In this way research, unwittingly, underscores the notion of deficit and confirms the status quo of a given organization, transmission, and, in particular, evaluation of knowledge.

Research very rarely challenges or exposes the social assumptions underlying what counts as valid knowledge, or what counts as a valid realization of that knowledge. There are exceptions in the area of curriculum development, but, even here, the work often has no built-in attempt to evaluate the changes. This holds particularly for the Educational Priority Areas "feasibility" projects in England.

Finally, we do not face up to the basic question: *What is the potential for change within educational institutions as they are presently constituted?* A lot of activity does not necessarily mean action.

I have taken so much space discussing the new educational concepts and categories because, in a small way, the work I have been doing has inadvertenty contributed to their formulation. It might be, and has been, said that my research, through focusing upon the subculture and forms of familial socialization, has also distracted attention from the conditions and contexts of learning in school. The focus upon language usage sometimes led people to divorce the use of language from the substratum of cultural meanings which are initially responsible for the language use. The concept "restricted code" has been equated with "linguistic deprivation," or even with the nonverbal child.

We can distinguish between uses of language which can be called "context bound" and uses of language which are less context bound. Consider, for example, the two stories below, which Peter Hawkins constructed as a result of his analysis of the speech of middle-class and working-class five-year-old children. The children were given a series of four pictures and they were invited to tell the story which the pictures illustrated. The first picture showed some boys playing football; in the second, the ball goes through the window of a house; the third shows a woman looking out of the window and a man making an ominous gesture; and, in the fourth, the children are moving away.

Here are two children's stories:

(1) Three boys are playing football and one boy kicks the ball and it goes through the window the ball breaks the window and the boys are looking at it and a man comes out and shouts at them because they've broken the window so they run away and then that lady looks out of her window and she tells the boys off.

(2) They're playing football and he kicks it and it goes through there it breaks the window and they're looking at it and he comes out and shouts at them because they've broken it so they run away and then she looks out and she tells them off.

With the first story, the reader does not need to see the four pictures which were used as the basis for the story, whereas, in the case of the second story, the reader requires the pictures in order to make sense of the story. The first story is free of the context which generated it, whereas the second story is much more closely tied to its context. As a result, the meanings of the second story are implicit, whereas the meanings of the first story are explicit.

Universalistic and Particularistic Meanings

It is not that the working-class children do not have in their passive vocabulary the words used by the middle-class children. Nor is it the case that the children differ in their tacit understanding of the linguistic rule system. Rather, what we have here are differences in the use of language arising out of a specific context. One child makes the meanings which he is realizing through language explicit for the person he is telling the story to, whereas the second child does not do so to the same extent. The first child takes very little for granted, whereas the second child takes a great deal for granted. Thus, the first child saw the task as a context in which his meanings were required to be made explicit, whereas the second child did not see the task as requiring such explication of meaning. It would not be difficult to imagine a context where the first child would produce speech rather like the second. What we are dealing with here are differences in the way children use language in the same context. We could say that the speech of the first child generated *universalistic meanings,* in the sense that the meanings are freed from the context and so understandable by all. The speech of the second child generated *particularistic meanings,* in the sense that the meanings are closely tied to the context and would be fully understood by others only if they had access to the context which originally generated the speech. Thus universalistic meanings are less bound to a given context, whereas particularistic meanings are severely context-bound.

Another example follows. When she controls her child, one mother places great emphasis upon language, because she wishes to make explicit and to elaborate for the child certain rules and the reasons for the rules, as well as their consequences. In this way, the child has access through language to the relationships between his particular act, which evoked the mother's control, and certain general principles and reasons and consequences, which serve to universalize the particular act. Another mother places less emphasis upon language when she controls her child, deals with only the particular act, and does not relate it to general principles and their reasoned basis and consequences. Both children learn that there is something they are supposed, or not supposed, to do. However, the first child learns rather more than this. The grounds for the first mother's acts have been made explicit and been elaborated; the grounds of the second mother's acts are implicit, unspoken. Our research shows just this: that the social classes differ in terms of the *contexts* which evoke certain linguistic realizations. Mothers in the middle-class (it is important to add not all), relative to working-class mothers (and, again, it is important to add not all by any means), place greater emphasis upon the use of language in socializing the child into the moral order, in disciplining the child, and in the communication and recognition of feeling. The first child is oriented toward universalistic meanings which transcend a given context, whereas the second child is oriented toward particularistic meanings which are closely tied to a given context and so do not transcend it. This does not mean that working-class mothers are non-verbal, but rather that they differ from the middle-class mothers in the *contexts* which evoke universalistic meanings. They are *not* linguistically deprived; neither are their children.

We can generalize from these two examples and say that certain groups of children, through the forms of their socialization, are oriented toward receiving and offering universalistic meanings in certain contexts, whereas other groups of children are oriented toward particularistic meanings. The linguistic realization of universalistic orders of meaning is very different from the linguistic realization of particularistic orders of meaning, and so are the forms of the social relation (for example, between mother and child) which generate these. We can say then that what is made available for learning, how it is made available and the patterns of social relation are also very different.

When we consider the children in school, we can see that there is likely to be difficulty since the school is necessarily concerned with the transmission and development of universalistic orders of meaning. The school is concerned with making explicit, and elaborating through language, principles and operations as these apply to objects (science subjects) and persons (arts subjects). One child, through his socialization, is already sensitive to the symbolic orders of the school, whereas the second child is much less sensitive to the universalistic orders of the school. The second child is oriented toward particularistic orders of meaning which are context-bound, in which principles and operations are implicit, and toward a form of language use through which such meanings are realized. The school is necessarily trying to develop in the child orders of relevance and relation as these apply to persons and objects, which are not initially the ones he spontaneously moves toward. The problem of educability at one level, whether in Europe, the U.S.A., or newly developing societies, can be understood in terms of a confrontation between the universalistic orders of meaning and the social relationships which generate them, and the particularistic orders of meanings and the social relationships which generate them, which the child brings with him to the school. *Orientations toward meta-languages of control and innovation are not made available to these children as part of their initial socialization.*

The Transmission of Knowledge and Meaning

I have stressed that the school is attempting to transmit uncommonsense knowledge, that is, public knowledge realized through various meta-languages. Such knowledge I have called "universalistic." However, it is also the case that the school both implicitly and explicitly is transmitting values, and their attendant morality, which affect educational contents and contexts of education. They do this by establishing criteria for acceptable pupil and staff conduct. Further, these values and morals affect the content of educational knowledge through the selection of books, texts, and films, and through examples and analogies used to assist access to public knowledge (universalistic meanings). Thus the working-class child may be placed at a considerable disadvantage in relation to the *total* culture of the school. It is not made for him; he may not answer to it.

I have suggested that the forms of an elaborated code give access to universalistic orders of meaning in the sense that the principles and operations controlling object and person relationships are made explicit through the use of language. Restricted codes give access to particularistic orders of meaning in which the principles and operations controlling object and person relationships are rendered implicit through the use of language (Bernstein, 1962). I have also tried to explain the cultural origins of these codes and their change (the most developed version is in Bernstein, 1965). If we now go back to our earlier formulation, we can say that elaborated codes give access to universalistic orders of meaning, which are less context-bound, whereas restricted codes give access to particularistic orders of meaning, which are far more context-bound.

Because a code is restricted, it does not mean that a child is nonverbal; nor is he, in the technical sense, linguistically deprived, for he possesses the same tacit understanding of the linguistic rule system as any child. It simply means that there is a restriction on the *contexts* and on the *conditions* which will orient the child to universalistic orders of meaning, and to making those linguistic choices through which such meanings are realized and so made public. It does not mean that the children cannot produce, at any time, elaborated speech in particular contexts.

It is critically important to distinguish between speech variants and a restricted code. A speech variant is a pattern of linguistic choices which is specific to a particular context: for example, when one talks to children, when a policeman gives evidence in court, when close friends talk together, or when people talk at cocktail parties or in train encounters. Because a code is restricted, it does not mean that a speaker will not in some contexts, and under specific conditions, use a range of modifiers or subordinations and the like, but it does mean that where such choices are made they will be highly context specific. Because a code is elaborated, it does not mean that in some contexts, under specific conditions, a speaker will not use a limited range of modifiers, subordinations, and the like. Rather, it does mean that such choices will, again, be highly context specific. For example, if an individual has to produce a summary (consider a précis), then it is likely that this will affect his linguistic choices.

Language and Socialization

The term "code" refers to the transmission of the deep meaning structure of a culture or subculture—the core meaning structure. Codes, in this view, make substantive the culture or subculture through their control over the linguistic realizations of contexts critical to the process of *socialization.* Building on the work of Professor Michael Halliday (1969), we can distinguish analytically four critical contexts.

1. The regulative contexts: these are the authority relations, in which the child is made aware of the moral order and its various backings.
2. The instructional contexts: here the child learns about the objective nature of objects and acquires various skills.
3. The imaginative or innovating contexts: here the child is encouraged to experiment and re-create his world on his own terms and in his own way.
4. The interpersonal contexts: here the child is made aware of affective states—his own and others.

In practice, these are interdependent, but the emphasis and contents will vary from one group to another. I am suggesting that the critical orderings of a culture or subculture are made substantive, are made palpable, through the form of its linguistic realizations of these four contexts—initially in the family. If these four contexts are realized through the predominant use of restricted speech variants pointing to particularistic—that is, relatively context-tied—meanings, then I infer that the deep structure of the communication is controlled by a restricted code. If these four contexts are realized predominantly through elaborated speech variants, which point toward relatively context-independent—that is, universalistic—meanings, then I infer that the deep structure of the communication is controlled by an elaborated code. Because the code is restricted, it does not mean that the users do not realize elaborated speech variants, at any time, but rather that *such variants will be used infrequently in the process of the socialization of the child in his family.*

The concept of code involves a distinction similar to the one which linguists make between surface and deep structure of the grammar. Thus sentences which look superficially different can be shown to be generated from the same rules. In the same way, although the linguistic choices involved in a summary will be markedly different from those involved in a self-conscious poem, which in turn will be markedly different from the linguistic choices involved in an analysis of physical or moral principles, or different again from the linguistic realization of forms of control, they may all, under certain conditions, point to the underlying regulation of restricted or elaborated codes.

Because the subculture or culture, through its forms of social integration, generates a restricted code, this does not mean that the resultant speech and meaning system is linguistically or culturally deprived, that the children have nothing to offer the school, or that their imaginings are not significant. Nor does it mean that we have to teach the children formal grammar. Nor does it mean that we have to interfere with their dialect. There is nothing, but nothing, in the dialect as such, which prevents a child from internalizing and learning to use universalistic meanings. If the contexts of learning, the examples, the reading books, are not contexts which are triggers for the children's imaginings, are not triggers for the children's curiosity and explorations in his family and community, then the child is not at home in the educational world. If the teacher has to say continuously, "Say it again, darling, I didn't understand you," then in the end the child may say nothing. If the culture of the teacher is to become part of the consciousness of the child, then the culture of the child must first be in the consciousness of the teacher. This may mean that the teacher must be able to understand the child's dialect, rather than deliberately attempting to change it. Much of the contexts of our schools is unwittingly drawn from aspects of the symbolic world of the middle-class, and so when the child steps into school he is stepping into a symbolic system which does not provide for him a linkage with his life outside.

Education as Universalistic Meanings

It is an accepted educational principle that we should work with what the child can offer. Why don't we practice it? The introduction of the child to the universalistic meanings of public forms of thought is not compensatory education—it is *education.* It is in itself not making children middle-class. How it is done, through the implicit values underlying the form and context of the educational environment, might. We need to distinguish between the principles and operations that it is our task as teachers to transmit and develop in the children, and the contexts we create in order to do this. We should start recognizing that the social experience the child already possesses is valid and significant, and that this social experience should be reflected back to him as being valid and significant. It can only be reflected back to him if it is a part of the texture of the learning experience we create. If we spent as much time thinking through the implications of this as we do thinking about the implications of the Piaget developmental sequences, then possibly schools might become exciting and challenging environments for parents, children, and teachers.

Over and beyond the issues raised so far, stand much larger questions: the question of what counts as having knowledge, the question of what counts as a valid realization of that knowledge, the question of the organizational contexts we create for educational purposes. For each of these questions we can add, "in relation to what age?" I have deliberately avoided adding, "in relation to what ability group?" because even if such a question at some point becomes relevant, the answer to it depends upon the answers to the earlier questions.

We need to examine the social assumptions underlying the organization, distribution, and evaluation of knowledge, for it is not the case that there is one and only one answer to the above questions. The power relationships created outside of the school penetrate the organization, distribution, and evaluation of knowledge through the social context of their transmission. The definition of educability is itself at any one time an attenuated consequence of these power relationships. To ask these questions is not to eschew the past, to foreshorten one's perspective to the strictly contemporary; it is rather to invite us to consider R. Lynd's question: knowledge for what?

Finally, we do not know what a child is capable of, as we have as yet no theory which enables us to create sets of optimal learning environments. Even if such a theory existed, it is most unlikely that resources on the scale required would be made available to make it substantive.

References

Bernstein, B. "Linguistic Codes, Hesitation Phenomena and Intelligence," *Language and Speech,* 5 (1962), 31.

———. "A Socio-Linguistic Approach to Social Learning," in *Social Science Survey*, ed. J. Gould. London: Penguin Book, 1965.

———. "A Socio-Linguistic Approach to Socialization: with Some Reference to Educability," in *Directions in Sociolinguistics*, ed. J. Gumperz and D. Hymes. New York: Holt, Rinehart and Winston, 1970.

Central Advisory Council for Education (England). *Children and Their Primary Schools*. London: Her Majesty's Stationery Office, 1967.

Central Advisory Council for Education (England). *Half Our Future*. London: Her Majesty's Stationery Office, 1963.

Fantini, M. and G. Weinstein. *The Disadvantaged: Challenge to Education*. New York: Harper and Row, 1968.

Halliday, M. A. K. "Relevant Models of Language: The Study of Language," *Educational Review*, 22 (1969).

Hawkins, P. R. "Social Class, the Nominal Group and Reference," *Language and Speech*, 12 (1969), 125–135.

Rosenthal, R. and L. Jacobson. *Pygmalion in the Classroom*. New York: Holt, Rinehart and Winston, 1968.

EARLY CHILDHOOD EDUCATION FOR THE DISADVANTAGED: WHAT RESEARCH SAYS

Helen F. Robison

Helen F. Robison reviews what research says about early childhood education for the disadvantaged and finds that, after more than a decade of efforts, there seems to be less certainty than ever about causes and cures, with the consequence that basic assumptions are being challenged and different kinds of research questions are now being asked. She discusses problems of comparability of target groups, the nature of control groups, conceptual frameworks, curriculum design, teacher training and supervision, and evaluation of outcomes.

In considering who are the disadvantaged in early childhood programs, Robison finds operational definitions are usually applied with low family income and ethnic or minority group status among the common attributes of populations designated as disadvantaged. She takes a sharp look at the "deficit" model of the disadvantaged child, suggesting that it needs considerable modification. Both the child and the school are in need of change. While the former's slow development of conceptual thinking is dysfunctional, the school must drastically alter its staffing, curriculum, and instructional strategies to supply a more adequate educational environment.

The theoretical bases undergirding many research designs are, Robison maintains, woefully weak: neither instructional nor learning theories are adequate. The theoretical bases for several research projects (for example, those of Bereiter, Deutsch, Gray and Klaus, Kamii, and Moore) are discussed, and the program results are assessed. Robison finds that most preschool programs with some structure and specificity produce results, but, unfortunately, "the public school has been successful in containing or washing out achieved gains."

The difficulties in setting up and comparing experimental and control groups of preschoolers and the consequent problems of understanding the effects of specific treatments are discussed. Curriculum designs range from programs in which explicit and detailed instructional tasks are spelled out to those which are relatively open-ended. Options available to children and teachers may be limited or many. Whereas systems analyses are being applied to instructional procedures, curriculum designs, and program sequencing, Robison indi-

cates that the results are not yet available to aid planners in selecting from competing programs.

Robison finds that the press for dissemination of new programs and the demand for new curriculum specifications result in popularity of prepackaged designs, many of which claim to be "teacher proof" in terms of prepared materials and resources. Teacher training and supervision of teachers are particularly critical in inner-city schools because of the high turnover of personnel. Finally, Robison details some of the problems of evaluation of new programs in early childhood, problems of instrumentation, design, and procedure.

Infancy studies, studies of the effects of improvement in the family's socioeconomic status, longitudinal studies of continuation of the optimum conditions delineated for preschool programs, stability of changes in young children—these are just a few of the many research areas Robison advances as needing further study. She concludes with a detailing of significant, researchable questions.

Helen F. Robison is Associate Professor of Education at Baruch College of the City University of New York.

EARLY CHILDHOOD EDUCATION FOR THE DISADVANTAGED: WHAT RESEARCH SAYS

Helen F. Robison

After more than a decade of research on early childhood education of the disadvantaged, there appears to be less certainty than before about causes and cures; basic assumptions are being challenged and the nature of research questions is changing. The "deficit" model of the child is increasingly viewed as inadequate and dysfunctional for program development. Other dilemmas concern the seemingly low potency of preschool programs in preventing educational retardation, parental roles in preschool education, and the relationship between economic improvement and academic progress. In addition to fundamental problems of theory and design of programs, urgent questions relate to criteria for evaluation of outcomes, as well as teacher training and supervision in implementation of new programs.

Polemical discussions frequently revolve around a global question in early childhood education of the disadvantaged: that is, should change be primarily a function of the child, or of the school, or both? It may seem obvious to the casual observer that this is a superficial question in the context of rapid change now operating everywhere in our society. Yet, this question turns out to be pivotal to many research designs. If it is assumed that the school will remain fundamentally unchanged, a more drastic model of child change is projected. At the other extreme, school and society changes may be seen as bridging the void to the present situation of the child in the slums, who remains unchanged while all environmental forces are shaped to fit his dimensions. In the latter view, preschool programs may or may not be important for day-to-day needs, but substantial social change becomes the catalyst which dissolves distressing problems of motivation, intellectual functioning, and applied intelligence. As a matter of fact, most research studies in education of young disadvantaged children seek to change the child's characteristic patterns of behavior in one or more aspects which are regarded as closely related to academic success. Along with hope for substantial change in the learner, concomitant requirements for school changes are frequently voiced.

Another point of view which probably has more support than would appear is the position that, since genetic factors, including prenatal conditions, account for most of the variance in IQ, changing the child is an exercise in futility (Jensen, 1969). Since, in this view, the child's malleability is limited, changes are required of the school in some important respect. It can be argued, from this position, either that further school segregation is required to isolate those of limited potential and to find ways to meet their limited abilities, or that drastic school changes are required to insure that this group actually realizes its admittedly limited potential; or it is possible to suggest that, with appropriate technology, the limited ability of even this group can be multiplied and elaborated, although to a considerably lesser degree than for those in the population who are better endowed genetically (*Harvard Educational Review*, Spring 1969).

This paper is concerned with the results of contemporary research on early education of disadvantaged children. Problems considered include comparability of target groups, nature of control groups, conceptual frameworks, curriculum design, teacher training and supervision, and evaluation of outcomes.

Target Groups

Who are these "disadvantaged" young children who are included in the various research studies? Are they a homogeneous population, or if not, what is known about the variability of these groups?

Operational definitions usually substitute for universal generalizations. Common attributes used singly, together, or in some combination to define "disadvantaged" groups include such economic and social characteristics as low family income (usually stated as about $3,000 for a family of four) or income primarily from welfare sources, ethnic minority group status, or deteriorated housing; and such academic characteristics as poor performance in school, reading retardation, limited linguistic ability, high rate of school dropouts, low rate of college admission, and low scores on IQ or achievement-type standardized tests.

Since low scores on IQ tests are so often used to identify "disadvantaged" children, it is interesting to note the range of mean IQ scores in the New York State Education Department's experimental prekindergarten projects, which are distributed over a wide geographic area. Among the Wave I children, who entered the prekindergarten classes in eight different school systems in 1964, Stanford-Binet pretest scores ranged from a mean IQ of 86.76 in one community to 95.07 in another. Wave II pretest scores, for the following year, for prekindergarten, ranged from 86.59 to 97.63 (Di Lorenzo, 1968, p. 113). Some of these projects are "integrated"; that is, middle-class children are included. In this situation, score changes after treatment are difficult to interpret. When mean scores change, is it possible that these changes primarily cluster in the subgroup of middle-class children? If one treatment seems to be paying off extraordinarily well, is this due primarily to the performance of middle-class children in the group? How can the impact of "integrated" education be compared with non-integrated education for four-year-olds unless the research design includes some subgrouping by academic or socioeconomic strata?

Deutsch's first group of four-year-olds had mean pretest Stanford-Binet scores of 99, both for experimental and control groups (Deutsch et al., 1968). How representative of the "disadvantaged" New York City black child population are these scores? How would they compare with other ethnic groups which contribute substantial numbers to the welfare rolls in New York City? The Gray-Klaus Early Training Project produced mean IQ pretest scores of 86 (Klaus and Gray, 1968), while the first Bereiter experimental group started with a mean of 95 (Bereiter and Engelmann, 1966). On the other hand, the Perry Preschool Project at Ypsilanti selected as its target group children in the "mentally retarded" range with IQ's from 50 to 85.

Children whose native language is not English may be untestable at the beginning of preschool programs. Many of the Spanish-speaking children cannot be tested by English-speaking personnel in New York City, various Texas communities, and in other states where there are concentrations of Spanish-speaking people. If pretests are administered, ridiculous scores are recorded, which inevitably produce fabulous change scores if the children learn to speak English. If pretests are not administered, change scores cannot be determined.

Thus a low pretest Stanford-Binet IQ score may mean different things, besides tester rapport and tester skill. Average scores may be just as complex to interpret. Prekindergarten enrollment is voluntary, and schools often complain that the parents who enroll their children are seldom among the most deprived families in the community. In one prekindergarten class, the teacher who had been visiting the families of the children described a number of families as middle-class, including fathers who were proprietors of one or more stores.

Problems in evaluating Head Start programs are instructive. As summarized by McDavid they included the following:

1. Head Start is a comprehensive, multi-dimensional program, not a stable, uniform, easily described form of intervention.
2. Goals are simultaneously pursued for immediate and ultimate impact.

3. There is paucity of information about the disadvantaged population.
4. It is extremely difficult to describe preschool program elements for clarity of comparison and contrast.
5. There is a conceptual problem of formulating researchable questions.
6. Methodological problems are many, especially the difficulty of sampling, in view of the non-random variations in the population, and the difficulty of locating control groups.
7. Logistic problems have to be considered. The nature of the Head Start programs requires evaluation to be unobtrusive and subordinate to program demands.
8. There are problems of middle-class researchers dealing with lower-class adults in data collection. (McDavid, 1968)

It may be noted that few studies feature limitations of the data as prominently as McDavid did in the Head Start evaluation. Few researchers note the vagaries of tester effect as Meier (1968) did. Caution is needed, therefore, in comparisons between and among the various research studies, since there may be considerable intra-group, as well as inter-group, variability. The low generalizability of these studies is usually ignored by those who cite them. Few studies are based on randomization of any kind of treatment, teacher assignment, or child assignment. Uncontrolled but significant variables are seldom identified or even mentioned, nor are unique aspects of any particular group. Numbers of children and teachers are usually small and these frequencies limit possibilities for data manipulation and interpretation.

Limited linguistic ability was identified as a characteristic of the "disadvantaged" population quite early. The "deficit" model of the child, and of the target groups generally, was based on a comparison of the low socioeconomic child with his middle-class counterpart, identifying the defects in the former (Hess, 1968, pp. 83–90). Deficits included lack of variety and clarity of stimuli in the home, which were regarded as conducive to cognitive growth. Children are not taken on trips to parks, zoos, and museums. There are too few objects and the environment is so permeated by static that children find difficulty ordering, categorizing, and classifying their familiar milieu. Other lacks include stimulating adult-child interaction and verbalization, sufficient varieties of adult models, motivation and stimuli for intellectual behavior, and environmental requirements for perseverance, deferment of need gratification, and task orientation. The deficit model has been elaborated by many researchers, despite the inferred nature of most deprivations and the difficulty of studying them directly. The Bereiter pattern drill program assumes all deficits are in the child and trains him to overcome the lacks which would otherwise unfit him for the school as it is.

It is not clear how such eminently passive experiences as visits to zoos and museums are thought to stimulate cognitive growth in young children. Children of migratory farm workers may be among the most-traveled of all youngsters, but such children tend to be among the very low scorers on standardized IQ tests and among the poorest bets for academic success in school. Bereiter avoids trips and real-life experiences of this type, chiefly on the ground that school time is limited and must be used selectively for the highest-priority deficits, which he finds in language and in logical thinking.

While the deficit model does not require the feature of irreversible retardation, there tends to be associated with it either an assumption, similar to Montessori's, that there are critical periods in the young child's development when stimulus deprivation can be crucial and result in irreversible damage to normal development, or that while no period is critical, early development is a time of greater plasticity and opportunity for enrichment for optimum growth and thus early intervention is more efficient, easier, and more reliable than intervention at later times. Deficits are sometimes viewed as specific, such as poor auditory discrimination, and sometimes as more global, such as retardation in development of representational and symbolic forms of cognition. Clearly, the deficit model requires changes in the child.

The opposite of the deficit model, which has been most clearly defined by socio-linguists, lacks a specific rubric. This positive model, if it can be called that, regards the linguistic behavior of the slum child as a valid, authentic language with its own complex structure and features, which happens to differ from the equally authentic dialect known as "standard English." Researchers who use a positive model tend to find other aspects of family and community living in the inner city equally authentic and beneficial. For example, young children in low socioeconomic areas are often found to be independent at earlier ages and more highly developed in responsibility for younger siblings than middle-class children. The extended family, supplementing the frequent matriarchal family, is viewed as an additional strength in child-rearing in the slums. Values cited include sharing, mutual helpfulness in financial and family needs, tolerance for a wide range of behavior, patience, and strength in the face of enormous adversity, whether of joblessness, poor housing, or ill health. Affectivity and close human relationships might be added to the list of authentic values of overcrowded slum living.

It may be noted that positive models do not necessarily require programs different from those deduced from deficit models. This may be because researchers are usually middle-class whites who find it difficult to conceive of successful coping in today's world without the skills and competencies which are the hallmark of the middle class. Or, it may be due to the realities of modern life, which currently seem to offer no alternative to increasingly abstract and symbolic forms of human behavior.

Ideally, it may be argued, the young child should learn reading and all skills and tool subjects in his native dialect, along with second dialect learning as a minor but important feature of his early education. One of the difficulties is that there are many different dialects lumped together as "non-standard English," so that it would be a rare teacher who would know more than one. Even where teacher and children who share a common dialect may be found—which must be possible in many Southern states, especially if a teacher could be selected from among the parents of the children—problems of encoding and decoding are difficult to overcome. Books and printed matter are written in the standard English dialect. The i/t/a programs overcome this problem easily, since the only change introduced is in orthography, not in syntactic structures or standard word spelling. Currently, there seems to be more profit in helping the speaker of non-standard dialect to learn to read the standard dialect.

Actually, as linguists and other researchers analyze the speech behavior of young speakers of non-standard dialect, they are challenging the stereotype of the "non-verbal" disadvantaged child and of the language limitations on his conceptual development. The Labov paper cited above describes the context within which non-verbal behavior and constrained responding are generated. Other data are available to suggest that, under favorable circumstances, a group of pre-kindergarten black children in Central Harlem were performing as well as, or better than, children from upper socioeconomic groups, particularly on sentence structure (Robison, 1968, p. 31). Other information about the verbal behavior of this group includes the findings by Rigrodsky and Morrison that the majority of the children had adequate articulation, as defined by the Templin-Darley scores for articulatory adequacy, with the most severely defective sound tested the voiced "th" in final position; and that the most common type of articulatory error, in initial, medial, and final position in words, was the substitution of one phoneme for another (Robison, 1969, pp. 36–40). Labov has noted that regional variations in standard English dialect pronunciations seem to offer relatively few obstacles to reading success. Speakers who pronounce "pen" as though it were written "pin" seem to have little difficulty reading it as "pen."

Audio-taped and video-taped recordings of the verbal behavior of the children cited in the preceding study offer overwhelming evidence that this population is highly verbal and, surprisingly, tends to use a high proportion of standard dialect along with varieties of non-standard dialect (Robison, 1969, p. 197). However, it must be granted that this group readily produces passive, non-verbal behavior for visiting psychologists, hurried testers, and poorly-trained teachers.

One transcription of a video-taped recording in an all-black prekindergarten class in Central Harlem in the spring of 1968 yielded 48 verbalizations by children in a discussion with the teacher about a carpentry project just completed. Of these 48 verbalizations, 21 were complete sentences of standard syntax, such as, "We could make a train out of it," "You can put another one on there," "We used a hammer," "No, we made a tunnel," and "We used a saw." There were quite a few one-word responses, which in context were appropriate to the teacher's questions; the use of full sentences would have resulted in unusually stilted and formal language structure. In fact, had full sentences been required, the rapid give-and-take of verbalizing about a just-completed activity would have been sacrificed, and drill in productive verbalization would have been substituted for actual practice in immediate recall; in sequencing events which had to be juggled symbolically, in words, because they were already past; and in using flexible forms of prediction of future possibilities. The appropriateness of the children's verbal responses, in content and syntax, are themselves proof that the children possess adequate receptive language for the cognitive purposes just described and that they are usually able to produce the forms that are needed. Problems related primarily to specific vocabulary words, which were not always available when they were required (Robison and Schwartz, 1971a).

There is a substantial middle ground which views both the child and the school as in need of change. While the child is viewed as adequate and teachable, his apparently slow development of conceptual thinking is usually regarded as dysfunctional and in need of change. However, the school is seen as woefully inadequate to supply the needed environmental and human impetus without drastic change in staffing, curriculum, and teaching strategies.

Conceptual Framework

The theory which supports a research design is often its weakest feature. This is only to say that where fruitful and suggestive theory is needed, but not yet developed, researchers must make do with the inadequate instruments available. Neither instructional theories nor learning theories are yet equal to the difficult tasks at hand. Piagetian theory of the process of epistemological development is strained to produce guidelines for learning, teaching, and curriculum selection.

It is a rare researcher who dares to build empirical knowledge without some kind of theoretical security blanket. Yet it is difficult to deduce any specific curriculum design from its "theoretical" base. Most of the research projects have tended to focus on similar classroom experiences, despite some variations in conceptual framework. Generally, research projects have selected such primary goals as language, perceptual and conceptual development, motivation, and self-concepts.

Bereiter's program (Bereiter and Engelmann, 1966) makes no attempt to use a Piagetian base. He claims to be an empiricist who constructed his pre-primary program to fulfill the requirements for academic success in the primary grades, as presently constituted. His goals are short-range and his program is properly characterized as acculturational, since he attempts to shape the child into the image he thinks is required by teachers in the first and second grades of public schools. He assumes that the schools will change very little in the forseeable future. Despite the much-publicized and specially funded projects designated as "innovative," it would be difficult to contradict Bereiter's premise that sedentary, verbal, abstract, and rote forms of instruction continue to be dominant in schools.

Bereiter's pragmatic approach led him to espouse pattern drill procedures, which are similar to popular forms of instruction in foreign languages. His assumptions that young disadvantaged children have neither language nor logic are being challenged. So is his premise that the young child develops logical thinking through his instructional strategies, which are primarily verbal. This is to suggest that other pragmatists may select the same goals as Bereiter, without inferring that his particular program is more effective than others. The first group of children to experience Bereiter's experimental curriculum numbered only fifteen. He has followed some of these children into primary school grades, reporting very successful academic functioning.

The Deutsch program uses terms such as "enrichment" and "therapeutic" to describe goals. Deutsch contributed rich detail to the "deficit model," spelling out areas of cognitive and affective deficits which required intervention in order to produce desired change. This program features many aspects of the traditional social-adjustment nursery school, while adding or emphasizing selected elements (Deutsch, 1968).

Deutsch's program presents the same difficulty as other complex programs, in that descriptions fall far short of including all important features generally assumed in schooling young children or actually featured in practice. This problem, however, is common to all descriptions of school programs, even those which choose to extract what the researchers regard as most important features. Some of the distinctive aspects of the Deutsch program include use of some auto-instructional devices, such as listening centers with headsets and tape recorders;

emphasis on specified concepts, such as size, shape, and time, as children engage in related and informal activities; extensive use of short trips to park, zoo, and other local resources to broaden the child's experiential base; informal methods of language training; and work with parents.

Analyzing and categorizing so complex a curriculum is a formidable task. Which elements are necessary? Are necessary elements sufficient? Is there more payoff from some educational strategies than from others? Do different teachers actually stress different aspects of this curriculum, depending on their preferences, skills, and understandings? How much "quality control" can be exercised over programs which fundamentally are developed more or less spontaneously by teachers as they initiate activity and respond to children's behavior? Even if "quality control" could be exercised, would it be desirable?

Despite the problems of encapsulating a program such as Deutsch's, its major thrust appears to be of the cognitive-developmental type, as Kohlberg uses this term (Kohlberg, 1968). That is, the program is less concerned with specific content teaching than with supporting and stimulating natural developmental progress. Long-range goals seem primary in this program, to facilitate maximum growth and utilization of intellectual potential (Deutsch, 1965). However, some specific content teaching seems to be included to prevent or arrest defined deficits, although the proportion of this "cultural training" to the "cognitive developmental" procedures cannot be determined from the available data. It is likely that, except where programs rely on technology or on similarly programmed material for specific content or skill teaching, it would be difficult to assess the impact of specific content teaching in any program without developing new instruments and categories for recording and analyzing classroom experience in early childhood programs.

In the Deutsch program, it might be noted, a control group of children not involved in the prekindergarten program regressed on the Stanford-Binet IQ test from the pretest mean of 99 to a posttest mean of 93, at the end of the year. The first experimental group's mean IQ rose from 99 to 102 at the end of the prekindergarten year, and to 104 at the end of the second year, in the experimental kindergarten program. On Peabody Picture Vocabulary Test scores, during the prekindergarten year, the control group had a mean posttest raw score of 37.9, compared with 44.9 for the experimental group. This, incidentally, is one of the projects in which the pre-primary IQ advantage by the experimental group was washed out in the primary public school program.

An interesting study by Karnes, Teska, and Hodgins (1969) compared three different programs, including Bereiter's, over a three-year period. Groups of children, who entered these intervention programs at age four, were randomly assigned to one of the three programs and were tested through the end of the first grade of public school. One group received what is described as a "traditional" nursery school program (T) in the research center, featuring incidental and informal learning. These children received no other treatment and went on to the "traditional" public school kindergarten and first grade. A second group experienced the "Amelioration in Learning Defects" program (A), which featured structured learning episodes where the major emphasis was on language development, in conjunction with the manipulation of concrete materials, and through game formats. There were three twenty-minute learning periods daily, focusing on mathematics concepts, science, social studies, and reading readiness, as well as language development. During the second year, this group attended the "conventional" public school kindergarten in the morning and returned to the research center for a one-hour afternoon "supportive" program, with two periods of learning, emphasizing academic achievement.

The third group experienced the Bereiter-Engelmann pattern drill program, here termed "Direct Verbal" (D), for two years, although a few parents insisted on sending their children to the morning public school kindergarten session and to the D program in the afternoon. This program emphasizes intensive oral drill in verbal and logical patterns, since the basic assumption of the program is that these are the major deficits of disadvantaged children, and minimizes visual and manipulative materials. The daily schedule is divided into three periods, one each for language, arithmetic, and reading, and in each period one teacher works very intensively and directedly with five children. Generally, children learn rules by rote, and then apply these rules in tightly structured sequences of increasing difficulty and variation, and with decreasing prompts. The teaching structure has been compared to that used in teaching a foreign language, that is, drilling on patterns and then requiring the child to use the patterns with growing independence in the tasks presented to him. The second year of this program was a more advanced variation of the first year.

All children attended a racially-integrated public school first-grade program during the third year, with no intervention from the research team. Since only 59 children remained at the end of the third year of the study, final results are based on small frequencies. Nevertheless, the results of these intervention programs are interesting. All three groups initially tested in the mid-nineties on the Stanford-Binet. At the end of the first year, the A and D program children scored at 110, considerably above the mean of 102.6 for the T group. At the end of the second or kindergarten year, the D group soared to a mean 120.6, while the A group declined slightly to 108.6 and the T group to 100. After a year of public school first grade, there were no significant differences in mean IQ among the three groups, although the D group remained highest at 109.7, the A group was second at 104.3, and the T group maintained its score of 100.

An analysis of children's IQ score changes by strata, based on small frequencies, indicated the A program seemed most beneficial for low-normal or slow-learning children, and this benefit was attributed to the stress in this program on physical manipulation of objects accompanied by appropriate verbalizations, instead of on verbal learning alone. The sharp drop of IQ gains in the D group was attributed to the change in instruction from intensive small-group learning in the research program to large-group instruction in the public school.

Using the Illinois Test of Psycholinguistic Abilities to test language growth, the study found no significant differences at the end of the three-year period, with regression in all three groups during the first grade in public school. The A and D groups excelled in number readiness scores on the Metropolitan Readiness Test at the end of kindergarten and on reading achievement as measured by the California Achievement Test at the end of first grade. The authors of this paper conclude, "This study provides little evidence to support the introduction of early reading programs for disadvantaged children" (Karnes et al., 1969, p. 23). Thus, the D program offered two preschool years of reading instruction, without any advantage at the end of the first grade over a program which had supplied only planned readiness activities instead.

The common element of both the A and D programs is considered by the researchers to be the major emphasis on language development through intensive, highly structured programming, with learning tasks designed to achieve immediate goals, and the child's repetitive verbal practice in direct teacher-child interaction. Here, as in other projects, with small frequencies in each cell, and with further subgrouping by ability strata, generalizability will require further replication. Program description is also required to delineate the so-called traditional nursery school program, since it is difficult to determine which particular tradition is actually being followed. The "traditional" kindergarten program is equally vague and ambiguous. Nor are there data readily available on program implementation which permit any empirical assessment of children's actual classroom experiences in the three programs which were compared. It seems essential to begin to match rigor of data manipulation with equal rigor in program design and in recording and analyzing the realities of classroom implementation. Before cause and effect can be claimed for program and published results, data are needed to substantiate the nature of the treatment actually administered.

The Early Training Project of Gray and Klaus has been one of the few programs where children's IQ scores were maintained at high levels through the second grade of public school despite decreases after public school entrance (Klaus and Gray, 1968; Gray et al., 1965). This project had immediate and long-range goals, including emphasis on changing attitude and aptitude variables. Attitude variable goals were listed as achievement motivation, delay of gratification, persistence, interest in school-type activities, and identification with achieving role models. Perception, concept development, and language constituted the aptitude variables. In this program, teacher guidelines specified small-group activities for perceptual and conceptual development and activities related to selected themes, to enlarge the child's background of general information. Mean IQ gains for the first experimental group averaged nine points, while two control groups, without preschool or kindergarten experience, lost three and six points, respectively. The Gray-Klaus program presents a complex mix of cultural training with cognitive-developmental goals of the long-range type. As in other designs, the specific curriculum defined is not the only possible derivation from the selected goals and theory.

Kamii has developed a curriculum with a very clear Piagetian base, although the relationship between the theory and the curriculum, as in the projects cited above, may not be one of logical necessity. In the "Piaget-Derived Preschool Curriculum," cognitive growth is featured, while social, emotional, and physical development continue to be important objectives. Teaching goals are to help children "integrate and elaborate their experiences so that they will have the cognitive structures into which future educational experiences can be assimilated" (Sonnequist et al., 1969, p. 2). The program features the child's own actions on objects or sensory-motor activities and their consolidation as a base upon which to build the more complex requirements of operational intelligence. The "skillful" and "creative" teaching required is suggested and illustrated but not defined. Its features, as perceived from illustrative material, resemble the Piagetian clinical method of testing to collect data on the development of intellectual structures. Thus, the objectives, the teaching role, the specified curriculum design, and the assessment of children's progress all appear to derive from Piaget (Piaget, 1954, 1962, 1965, 1967).

Questions can be raised about the extent to which Piaget's epistemological studies contribute fruitfully to teaching methodology or curriculum sources for the young disadvantaged child. For example, for such goals of cognitive functioning as classification, ordering, or conservation, is it functional to ignore the bodies of knowledge known as the disciplines, where, in science and mathematics, for example, considerable experience is available in contemporary curriculum studies to offer rich content for children's learning? If language development is a goal, it is difficult to see how curriculum can be derived from the Piagetian studies so far published. Furthermore, Piaget has studied how mature forms of thinking have developed, not alternative or experimental forms. Neither has he differentiated disadvantaged populations in his studies, which focus on the normative.

If the Kamii study is enabled to follow the experimental groups through the primary grades, it will be interesting to find out how the groups fare in school. However, the problem of criteria for evaluation remains. Will comparisons continue to be based on IQ scores or on Piagetian-derived clinical tests, or will there be a shift to achievement scores on standardized tests of reading, arithmetic, and other subject-matter content? Until finer instruments of evaluation are fashioned, it will continue to be difficult to make meaningful comparisons of the effects of different curriculum designs.

A complex design is found in the New Nursery School Project at Greeley, Colorado, where three experimental groups of deprived, predominantly Spanish-speaking children are compared with three middle- and upper-class "contrast" groups and one deprived group without nursery school experience. The progress of these groups will be followed throughout the elementary school years. The experimental groups are offered a fairly traditional nursery school program, combined with the Edison Responsive Environment (ERE), popularly known as the "talking typewriter." The contrast groups are also using the ERE (Meier, 1968).

Meier reported that, on the Stanford-Binet, experimental groups averaged about ten points above the equally deprived stay-at-home control group but about fifteen points below their more advantaged contrast groups. At the end of the kindergarten year, the public school administered the Metropolitan Reading Readiness Test, and the experimental group scored at the 70th percentile while the disadvantaged control group scored at the 35th percentile. An interesting finding, comparing the experimental with the middle- and upper-class groups, was that the latter spent significantly less time in the typewriter booth but their average mastery level was significantly higher.

Very few programs are being assessed in as great detail as the New Nursery School Project, and very few programs lean so heavily on technology for language and reading instruction. With such an interesting research design, one could wish that it had been possible to add another contrast group, that is, a deprived group in a program without the ERE, so that the impact of the technology might have been more specifically evaluated.

The theoretical base for the New Nursery School Project design is difficult to delineate. O. K. Moore (1962), who developed the technology of the ERE, found it was premature to publish a full-fledged theory. Moore cited various sources of theoretical inspiration, especially George Herbert Mead and Georg Simmel, and specified basic assumptions of a responsive environment for young children, but if these generate a "conceptual framework," Moore has been loathe to claim it. In fact, Moore's description of programming the ERE reflects assumptions alternative to some of his initial premises, especially where the "exploratory" freedom of the child is suddenly changed to permit only responses to programmed procedures. The use of this technology on a limited, voluntary basis, in the context of various kinds of nursery school programs, will surely contribute rich data for future theory building.

Moore's interest in "developing an experimentally grounded theory of human problem solving and social interaction" did not mislead him into regarding this complex goal as easily attainable (Moore, 1965). Nevertheless, he has probably made considerable progress toward this goal in defining what he calls "theoretical notions."

A brief, and very inadequate, summary of Moore's theoretical ideas suggests the very fruitful notions he has been developing, which have surely contributed some suggestions, so far few in number, to instructional systems which have been designed for young children. His intriguing notion of man as the theorizing animal assumes that theories are usually learned from other people in the form of abstract models, which are closed in "critical features of our environment." Children "play their way to social competence," learning theories through "folk models," which consist of such forms as puzzles, games of chance, games of strategy, and the normative qualities of esthetic experiences (Moore, 1965, p. 108).

Moore's important contribution to fashioning environments to offer specified forms of experience has been little studied by those seeking to prevent or ameliorate educational retardation or disadvantage. It may be that there has been too much concern with Piagetian developmental theory and too little concern with theory and research, in various disciplines, which have dealt directly with environmental restructuring and change. The current trend to more interdisciplinary types of research teams may help to correct prior imbalance and to introduce some of the fresh thinking emanating from such diverse fields of study as urban planning, esthetics, architecture, anthropology, and socio-linguistics.

There are other interesting program studies with disadvantaged young children, including some in which children have an "integrated" school experience in a newly-devised curriculum with middle-class children, and others which vary different aspects of the curriculum or the program. In all cases, there are problems of homogeneity of target groups, of specificity of program design and of the extent of its implementation in the classroom, and of fine enough standardized instruments to differentiate results from different programs. Most preschool programs with some structure and specificity seem to produce similar results, and, generally, the public school has been successful in containing or washing out achieved gains.

Control Groups

Earlier studies compared children in preschool programs with children who stayed home. The current trend is to compare results from one program with the results of other programs. Comparing children in school with stay-at-homes is unsatisfactory because the school children necessarily learn how to take tests and how to respond to requests of an academic nature. The resultant "IQ change" often looks spurious when the stay-at-homes catch up during the following year when they attend school.

Control groups of stay-at-homes often appear to differ in some important way from the experimental group in school, even when a random assignment can be made. It will be increasingly difficult to make such assignments as school opportunities expand for young disadvantaged children and stay-at-homes increasingly constitute a qualitatively different group of children, in families with little motivation to seek schooling.

When different programs are compared, with the same population —so that, in effect, each program constitutes a control for the others— resulting differences might be very meaningful where assignment of children, teachers, and treatment can be randomized. This is seldom possible in practice, for administrative, teacher, and parent-related reasons. When different programs are implemented either in the same school building or within a small geographical area where teachers tend to meet, visit, and interchange experiences, program design may be blunted by a homogenization procedure which operates through social and professional contracts of teachers, efforts of supervisors and principals, and, in some cases, pressures from parents. Where all comparisons include "experimental" treatments, the Hawthorne effect tends to be uniform and therefore should contribute less to differentiated results than where experimental programs are compared with none or with "traditional" ones.

There will continue to be serious problems in setting up and comparing experimental and control groups. Parent groups may be among those who offer the strongest resistance to enrolling a child in a control group, as the pressures for school achievement remain undiluted.

Curriculum Design

All curriculum designs come to terms, sooner or later, with the young child in his need for movement and change, for warm adult relationships, and for resistance to constraint and imposition. In some programs, the area of choices open to the child is very wide, whereas in other programs it is narrow.

Some designs are explicit and detailed in curriculum experiences, notably the Bereiter program, which is equally clear about teaching role and teaching strategy. The teacher sets the pace and controls the learning episode, and she reinforces desirable behavior with praise. No alternatives or choices are available to the child in lieu of the prescribed drill program. Instructional tasks are clearly defined, and so are subgrouping and time periods. Arithmetic, language, and reading are the selected content areas, and specific aspects of each of these areas are identified. Teacher training should be relatively easy and rapid, except for teachers unwilling to transform their teaching styles to accord with the prescribed procedures. Supervision seems equally uncomplicated, since decision-making by child, teacher, or supervisor must necessarily be limited in this design.

Most designs are far more complex than Bereiter's, with either undefined subject matter or more selected content areas, often including science, music, art, and some social studies. In the Kamii program, curriculum is developed by researchers and the teaching staff in weekly meetings, and evaluated in subsequent meetings. Content areas are undefined and classroom experiences are apparently devised primarily to meet specified cognitive goals, without regard to patterned use of curriculum sources. The Gray-Klaus curriculum seems to be similar, although there appear to be more prescriptions than in the Kamii design, more structured drill or practice games, and fewer decisions open to child, teacher, or supervisor.

The Deutsch curriculum appears to be one that has evolved out of teachers' empirical classroom experience, although the program itself evidently has some clear goals in teaching various skills and behaviors. Options to child, teacher, and supervisor seem to be wide. Content areas are apparently undefined, with cognitive and language goals the main determiners of the appropriateness of classroom experience.

Some systems analysis is now being applied to instructional procedures and to curriculum design and sequencing; but results are not yet available to assist in the patterning of curriculum for young children along more rational and replicable lines than those described above. Systems analysis may be helpful in two ways. Hierarchies of learning goals may provide more specific and helpful objectives for program development than teacher guesses and hunches. A parallel structure could be composed of hierarchies of sets of classroom experiences, interchangeable as to level of cognitive complexity, but differentiated as to content or materials use, or other such important instructional components. The advantage of such analysis is that it would make it possible to program those aspects of instructional design which the machine can be trusted to handle, while the flexibility required for informed judgments would be left to teachers.

Early childhood curriculum design will undoubtedly begin to receive more systematic study than it has heretofore. School systems which seek information about competing programs, and evaluators who are designated to assess their results are among a growing group of consumers who are in need of more informative criteria and better guidelines than can now be found.

Teaching and Supervision

To design a new program is not enough. Unless teachers can learn to implement it, and are willing to, the design cannot become reality. The simplest and most obvious types of new designs have considerable advantages over complex ones. If the design offers a "teacher-proof" package which relies largely on prepared teaching material in the form of film, tape, or equipment, quick, widespread implementation seems assured. If, however, a complex design relies on informed teacher judgments, with many options available, the need to retrain teachers to understand and master aleatory or unpredictable forms of behavior may consign such a program either to unrecognizable transformations or to non-use. The press for dissemination of new programs and the widespread demand for new curriculum specifications tend to favor designs which can be prepackaged and produced in considerable detail. This is the mass production syndrome—interchangeability of parts and rigidity of component specifications. Often what emerges as a fresh creation from the designing board losses its playfulness and flexibility in the process of reproduction.

Supervision is a key role in curriculum development and implementation. If supervision is conceived as a teaching strategy, to help teachers to acquire new understandings, skills, and attitudes, it seems essential to include supervisors in new program implementation. Support and facilitation in changing one's teaching behavior is required to ease the painfulness of transition and insecurity. Retraining teachers is a continuous requirement, even in experimental programs, because teacher turnover is high in so many communities, especially in slum neighborhoods.

Evaluation

Some of the problems of evaluation of new programs have been mentioned above. The use of IQ scores as criterion measures for intervention programs has proven unsatisfactory to most researchers. Unresolved problems about what IQ scores measure are compounded by differential goals of different programs and the lack of reliable standards by which to evaluate children's progress toward identified goals.

If the IQ is regarded as a fairly direct measurement of genetically determined intellectual ability, changes in IQ must of necessity be spurious, unless deprived environments are viewed as contributing to inefficient use of native intelligence. In such a case, posttest IQ reflects a truer measurement of intelligence, and it is the pretest IQ which is spuriously low. If the IQ is viewed as subject to considerable variability due to environmental deficits, as Bloom contends, one can accept his estimate that the effect of extremely poor environments on IQ scores can be as much as 20 IQ points (Bloom, 1964, p. 89). Environmentalists may regard the increased IQ scores as reflecting either increased intelligence due to environment enrichment or more efficient use of the same intellectual equipment, depending on their basic assumptions about intelligence.

Piagetian theory supplies another conception of intelligence. This theory views intelligence as a series of successive balances resulting from interaction between the child's assimilative and accommodative activities (Piaget, 1962 and 1965). Environmental and genetic forces both contribute to the development of intelligence, which can be viewed as having a specified structure at any point in time when the child may be asked for examples of intellectual functioning. This is a dynamic view of intelligence as a growing process, with a structure that comes into being and changes with experience, over time. Through the child's growing years, intelligence is always in the process of becoming and of being transformed into a more complex instrument. By contrast, the concept of IQ, or intelligence quotient, is a statistical one, static rather than dynamic (Elkind, 1969). Another view is that IQ is an abstract model of intelligence, substantially lacking in isomorphism with reality and incapable of reification.

School achievement scores on standardized tests may generally be more useful than IQ scores for purposes of comparison. Problems in using achievement scores for young children include floors too high to measure achievement of four- and five-year-olds; irrelevance of most achievement criteria to most preschool curriculum designs; varieties and non-comparability of different achievement tests; difficulties of administration of these tests, which often require child literacy and ability to write numbers, words, or other standard symbols; and the lack of fine calibration of such tests to differentiate results clearly.

We have seen recently a spate of new tests come onto the market which attempt to fill the great need for adequate evaluation of preschool programs. Some of these require administration in one sitting, lasting as long as forty-five minutes or an hour. Teachers of young children are properly dubious of such tests, which so overtax the child's ability to attend and to stay put. Some "non-verbal" tests require complex tester verbalization on tasks and procedures. A new achievement-type test which was recently developed to evaluate a specific new curriculum design had a test-retest reliability of only .49 (Robison and Schwartz, 1971b). Tester effects are considerable, not only for new testers but also for experienced testers. School provision for adequate test conditions is frequently inadequate.

What about the test results of programs that seek immediate goals as compared with those that feature long-range goals of efficient cognitive functioning? Does a fast payoff mean ephemeral gains? The data so far cannot answer most of the questions researchers and educators are asking.

Directions for Further Research

The concern with the three-to-five-year age range in "preschool" programs is broadening to include earlier and later ages, parental and community changes in attitudes and aspirations, and greater urgency to restructure schooling for all, not just for the children of the poor.

Infancy studies are growing rapidly on many college campuses today. Early education is being redefined to mean education and collaboration of parents-to-be as well as schooling of infants and toddlers from birth onward. European experience with infants and children under three is being studied by those who would develop viable models for American children. Scandinavian, Soviet, and Israeli experiences are of special interest to American researchers because of the substantial history of group care of very young children in these countries.

Interest in infancy and toddlerhood reflects hunches and evidence that parents really are more important in their children's early educational experience than anyone else, or than any other agents of educational experience. It also reflects hunches that motivation is established very early in life and that habits of linguistic and cognitive functioning may also have such firm, early roots that these must be nurtured as early in life as possible.

One project which was funded on a small scale by the Office of Economic Opportunity provided cash income for a sample of families, without any welfare strictures, to find out whether assurance of income over an admittedly short period of time might make a weighty contribution to progress in overcoming poverty. It would be helpful to establish whether decreased economic insecurity contributes to increased motivation for learning among the children in the family.

An obvious need in research on education of disadvantaged young children is a design which can distinguish differential academic progress among groups where the independent variable is improvement in the family's socioeconomic status. Other things being equal, as economists are wont to say, what happens when family income changes from welfare to earned sources and rises at the same time? What happens when the family's chief breadwinner moves from an unskilled to a semiskilled occupation, or even into a skilled, clerical, or professional job? It might be an oversimplification to look to such economic factors for the most drastic sources of change in motivational and aspirational aspects. Parent participation in children's schooling might be required in addition to economic improvement if desired goals are to be achieved. There may be other requirements as well.

A further need is a longitudinal study of a school experience which maintains throughout the elementary school years the optimum conditions delineated for preschool programs. In effect, a considerable restructuring of the school would be featured.

A host of specific research questions remain to be pursued. For example, is self-concept a class-based variable for young children? Does self-valuing change to any significant extent as a function of preschool education of a specific type? Are there reliable ways to ascertain the young child's self-concept? What is the relationship between self-concept and various criteria of academic functioning?

Is the evidence that so many preschool programs appear to have only transitory effects due to the overly narrow base of evaluation usually employed? Should more effort be channeled into devising better tests of motivation, social learnings, coping skills, or Piagetian-type cognitive functioning? Can we develop evaluative instruments fine enough to detect small but important changes in cognitive functioning; for example, a change from unstable counting of size of sets to stable counting based on one-to-one relationships?

Would it be more efficient for preschool programs to concentrate on immediate goals rather than long-range goals? If so, which immediate goals should have the highest priority? Should it be verbal statements of logical reasoning, early decoding instruction, social learnings, problem-solving, creativity, independence, responsibility, or sensory acuity?

If long-range goals are higher priority than immediate goals, what success criterion should be employed? Should it be achievement scores, addiction to reading outside of school, aspiration for graduate work, IQ scores, functioning on Piagetian tasks, or yet-to-be-constructed tests of applied intelligence?

Finally, what about environmental restructuring of a substantial nature? If O. K. Moore, or other imaginative researchers, can continue to spin off interesting theoretical notions which can develop into an integrated theoretical structure, will there be a more fruitful conceptualization of instructional systems, upon which more productive research designs can be built?

References

Bereiter, C. and Engelmann, S. *Teaching Disadvantaged Children in the Preschool.* Englewood Cliffs, N.J.: Prentice-Hall, 1966.

Bloom, B. *Stability and Change in Human Characteristics.* New York: John Wiley and Sons, Inc., 1964.

Chittenden, E. A. "Research Memorandum. Some Implications of Piaget's Research for Testing Young Children." Princeton, N.J.: Educational Testing Service, March 1969.

Deutsch, M. "Social Intervention and the Malleability of the Child." Fourth Annual School of Education Lecture, Cornell University, May 6, 1965.

Deutsch, M., I. Katz, and A. R. Jensen (eds.). *Social Class, Race and Psychological Development.* New York: Holt, Rinehart and Winston, 1968.

Di Lorenzo, L. T. and R. Salter. "An Evaluative Study of Prekindergarten Programs for Educationally Disadvantaged Children: Follow-up and Replication," *Exceptional Children,* 35, 2 (October 1968), 111–120.

Elkind, D. "Piagetian and Psychometric Conceptions of Intelligence, *Harvard Educational Review,* 39, 2 (Spring 1969), 319–337.

Gilmer, B. R. "Intra-Family Diffusion of Selected Cognitive Skills as a Function of Educational Stimulation." *DARCEE Papers and Reports,* Vol. 3, No. 1, 1969. Nashville, Tenn.: George Peabody College for Teachers.

Gray, W., R. A. Klaus, J. O. Miller, and B. J. Forrester. *The Early Training Project: A Handbook of Aims and Activities.* Nashville, Tenn.: George Peabody College for Teachers and Murfreesboro, Tenn., City Schools, 1965.

Harvard Educational Review, 39, 2 (Spring 1969), 273–356.

Hess, D. and R. M. Meyers (eds.). *Early Education.* Chicago: Aldine Press, 1968.

Jensen, A. R. "How Much Can We Boost I.Q. and Scholastic Achievement?" *Harvard Educational Review,* 39, 1 (Winter 1969), 1–123.

Karnes, M. B., J. A. Teska, and A. S. Hodgins. "A Longitudinal Study of

Disadvantaged Children Who Participated in Three Different Preschool Programs." Paper read at AERA meetings, Los Angeles, Calif., February 1969.

Klaus, R. A. and S. W. Gray. "The Early Training Project for Disadvantaged Children: A Report After Five Years." *Monographs of the Society for Research in Child Development,* 1968, Vol. 33, No. 4.

Kohlberg, L. "Early Education: A Cognitive-Developmental View," *Child Development,* 39, 4 (December 1968), 1013–1062.

Labov, W. "The Non-Standard Negro Vernacular: Some Practical Suggestions." In *Position Papers from Language Education for the Disadvantaged, Report No. 3,* NDEA National Institute for Advanced Study in Teaching Disadvantaged Youth, June 1968. Pp. 4–7.

———. "The Logic of Nonstandard English," in *Language and Poverty,* ed. J. Williams. Chicago: Markham Publishing Co., 1970. Pp. 153–189.

McDavid, J. W. "What Kinds of Changes Occur in What Kinds of Children Under What Kinds of Programs: The National Evaluation of Head Start." Washington, D.C.: Project Head Start, U.S. Department of HEW, Office of Education, 1968.

Mackler, B. "The Little Black School House, Success and Failure in a Ghetto School." Department of Urban Affairs, Hunter College, City University of New York. Undated.

Meier, J. "Some Results of New Nursery School Language Research," *Childhood Education,* 45 (December 1968), 228+.

Moore, O. K. "The Special Child in Century 21." Paper presented to Second National Northwestern Summer Conference. Seattle, Wash., August 1962.

———. "The Responsive Environment Project and the Deaf," *American Annals of the Deaf,* 110, 5 (November 1965), 604–614.

Nimnicht, G., O. McAfee, and J. Meier. "A Summary of the Evaluation of the Experimental Program for Deprived Children at the New Nursery School Using Some Experimental Measures." Greeley, Colo.: Colorado State College, December 1967. Mimeographed.

Piaget, J. *The Construction of Reality in the Child.* New York: Basic Books, 1954.

———. *Play, Dreams and Imitation in Childhood.* New York: Norton, 1962.

———. *The Child's Conception of Number.* New York: Norton, 1965.

———. *The Child's Conception of Space.* New York: Norton, 1967.

Richmond, J. "For the Child of Poverty," *American Child,* Vol. 5, No. 2. (Spring 1966).

Robison, H. F. "Project CHILD: Evolution of a Curriculum to Heighten Intellectual and Language Development." Paper presented to National Association for the Education of Young Children Conference, Salt Lake City, November 15, 1968.

———. "Rationale for the CHILD Curriculum," in *Conceptualization of*

Preschool Curricula, ed. R. K. Parker. Boston: Allyn and Bacon, 1971.

——— and S. L. Schwartz. *Curriculum for Learning at an Early Age: Program to Heighten Intellectual Development*. New York: Appleton-Century-Crofts, 1971(a).

———. *Learning at an Early Age: A Programmed Text to Prepare Teachers for Young Urban Learners*. New York: Appleton-Century-Crofts, 1971(b).

Sonnequist, H., C. Kamii, and L. Derman. "A Piaget-Derived Preschool Curriculum," in *Educational Implications of Piaget's Theory: A Book of Readings*, ed. I. J. Athey and D. O. Rubadaw. Waltham, Mass.: Blaisdell Publishing Company, 1969.

Weikert, D. P. *Preschool Intervention: A Preliminary Report of the Perry Preschool Project*. Ann Arbor, Mich.: Campus Publishers, 1967.

UP FROM POVERTY: THE PRICE OF "MAKING IT" IN A GHETTO SCHOOL

Bernard Mackler

Bernard Mackler reports on a study aimed at finding out how a school in a ghetto area functions, especially in terms of how it aids and facilitates "successful" pupils. In a school in which the vast majority of the pupils were failing, what processes operated to result in success for some children? The research team believed that understanding how black ghetto children succeed against considerable odds would provide insight into what "the world was doing to them and what, in turn, they imposed upon the world to change their own future."

The chief findings deal with the way in which the school is administratively designed to socialize youngsters. The staff insists that pupils be passive, listen, be polite, and follow all rules. Pupils who do behave in this fashion in kindergarten and who also demonstrate ability to read are chosen for the "top" first-grade class; those who do not attend kindergarten or do not read are assigned to bottom classes where they join with pupils who are expressive, demonstrative, and unable to keep pace with pupils in other classes insofar as reading is concerned. Social behavior grades are related to academic grades. The message the teacher conveys to the child is that "to do well in the academic area, one has to behave." Nor is conformity restricted to student-teacher relationships; Children who are rejected by their peers (negative sociometric ratings) are the same pupils who score low on social behavior.

Mackler found that for the top classes, teacher grades are related to achievement; however, for the average and lower classes, grades are inversely related to reading achievement. These results suggest that children who are potentially able may be poorly motivated due to personal problems or poorly taught by their teachers. On the other hand, it may simply mean that teachers are marking primarily on the basis of conforming behavior or for effort without regard to objective ability.

The top class or classes in each grade tended to have the "best" teachers, assuming the "good" teacher to be competent and sensitive to pupils as individuals. Teachers for the poorer sections at each grade tended to be moved around in those sections, while the better teachers generally stayed with the best sections. Mackler viewed the success of the IG (Intel-

lectually Gifted) class as evidence that the system can produce results. However, "for those who are not chosen for the top groups, the price is virtually being given up as lost in school, and, therefore, almost certainly in life."

Mackler views the basis of success for the ghetto child as prior success: "Confidence comes from mastery, and these pupils have been able to master the school's demands." From the beginning of their school careers, they have been told that they are the "best," and the organization of the school contributes to reinforcement of success through assignment of the best teachers and of conforming, adopting peer relationships. He concludes that "the school, the home, the environment, the mass media, the nation, and, in turn, the child all need to be altered" if success is to be expanded beyond the limited few who do make it in a ghetto school.

Bernard Mackler is Professor of Education at Hunter College of the City University of New York.

UP FROM POVERTY: THE PRICE OF "MAKING IT" IN A GHETTO SCHOOL

Bernard Mackler

When this study began in 1963, the schools were problematic, but one never imagined a three-month strike or policemen guarding the entry to some schools or helping close others. The schools seem to be the hot spots of the late sixties, not unlike our overseas embassies and agencies in the early sixties. Vandalism and destruction is the hallmark of what has occurred and, unfortunately, will continue to occur. This study can shed light on what schools do and don't do for ghetto children when there is no flak in the air. Assuming that equilibrium is restored (if that is not the case, chaos will reign and the schools will be unable to do anything systematically), how does a school in Harlem function, and what impact does it have on the lives of its young occupants?

This study was aimed at finding out how a school in a poor area functions, with particular attention to how it aids successful pupils. This emphasis on why some black children do well did not arise from our Pollyanna wish to pat these pupils or the schools on the back for a job well done; rather an approach was designed to understand the process of schooling for the successful, and their average and failing peers. By white standards, the majority of black children are failing, which is easy to understand considering the self-fulfilling prophecy of failure and inferiority. Yet there were those who had the courage to stand out—to brave failure and try to succeed. This existential stance suggested a new way of looking at this difficult and old problem of failure. Our research team believed that individuals, children as individuals, could see the way provided that there were persons who would shed some light. We assumed that there were adults at home or in school who might work against all odds to try to bring a young seedling to flower.

The Successful Child as a Guide

We believed that ghetto children could succeed, and that they might explain to us what the world was doing to them, and what, in turn, they imposed upon the world to change their own future. We did not posit supermen, but children who had personal convictions of their own ability, their own destiny. We hoped to begin to learn who was responsible for success and for failure in the ghetto schools.

We chose for our study a school in Harlem having achievement patterns typical of the ghetto school. We began to observe and become part of the school. We interviewed staff members. Achievement, creativity, and intelligence tests were given to the children. Sociometric measurements were taken. We observed and tested throughout the school for a period of one year (1963–1964) and visited the school periodically over the following two years to watch for trends in achievement, teacher and pupil mobility, and general tempo of the school. During the third year of our study we made intensive evaluations of a sample group of pupils considered successful over the entire period of the study. These youngsters were interviewed and given personality tests. Their teachers were asked to rate their behavior. Groups comparable in age and sex of average and of failing students were given the same tests and interviews. One final procedural note: since this was initially an elementary school study of over 1,000 pupils from whom the longitudinal sample of 154 successful, average, and failing youngsters was drawn, we decided to add a sample of 300 high school pupils to give us continuity through the academic career. Thus, we traced the careers of 300 ghetto youngsters from first grade on through high school to see what made some succeed and some fail.

The major findings of this study concern the way the school is administratively equipped to socialize the youngsters. Observations and objective scores indicate that the price for success is behaving in a way acceptable to the school. The school staff wants pupils to be passive, to listen, to be polite, to adhere to the rules. Those pupils who exhibit this behavior in kindergarten and who demonstrate ability to read are selected for the "top" first-grade class. Those who do not are assigned to "average" classes. Those who do not attend kindergarten go to the bottom classes. Once there, the road to the top classes is an arduous one. In the bottom classes are those who are expressive and demonstrative and who cannot learn their reading assignments at the same pace as the pupils in the top classes. Much of the teacher's time is spent trying to meet the needs of these pupils and less time is spent on reading assignments per se. It is difficult for a pupil to "catch up" or "shine" in such a situation. If he does, he goes to the second best class and perhaps to the top class by the third grade. No one makes it to the top from the third grade on, except those who were in the top classes in previous years. The pupils are graded for their social behavior, and, as is apparent in Table 1, these scores show marked increments in their relationships to achievement scores.

TABLE 1. Factor Loadings of Social Behavior Grades and Work-Study Habits with Academic Grades for All Six Grades

	Grades					
	1	2	3	4	5	6
Grade-Point Average	.95	.92	.96	.86	.91	.73
Social Studies	.90	.87	.94	.73	.73	.61
Science	.86	.81	.93	.80	.67	.61
Mathematics	.76	.75	.90	.71	.69	.65
Work-Study Habits	.69	.75	.86	.46	.64	.44
Social Behavior	.34	.58	.83	.26	.42	.26

Social behavior grades are related to academic grades for all six grades of the elementary school, with the factor loading increasing from grades one to three, then decreasing and stabilizing (see Table 1). Social behavior grades are distinguishable from work-study grades, except for the third grade, adding validity to our notion that teachers are not highly influenced by the halo effect for social behavior rating and schoolwork or work-study skills. The ratings are being made for separate behaviors (see Table 1). Social behavior is related to other scores throughout the six grades, especially to sociometric negative choices. In the first grade, students who score high for their good behavior score low on creativity and moderately high on reading, are preferred by their classmates, and are rarely nominated as negative choices on the sociometric. This is true throughout the six grades.

In the third grade, social behavior is highly related to academic grades. In fact these are almost indistinguishable, probably meaning that social behavior grades and academic grades are measuring the same aspect, or that the teachers' evaluations of one affect the other. Before the third grade, teachers may have been grading for behavior and ability separately. Now the children need to express themselves and become more assertive, seeming to call for more stringent controls by their teachers. The teachers seem to be equating ability and behavior, and, because academic work has become so important, demanding more and more attention and obedience from the pupils. The teacher is saying that to do well in the academic area, one has to behave. The children internalize this and begin to avoid other pupils who are not behaving well in class. This becomes very evident in the fourth grade and remains constant for the remaining school years. After the fourth grade, the teacher's rating of ability seems to be related to achievement, per se, and less so to behavior.

For the first three grades, teachers' academic ratings are related increasingly to behavior. This then gets stamped in by the teachers in the third grade. From the fourth grade on, the teachers' assessment of ability is more closely tied to "objective" ability, although behavior still plays a role, albeit a lesser one.

Social behavior is important, as we will see in how the top fourth grade class (the intellectually gifted class—IG class), culled from this and two neighboring schools, begins to behave to get ahead. The pupils have learned the rules of the success game; they are motivated to work hard. During the group and individual testing sessions we held, as well as in our participant-observations, we noted that they not only worked hard, but sat quietly and listened attentively to instructions, did not distract fellow classmates once work began, and usually raised their hands to ask a question. They all knew that they had been singled out for their "good" schoolwork and felt, collectively, that their special status made them different from the rest of the school. Their teacher certainly reinforced this by reminding them often of how special they were.

The Significance of Social Behavior—Peer Relationships

How these aspects may have functioned in this class can best be seen in the interactions between social behavior and peer relationships. In our observations of the other classes in this school by grade, by ability grouping, and by class, we noted the high factor loadings between teacher grades on behavior, academic grades, and peer selection. We also noted that by the third grade the teachers' academic grades and social behavior grades are nearly identical, but, in the fourth grade, the teachers' social behavior grades become more related to peer selection than to teacher selection. For the special IG fourth-grade class, that is exactly what happens. The highest factor loading, for any class, of social behavior grades with sociometric positive selection by classmates occurs here. This means that for this class, the relationship of pupil behavior to popularity is higher than for any other class. And, ironically, these students were picked partly on that basis in the first place.

In other words, the most able and best-behaved students are put in the IG class, and these students value behavior more than the other students in the fourth grade do. The influence of the past, in teachers' rewarding pupils who behaved well in the first three grades, is still operating on how pupils interact with, select, and avoid each other. Furthermore, the class has all "model" children, which means that they have to be more sensitive to teacher pressures to behave, for there are no "bad" children in the class. The degree of conformity seems to be most intense in a class in which the limits of behavior have been defined for three years with the children partly grouped on that basis, and yet, the pupils are still strongly influenced by good behavior.

The children who were rejected by their peers (negative sociometric) in the IG fourth-grade class were the same ones who scored low on social behavior. And here, for the first time, students were rejected who scored poorly on work-study habits as well. Students who were considered ideal as playmates scored high on work-study habits as well as on social behavior. Students who scored low on the *Circle Creativity Test,* on all four scores, were likely to be among the more popular. The remaining creativity tests, *Ask and Guess* and *Tin Cans,* yielded no social relationships, but were related to math and reading achievement. IQ and creativity were not related.

For the top ability classes in all grades we noted no relationship between IQ and reading achievement. For the special IG class one would expect a relatively high correlation, since the youngsters are selected on both. The correlation coefficient for scores on the Lorge-Thorndike Intelligence Test and the Metropolitan Reading Achievement Test is .52 and, for the Peabody IQ and the Metropolitan, it is .33. Both are moderately high, but not as high as one might expect. (This special IG class stood apart from the regular ability-ranking system of the school; nevertheless its ability level was one notch above the "top" regular class in its grade.)

The number of children who are above the 50th percentile in reading is not much higher for the top ability, or "1," class in the fourth grade than for the special IG class. This can be explained, in part, by the way the IG class was selected on achievement *and* IQ (and behavior), while the "1" class was selected on achievement (and behavior). The sociometrics indicate that pupil popularity, teacher choice for future success and responsible tasks, and ability all are intertwined. The less popular are among the less able, with the teacher-rejected pupils typically less able and isolated from their peers. Our classroom pattern for pupil popularity and pupil rejection is obviously at work here.

Having looked at many classes, we believe that the IG class can be viewed as *the* prototype for academic success. The fact is that this class is a grade ahead in reading and is the only class that can boast of that achievement level among the classes that we studied.

Groupings Are Confirmed by Results

Only the top class in the first, second, and third, the IG class in the fourth, and the top class in the sixth grade have mean reading achievement scores on or above national norms. These five classes are but one-seventh of the total number of classes in this school. Naturally, these top classes are at the top of each grade by school grouping, so that the homogeneous grouping that the school works so diligently at is objectively confirmed by the sharp differences between classes. And these differences are there for each grade.

For instance, in the first grade, the mean reading score for the top class is 1.8 (one year, eight months),* while the rest of the classes range from 1.4 to 1.1, the 1.4 having been attained by the second highest class. This means that, initially, there are differences in what the children bring to school. By grouping homogeneously, the initial differences between children will be exaggerated over the years. Hence, what youngsters bring to each other in a homogeneous class will, in turn, increase or decrease future aspirations.

For example, if a child goes to kindergarten and is rated "potentially able" and is also "well-behaved," he enters the top first-grade class. Here he has peers of comparable ability, all of whom are geared to learn, and the teacher does her best to teach academic subjects. They come to school ahead and they stay ahead. At the end of the first year, this class has a mean reading score of 1.8, with a majority of pupils above the 50th percentile on reading. However, the rest of the classes, especially those from the third class on down, have few pupils who are on or above the national average. The bottom two classes, and particularly the lowest class, consist primarily of pupils who did not attend kindergarten. While their teachers work equally hard at teaching, these children have not learned what it is to sit still, the requisite behavior for school and learning. It is a logical conjecture that these teachers spend an inordinate amount of time teaching behavior and meeting the needs of children who were unable to attend kindergarten.

Often these children did not attend because the family moved often, or the parents were unable to get the child to school regularly, or family problems made kindergarten low on their priority list, or the parents were not motivated to get their child to school. Regardless of reason, these non-kindergarten children have an exciting school year in the first grade, but fall way behind their peers in the top classes. The differences in reading achievement are of a few months to over one year by the end of the first grade. In fact, the mean difference between the top and bottom class is seven months; it is three months between the top two classes. This gap is never closed, for the children in the bottom classes have a hard time receiving the extra individual attention needed to get to the top classes. Even the best of teachers have a difficult year in this situation.

At the end of the first year, the top class invariably stays together except for those few who do not do well. The majority of students are placed the same way in the second grade. The pattern of second-grade reading scores is identical to the first, with the gap between the top and the bottom class increasing from seven months to 14 months.

*Reading grades are computed on a ten-month school year.

By the third grade, the gap is 20 months. In the fourth grade, it is 28 months between the IG class and the bottom class and 15 months between the regular "top" class and the bottom. Eighteen months separate the top and bottom classes in the fifth grade, and 29 months separate the top and bottom classes in the sixth grade. Since these are mean differences, one can expect substantially greater individual differences between the top and bottom pupils for any grade. Also, the mean differences for the fifth and sixth grades are even slightly greater than indicated, for 18 students in those two grades attained reading scores so low that they were arbitrarily given third-grade achievement scores. Their raw scores were so low that the national norms had no conversion scores for them. Obviously, they were all reading below the third grade level. Individual reading tests would have provided greater precisions, but they would have presented problems of equivalency scores with the tests used for the remaining 900 plus students. We decided to lose some precision and maintain comparability for such a small and obviously failing group.

The first and second grades are the only grades with *two* classes at or almost at grade level. It is the second highest class in the first and second grades that comes close to being at grade level. The third grade has but one class above grade level, and the difference between the top two classes is substantial: the top class is at 3.6 and over a year higher than the next at 2.4. The second grade has four classes with mean performances on a first-grade level (1.3 to 1.5) and the third grade has three classes still on a first-grade level (1.4 to 1.7). The way to stay above grade level appeared to be to stay in the top class for the first three years and not get transferred to a lower class. Once ahead, a child can continue to stay ahead.

By the fourth grade, the road to success is the IG class where the most able pupils from three schools are combined. It should come as no surprise that "the cream of the crop's" mean performance is well over one year ahead of the ordinary top class, 5.1 for the IG class and 3.8 for the "1" class. The "1" class is almost on grade level, while the IG class is way above grade level and national norms. No other class is doing as well. The first three grades combined have a few classes above grade level, while the upper three grades combined have only one class (other than the IG class) on grade level—the top sixth-grade class. There are no classes above grade level in the upper grades. The top fifth-grade class mean is 5.0, but at the time of testing the children would have had to score 5.2 to be on grade level.

We may have used a good deal of space describing the IG class, but the reasons for this can now be understood. This class is the surest route to continued success: From the fourth through sixth grades, these children will stay together and not only influence each other, but will be taught by the teacher most able to see to it that these pupils continue to stay well above grade level. Call it success or achievement-orientation, for the pupil it is the surest way to stay on an academically-oriented route, one that will set patterns of learning leading to junior high success, a high school academic diploma, and college entrance eventually. To a lesser extent, the top, or "1," classes for the fourth, fifth, and sixth grades hold out these same possibilities. However, for the rest of the classes of the upper three grades, the doors to success begin to close. So far, we have reported only on reading, but the same patterns persist for arithmetic. In that subject, only the IG class is *above* grade level and only one other class, the top sixth grade, is on grade level. The top fourth- and fifth-grade classes hover close to, but are, in fact, slightly below, grade level, while the remaining 14 classes are between four months to almost three years below in math with most classes over one year below.

For the "1" classes, teacher grades are related to achievement; but for the average and lower classes, grades are inversely related to reading achievement. These are peculiar findings and mean that in the higher-achieving classes, teacher grades approximate other objective measures of performance; children who have the ability and work diligently receive "good" grades. However, for the average- and lower-achieving classes, the students who receive higher grades are typically performing lower on reading tests, while in the same classes the relatively more able students are receiving lower grades. This could mean that children who are capable and potentially able are either poorly motivated because of personal problems or poorly taught by their teachers. It could also mean that teachers are not grading for ability in the average and lower classes, but primarily for conforming behavior or for effort, regardless of objective ability.

Teachers and the Grouping System

This school grouped its students according to an "exponent system"—those who were felt to have the highest degree of desirable qualities such as good behavior and ability were put in 6-1, for example. Those in 6-2 would be slightly less "qualified" and, so on, down to the 6-6 bottom. Given this structure, we expected to find the "better" teachers placed with the most able groups and vice versa. Our assumption proved generally, but not completely, true, perhaps because some of our teacher evaluations did not jibe with the school's.

Considering "good" teachers to be competent and sensitive to pupils, it seemed that in each grade the first, and sometimes the second, exponent classes had good teachers. These teachers gave the impression that they expected a good deal from their students in the way of learning and growth and believed that the expectation could be fulfilled.

Our feeling that the lowest exponent classes would, consequently, get the poorest teachers also had considerable, but qualified, validity. There were a few very fine people working with these children, but they were outnumbered by those who were mediocre or worse, while the upper levels were kept quite pure. It would be cute to say "in the middle were the middling," but more accurate to say "were the mixed" —some good, some not so good.

While there was some shifting of teachers in grade and exponent at the beginning of each school year, the change in distribution of better and poorer teachers did not appear to be significant. There did seem to be a tendency to move a few of the better teachers to the lower exponent groups, but since they were replaced with teachers of equal or near equal ability, the overall quality on the top remained pretty much the same. With usually five or six exponents for each grade, there was enough room to shift the displaced lower-exponent teachers around without letting them rise too near the top. The few that did move far up were almost invariably from that small group of good low-exponent teachers. As far as we could see, there seemed to be only one or two occasions when someone we considered a poor teacher was moved to a high-exponent class. In short, it appeared that the school had decided that if a chance was to be taken on a teacher's quality, it would not be at the expense of the students in the highest-exponent classes.

Teachers of the lower-exponent groups voiced far more awareness of the specific exponent number of their classes than those who had higher-rated groups. They seemed to feel that they were somehow bound by the exponent number, and several, early in the year, predicted a dismally unconstructive ten months for themselves because they had a low class. In one instance while giving a test to a class in October or November, we remarked to the teacher that his class seemed to be doing quite well. He replied that if we really wanted to see good students, we should see the "1" class on his grade. His group was inferior to them, he went on, and "didn't have the right attitude about school." In a lunchroom conversation earlier in the year, one woman said to a colleague that she felt she was going to "have a bad year because she had a '4' class." On another occasion, we were in the hall with the "1" and "5" exponent teachers from the same grade viewing some paintings done by the "1" class. After some favorable comments, the "5" teacher said, "Yeah, but look at the kids you got."

Some teachers were probably not totally unjustified in their negativism. After knowing nothing except poverty, discrimination, and general unhappiness, many children do become difficult to reach in school. But, to a considerable extent, the school and teachers contribute to the troubles they bemoan through their exaggerated concern with the exponent system. It seemed natural for the teachers to refer to the classes in terms of the exponent number, not as Mrs. So-and-So's class, or the class that this boy or girl is in, or Mr. X's class from last year. Individual children, and even teachers, were becoming less significant than an exponent number. Although there has been some movement in the past two or three years to tone this down by listing classes by room number (6-307) rather than exponent (6-5), the new listings are still usually in order from highest exponent down.

Gearing ghetto schools to the talent-loading exponent system may make sense, on the surface, in terms of the limited resources which most of them have. The IG class seemed to be proof that the system can produce results, but at a cost. For those who are not chosen for the top groups, the price is virtually being given up as lost in school, and, therefore, almost certainly in life. For those who are chosen, it often means conforming to the rigid propriety demanded of those living in fishbowls and also losing, giving up, or forgetting the aspects of one's life that might cause any observers to doubt that they really were in Bronxville. Moreover, for ghetto schools, playing the exponent game toward success in society is simply feeding the fires destroying them. It is saying that, "Because only so many of our children will make it outside school, we are only going to let so many make it inside school." The status quo remains unchanged.

The principal corroborated in an interview our observation that he assigns better-than-average teachers to lower grades. He stated that the lowest ability classes also get better-than-average teachers. The upper grades, in particular, and the entire school's average classes (third, fourth, or fifth exponents, depending on the grade) have the poorest teachers. Also, the classes that had teacher turnover during this particular school year were the third grade's fifth and sixth classes. These children had a flow of substitute teachers before a somewhat stable situation was established. The 3-5 class was almost bedlam for a while with six teachers in a two-month period.

One of us took over the 3-5 class one morning in May so that the teacher could be interviewed. The teacher, who had been with the class since February, still could not assert herself, and the damage had been done. On this day, the pupils were almost out of control, especially one boy who threatened to jump out of a window that had tightly-strung wiring across it. The girls worked diligently at their desks, but every 20 minutes they would bring a pointer to "shape up" the errant boys. In a half hour, as the substitute began to read aloud a book the class had requested, the class returned to tranquility.

It is unfortunate the ghetto schools get their reputation from such a classroom, only one of 36. Perhaps mass media is to blame, for newspapers and television are quick to point out what is dramatic or what creates interest. The "good" classrooms are boring news items or so typical that they are not worth reporting about. However, the public does not have this perspective and quickly assumes that Harlem schools are all wild.

The superior teachers stay with the top classes from year to year; therefore, the more able students have six years of better teaching, while the average students may have the weaker teachers for six years. If they are totally unfortunate, they may have many substitutes, for the weaker teachers not only teach poorly, but are "sick" often, or go on leave, or transfer to another school during the year. Imagine that this happens during one year in a pupil's six-year elementary school career: it is a year in which little academic learning may occur. Another kind of learning is occurring, however. That is that, "No teacher cares to stay with us for the year." Imagine if this befalls a pupil twice, or more often, in his six-year elementary school career. Contrast this with the top classes, which tend to have the superior and more responsible teachers, and the contrast in education for the top and average pupils is clear.

The choice that this principal made is not inconsistent with what happened and is happening in America today. Often in the high schools there are "honors classes" for the gifted pupils, and the superior teachers teach these classes. In urban centers, the more experienced teachers do not want to teach in ghetto schools. If forced to teach there, they quickly find their way to the suburbs. What are principals to do with the staff they have? And, even if all 36 teachers were superior, we noted that the bottom class in the first grade brings the additional problems of not having attended kindergarten. Superficially, this means these children did not learn about school, classroom, cognitive skills, socializing, and so on. More important, it tells us that these children come from homes which are not sufficiently interested in education to send their children to kindergarten or which cannot get their children off to school because of their own personal problems. As to the IG classes, the principal saw them as lifting the morale of staff and pupils; he would assign a superior teacher to these classes and saw no major shortcomings to this procedure.

In our interviews teachers from different ability groups were compared. Of the 19 factors culled from our interviews, only one showed a significant difference. This factor involves "professional orientation." The most professionally alert teachers are teaching the top, bottom, and fourth ability group. The least informed were teachers of the third ability group. Very little can be concluded from this since the remaining comparisons showed no significant differences.

Only three specific items indicated differences between teachers of ability groups. The first item asks, "Where are you presently living?" Surprisingly, the teachers of the top classes (five out of six) live outside of Manhattan, while the teachers who teach the bottom classes live in Manhattan, and most live in Harlem. The residences of teachers of the "average" classes are equally divided between Manhattan and outside Manhattan.

On the second item, which deals with grading, the teachers were asked to grade a "Mary, who behaves very well in class and does poor schoolwork." The teachers in the top classes all (six) graded this fictitious student on her schoolwork while 13 of the teachers from the remaining ability groups (roughly half) graded "Mary" on her behavior and ability. Mary received a grade of "D" from the teachers of top classes and a "C" from the 13 other teachers. In interviews, the teachers commented that they saw through this item and that they graded solely on ability. The fact that all of the teachers said this, but 13 of them then went on to grade on behavior corroborates our earlier findings that grading and grouping is a combination and contamination of ability and behavior. Since the top classes have already been sorted, it makes sense that these teachers would grade solely on ability. The behavior problems have been weeded out and those children who will not listen are no longer there; the teachers need concern themselves less with behavior problems since the more conforming and more able students are in their class.

The third item that clearly differentiates the teachers of top classes from the rest asks, "Do you prefer to be told in advance when a supervisor is planning to observe your teaching in the classroom?" The teachers of top classes all answered "Yes," while of the remaining groups 8 out of 22 teachers said "No." This may mean that the top teachers like to be at their best when they are evaluated. It can also mean that the most ambitious teachers, those who want to be at their best when evaluated, are in the top classes. It could also be that the more spontaneous, more open, less upwardly mobile teachers are not in the top classes.

The Ghetto School Children

We have looked at the school, and now we will look at the children. The most immediate impression we have after analyzing all the material, qualitatively and quantitatively, is that we did a lot of work to show that black children and their families, regardless of their housing and economic plight, are quite like their white counterparts. They want to get ahead; they dream the American dream of success. All the youngsters want the best of all possible worlds, but the successful pupils, and to a lesser extent their average peers, work to make their dream come through. It is not that the failing pupils would not like to work if they but knew how, and if they felt they would get somewhere if they did.

The success route is not a one-person affair. The children who succeed are more independent about themselves, their future, and their environment; yet they have become so because of their reliance on others in the past and the present. Confidence comes from mastery, and these pupils have been able to master the school's demands. In the early years of school they met with rewards, not materialistic, but in the form of praise. They were told that they were in the "best" classes because they worked hard and could do the work. They were told again and again that this is the route to a better life. Once on this route, they saw that they had the ability to stay on course. The influence of their classmates only enhanced what the adults, their parents, teachers, older siblings, and relatives kept saying. The desire to do well is obviously not innate but acquired. Once acquired, new and additional reinforcers act to increase this desire.

We noted the stability of the pattern—whether of success, average performance, or failure. Once established, usually by the first grade and typically no later than the second grade, the life in school is predictable. The kindergarten years feed into this pattern, molding not only the ability but also the behavior requisite for school accomplishment. We noted that the home life prior to kindergarten and after school entry is critical. Where is the pupil to learn how to behave appropriately for school, how to get a positive view of himself and of the values associated with school life and schoolwork? Naturally, there are those precious few who succeed mostly because of school influences, when the family had little positive influence. But these are rare.

The many studies on what leads to academic success among white and black youngsters, in elementary, secondary, and higher education; from low- and middle-, or higher-income brackets all share the following findings: good self-concept, adequate controls, directed effort, and acceptance of demands by authorities, notably teachers and parents. This we already knew; what is new in our findings is how this affects the youngsters. We noted that in our sample, relatively early in life, a successful pupil sees himself differently from average or failing youngsters. He not only is proud of himself, but he wants to learn in order to get ahead, to go to college, to become a teacher, doctor, or lawyer. We are not saying that the average or failing child is not as worthy of respect, but that his life begins to be shaped differently. He learns early that he has fewer opportunities. This may or may not be true objectively, but the fact remains that he believes he is not worth as much to himself and to others. The average pupil tries hard, he wants to get to the top, but there is a persistent notion of frustration and futility that eventually catches up with him. He tries to emulate the front-runner and keep pace with him, but he knows that this is tougher with each year. After a number of years, he comes to realize that he can no longer fool himself. He must accept the reality of "being average," going for a general diploma, and not going to a regular college.

The failing pupils are greeted with "reality" far sooner than the average pupils. They know early what the scene is, what the rules of the game are, and what they mean to them. They want to be "good" and to do "good" in school, for to fail means to be "bad," and to be "bad" means admonishment in school and certainly no praise, and at best, false or superficial jubilation when a minor hurdle or obstacle is overcome. At home, life is not as good as it could be. Parents get irritated, scold, punish, reject, even whip when the news is bad, and, after many poor report cards, the youngster wonders how he can keep his head above water. To drop out seems a desirable course, for when the youngster becomes of age, it seems better to drop out then to hang around for more blows.

Yet the fact that the failing youngster shares the same values as the other youngsters, that he too would like to make it, can be used creatively by school staff. Far too often these shared values are ignored. And the results are too well known—failure leads to a spiral of repeated failure, poor self-concept, and a need to so something well even if that something is misguided. Too often dropouts eventually succeed in their own world of shooting pool, loan-sharking, pimping, hustling, or pushing. Certainly not every dropout begins a career in crime, but the employment records of those who avoid crime consistently show poor paying and non-skilled jobs even for those who want to make the best of their situation.

Making It—Why?

We should have, by now, a good feeling for the school as an institution and as a system. But institutions and social systems are made with and by people. We have seen how the major performers behave and have some insights as to why. There are other forces to be sure, such as mass media, society as a whole, the question of race relations domestically and internationally, the parents, the homes, the neighborhood. However, we have focused on the school in its crucial functions from 9 A.M. to 3 P.M. every day. But we still have not touched upon one important ingredient with any profundity: motivation. We originally felt that the heart of the study, *the early desire to succeed academically,* could not be readily assayed. We are convinced of that now. We can see how only 35 pupils out of 1,000 stay "successful,"* what they do, and how they see themselves, their peers, their teachers and parents, and their future. Then we analysts and interpreters try to understand the *why*—why the decision to be one sort of a person rather than another. This desire, this drive to get ahead, to "make it," is the fuel that makes the difference. We can see the necessary (but often insufficient) conditions: good self-concepts; parent(s) who care, who prod and push—especially and emphatically the women in the household, usually the mother, but sometimes an aunt who acts as mother or the grandmother; the ability to listen to authority figures; and the internal discipline. However, these all need a key to start them, and what that key is varies with each child. Some want to get out of the ghetto and lead a better life; some desire to improve the lives of others; some have a thirst to learn; some have a hunger to dominate language and to master school tasks; some seek success to be loved by their parents; some combine these goals and desires in unique ways. It is no small wonder that psychologists have difficulty in evaluating motivation, for not only is it elusive, but there is a uniqueness to it as well, making it difficult to generalize, especially with tests that are so undynamic. Motivation is movement, and the evaluation of it by paper and pencil tests is static. This adds to the difficulty of comprehending what makes a child do what he does.

We can generalize about motivation if we avoid uniqueness and say that the black children desire to succeed for the same reasons that white children do. They want to master themselves and their environment. The fact that this may be more difficult for them, which, therefore, forces the success-oriented child to try harder, does not negate the similarity in desire. Those who do succeed are not supermen, but they are willing to choose a different kind of life and do see the possibility of getting there. Success along the way certainly helps in moving toward the fulfillment of the dream.

Our initial goals were to document different patterns and pinpoint some of the underlying reasons for achievement. It would appear that the circle of impoverishment can be broken, but this requires an exceedingly strong desire nursed and fostered by a parent who unselfishly gives her all. And the school must be facilitating too. Unfortunately, it apparently only aids a few, the most able, the best behaved, and the most confident. This route to success was available when we began the study and is available today, but the hardships encountered during the journey allow only the hardiest to survive. Of course, we

*The criteria for success included reading above grade level on our tests, being in the IGC, and top classes except for the first grade, and academic grades above B+.

could recommend ways in which parents can facilitate their child's personal and social growth prior to and during school. Yet, as crucial as that is, it is not enough.

Our stress on comparison, looking at successful children as well as failing and average students, has pointed to the strengths and weaknesses of the children, but, more important, of the schools which they attend. We have learned how the school aids or fails the child. By this method, we have tried to go beyond our colleagues who have looked only at failure. It is obvious that this school, try as it might, has not fared well. And we dare say that the performance of its pupils is typical of black youngsters in big-city ghettos.

We feel we have added to the literature. We have added to an understanding of how the individual, here the black child, meets and interacts with social institutions. This intersection of person and social structure points to a few fundamentals: the strengths of an individual, the resources he can call upon to surmount social and environmental obstacles, the social institution which stands ready to aid or impede youngsters. We now can see more clearly the limits of a person as he encounters an institution, and we can see how the needs of children are met or neglected from the institutional side.

The school, the home, the environment, the mass media, the nation, and in turn, the child all need to be altered. Economic and personal opportunity through education is wanting. But our idle (or even active) words will not turn the tide. The stakes are great: racial tension is such that little or no change, except piecemeal approaches, will occur in the next decade from the white community. Our study began on a hopeful note back in 1963 when the civil rights movement was at its peak. Solutions for the problems of the schools, employment, and housing seemed possible through legislative means. Integration was the key, or at least it seemed so then.

The future of America may well rest on how the country moves in the next few years. Reports and studies and platforms and speeches and promises can no longer be seen as great leaps forward. Only action will move Black America to realize its goals of pride, respect, enrichment, enhancement, and growth. Whites can choose to either facilitate or impede this growth. There is no room in between. Once these goals are attained, then and only then, will more blacks succeed in schools. And, community control of schools is the only viable possibility for that to occur.

In our conclusion, we have moved swiftly from the schools to society, for we do not agree with Dewey's notion that schools move society. Schools do no more, and no less, then what society expects or demands of them. The facts that so few black children read on grade level, that the schools have stayed segregated contrary to the law of the land, and that the officialdom controls them, all document our point. The white racist society wants to keep the black people down, way down. The few who make it are exhibited with pride by the whites, for in this way they can say that they are truly liberal and are trying to be helpful. Whenever blacks fail, it is the result of family and environmental circumstances and, perhaps, the system, too, but to a lesser degree.

The schools of the present do what society expects them to do. We live in a society in which materialism and productivity count. Our schools stress achievement, products, performance, and conforming behavior, and thereby reflect the values of our general society. We would expect black-run schools to reflect the same. Once they are on a par with or exceed white schools in performance, we may then ask how dull or stultifying all our schools are. However, it is only when our values change that our schools will change. The non-intellectual, non-creative, non-feeling atmosphere of our society is reflected everywhere we turn, and the schools are no exception. When our values change, when we see each other and children as human beings and see and respect each person as an individual, then the teachers who convey our values will in turn educate and lead our children differently.

TOWARD A DEFINITION OF "STRUCTURE" IN THE EDUCATION OF DISADVANTAGED STUDENTS

Russell C. Doll
Daniel U. Levine

Russell C. Doll and Daniel U. Levine take the position that "better education for the disadvantaged student is dependent on providing a relatively large amount of structure in his educational experiences." They argue that the term "structure" needs more explicit analysis and that its implications and of the characteristics of such students and the problems they encounter within and outside of school to indicate the necessity for providing disadvantaged students with educational experiences and environments which have been carefully and consistently ordered to provide step-by-step guidance leading to clearly defined classroom goals.

To identify the elements of structure in an educational program for disadvantaged students, a case study is presented. A description of the experiences one of the authors had in an inter-city classroom is given, with rationale provided for particular actions taken. Referring to Redl's zones of behavior—green, wanted and sanctioned behavior; yellow, behavior not accepted, but tolerated for special reasons or in special cases; and red, unwanted and unsanctioned behavior—the authors indicate how procedures were set up carefully delineating the behavior zones and describing the sanctions which might occur. How the teacher moved the class from continuous chaos to effective inquiry and learning is described through the case study presentation.

Finally, Doll and Levine present four components of structure and indicate that what is involved is (a) the choice and sequencing of instructional experiences and materials in accordance with the specific needs and problems of particular students; (b) the initiation of procedures and conditions aimed at developing order so that teaching and learning can occur; (c) the systematic choice and creation of situations and selection of resources so that success is experienced by disadvantaged students; and (d) the ground rules defining expectations which are realistic, student participation in setting subsequent rules is facilitated, and students are enabled to understand the rationale underlying activities and assignments.

Doll and Levine close with six cautions which the teacher of disadvantaged students must keep in mind as he moves toward structuring teaching and learning in the classroom.

They observe that the real problem in inner-city classrooms is not simply to maintain order but to create a structure that facilitates student participation and activity. This requires careful and thorough planning of educational experiences and and environments. This, they observe, may simply be a "roundabout way of saying that the inner-city teacher should be a good teacher." However, the inner-city teacher has a particular responsibility for successfully motivating and guiding pupils to become more effective learners.

Russell C. Doll is Assistant Professor of Education at the University of Missouri at Kansas City. Daniel U. Levine is Director of the Center for the Study of Metropolitan Problems in Education at that institution.

TOWARD A DEFINITION OF "STRUCTURE" IN THE EDUCATION OF DISADVANTAGED STUDENTS

Russell C. Doll
Daniel U. Levine

Recently, professional as well as lay journals dealing with education have included a good deal of material arguing in favor of educational approaches and practices variously labeled such things as "learning at random," "free learning," and "spontaneous learning." The arguments put forth in such publications reflect, of course, a recurrent theme in a continuing educational debate, but they have become more urgent and appropriate as we become more cognizant of the many deficiencies inherent in present educational methods and systems, which in many respects do more to process than educate students.

Need for a Definition of "Structure"

Assertions that we should be more "creative" and "free" in the public schools occur with some frequency in writings and discussions dealing with the education of economically disadvantaged students, for it is here that our educational system most obviously is failing to achieve a minimally-acceptable level of success in preparing students for participation in our industrial society. Whatever one thinks are the most important causes or mixtures of causes for the unsatisfactory academic performance of many disadvantaged students, all can agree that educational programs for the disadvantaged must be radically changed and improved.

It should be clear that we are not opposed to "free learning" or "spontaneity"—and certainly not to "creativity"—in the classroom, depending on how such terms are defined and what they mean when translated into specific educational methods and practices. There is reason for serious concern, however, about the possibility that the desirable concepts underlying progressive educational philosophies will be naively applied in a manner detrimental to the education of disadvantaged youngsters, particularly by new teachers whose good intentions or ideological predispositions may far outweigh their first-hand awareness and knowledge of the problems disadvantaged students tend to encounter inside as well as outside the school.

To be more specific, there is reason to believe that better education for the disadvantaged student * is dependent on providing a relatively large amount of structure in his educational experiences. If this is so, it is a serious mistake for a teacher to assume that good educational principles are incompatible with the provision of structure in school programs for disadvantaged students. This also means that the term "structure" must be analyzed more explicitly and its implications and meanings spelled out more definitely than heretofore by educators interested in school programs for the disadvantaged.

Although we do not know of any source in the literature on educating disadvantaged students which gives very systematic attention to issues or definitions involving the provision of structure in school programs for these students, awareness of the importance of structure does seem to be fairly widespread among practitioners, writers, and researchers concerned with improving education for the disadvantaged. For example, the authors of a recent paper which reported substantial gains in achievement and learning habits among 159 socially and/or economically disadvantaged Negro teenagers enrolled in a compensatory education program in the South interpreted their findings as "evidence of the effectiveness of a program . . . guided by the philosophy that student activities should be carefully and thoughtfully structured" (Comer, Harrow, and Johnson, 1968, p. 38). Although the authors of this report did describe some of the program characteristics which presumably led them to characterize the program as "structured" rather than "unstructured," they did not attempt to systematically identify the elements or dimensions which should be included in an explicit definition of "structure" in educational programs for the disadvantaged.

Before attempting to delineate the meaning of "structure" in educational programs for the disadvantaged, it is appropriate to emphasize briefly some of the general reasons for believing that structure is a suitable and desirable aspect of such programs. Basically, these reasons are related to the characteristics of disadvantaged students and of the family, community, and educational environments in which they live and go to school.

*The term "disadvantaged," as used in this paper, refers primarily to students who are educationally as well as economically disadvantaged in the sense that they are academically at a disadvantage in relation to groups of students who encounter fewer problems in existing school programs. Not all low-income youngsters are educationally disadvantaged, nor are all educationally disadvantaged students from low-income families. But for reasons which by now are widely recognized, youngsters who are disadvantaged either economically or socially, or both, tend to be educationally disadvantaged as well.

One of the terms which appears most frequently in descriptions of the lives of disadvantaged youngsters and adults is "chaotic." For many of the poor, chaos in daily life is a direct and inescapable effect of poverty. For example, the future obviously will seem disorderly and unpredictable to the members of families constantly on the verge of being evicted from their living quarters for non-payment of rent. Among the other conditions which make the lives of low-income citizens disorderly and chaotic are unemployment, poor health, and overcrowding in home and community.

A second and related characteristic of the disadvantaged is the general sense of insecurity produced among individuals when short-range as well as long-range physiological and psychological needs frequently are unsatisfied or only inconsistently fulfilled. One way in which such feelings of insecurity are manifested in continual disruption of the inner-city classroom has been perceptively described by Herndon (1968) in the following passages from his account of his experience as a teacher in the inner city:

> Why would a kid, or a whole row of kids, become frantic because they weren't getting any pencils? Why was it no one could pass out paper for a routine assignment without all the kids in the back rows pushing up to the front, grabbing at the paper, crumpling it and spilling it out onto the floor out of fear they wouldn't get any? Certainly it was clear by now that they were going to get paper and pencils, wasn't it? They always did, every day, every period, all year long.
>
> . . . [One reason for this behavior was their] concern to get their fair share of whatever was being passed out, passed out officially, what you were spozed to get in school, at Juvi, as an American, from the government, city, county, from the school, from the teachers. What was being passed out today, what probably would be passed out tomorrow, but on the other hand just might not be. What was being passed out one at a time. For actually, of all the things that were being passed out to them, it was always one at a time; there never was a surplus. (pp. 62–63, 65)

In a series of studies conducted at Syracuse University, psychologist David Hunt (1966) found that disadvantaged students tended to function on a lower "conceptual level" than did students with more privileged backgrounds. Students functioning at a low, or relatively undeveloped, conceptual level, according to Hunt's definition and measures of this variable, seemed to be preoccupied with immediate needs and therefore had difficulty in understanding others' points of view and in concentrating attention to perform abstract tasks.

Another frequently noted characteristic of the disadvantaged student is his short attention span when confronted with the traditional kinds of tasks and materials still typical of school programs. Compared to more advantaged students, he generally has had little experience attending to complex verbal explanations or following complicated sets of oral or written instructions. Elkins (1969) points out that, unable to accomplish school-related tasks which he has not been prepared to handle and teachers have been unable or unwilling to modify in accordance with his particular background and experience, the disadvantaged student begins to see himself as a failure in school, and his low self-concept as a learner in turn "causes him to avoid uncomfortable competitive situations. Rather than confront the challenge which holds great possibility of more failure, he withdraws or becomes hostile" (p. 595). The concrete though subtle and pervasive classroom effects of a long procession of failures and of feelings of inferiority as a learner which disadvantaged students experience in the school are succinctly described in the following passage from Herndon's analysis of the situation in his most difficult class:

> The heart of their problem as a class was the simple skill of reading. . . . They were unsure if they would be able to avoid derision at any given moment, and so tried to assert their superiority over each other in the very area of their common incompetence. Any time we tried to work on beginning word recognition, letters, sounds, the majority sounded off about "that baby stuff," and as a result the nonreaders had to sound off about it too; they couldn't admit not knowing how to read and so they couldn't ever begin to learn, because in order to learn they'd have to begin, right there in class, with simplicities, easily identified by all as "learning to read," and open themselves up to scorn. Nothing doing. (p. 91)

It would be easy to continue listing and illustrating the characteristics of disadvantaged students and the problems they encounter inside as well as outside the school. Enough has been said, however, to indicate why teachers who work with low-income students and observers who study low-income schools generally have an intuitive understanding of the necessity for providing disadvantaged youngsters with educational experiences and environments carefully and consistently structured to constitute an orderly environment in which they can feel secure and comfortable and in which they receive step-by-step guidance leading toward the mastery of clearly-defined goals in the classroom. (See Bloom, 1966.) Merely recognizing the desirability of providing structure in educational programs for disadvantaged students, however, does precious little to help teachers acquire practical understandings of what the principle implies in making decisions concerning the conduct of instruction in the classroom. Until the principle is translated into relatively concrete prescriptions to inform and guide the decisions and behaviors of teachers and students, it is little more than a slogan which may be applied only occasionally and inconsistently—and therefore ineffectively—in the classroom. To make the principle meaningful and useful for teachers, conversely, it is necessary to identify, as clearly and explicitly as possible, the major elements which come under the general rubric of "structure."

What, then, are the most important facets of a strategy for providing structure in the education of disadvantaged students? To identify these aspects of what structure should mean in designing or conducting educational programs for the disadvantaged, our approach will be to utilize a case study. The following section contains a description of the experience of one inner-city elementary school teacher who apparently succeeded in using a structured approach to improve the performance of his disadvantaged students. The final section then presents our classification of the elements or aspects of structure which we believe were most responsible for the relatively high degree of success he experienced.

A Case Study

One of the authors was assigned to a classroom in a low-income school two months after the spring semester had begun. It was an eighth-grade classroom with overage children who had experienced many years of failure in school and were somewhat hostile. The class had already disposed of two other regularly assigned teachers. Each had lasted approximately one month and then fled in tears. The week before the writer had taken over the class, the children had had a number of substitute teachers.

The classroom at this point was in chaos. Some members had kicked a hole about two feet in diameter in the lower part of the back wall. Books would go flying out the window onto the busy street located below, sometimes to be returned by passing pedestrians. The custodian would check each night to see that all the books had been removed from the large corner wastebasket. Children got up and walked around the room and out in the halls when they felt like it. Dismissal time resembled a stampede in a Western movie. Younger children were often hurt. Children from this third-floor room would occasionally dart up the ladder stretching from the floor to the trapdoor in the roof and run around on the roof until they decided to come down to the room again. Bulletin boards were a shambles, with phrases like "Screw you" or "The teacher is full of shit" scratched in them. The blackboards had suffered a similar fate. Someone had relieved himself in the science crock in the cloakroom.

The teacher was in the room for no more than twenty minutes when, exasperated already, he told one boy to "Be quiet," and the boy replied, "Be quiet yourself, you bald-headed, four-eyed bastard." And so, on that note, and under those conditions, the teaching was to begin in this room.

The first two weeks, with the help of tranquilizers, the teacher held the line. Certainly no teaching was taking place, but at least the students were in their seats most of the time. No books sailed out of windows; no one romped on the roof; dismissal times were not as great a danger to life and limb. But things could not profitably nor practicably go on as they were going. The students were staying in their seats because of busy-work (which was not the wrong assignment at this stage; why it was not will be explained later). The room was no longer chaotic simply because of tactics of coercion.

The problem was how to change this classroom into one with an environment for learning and teaching. This change, to be effective at all, had to take into account the needs of the children; could not be unnecessarily punitive or coercive; and had to build on the children's strengths and on their desire to be a part of the change. In this case study an attempt will be made to show how this change was brought about through careful planning and structuring procedures. Because of space requirements, more has been left out than should have been. It is impossible to include all of the kinds of planned interaction that took place and the care taken to insure the "quality" of these interactions. For example, it is not possible to adequately tell of the carefully planned and phrased statements of understanding which preceded any type of correction, advice, or even instruction, or how the contacts were planned to both alter the situation and maintain the child's and teacher's self-respect. It is hoped, however, that the examples included are practical and helpful, since we in education have for too long skirted the teacher's real problems by offering clichés such as "Show More Understanding," "They Need Attention," and "Make Things Interesting So They Want To Behave And Learn."

After several sleepless nights, the writer saw that he had to change the children's attitudes toward themselves, provide them with some academic success, modify their behavior so that genuine praise could be offered, show them their potential for success, and prove to them they were worth something.

The first problem was simply to maintain order in the room. There were a number of evident reasons for the disorder. The students were behaving as they were because they were living up to their reputation in the school. This was leading them in a vicious circle. Somehow the writer had to begin to change this reputation. Another reason for their behavior was the complete lack of routine in their day. They lacked knowledge regarding the bounds for their behavior and were unaware of a *predictable* and understood series of sanctions regarding behavior. Everything seemed arbitrary and almost unreal. The lack of routine and their not knowing what to do were helping to cause the chaos in the classroom.

To break the hold of their reputations on themselves and the faculty, they needed success experiences which could lead to legitimate praise. To help them achieve this success, they needed procedures they could follow and understand. The writer sat down one night and began to carefully plan procedures which would lead to success and recognition. The procedures mentioned in the following discussion are not easily distinguishable from one another. Each planned procedure or event was taking place within the same general time period. The procedures for success within the school, and for recognition within and without the school, were planned so that one event built onto and reinforced the other.

The first thing needed was to provide the students with a definite set of procedures and expectations for classroom routine. Until procedures were understood and mastered, there was little chance that an adequate teaching and learning climate could be established. As it was, a great deal of time was being wasted taking care of accidents, fights, and calming general bedlam. The potential for student-student and student-teacher conflict was very high. For example, the children's game of beating each other to one coat hook was the cause of several confrontations between classmates, causing some rather serious moments.

Fritz Redl has referred to "three zones of behavior": the green zone, which is wanted and sanctioned behavior; the yellow zone, which is not acceptable but is tolerated for special reasons or in certain cases; and a red zone of unwanted and unsanctioned behavior. Based on this idea, guidelines for classroom behavior were delineated and sanctions described so that children would understand the boundaries and what would happen if they were crossed. Procedures for passing and entering the room, sharpening pencils, collecting papers, and taking care of books were set up. For example, the simple procedure of placing a name by each coat hook and making sure each coat was on the right hook eliminated the game of "The Hook." Having the children cover their books, and allowing them to draw their own designs on the covers, numbering the books, and making specific book assignments eliminated the book throwing. Thus, structuring movement within the class led to a decrease in the general chaos.

Mundane things? Maybe. But successful accomplishment of these things was the first break in the cycle of failure in which these students were immersed. By instituting these procedures the writer established reasons for offering praise and set up a situation in which other teachers could praise the children. The "success" provided the teacher with the first genuine opportunity to offer legitimate praise the students *knew* they had earned.

Success in entering and leaving the room and improvement of behavior in the halls led to another step in the progression from low men on the totem pole to people with some self-respect. As soon as their first real success was achieved in these "mundane" tasks, another teacher was asked to stop in and compliment the group. The effect was devastating. Usually teachers had entered to damn, here a teacher entered to praise. This allowed the writer the opportunity to build on or point to their potential for other things. It is important that the teachers plan, or set up, praise from other members of the faculty and the school.

To summarize,

1. Procedures for structuring simple success in behavior led to a break in the cycle of failure. Plan for these "mundane" but critical procedures.
2. Success led to the opportunity to give praise. Deliberately plan for praise through structure and look for the first opportunities to legitimately offer praise.
3. Success led to a deliberately planned situation in which the writer had set up praise from another teacher. Plan in advance for the teacher's praise to be reinforced legitimately by other faculty members.
4. Praise from other faculty members provided the writer with the opportunity to continue to build success in behavior. Plan for a continuing sequence of praise for success.

To eliminate the possibility that procedures will seem to be only punitive, it is necessary to provide a rationale for almost everything planned. Some kind of structure and meaning must be given to the seeming irrationality of the demands of school life and the sometimes irrelevant demands of academic work. This rationale must be stated in terms of the children's self-interests. It is not enough to say that certain things will be *expected* of them in the classroom. They must know *why* these things are expected and the "why" must answer many of their concerns or be advantageous to them in some way. For example, it was not enough to say we were going to enter the room or pass in a certain way. It was necessary to say why, and the why was offered with the rationale that it was for *their* own safety, and that the teacher was doing this because he was concerned about *them* and was not going to allow *them* to injure themselves, that he knew their potential and was not going to allow *them* to ruin themselves, especially when *they* could be the leaders in the school.

The teacher also provided a rationale for academic demands in this way. Before he had come to the room, no one had bothered to complete a paper or to make any work legible. These youngsters were being allowed to commit suicide as far as their future was concerned. But the teacher now held them to doing work and to completing work. In the process, a rationale for these demands had to be set up. The teacher used as a paperweight a piece of "scrap" from a machine shop, which if "good" would have been worth about $250.00. He had it there for a reason, and had planned ahead to use it as the rationale. The first day of the new regime of demanding that schoolwork be complete and legible (at least the heading), he used that piece of "scrap." The man who made the piece was only a fraction off on his measurements and he had turned out twenty of these pieces. He lost his job. The teacher drew a rather tortured but effective parallel between his demands and the "payoff" for the "job" in the class. (Payoff was the granting of a privilege.) He also attempted to point out the relationship between the demands of the school and the demands of the outside world. This procedure, as awkward as it was, was better than only demanding work. The teacher was not put in the position of initiating an irrational demand. Students were at least given an idea of why care was needed and asked for and how it could have a payoff. *But most important, and the real reason for the procedure, was that it gave the writer the opportunity to demand legible, careful work without a punitive stigma.*

It is then necessary to capitalize on this planning in regard to demanding work. Once the rationale provided the class produces the least glimmer of success in the students' work, get the work up on the bulletin board immediately. The bulletin and blackboards were chosen because the students had once used these as a target of their wrath. The papers of those who led these attacks on the boards were sure to be put up. The "Battle of the Boards" stopped almost overnight.

A great deal of success in the classroom relates to maintaining consistency in regard to demands for academic work. It also involves consistency in the application of sanctions when the legitimate demands for academic work are not met. And, it includes being consistently fair and just in the treatment of students who have sanctions applied to them. For example, many students did not do either classwork or homework. Those who did the assignments did them in a haphazard, perfunctory manner which negated the purpose of the work. To have the students realize that work must be done, a definite structure of expectations was set up for them. Assignments were given them which were easy to understand and in which there was little possibility for failure. Individual assistance was given to those having difficulty, or their assignments were modified. The assignments were not given to make an assessment of their capabilities. The idea was to get them into the habit of doing their work, and of expecting that certain sanctions would be placed on them if they did not perform. The students were given a rationale for the work and were advised of the procedures that would be followed regarding incomplete work or work not turned in.

When, after establishing these procedures, the teacher was faced with little classwork and no homework, he followed through by asking for the work (which never had happened before—it had only been assigned by most of the teachers) and then he followed through on his sanctions, which were carefully planned in a graduated sequence both over time and in severity. The sanctions ranged from individual conferences to see if students understood and needed help, to mimeographed notes having to be signed by parents, to visits to the home, to suspensions. There were no cases that went past the home visits. That the teacher had actually proceeded through the steps as he had told them he was going to do astounded the class. They couldn't believe it because no one had expected anything of them. Also, no excuses were accepted from the "goodies" in class or from those with notorious reputations. This, too, astounded those usually in trouble, as it astounded those who didn't cause trouble and had always been left to coast.

A number of things were accomplished by these procedures:

1. Providing the students with legitimate rationales allowed them to see some meaning to what was being asked of them.
2. They began to see that what they were doing meant something to someone.
3. They began to feel some degree of security in knowing the bounds within which they could operate and knowing that there was an orderly sequence of procedures if they overstepped the bounds. Although the yellow zone was very large initially, the red slightly smaller, and the green the smallest, by the end of the semester most of the behavior which had been in the red zone had shifted to the green because students could now handle it in a non-disruptive manner.
4. Making certain they achieved success in academic work allowed the teacher to use the symbols of success (good papers) to provide some means of identification with the room.
5. The setting up of procedures set a tone of consistency, fairness, and firmness within the developing structure.
6. The procedures and the resultant success offered the writer an opportunity to set the room apart from the other chaotic classrooms and use this to build their self-concept and morale.

7. It set an academic tone to build onto the tone of order which was developing.

Unfortunately, in all classrooms, some degree of coercion is needed. The planning to bring order from chaos sometimes ran counter to what the children had been used to. During the periods the writer was getting control of the class and giving the students procedures for success in behavior, the writer was often forced into giving what is usually called "punishment." He was very careful in the matter of punishment-coercion, and a hasty but effective approach was planned to lessen the detrimental effects of punishment-coercion.

The approach was to simply not use the term "punishment" and to try not to put the "blame" on *them.* The teacher accepts the blame instead! For example, during the period when the teacher was trying to structure their success in passing so he could praise them, the students had a hard time extinguishing the bedlam and the stampede behavior. The second time they stampeded, after the teacher thought things were going well, he knew that the rational route was out and a good talking to wouldn't work either. Keeping them in for recess and saying it was punishment would only worsen the situation. Instead, he told them that what was happening was *his* fault and not *theirs.* He told them he had just not explained things well enough, nor had he given them enough practice. Since he didn't want them blamed for his failings, he must act immediately. They would have to practice. But since they couldn't practice during school hours they could do so only during recess periods. So they "practiced" during two recess periods. The writer was as accepting of them as before. He praised them for their good lines and called other teachers' attention to the fine practice, stating that they were great kids to do this. Soon their frowns turned to grins and their grins to large smiles. The message had come across and they had accepted it. They knew they had lost two recess periods but they knew why and they knew how to get the recess periods back. The next dismissal period the lines were such that no one's safety was put in jeopardy. Yet there was no resentment since the blame for the whole matter was not placed on them. The message came across more as a "con," and they accepted correction in this framework. All the correction in the room was handled in this general manner, although sometimes the kids out-conned the writer, which was all right!

During the period of striving for control, it was still necessary to correct individual students. It was important to show the student he was still acceptable after the correction. In circulating around the room during work periods, time was planned so the writer could stop by, kneel by, touch, or help those whom he had had to control earlier. He made himself walk in the aisles, smiling and whispering with those with whom he may have had some difficulty. He made a genuine effort to assist them individually. In other words, he structured positive individual contacts so that these could be used to counteract negative ones.

Sometimes, as in all relationships involving close and prolonged contact, serious, direct confrontations cannot be avoided. Tempers are lost. The teacher may find himself controlling from a position of power, shouting at a child, "pulling rank," "putting the child down." Such confrontations can have disastrous long-range consequences (not to mention immediate consequences). Plans must be made *in advance* to try to stop the immediate disaster and head off the long-range effects. The writer attempted to do this in two ways. To head off the immediate reactions during the very first week, he made it clear to the class that he could make a mistake in correcting someone. It was pointed out to the students that some misunderstandings will occur just as they do at home and with buddies. Further, these misunderstandings will not mean he rejects them as students but that it is the situation to which he objects. Conversely, they will dislike what he does sometimes, but they should be assured that he will understand this. At these times, strong words may be said, but they should be forgotten when tempers cool. In this way, the writer attempted to point out to them that confrontation is sometimes an inherent part of any situation and this does not mean either party is wrong or should be rejected.

To head off the long-range effects of serious confrontation, it was necessary to build up a child if he had been "put down." The writer made an arrangement with a group of other teachers to establish a system whereby they would cooperate not only to help the child but to take pressure off the teacher involved in the confrontation. It was called by the teachers "Operation Build Up," and, at times, "Operation SOS" (Save Our Skins). The rebuked child would be sent to a cooperating teacher's room on a trumped-up errand with a note which covertly told the teacher "SOS" time. The teacher would then have the child perform a task, praise him, ask how things were going, and so on. In turn a note of praise for a job well done would go back to the sending teacher. This allowed the sending teacher to praise the child and set the stage for a rapprochement. This series of "Build Up" situations helped to let his peers see that things were, at least on the surface, back to normal again between student and teacher. It also took the pressure of retaliation off the student, a pressure many did not want anyway.

One problem plaguing inner-city classrooms is that of student grievances. Often these are expressed vocally and in a fashion which is upsetting to the class and leads to unnecessary confrontations. To offset this problem, a plan was set up whereby the students understood they could be heard and could influence things in the classroom. Since the writer had made it clear that he was not perfect and that mistakes could be made, the students were able to feel free to raise grievances and the teacher felt less threatened in making changes. Grievance procedures must include an understanding that instant explosions can be postponed until a break time when fair hearings can take place and tempers have cooled. But in order for this to be successful the students must know the teacher will be fair even to the point of reversing himself on some matter and apologizing in front of the class for something he has done wrong. In fact, it may be a good idea initially to plan a situation in which he will indeed reverse himself and make an apology.

A number of things are accomplished through the procedures described above:

1. Placing the blame for punishment on his own shortcomings avoids placing the teacher in an overt punitive position, even though punitive action may be taken. Though children see through the game, they accept it as a "con" and are less resentful.
2. Not only is control enhanced by planning to circulate and make individual contacts through assisting children in their work, but this approach also helps heal any real or imagined slights which the students have experienced. This healing helps to counter a build-up of silent hostility which might explode later.
3. By making provisions, both within and without the classroom, for building up the student after a confrontation, the teacher can avoid an ongoing state of warfare between himself and the student.
4. By creating avenues for grievances and by letting the students know they will be heard, the teacher can avoid the explosions of frustration which frequently occur during lessons or during periods of the day, and which force both parties into unwanted confrontations.

Procedures for Improving Children's Self-Concepts

Efforts to structure behavioral success could be ineffective if the teacher did not, at the same time, work on procedures for improving the children's self-concept. To do this the teacher should work on building up an esprit-de-corps within the room, a feeling that the children are different, that they can do things others can't.

One obvious way is to decorate the room as attractively as possible with the students' work. A not-so-obvious approach is to lessen the chances of their recognizing symbols of failure that they may have created or to eliminate these symbols, thereby making praise more valid. Many inner-city classrooms have their own equivalents of the decimated bulletin board and the two-foot hole in the wall which children see daily. These ever-present symbols of failure negate praise. To a degree, they stifle attempts by the teacher to make an approach to improving the children's idea of themselves so they can begin to feel secure enough to tackle classwork. Therefore, one of the first things the writer did was to have the students assist him in covering up that hole as part of a general renovation. The writer covered up the "cuss" words on the bulletin and blackboards as part of the total change. He made sure he covered them up with students' work and things that seemed to be important to them. And they weren't covered up because they were "cuss" words or because it was a hole, but because all these things were *symbols of their past hostility, rebellion and, in their eyes, failure.*

The other symbols of failure were the principal and teachers who checked up on the writer periodically to see if he was in one piece. Every time the door opened, this told the kids that they were no-good-troublemakers. The writer knew it was important that outside influences not be allowed to negate attempts to build up the children, so he had a long talk with the principal and other teachers. He asked them to enter the room only when they could say something good, to handle all problems with him after school or at lunch, and to please praise the children when he asked them to and when the children had performed in a way warranting legitimate praise.

Once the outside influences are curbed, an attempt must be made to develop a feeling that all members of the group, teacher and students, share something between them to which no one on the outside is privy. The only way this can be effectively done is to handle all problems, as much as possible, within the confines of the room. The children are told that problems will arise but, as with families, the problems are nobody's business but their own. For example, one day the writer was "chewing out" the class for something and the principal walked in and asked how things were. The writer replied they were fine, never better, and the group was a great group. After the principal left, the writer explained that the problem was their "family" problem, their own business. The students appreciated the confidential atmosphere and at the same time knew the praise was warranted because, thanks to the structure and demands regarding the "mundane" things, they were "proving" themselves to others outside the classroom. Little by little a "we" feeling grew. The idea of a "room family" was worked on until it became an effective theme which assisted the writer in building up a group spirit, even a mystique, among the students.

This mystique provided the writer with the opportunity to avoid making individual students the focal point of talk concerning misbehavior outside the classroom. Instead of having to say "What did *you* do?", he could say, "The room really looked bad with that stunt," or "How do you think your buddies will look when someone says '*Somebody from Room 302* goofed up'?" The pressure was taken from the writer since he did not have to make things personal. Further, many of the "problem students" were relieved of pressure as well, since adhering to the norms of the group let them "safely" perform in an acceptable manner (which they really wanted to do anyway). The idea of their being a "special group" allowed the writer to begin to demand more of the students with regard to academic work and general social responsibility. It also provided him with additional rationales for these academic demands. As the idea of their being a special group increased, morale and behavior improved, and the writer could ask why this improvement could not be duplicated academically. Students soon began to ask this question themselves.

Yet in-school factors can go only so far in increasing students' sense of worth and usefulness. By utilizing opportunities raised by events or situations outside of the school, the teacher can give them a sense of being a worthwhile part of the larger society. He can also use their participation in these events to increase their standing in the school, as well as provide meaningful learning experiences. The teacher must, therefore, be on the alert as to how he can structure their interests to serve these many different ends.

For example, during this period of time the temples of Abu Simbel were being moved to save them from the flood waters of the Aswan Dam. The writer and students began immediately to study Africa, concentrating on Egypt. The temples of Abu Simbel were discussed, as was the need for money to help move them. The children began to see some worth in saving them and a few suggested a collection. The writer seized on this immediately to challenge the class. He would match what they gave. They gave, in a two-week period, eight dollars and sixteen cents. The writer had already decided not to send the money to the fund-raising organization but to one of the city's newspapers to forward to the organization. The hoped-for happened. A reporter and photographer from the newspaper came to the school, photographed the class, interviewed some children, and wrote a lengthy human-interest feature article entitled "Kids Chip In Dough to Save Temple of Abu Simbel." Suddenly, this group of children, who had been "troublemakers," was visited by a reporter and photographer and became the subject of a feature article which was posted all over the school. Other teachers and the principal praised them, and the leader of the archeological expedition sent the class a huge autographed picture of the Temple. The picture and article were framed and, of course, went onto the bulletin board.

Another "calculated happening" was the class activity involving sharing Thanksgiving with the "poor people." ("I thought we were the poor people," said one bewildered class member.) These children had "received" for so long, they jumped at the chance to "give." A large box with the room number was placed in the room for them to put canned goods into. It was intentionally placed on the floor, near the covered hole. Mention was made of how far we had come—from the "hole" to the ability to share with our fellowmen. (By now all reference to the room, good or bad, was in terms of "we.") The box was taken by a group of students to the Salvation Army. The writer had called earlier and requested that the director send a note of thanks to the group. He complied and the children could again feel a sense of worth and usefulness. If, however, the director had not complied, the writer would then have written the letter and mailed it to the group. Calculated and gimmicky? Yes, but very needed and very effective. Along with the success experienced in developing order in the classroom, they now began to experience success in the world outside their classroom. They began to internalize what they were once forced by others to do and never did. They were asking and expecting more of themselves.

A vignette of an incident outside the school provides an example of this developing pride and the beneficial spin-off in out-of-school matters. The writer would periodically stop at the corner tavern after school for a bag of potato chips. At the beginning of the semester, the tavern-owner complained vociferously about the children in the class. They were raising general hell inside the tavern, where they played the pinball machine, and outside the tavern, where they pitched pennies and observed life passing their corner. After a while, however, the writer noticed that the complaints ceased and some grudging compliments were given. The owner related one incident in which he had told some of the boys that they were at last beginning to behave like human beings and one answered, "Yeah, we're from Room 302."

Situations exist in the classroom which have inherent within them possibilities for confrontation, punitive action, and the raising of general problems. It is these types of situations that a teacher must carefully analyze to see what lies at the root of the problem, how correction of the problem can be made without damaging relations, and, most importantly, how correcting the problem can be structured in such a way as to assist the teacher in his efforts to develop a positive classroom climate. Two such examples of problems and of the structure provided to solve them follow:

One concerns the habit the students had, when the writer took over the class, of shouting greetings to all who walked into the room. It was, of course, not only a carry-over from the anarchy of the other two teachers, but also a testing of the current teacher. At first, this greatly disturbed the writer since the room sounded like the subway at rush hour. It took at least ten minutes to get the children quieted down. After their initial successes and resultant praise upon mastering the "mundane" tasks, they became more receptive to strong "suggestions" to tone down their greetings. But this approach did not really provide a solution because it was based on coercion and it was leading to a continuing game of "Shout and Stop." Was there a way of stopping the minor bedlam by using it to enhance relations between students and teacher?

The next day it was explained to the class that the writer now understood that they had only wanted to be friendly and he apologized for not recognizing this sooner. Then he suggested that there were other ways to greet people; he remembered a school in which the kids stood up by the side of the desk when a teacher or adult entered (which was a lie). The room echoed with moans and groans and sour faces, as overgrown eighth-grade boys slouched further in their seats with Cheshire-cat grins on their faces. The writer then dropped the idea.

Interest soon revived, however, when the writer casually let word drop that such a procedure might be fun since there was a possibility of sending an unsuspecting teacher or principal into cardiac arrest when a whole room suddenly arose as if to attack. This was something they liked and that held a payoff for them. On this basis, it was decided to try the "Great Uprising," as it was dubbed by the rest of the faculty. The room practiced how they would stand. The writer entered the room a couple of times and pretended to be surprised, hamming it up. Meanwhile, arrangements had been made with another teacher to enter the room when notified. The teacher had been told to register surprise if the room stood up, but to register no surprise if they did not stand up. When she entered only two people stood up. No surprise was registered. The teacher was sent back out and then invited in again. They stood up. The teacher acted her part beautifully and the kids were pleased. The standing soon became a trademark of the room, with the principal bringing in visitors just for effect. The students accepted the procedure as one more bit of evidence that they had a "swinging" room, different from others, and were provided with more positive reinforcement. The writer could continue to emphasize the idea of their being special and to relate this uniqueness to academic demands.

A second example concerns the chaos caused by 42 children, some overage, in movable desks, which had the writer pinned against the blackboard at the end of the day and which led to innumerable disruptions and control problems, many of which the children did not want to happen but were preordained by the seating arrangements. This problem could be handled immediately. The desks were arranged in rows, on a Friday afternoon, with the help of the custodian. The children were notified there would be a change. (Rows were decided upon since 42 children in an average-sized classroom canceled out the intended function of movable desks, to allow flexibility in grouping.) Tempera paint was put on the floor at the front legs of each desk so the children could not mistake where they were supposed to be.

That Monday they were reminded, after each lesson period, to straighten out their desks. The writer made sure they could not and did not fail, so that at the end of the day he could offer genuine praise, point out how chaotic things used to be, and discuss their potential for improvement. This event was one of their first success experiences. The discovery that a day could end on a positive, friendly note, with a word of praise and congratulation, was a new and bolstering experience for them.

Gradually, all of these procedures began to pay off in regard to the academic tone in the classroom. The students began to listen, pay attention, and stop the chaotic pandemonium and the self-destructive behavior. Papers and work were being turned in by those who had never done so before. The whole tone of the room changed. The writer could begin to ease off on his demands, since the students had internalized the patterns of behavior and had begun to demand these patterns of themselves and their peers. This change allowed the writer to begin to offer individual assistance to those who needed help. Also, he could begin to utilize students as tutors, since attitudes toward one another had changed. He was able to leave the room to talk to parents and not find books in the hall and a fight in the aisle when he returned. After a while the class chairman, on his own, began to take over while the teacher was outside, in order to continue with the class.

At the end of a semester and a half most of the students were working at grade level, or near grade level, in arithmetic. For a great majority this meant a leap of over two years. Almost all showed exceptional gains in English and social studies and, although still not up to grade level in these subjects, the gains were significant. Since the children changed rooms for reading, this change could not be measured very precisely. However, a crude comparison showed that those children who stayed in the writer's room for reading made significant gains over the homeroom children who went to other, more chaotic, less demanding and less "prideful" classrooms for reading. Both groups performed better than did the children from other classrooms who came to the writer's room for reading. Another crude comparison showed that homeroom children who were sent to other rooms performed better than did the children in those other rooms.

This, of course, is what the end result of all the above procedures should be: the creation of a learning climate, the development of the will and pride to learn, and the confidence to make a beginning. Otherwise it is all manipulation and order for order's sake. The reason for all of the above is to enable the teacher to work to improve academic skills so that students have an opportunity to take their place in a technological society and reap its benefits if they so choose. It also should be kept in mind that nothing improves self-concept like the success students experience in their academic work once a learning climate has been established. Success, however, does not come overnight. Success in academic work has to be carefully planned and procedures have to be worked out so that students are assured of some degree of success.

The first thing that was needed was to provide some type of work in which they could not fail. At first the demands of the writer were for the simplest of procedures, that of getting a heading correctly on a paper. After each student had been provided with a sample heading to keep in his notebook, the writer checked only for correct headings. Even the poorest readers and most academically retarded youngsters got this correct and their papers immediately went up on the bulletin boards to help overcome these symbols of failure. Children who had never had a paper recognized in their lives saw one recognized.

The next demand was for lightly structured assignments initially intended to serve a number of purposes:

1. They kept students in their seats during the crucial first two weeks.
2. They were almost fail-proof and were not threatening, and therefore the students did not try to avoid the work.
3. They provided students with initial success.
4. Such assignments allowed the writer to relate to individual problem students during the first two weeks.
5. Such assignments allowed the writer to offer individual assistance, and they allowed students to see a payoff from this assistance.

These assignments included doing simple review problems in arithmetic, copying definitions in English, copying spelling words and definitions, and so on. The rationale given to the class for the busywork was that the writer wanted them to be able to have a chance to review work and to be able to do their best.

After a two-week period of intensive remedial work with many students, a gradual introduction to more complicated work and independent work could begin. Because of the procedures and planning mentioned earlier, order was being restored and pride instilled. Having experienced moderate success in the structured academic work, students proceeded with a degree of security to more challenging assignments, and the writer could spend more time in explanation and assistance. At this time the writer did not enter any marks on the papers. He did check work for his own diagnostic purposes, to see who needed help in what. Instead of marking or "red inking" the papers, the writer entered written comments in his record book so that papers could continue to be put on the boards and so that the students who had been successful during the "busywork" time would not be overwhelmed during this period of increased academic demand. However, each child was individually given help on aspects of his work which diagnostic checks showed he needed.

After a while the writer found he could use student tutors to help him provide individual assistance. It was important that plans be made to prepare the students for help from their peers and then to give the peers help in assisting others. This help should initially be performed in non-threatening tasks not directly related to academic work. The students helped others in such things as art, music, or sports, subjects which do not carry the stigma of being a dummy if you need help in them. Also, many of the students who couldn't help in academic work could see themselves in a contributing role. After this, the writer had students helping others in academic work. This help came last, since many students seemed to be most resistant to offers of help from other students. This resistance bordered on hostility (since many had the idea that only "teacher's pets" helped) and was overcome only by the gradual plans made for the introduction of student tutoring.

To structure tutoring by students to make it more effective, the tutors were provided with assistance in the form of individual help before they tutored. The teacher let them know what had to be worked on and provided them with work-sheets or page numbers. He let them put the instruction in their own words, but he gave them some guidelines. And, most important, he got the permission of the learner before assigning the tutor.

In their academic work the class had proceeded from "busywork" to the stage just described. They were ready to proceed to the third stage a little past mid-semester. This was the stage when they would enter into some degree of independent work. It was crucial at this stage that the writer provide them with models to follow so that the potential for success would be increased.

For example, the class was to have a panel discussion. No more than five minutes had passed before the "discussion" almost erupted into open warfare and fisticuffs. The writer stopped the panel. His first reaction was to think the students incapable of any such activity. However, after further thought it became evident that the children had never seen a panel discussion. Also, they had not had practice in the kind of verbal give-and-take that middle-class children have in their home situation and in other areas of their experiences. For middle-class children, the panel discussion is a familiar thing and often an extension of a verbal communication pattern they experience over the breakfast and dinner tables. For the writer's children such verbal challenges were signals for a fight. Obviously, the children needed a model to follow.

Community people with whom the writer had established contact (minister, boys club director, park district coach, mother) were asked to present a panel discussion. Here the children had an opportunity to see that probing questions could be asked and opinions exchanged without this being a challenge to a fight. The second student panel was still bedlam. A third panel was scheduled with community people, students from the class, and another teacher. This seemed to do it, for the third panel worked perfectly. Students again discussed a topic they had chosen, but this time with an openness, feeling, and intelligence that both they and the writer previously would have thought they were incapable of attaining. This success came about because a model was given.

During the course of the semester the children were successfully engaging in independent library work out of the room, holding committee meetings in the hall, setting up study committees, electing groups to assist the teacher to plan curriculum, and helping choose textbooks and other learning materials, such as newspapers, magazines, and comic books. Lessons could be given utilizing folk music, students' own stories, and a host of other things which had seemed impossible at the beginning of the semester. But the success of all these "novel" (for them) approaches was probably due to the fact that the writer structured procedures and provided models to follow. Students knew what was expected of them in library work because a model of how to conduct library research was provided them by "neighborhood hero" high school athletes the writer asked to help him. A model for committee work was provided for them by the boys club director and his staff when they presented a mock committee meeting to draw up the season's basketball schedules.

The idea of providing a model becomes crucial when the children enter the inquiry stage. The writer made the mistake of following the advice of some textbooks and experts on inquiry in various subject matters. When he began "inquiry," the inductive approach to subject matter, the children retreated immediately. Deadly silences and pained looks followed each question designed to elicit the answers on which to build a generalization. Once again they began to feel like failures. Then the writer reversed the procedure. He gave the generalization first and then proceeded to work from there, showing how inquiry produced it. He took them step by step back through to the original problem. After a number of such examples, the students began to see what it meant to engage in inquiry. After providing these models, the writer presented a problem and carefully worked the class through to the generalization. Soon the students were able to do this themselves and to apply this process to solving or analyzing different problems raised by the group itself, including the problems of their society and their life.

When the writer had to leave the school, the room was a far different place than it had been before. Students and teacher had been rewarded by behavioral and academic successes. The students presented the writer with a plaque inscribed, "To The World's Greatest Teacher—Room 302." But what brought a lump to the writer's throat were the rather shy statements from two students who said, "I'm glad you were our teacher because you made us behave and learn" and "Yeah, you taught us."

Fundamental Elements in a Definition of Structure

Although we have not undertaken to carry out a formal analysis of the preceding material, we believe that a careful reading of it indicates that there were at least four fundamental ways in which the teacher in question endeavored to structure the educational experiences and environment of his classroom to bring about improved performance on the part of his disadvantaged students. We further believe that each of these four elements or dimensions of structure is a basic and perhaps indispensable component which should be included in any plan for structuring education to help disadvantaged students perform more effectively in the classroom. No claim or pretense is made that these four aspects constitute an exhaustive definition of structure or that they are completely discrete from one another. Nevertheless, we believe that a definition of structure which breaks the term down into these four component elements is considerably more useful for classroom teachers than are customary usages in which the term tends to be defined so generally that it has little if any meaning. Without a systematic classification of the most important dimensions of structure which teachers should be providing for disadvantaged students in their classrooms, teachers receive little practical guidance from those who advocate the use of "structure" in educating disadvantaged students.

1. *Structure involves the choice and sequencing of instructional experiences and materials in accordance with the particular learning problems and characteristics of disadvantaged students.*

One reason why this aspect of structure is so important is that it is so closely related to the special characteristics and experiences (e.g., short attention span, high distractibility, unfamiliarity with standard middle-class language and concepts) of students from low-income homes and neighborhoods. Several recent publications have provided useful analyses and illustrations of such matters as the structuring of curriculum materials to build "redundancy" into instructional sequences (Beilin and Gotkin, 1967) or to allow for individualization in instructional strategies (Blank and Solomon, 1969) for disadvantaged students, and we do not feel that any analysis or examples we might add would differ substantially from those already available in these sources. We, therefore, did not choose to include case study material giving much attention to or many examples of this aspect of structure.

2. *Structure involves the initiation of procedures and arrangements to obtain order, so that teaching and learning can begin to take place.*

It is much easier to say that the teacher must utilize definite procedures to achieve and maintain order than it is to identify effective procedures and to utilize them successfully for this purpose in a particular classroom, particularly among disadvantaged students in the inner city. It would be no trouble at all to find thousands of well-intentioned inner-city teachers whose experience would attest to the foolishness of any claim that the task of maintaining an orderly environment in the inner city can be solved merely by resolving to structure school experiences to achieve this goal. Nevertheless, the success achieved by teachers who have set out consciously to do this by utilizing methods such as are described in the preceding section shows that the task is not impossible.

We do not agree with the arguments of educators who seem to believe that any specific or direct effort to establish order in the classroom is necessarily repressive of creativity or discriminatory to the interests of most disadvantaged students. We do agree with those who believe that a minimum amount of order facilitates rather than inhibits the intellectual, social, and emotional growth of disadvantaged students in the classroom. We also agree that order should be organically achieved, insofar as it is possible to do so, by providing experiences which are interesting and intrinsically motivating for the disadvantaged child.

In considering whether it is somehow immoral or undesirable to systematically structure educational experiences and environments for the purpose of achieving order in the inner-city classroom, teachers should take into account the findings of research and evaluation studies which usually attribute at least part of the success of outstanding teachers of the disadvantaged to their skill in utilizing structure to maintain order. Such findings have come as no surprise, of course, to most observers familiar with the problems of educating disadvantaged students.

The constant danger in working to achieve order in the inner-city classroom is that efforts to structure learning for this purpose will become an end in themselves. Since teachers have to struggle very hard to maintain an orderly environment, many come to feel that their teaching responsibilities have been discharged as long as open warfare among students or between students and teachers has been averted. When this happens, structure is no longer a means to make learning possible but has degenerated into custodial procedures and busywork which accomplish nothing more than smoothing the passage of time. After summarizing the advice given to him by colleagues who had fallen into the error of working out methods to control behavior in the classroom but were unwilling or unable to devise instructional experiences to overcome the fundamental learning problems of their disadvantaged students, Herndon (1968) remarks how he came to realize that an approach limited only to the goal of attaining order was "a failure and was going to be a failure. . . . I knew damn well that they'd been getting this treatment for the past six years, that during this time they'd learned practically nothing about the 'skills' this type of order was spozed to produce—no adverbs, not how to spell, no punctuation, not adding, subtracting, multiplying, or dividing; many hadn't even learned how to read" (p. 106).

3. *Structure involves the systematic choice and creation of situations and educational materials which provide disadvantaged students with experiences of success in the school. Efforts to plan and provide experiences from which disadvantaged students can derive a feeling of success should not be limited to the rather obvious imperative to utilize appropriate instructional materials but should permeate every event or activity which takes place in the school, from mundane matters, such as following a set of simple instructions during recess, to more complicated matters, such as the preparation and carrying out of an assembly program or classroom discussion group. In doing this, teachers of the disadvantaged should utilize all available means of recognizing and rewarding students which prove to be effective in increasing students' motivation and raising their self-concept.*

One of the questions frequently debated among educators concerned with the disadvantaged is whether it is either moral or wise to use material rewards, such as candy, prizes, tokens, stars, and so on, in the inner-city classroom. Those who believe that material rewards should be avoided argue that the students must become intrinsically motivated if they are to succeed in the school and that external rewards not only do not help a student become intrinsically motivated but may even fixate students at an undesirable stage of development. Those who believe that material rewards should be utilized argue that extrinsic motivation not only can be transformed into intrinsically motivated behaviors but actually facilitates the development of these latter behaviors by setting the stage for successful learning experiences in the inner-city school.

Apparently psychologists have not fully resolved this dispute over whether extrinsic motivation hampers or facilitates the development of intrinsic motivation among advantaged or disadvantaged students. Nor have they identified the conditions which may make extrinsic motivation either effective or ineffective. Until they do, we believe it is wise to side with the inner-city teacher who, in systematically structuring educational experiences and environments in his classroom, utilizes external rewards as well as less visible methods to help his students gain a feeling of success in the school. Our reasons for taking this position are that (a) the need to structure success experiences for disadvantaged students simply is too overwhelming, (b) the negatively motivating experience of failure in school and society among these students simply is too pervasive, and (c) the instances of success reported to us by inner-city teachers who have used extrinsic rewards in a systematic manner have been too convincing and encouraging to allow us to reject potentially valuable motivation devices without conclusive evidence that a particular approach is harmful either from a short-range or a long-range point of view.

As in the case of the second dimension of structure described above, the constant danger in using extrinsic as well as intrinsic rewards which might give disadvantaged students a feeling of success in the school is that a teacher will be satisfied if these rewards apparently result in improvements in the behaviors or attitudes of students in his class and will not put much effort into planning and providing experiences which might develop more self-directed behaviors or otherwise lead to actual improvements in the learning among his students. It goes without saying that a teacher who found ways to help disadvantaged students experience success merely in order to make them happy or to maintain order in the classroom would be making only a small and inadequate gesture toward fulfilling his responsibilities to his students and his employers.

4. *Structure involves the use of requirements and ground rules in such a way as to (a) clearly define what students are expected to do;*

(b) require initial participation on the part of the student; (c) provide for increasing student participation in setting subsequent ground rules and requirements; and (d) ensure that students understand as thoroughly as possible the rationale underlying the activities and assignments in which they participate in the school and classroom.

The reason why we have listed all these goals under a single dimension of structure is that they are so closely interrelated to each other. Educators who work with disadvantaged students, not to mention the students themselves, generally report that pupil performance is most likely to improve when clear and definite requirements are set down concerning such matters as the time schedule for assignments; and expectations thus spelled out are adhered to as closely as possible. Many disadvantaged pupils report that clear and enforced definitions of their responsibilities help them get started on and maintain a certain amount of momentum in their academic studies. This means that definite arrangements also should be made to provide students with a place and time to study, knowledge and skills they need in working on their assignments, and other concrete forms of help in developing academic competence. The teacher who merely lays down clear and definite requirements without making many kinds of arrangements to ensure that disadvantaged pupils can live up to them may be in for a rude shock.

Yet, clear and definite requirements and a situation which is conducive to their completion will get teachers and students only so far. Students need to develop a clear picture of the reasons for engaging in one or another activity in preference to others, particularly in the case of disadvantaged students who tend to be relatively unclear concerning the ways in which skills and understandings are built on one another. They need knowledge of, and skills in, carrying out the role of student. One of the best ways to help an individual understand and master a role is to have him participate in the decisions which define and delineate it. As early as possible in a particular classroom, disadvantaged students should participate in making the decisions which determine what will happen in that classroom.

As is true with respect to our conclusions concerning the need for structure in choosing and sequencing instructional materials, establishing and maintaining order, and utilizing external rewards and intrinsic motivation, there may be critics who feel it is somehow demeaning to the individuality or creative potential of the disadvantaged student to impose requirements and expectations other than those which might arise naturally from his curiosity or his urge to participate in a specific activity. In each such dispute, we believe that most teachers who do not make a systematic attempt to structure arrangements, procedures, and situations in ways such as are described in this paper are not fulfilling their obligations to their disadvantaged students.

We agree that the goals toward which education should aim are better embodied in such terms as *self-direction, self-discipline,* and *creativity* than in such terms as *classroom order* and *requirements*. The central problem, however, is always how to get from here to there; from a situation in which many disadvantaged students generally are learning little but alienation in the school, to a situation in which they become active and willing learners. The distance to be traveled between *what is* and *what should be* is even greater in the inner-city school than in the middle-class school. The longer and more distant one's destination is in undertaking a voyage, the more he needs a map to help him get there. *Structure,* in this sense, can help provide the map disadvantaged students need in negotiating and overcoming the obstacles and problems they will encounter in schools where educators are determined to help them become more proficient learners.

Lest the statements we have offered about structure be misunderstood or distorted to support conclusions which might be detrimental to the education of disadvantaged students, we conclude with six cautions which should be kept in mind when thinking about the topics raised in this paper. These points are not tacked on as footnotes; instead, we consider them to be extremely important qualifications which, if not adequately taken into account, would make plans to emphasize structure in the classroom not only simple-minded but potentially damaging to disadvantaged students.

1. *Not all economically disadvantaged students are educationally disadvantaged.* As in any other group, a class of economically disadvantaged students includes individuals who differ widely in motivation, level of development, and other ways. Like any other teaching decision, approaches aimed at providing structure in the inner-city classroom should recognize and deal with variations and differences among students.

2. *Providing structure in the classroom facilitates but does not in itself constitute a solution to problems involved in stimulating learning among the disadvantaged.* Creative and innovative curricular materials must be provided, or disadvantaged students will tend to be negative and uninterested in education. Structure does not justify the use of physically or psychologically punitive methods in the classroom, nor does it in any way obviate the need for inner-city teachers to be flexible in working with their students and to treat each student as a worthwhile human being.

3. *Structuring classroom experiences and environments does not prevent a teacher from building on or encouraging the expression of the spontaneous interests and impulses of disadvantaged students.*

Whether an educational program is structured or unstructured, most classroom activities can and should not only allow for, but also encourage the free expression and pursuit of ideas, concepts, and interests among a particular group of disadvantaged students.

4. *In most situations involving a subordinate-superordinate position (real or implied) there exist possibilities for the development of hostility on the part of those in the subordinate role.* These possibilities become especially acute in an inner-city school during the time an academic climate is being established. It is necessary for the teacher to provide avenues or opportunities for the channeling of this hostility. It will also be necessary for the teacher to show great understanding regarding hostile outbursts and to exercise judgment regarding what things to overlook and what things to give attention to. Setting up opportunities to laugh with the class is critical to the development of rapport. Often it is necessary to arrange situations which allow for a "positive" release of hostility directed at the school and/or teacher and to use these situations to laugh with the students and let them see the "human" side of the teacher.

5. *A teacher must work toward developing a reputation in the school regarding his expectations, his interest in the children, his fairness and his understanding.* Once a reputation is established, the necessity to enforce a structure for establishing an academic climate may be significantly reduced.

6. *Some inner-city teachers may be more effective in an unstructured rather than a structured classroom.* Not all teachers are alike, and a few of those who may be temperamentally unfitted to work in a structured framework might also have some rare knack for making an unstructured approach work successfully in the inner city.

One additional point to which attention must be drawn in a discussion advocating the use of structure in school programs for disadvantaged students is that the choice of such an approach has definite implications for the role and behavior of the teacher. Among the most important of these implications are the following:

1. If teachers are to succeed in attempting to systematically incorporate structure into classroom programs for the disadvantaged, they must be given much more time for planning and testing the arrangements and strategies they may decide to use in the classroom than is now available to them in most public schools.

2. Inner-city teachers must take the initiative in learning as much as possible about the actual family and neighborhood conditions in which their students live, or the structural procedures and arrangements teachers devise and introduce may be inappropriate and may have little or no effect in inspiring, controlling, rewarding, or guiding their students. Besides learning about the family and neighborhood,

it is important that the teacher take part in activities related to neighborhood life. For example, the teacher in the case study attended meetings of neighborhood councils, went to churches in the area, and shopped in the area during Friday and Saturday rush times. All of these activities were designed to provide the teacher with a great amount of contact and exposure to students and parents so as to develop an understanding of the area as well as to develop a "reputation" among students and parents as a concerned teacher. The structuring of contacts to develop a reputation concerning out-of-classroom matters is an essential ingredient in developing acceptance in the classroom and in obtaining student acceptance of the structuring of academic and behavioral demands.

3. As outstanding teachers who have described their experience in the inner-city have been quick to realize, one or even a few successful teachers can have little long-range impact when their disadvantaged students return to school and non-school environments which do not reinforce the gains made in a particular classroom. Particularly since disadvantaged students encounter a great deal of conflict or at least inconsistency between the various expectations held out for them in moving between their school, family, and neighborhood environments, it is necessary that an effectively structured school environment be as consistent as possible throughout the school if students are to learn to perform well in their roles in the school and classroom (Levine, 1968). This implies, of course, that the entire faculty in the inner-city school should work together in a carefully and closely coordinated manner if they desire to utilize structured educational programs to improve the learning of their disadvantaged students.

In Conclusion

The purpose of this paper has been to define the term "structure" with more precision than has been customary among practitioners and researchers working with disadvantaged youngsters. Despite considerable agreement and evidence concerning the importance of structure in school programs for disadvantaged students, the term generally has been used without clearly specifying its underlying meaning or the major elements in its definition.

Case material on an apparently successful inner-city classroom was presented, which supports, we believe, the conclusion that plans to structure education for the disadvantaged should have at least four major dimensions or aspects: (1) choosing and sequencing instructional materials and experiences in accordance with the particular learning problems and characteristics of disadvantaged students; (2) devising and using procedures and arrangements to obtain order in the school and classroom; (3) systematically choosing and creating educational situations and materials which provide disadvantaged students with experiences of success; and (4) setting clear and specific requirements which students help to define, and acting to arrange schedules and provide resources which not only permit but also encourage successful completion of these requirements.

We recognize that this definition must be viewed as provisional and that it omits several important meanings which might have been included in it. Readers may wish to identify additional elements or aspects of structure which should be taken explicitly into account when planning educational programs for the disadvantaged. We do believe, however, that it is vitally necessary to include each of the four major elements identified above in conducting a structured school program for disadvantaged students; from this point of view, effective education in the inner city is contingent on the utilization of all four types of structure. When sufficient amounts of the right kind of structure are provided to maintain order but structure is not equally well used to sequence instructional materials, to provide many kinds of success experiences for students, and to help pupils understand and learn how to function in the role of student in school and classroom, few or no gains may be made in improving pupil performance. In fact, structured arrangements and procedures designed to maintain an orderly classroom often will not succeed in accomplishing even this limited goal unless simultaneous efforts are made to structure the classroom environment so that disadvantaged students experience some success and feel they are learning something in it.

Similarly, the major problem in many inner-city classrooms is not so much maintaining order as encouraging student activity.* In these cases it is obvious that structure must mean much more than the attainment and maintenance of order if disadvantaged students are to perform more effectively in the schools.

By now it probably is very clear that the essence of "structure" in the school programs for the disadvantaged is careful and thorough planning of the educational experiences and environments provided for students. It should also be clear, furthermore, that our assigning to

*One particularly good description of such a situation has been provided by a junior high department chairman: "the class is not unruly; it is not loud; it is not filled with leering exhibitionists. On the contrary, the class is orderly, quiet, and filled with many who do not wish to be seen. The problem turns out not to be one of noise, but of silence. . . . This lack of response, I am convinced, is not because so few know the answer or have no contributions to make. Rather, it stems from a peculiarity of the inner-city high-school student. The psychological and sociological forces which have molded him require that he protect himself at all times. The world is hostile, school is hostile, the teacher is hostile. If he answers a question or makes a judgment, he has let down his defenses and becomes vulnerable. Experience has taught him that it is better not to volunteer an answer, for the answer may be wrong" (Glovinsky, 1968, p. 106).

the teacher responsibility for exercising as much systematic foresight as possible in order to structure learning sequences effectively and to guide pupils toward participation and success in an orderly and psychologically secure setting might easily be used to describe the parameters of good teaching in any school. In a sense, then, our attempt to define structure is nothing but a roundabout way of saying that the inner-city teacher should be a good teacher.

In another sense, however, a definition of structure *does* have particular importance for the inner-city teacher. A number of observers, among them Fantini and Weinstein (1968), have rightly remarked that education in middle-class schools tends to be no less ineffective and inadequate than are present school programs for the disadvantaged, but the fact that middle-class students are not so obviously marking time as disadvantaged pupils are inhibits public awareness that our schools could and should be much better than they are now. Teachers and administrators in middle-class schools probably can continue to pretend, at least for a while, that these schools are effective institutions. ("Look, parent, look: 80 per cent of our graduates go to college. Five of them won Merit Scholarships. Shhh! Don't worry about those who report they are being processed through their classrooms or who are beginning to criticize an education which they find to be uninspired and meaningless.") In the inner-city, on the other hand, this leeway does not exist; here we have hardly any time left to re-examine, plan, structure, and re-structure school programs which successfully motivate and guide pupils to become more effective learners.

References

Beilin, H. and L. Gotkin. "Psychological Issues in the Development of Mathematics Curricula for Socially Disadvantaged Children," in Passow, A. H., M. L. Goldberg, and A. J. Tannenbaum. *Education of the Disadvantaged: A Book of Readings.* New York: Holt, Rinehart and Winston, 1967. Pp. 287–306.

Blank, M. and F. Solomon. "How Shall the Disadvantaged Child Be Taught?" *Child Development,* 40 (March 1969), 48–60.

Bloom, B. "Stability and Change in Human Characteristics: Implications for School Reorganization," *Educational Administration Quarterly,* 2 (Winter 1966), 34–49.

Comer, J. P., M. Harrow, and S. H. Johnson. "Summer Study Skills Program: A Case for Structure," *Journal of Negro Education,* 38 (Winter 1968), 38–45.

Dvorky, D. "Experts Use the Second Chance to Make Job Corps Succeed," *Education News,* November 13, 1967, p. 15.

Elkins, D. "Instructional Guidelines for Teachers of the Disadvantaged," *The Record,* 70 (April 1969), 593–615.

Fantini, M. and G. Weinstein. *The Disadvantaged: Challenge to Education.* New York: Harper and Row, 1968.

Glovinksy, A. "Views of a Department Head," in *New Teachers in Urban Schools,* ed. R. Wisniewski. New York: Random House, 1968. Pp. 102–112.

Goodman, M. E. and A. Beman. "Tracktown Children," in *The Negro Family: A Book of Readings,* ed. C. V. Willie. Columbus: Charles E. Merrill, 1970.

Herndon, J. *The Way It Spozed To Be.* New York: Bantam Books, 1968.

Hunt, D. E. "A Conceptual Systems Change Model and Its Application to Education," in *Flexibility, Adaptability and Creativity,* ed. O. J. Harvey. New York: Springer Publishing Co., 1966.

Levine, D. U. "Cultural Diffraction in the Social System of the Low-Income School," *School and Society,* 96 (March 30, 1968), 206–207, 210.

THE DEATH OF INTELLECT; OR HOW TO CHANGE TEACHERS INTO CRETINS WITHOUT REALLY TRYING

Larry Cuban

Larry Cuban observes life in the inner-city school and finds that each of the four "models" into which current literature on the subject can be categorized (i.e., the pornographic, Up-the-Down-Staircase, death-of-the-black-child, and confessions-of-a-new-teacher) is incomplete in some ways. Cuban argues that there is much about teaching and learning in the ghetto school that is neither exotic nor bizarre, much which is monotonous and routine, and yet encompasses for both teachers and students considerable vitality and responsiveness as well as frustration and anxiety.

Cuban focuses here on a small slice of what happens intellectually to teachers in the inner-city schools and suggests things which can be done to halt "the persistent shrinkage of minds." Any basic reform designed to expand opportunities for the disadvantaged is more or less doomed, he believes, unless what happens to the teachers intellectually is examined and understood. Thus, he presents a vignette of "A Teachers' Day . . ." and follows a seven-year veteran teacher through his typical daily schedule, and then examines the basis for his ineffectiveness. To Cuban, the teacher's ineffectiveness and drabness probably have developed from the interaction between the system (its structure, rules, and relationships) and the individual himself. Authoritarian administrative leadership is the mode rather than the exception, with the consequence that only a dull conformity survives.

A pattern of do's and don'ts, communicated through bulletins, bells, and regulations and promulgated by principals and supervisors who are themselves caught up in the "system" yield teachers who are technicians and children who cannot be trusted with responsibility or be given independence to act on their own.

Cuban maintains that the daily schedule and teaching assignments curtail intellectual growth, "keeping teachers docile and child-like by isolating them from one another." This planned isolation and insulation, deliberately or otherwise, causes promising new teachers to starve to death intellectually. They have little or no time to read, think about, discuss, analyze, or otherwise deepen their understandings of theory and practice of teaching or closely related matters. Most in-service activities, Cuban finds, are of little value, and changing the name to "staff development" will have little impact unless the problems related to intellectual sterility are attacked.

There are three kinds of teacher growth with which in-service education must deal, Cuban believes. These involve: (a) internalizing the skills of reflective thinking; (b) examining one's own attitudes and feelings concerning low-income youngsters, race, and minority group status; and (c) analyzing systematically one's own teaching in terms of what is used and how it is used. Such periodic and systematic self-examination, Cuban suggests, will result in "a person who is curious, aware, and thoughtful, whose goal is continuing self-renewal."

Cuban sees college courses and sensitivity training sessions as having limited value. He proposes two alternate strategies for teacher growth. One is designed to encourage teachers to do research and develop instructional materials for their own students. The second involves providing time, money, and support for teachers to analyze their own teaching behavior under conditions which are supportive rather than destructive. Cuban assumes that teachers in the inner city do care and do want to grow and that the conditions for such intellectual growth must be created by the system itself.

Larry Cuban is a high school teacher in the District of Columbia public school system.

THE DEATH OF INTELLECT; OR HOW TO CHANGE TEACHERS INTO CRETINS WITHOUT REALLY TRYING

Larry Cuban

The growing literature on inner-city schools * runs broad and deep. In the developing genre of writing, four strains have emerged.

First, there is the pornographic model. Evan Hunter's *Blackboard Jungle* spawned an enormous litter, from *White Teacher in a Black School* to the latest exposé of sex, violence, and drugs in the schools. This type depicts schools as zoos where barbaric behavior prevails and educational perversion dominates. Seldom does analysis intrude upon description; the reader is often left with the feeling that sick kids get what they deserve.

Second, there is the *Up-the-Down-Staircase* model. This is the type of book that artistically attempts to recapture the chaos, frustrations, and anxieties of teachers thrust into impossible situations. The tone is usually mocking, light, and even impish. The bias is anti-administration, pro-teacher and student. The villain is generally the Admiral Ass character or simply the Bureaucracy. The hero or heroine is a teacher who rises above all the frustrations and obstacles, even rejecting a safe job in the suburbs to remain in the hectic classroom. James Herndon's *The Way It Spozed To Be* reverses the formula and gives us a lovable anti-hero who gets tossed out of school because he does succeed with students.

The third model passionately attacks ghetto schools for their destruction of black children. Jonathan Kozol's prize winning book is representative of this death-of-the-black-child-as-seen-by-the-inmates-of-the-public-schools model. The vehicle for Kozol's attack is the

* "Inner-city schools" refers to those schools enrolling large numbers of low-income children of both races. For the most part they are racially isolated. I have tried to avoid adjectives that wave a red flag, like "lower class," "ghetto," "disadvantaged," "culturally deprived" (or depraved as one teacher informed me), because such labels open sores and close minds. More important, these terms exaggerate the difference between children and ignore their many basic similarities. Certainly, "inner-city" is imprecise and probably euphemistic, but at this point in the growing concern over education for the poor there is no sense in obscuring the issues by using even more loaded, inaccurate words.

description of an elementary school by a former teacher aide who candidly admits that he watched the kids die. Books such as this detail the twitches of the corpse as *rigor mortis* sets in and the uncaring teachers and administrators watch the process. Such descriptions scathingly reveal the hypocrisy and insensitivity of whites toward blacks of all ages.

Fourth, there is the Confessions-of-a-New-Teacher model. While Kozol, Herndon, and others were new teachers, they rejected the diary format for exposition and analysis structured to make their points. In this model, however, through tapes, diaries, and letters new teachers describe their stream of consciousness impressions, the changes they endure, and the numerous experiences, both painful and pleasurable, that they encounter.

The four categories are imperfect. No doubt there is slippage and overlapping among them, and perhaps there are some that defy typing; but the fact remains that an enormous literature on what inner-city schools are like has been produced. Out of hundreds of thousands of words—some of which are superbly eloquent and some appallingly shallow—where is the truth? What is it really like to teach in such a school?

Shards of truth appear in many of the books, but put together they create an abstract mosaic—with missing pieces, I might add—not a complete rendering of reality. There is much about teaching and learning in inner-city schools (and both, indeed, do happen) that is not bizarre or exotic; that does not make headlines or book-club selections. There is the dull, monotonous routine that goes unreported. There are the subtle cruelties that students and teachers—out of frustration and anxiety—inflict upon one another. There is the callousness that develops. And there is the vitality of diverse young people who connect up with responsive teachers and soar. To capture all of this, the Great American Education Book remains to be written. I, unfortunately, cannot write that book.

What I can do, however, is sketch out one narrow slice of what happens to teachers intellectually in inner-city schools and what can be done to halt the persistent shrinkage of minds. Here is a dimension of inner-city education that seldom is examined, yet remains critical to the success of any basic reform proposed to expand opportunities for the disadvantaged.

A Teacher's Day . . .

Consider David Brown (not his real name), a seven-year veteran teacher in a Midwestern inner-city school. A graduate of the city's teacher training institution, Brown worked his way through college and he is proud of it. On a recent questionnaire, he replied that he enjoyed teaching although he was uneasy about the low caliber of new students, was satisfied with the working conditions, and liked the children in the school. If Brown is typical of any group, it is of those individuals who try to do a good job in the classroom yet do not fully understand how the school system and he inevitably conspire to erode his intellect and compromise his effectiveness.

Arriving at 8:30, he signed the time sheet, picked up the keys to his homeroom and the notices in his mailbox. In his room (this year, Brown has it the whole day; last year he shared it with one other teacher; and the year before he "floated" from room to room to teach his five classes), he began reading the daily bulletin.

BULLETIN No. 27
October 13, 1967

THOUGHT FOR THE DAY:
Difficulties strengthen the mind as labor does the body (Seneca)

[*Whoever Seneca was, Brown thought, he knew about this school.*]

1. Do not admit to class without a note from Mrs. Jones:
Raymond Miller 417
Forest Pettigrew 203
Timothy Calloway 409

[*Pettigrew is in my fourth period class. I wonder what trouble he's in now. His whole family is bad news.*]

2. TIME CORRECTION: Senior Class will have rehearsal for the Convocation today at the 2nd period.

[*Well, there goes that class. And I stayed up late last night clipping those pictures for the lesson.*]

3. CANDY SALE: Please turn in all your candy money NOW.
4. Varsity football at home. Students with tickets will be excused the 7th period.

[*I figured they'd do that; I didn't prepare for that class anyway.*]

TEACHERS
1. All male teachers are expected on duty at the football game today. Mr. Smith will be around with the sign-up sheet.
2. Beginning TODAY daily absence sheets will be placed in each teacher's box and may be picked up at any time after 11:10. Students will make **no** more deliveries.

[*I guess the kids found another way of cutting class.*]

3. No teacher is to send a student on an errand outside the school **without express permission** from the office.

4. Faculty meeting next Wednesday. Be prompt. Attendance will be taken.

[*Oh, hell, another afternoon shot. If he reads to us like he did last meeting, I'll walk out. Aw, I won't. I always say that but never get my ass off the seat.*]

5. Some homeroom teachers have failed to complete attendance cards, Request for Information Sheets, and triplicate program cards for each student. Students are ABSOLUTELY not to fill these cards out. Do not use ball-point pens to complete forms.

[*That's me, I'll have to take those damn things home this weekend to finish them.*]

6. The following schedule for the submission of records and reports for upcoming report card grades is listed for the information of all teachers:

Grading period closed on November 9, Thursday.

Thursday, November 9 —All attendance cards are due in Room 109 at 9:45 a.m.

Monday, November 13 —All Form 40's are due in the Business Office at 8:45 a.m.

Thursday, November 16—Report Cards will be distributed to pupils at 2:50 p.m.

Friday, November 17 —Form 39's and Form 40's are due in the office at 9:00 a.m.

[*Oh, God!*]

Brown finished the bulletin as his homeroom began to fill up with youngsters. His 37 youngsters are with him about twenty minutes and then they move into their first-period class. He is supposed to provide guidance for members of the homeroom, but rarely does he have time to lift his head from the records he must complete for the office. While he took roll (since it was Friday, over eight students were absent), the tardy bell rang. Two latecomers appeared. To one who had been chronically late, he assigned an after-school detention. He does not like the idea of a detention hall, but Brown feared that the others in the homeroom might come late if he didn't assign detentions.

He called the homeroom to order, read the announcements, and asked for comments or questions. Since there were none except from the stout girl in the last row who wanted to go to the bathroom (permission granted), Brown asked all students to take out their books and study or do homework until the bell rang. Some did that. Others put their heads down and went to sleep. A few copied homework from one another. And the rest ignored what Brown had said and began talking. Sharp glances and a warning from Brown ended the conversations. (Brown runs a tight classroom and is proud of it.)

In the remaining minutes of the homeroom period, he wrote assignments for his five classes on the blackboard. He has three eleventh- and two twelfth-grade English classes. Though it seems to the layman that he would only have two different weekly preparations —one for eleventh and the other for the twelfth—for the twenty-five classes he teaches a week—he really has more. Or at least he did at one time. Two of his five classes are college preparatory; two are general academic; and one is in a business curriculum. When he first began teaching, he prepared detailed lesson plans, reading background materials, and the like. But the caliber of students changed and academic standards seemed to fall and he got married and, well, he does not have five preparations now; he has two. He still feels uneasy about all eleventh-graders reading *The Scarlet Letter* and his twelfth-graders analyzing eighteenth-century poetry, but he has learned to live with it.

The first three periods of the day went well enough for a Friday. Two P.A. announcements ("Will June Taylor of homeroom 201 please report to the office immediately," and "There is a blue Mustang blocking the principal's car in the parking lot. Unless it is moved, it will be towed away.") interrupted his first-period class. But it was not more than a nuisance since the class was answering questions on the character of Hester Pryne that Brown had lifted from an English literature workbook.

He did get irritated, however, in his third-period class of Business English. Four students left for the Nurse's office in the middle of a discussion on symbolism in Alexander Pope's poetry. It was not exactly a discussion since only five of the thirty students present were answering the questions that Brown had assigned; the others had not done their homework. What irritated Brown was that of the five who left, three had been active in the discussion. Now he was left with a small three-way conversation in a class of thirty. Again, it seemed to Brown that the quality of youngsters in the school was deteriorating.

At lunchtime (the teachers' union had secured 40 minutes of uninterrupted time), Brown joined the "gripe" table. Four to six veteran faculty members would often spend the period complaining about the latest stupidity of the administration or bizarre incident in school or an encounter with a troublesome youth. Consensus was invariably reached that if parents were more interested in their children then the teacher's job would be much easier. But Brown always felt uneasy when the griping turned to uninterested parents, mainly because he had met so few (only twelve parents had visited him out of 150 students at the last PTA meeting) and because of the memory of how difficult it was for his folks to attend school functions. Anyway, it was different for these parents because many were on welfare. His parents, although poor, never took handouts.

The next class was a disaster. The homework he had assigned two days ago was still undone by a majority of the class. He gave them a sermon about responsibility, the importance of education for "you people," why laziness leads to dropping-out, etc., etc., and ordered the whole class to open their textbooks and begin doing the homework. Most students complied, even the ones who had already done the assignment. But within ten minutes a few students had their heads down on their desks ("resting my eyes," one student told Brown). Clusters of buzzing kids materialized. Brown rose from his desk. He walked back and forth in front of the class for the remaining 25 minutes, glaring at individuals when they began talking.

Finally the bell rang. Brown went to the faculty lounge. It was his planning period, and he usually graded papers or caught up on homeroom records, but today he didn't feel like it. He needed a smoke. In the men's lounge (it was a school built over fifty years ago and the lounges were still segregated) a few of the men teachers were playing bridge, one was snoring on the divan, and a small group was gossiping about the school. He joined the last group. He stayed for two periods since his last class was excused early. In the middle of the last period of the day, a P.A. announcement called him to the principal's office, generating some humorous remarks among the loungers.

Brown knew the call had to do with his application to a federally-sponsored institute for teachers of the disadvantaged operated by a local university. It did. The principal showed him the strong recommendation he had written to the director of the institute. The principal had singled out Brown as a stalwart of his staff, responsible in fulfilling professional obligations (he turned in most of his reports on time), of high moral character, an effective teacher, etc., etc. Even though the principal had seen Brown teach only twice in seven years, and at that, was in his classes for no more than twenty minutes all together, the principal knew that Brown controlled his classes and rarely sent youngsters to him for disciplinary measure. The principal gave Brown a copy of the recommendation and wished him luck. Just then the final bell rang. He returned to his room to clear his desk. At 3:30, David Brown turned in his candy money and signed out.

David Brown is a nice guy. His principal rated him superior. His colleagues respect him, but his students yawn. And the sad truth is that as nice as Brown may be, he is ineffective. He does not stimulate interest and involvement in what is being taught or learned (the two are not the same); he sees the control of a class only as a nasty task to perform; he does not listen well or change methods or materials; he does not communicate clearly. Turning this around, were Brown an effective teacher, he would be able to involve youngsters in what is to be learned and to communicate clearly knowledge, skills, and attitudes through a broad repertoire of approaches and materials. The benchmark of these measures of effectiveness would be improved performance.

Teacher Ineffectiveness and School Leadership

Does ineffectiveness stem from Brown's genes? His socioeconomic class? Probably not. My guess is, and it is only a guess, that whatever drabness Brown possesses has developed out of the interaction between himself and the school system. Consider the administrative structure and the rules that he works within.

In many schools, the principal and his assistants call the shots. They arrange the teaching schedules, set the agenda for the faculty meetings, disburse funds from the school's kitty, and enforce the curriculum. Of course, the more enlightened administrators consult, seek advice, and weigh the pros and cons; they smooth out the rough edges of authoritarian decision-making. But when you get right down to it, the principal decides.

This observation of authoritarian leadership—rough-edged or gilded—is not new nor meant critically. It is an observation made by many who are more eloquent and caustic than I am. With the principal's having responsibility for the school, authority is placed in his hands. Fine. Yet authority is double-edged; it cuts both ways. In many schools, buttressed by rules and administrative measures, authority strangles initiative. Only dull conformity survives. Administrative power can, however, generate imagination, spontaneity, and esprit.

Unfortunately, in inner-city schools, the pattern is that all the do's and don'ts only oppress teachers—not loudly, beating them over the head with a sledgehammer, but, like the drip of a leaky faucet, slowly, silently, and relentlessly. It numbs brains and paralyzes independence.

Consider what bulletins, bell schedules, and regulations communicate to teachers. First, they say he is a technician, a mechanic, at best. He cannot be trusted with too much responsibility. This silent language of the school quickly and effectively contradicts all that garbage from university courses on professionalism given to prospective teachers. After all, how many professionals do you know who would tolerate the language of David Brown's bulletin—written in the second person imperative, no less. Bells at odd minutes (9:23, 2:56) suggest factory efficiency, but at the cost of telling teachers with every gong, clang, and buzz that they are incapable of deciding when to begin or end the class.

Second, the silent language of bells, rules, and bulletins says clearly and loudly that teachers are dumb children. Teachers cannot read bulletins carefully; that is why there is a public address system to repeat what is written in the bulletin. Teachers cannot follow directions; that is why faculty meetings are held to impress upon them the importance of certain tasks. Teachers are not permitted to collect or spend money without the permission of the principal. Child-like dependency results from strictures and demands.

Third, regulations, especially those concerning petty details or those governing behavior of children and teachers, signal distrust. Seldom are such regulations drawn up cooperatively.

That distrust—a feeling that fathers an elaborate spider web of rules, which, in turn, encourages more dependency—is not peculiar to teachers; it extends throughout most school systems. Christopher Jencks caught its spirit when he observed:

> Every member of the organization is concerned with keeping his superior happy, and he develops . . . an elaborate con game. Nobody is interested in real problems of the "outside" world. Rather, students are interested in figuring out what the teachers want and trying to give it to them, the teachers do the same with the principals, principals with the superintendents, and the superintendents with the school boards. . . . [Because very little faith exists between the members of the system], school personnel at every level tend to centralize authority in their own hands. Thus, it becomes natural for the superintendent not to allow his principals to make up their own budgets, for the principals not to allow their teachers to make up their own syllabuses, for the teachers not to allow students to choose their own readings. . . . (quoted in Harvey Pressman, "New Schools for the Poor," January 1966, mimeo, p. 15).

The roles of administrators, supervisors, and curriculum workers do not escape this distrust and network of rules. Their roles are so structured as to limit their maneuverability and their independence.

While principals appear to have a great deal of autonomy, they are transfixed by a peculiar double vision. One eye focuses upon pleasing supervisors, for advancement in the system goes to those who "play ball with the team" (schools, like prisons, as some have observed, pay off for good behavior); the other eye focuses upon running a tight ship—no boat rocking from students and teachers since waves cause trouble.

Subject supervisors are also trapped by the system's endemic distrust and regulations. They are powerless to effect changes. Therefore, to those who need help, they are irrelevant. Teachers need fewer students and more contact with those they have. They need fewer classes to teach, no clerical duties, and more time for planning. These basic problems supervisors cannot solve. Charged with responsibility, yet empty of authority, supervisors can only advise, cajole, and supplicate. Confronted by powerlessness, supervisors turn inward. They conduct workshops, collect information, visit classes, and prepare sample lesson plans. Like loyal house slaves, administrators, supervisors, and the like are devoted, dependable, and nice to have around.

Returning to the teacher, the bells, bulletins, and administrative rules they are required to follow (many schools still require teachers to sign in or punch in on a time clock) are but the tip of the iceberg that extends deep throughout the school system.

Nurturing the Teacher's Intellectual Growth

Consider how the teaching load and daily schedule curb intellectual growth, keeping teachers docile and child-like by isolating them from one another. At the elementary level—even with all the talk about team-teaching, non-gradedness, and individualizing instruction—most teachers still have self-contained classrooms. For five hours a day, the teacher prepares at least seven different lessons, interacts over one thousand times with thirty kids, and conducts the necessary business of getting materials and children ready for learning. At the secondary level, teachers will have five classes with about 150 to 175 students, two to three preparations, an additional assignment, and clerical trivia.

Such teacher loads and scheduling conspire to separate teachers from one another. They are locked into their rooms (or lounges, out of desperation) and prevented from dealing with colleagues cooperatively. The low level of intellectual give and take, the simple conceptual framework that teachers use to explain what goes on in class and school (see Philip Jackson's *Life in Classrooms* on this point) stems not from any inherent incapacity to deal with issues but from lack of opportunity to play the game of intellect. It is quite easy to come to school at 8:15 and leave at 3:30, five days a week, and not have one chance to discuss meaningfully and undefensively an instructional or curricular or student problem. Seldom are there opportunities for teachers to grapple with the tangled issues of identity, child and adolescent development, and behavior as affected and shaped by the school program. No time is available.

In short, *many promising teachers enter the profession and starve to death intellectually*. It is as if the brain shrank to the size of a pea while the rest of the body continued operating as usual. The fact is, as teachers know so well, that they have no time to read, write, or think about theory or techniques. The cliché about the twenty-year veteran teaching the same thing twenty times touches upon the intellectual sterility of teachers. The onerous teaching load confronting teachers is just another structural support of a system that keeps teachers docile. If this is the case, one can ask legitimately and angrily, How can teachers who are restrained from growing mentally be charged with the responsibilities of stretching disadvantaged youngsters' minds? It is a rhetorical and loaded, yet valid, question. Few ask it; fewer still answer. It is a critical question for inner-city schools, where teachers and facilities are believed to make a difference in childrens' lives.

If this description of how teachers' intellect atrophies is accurate, and I think it is, then what can be done? There is, however, a prior question: Why is it essential to provide growth for teachers and, in effect, recharge their intellectual batteries? The answer is self-evident. There will be no improvement in learning, instruction, and education for the disadvantaged until the quality of the teacher's performance is raised. And, a teacher's performance is linked to his grasp of reflective thought, his repertoire of verbal skills, his ability to deal with individuals and groups, and his awareness of himself. Unfortunately, I have little data to support this assertion: no regression analyses and no standard deviations. All I have are some strong hunches based on my experiences and the illusive data from the Coleman report on the impact of teachers upon student achievement. Those data suggest that reducing class size, improving facilities, renovating curricula, and refashioning school organization—all of which are worthwhile and well within the mainstream of educational reform—inevitably hinge upon the caliber of the staff. But this is almost a cliché. It does, fortunately, bring me back to the original question: If nourishing the intellect is crucial, what can be done?

Here, from the forgotten corners of the educational bureaucracies, emerge the in-service training managers. Next to Motherhood and Old Glory, there is nothing in education more guaranteed to bring forth a gushy cliché, a tear to the eye, or a clinched fist to the breast than in-service education. Everyone agrees that it is essential. Yet, seldom is a fraction of one per cent of a school system's operating budget allocated for it. High in priority, low in dollars. Not surprisingly, what occurs is both inept and inappropriate, much as if a carpenter prescribed aspirin for lung cancer.

What passes for in-service education usually includes dull faculty meetings dealing with candy money, after-school workshops where speakers drive eyelids down and blood pressure up, annual conference days set aside for teachers to listen to a national expert in a cavernous auditorium, and courses offered by the local college or school system itself, often taught by tired schoolmen. In general, it is a sad, sad tale.

A movement is now afoot among school administrators to upgrade in-service education, complete with a change in name. The phrase "staff development" has gained acceptance quickly and quietly. Not unlike, I guess, calling hamburger "chopped sirloin."

Few staff development programs—as they have begun to emerge in large school systems—have developed coherent strategies for dealing with the intellectual sterility that pervades public schools in general and inner-city schools in particular. I am convinced that a school system can generate a vibrant intellectual electricity within its staff, thereby stimulating growth. And teachers themselves—at least those who choose not to drop out and who perceive the slow erosion of their own intellect—have it within themselves to generate personal growth. That a system and its teachers can, obviously, does not mean that it will.

Before dealing with what the system and teachers can do, let me briefly describe three kinds of teacher growth to which I refer:

> —Unless a teacher has internalized the skills of reflective thought (how to analyze problems, validate hunches, identify assumptions and inaccurate conclusions, and so on) there is little he can do to teach youngsters the skills of thinking.
>
> —Unless a teacher has examined himself with regard to his attitudes toward low-income youngsters, his feelings about race, and what he has to offer, much of his instruction and the content he deals with will be interlaced with unexamined feelings that inevitably block both teaching and learning.
>
> —Unless a teacher systematically and periodically examines his teaching in terms of what he uses and how he uses it, what imagination and vigor he may initially have had will suffocate and disappear.

Notice that nothing is said about getting more content or learning about innovative programs. Why? If self-examination of attitudes, instruction, and materials is linked to the grasp of the process of thinking, we may well have a person who is curious, aware, and thoughtful, whose goal is continuing self-renewal. If so, the usual content areas of in-service training would take care of themselves. Quixotic? Perhaps.

There is a flaw. A first principle of individual growth is that the learner—be he adult or child—must feel the need for growth in the areas mentioned. If this does not happen, then we have the familiar story of programs being stuffed down teachers' throats, and, as people are wont to do when they are choking on unwanted material, they cough it up undigested at a later point. Thus we come, finally, full circle to our original but not amended question: How, then, can teachers be helped to grow in the desired directions?

A number of strategies have developed in the last few years. First, there is "sensitivity training." With teachers accused of racist attitudes and low expectations of poor and ethnic children, many school administrators, eagerly grasping for instant growth, passionately embraced "sensitivity training." Teachers' attitudes are confronted and dealt with directly in an effort to get individuals to reassess themselves. Everyone has his own horror or success story. I suspect both are true, given the variation of expertise among trainers. The point is that clubbing teachers over the head with their alleged deficits—aside from the arrogance of the strategy—is about as effective (or sensitive) as telling kids that they are dumb and should get smart. In the rush for group dynamics, T-groupings, and human relations workshops, administrators and trainers have often frustrated the very results they wished to achieve—by judging attitudes, by increasing anxiety excessively, and, finally, by planning few follow-up activities. Undoubtedly, sledgehammer attacks will cause some teachers to examine themselves. But the costs are such as to make one doubt that such a strategy is efficient, much less effective.

A second strategy is sending teachers to colleges or bringing professors to school to conduct after-hours seminars. How ironic. So often the limited intellectuality of teachers is, in part, due to the pap that many of them endured at their alma mater. Professors lecturing a second time to teachers about inner-city schools (an area where few colleges have respectable track records), is a bit bold, if not presumptuous. Yet the intellectual resources of a school system are so slim that they must lean upon institutions with little credibility among schoolmen.

Strategies for Teacher Growth

Clearly, there are other strategies. Often they are random, fragmented, and limited. Unfortunately, few school systems see as their job the planning and operation of a total program of staff development. Responsibility for staff improvement rests with the school system, not the colleges or the community.

If a school system accepts the responsibility and decides to do something about upgrading instruction, it would do well to explore two approaches that offer promise in moving inner-city teachers off dead center. A qualification is in order: The enormous problems confronting inner-city schools will not be erased by what I describe. If used, though, it could equip teachers with the tools necessary to make a difference in the intellectual lives of their children and thereby expand their opportunities.

The basis for the two approaches is simple: teachers need to work on familiar tasks they feel are important. Tasks become the vehicle with which to leapfrog the mundane and reach the essential. Not exactly innovative, but a reliable strategy nonetheless.

The first approach is for teachers to research, develop, and, where-ever possible, produce instructional materials for their own students. I do not mean curriculum guides, syllabi, and resource units. I mean materials in the form of short units to be put into the hands of students —readings. photos, or other materials such as films or tapes. In most cases, these units are presented as a student manual with an accompanying teacher's manual. Classroom teachers need materials every day. Many want diversity. Few know how to prepare their own.

To create an instructional unit forces teachers to ask basic questions of instruction: What should students learn? Why should they learn it? How should it be learned? Was it learned? Too often these questions are asked and answered by textbooks or other commercially produced materials. Teachers become technicians. But to equip teachers with the knowledge and skills of designing instructional objectives, selecting content that appeals to students, and constructing questions will push teachers to think. While there is much that is mechanical in teaching, creating one's own material generates an intellectual electricity that jiggles teachers into examining their choice of content and method. Inevitably, issues of attitudes toward kids and how they learn and feelings about one's self surface. Development of instructional materials is staff development; the process becomes just as important as the product.

What are some of the problems? Teachers have good cause to shy away from preparing curriculum materials for their classes. Count the reasons:

—No time for research.
—No space and materials to prepare lessons and units.
—Supervisors often want teachers to follow the course of study.
—City-wide tests.
—If prescribed materials are diverged from, students won't be prepared for college.

Like all obstacles, these can be perceived as barriers to overcome or excuses to do nothing.

Lack of time and assistance are valid reasons. Fear of constraint from supervisors is largely myth in inner-city schools since they do not have line authority over teachers and are not around enough. Even the most ambitious, most aggressive supervisor or department head would not be able to visit a particular teacher's class more than once a month and that is a generous estimate. Even were the supervisor to visit more often, sharp teachers ingeniously prepare for such visits—the word of a supervisor's arrival spreads quickly—by prepping kids or trotting out conventional lessons.

If anything, a strange, eerie freedom pervades most inner-city classrooms. Once the door closes, teachers do pretty much what they want to do, and only the student grapevine reveals peephole glances into what goes on in a class. In most cases, teachers follow the text or guidelines laid down; some chuck these aside and use what they can salvage in an attempt to teach creatively; still others could teach a racing sheet to students and no one would know the difference. Recent student protests across the nation, of course, opened the classroom door somewhat and broke the conspiracy of silence over what does happen inside.

If freedom is a false issue, so are College Boards and city- or state-wide tests. Teaching academic and problem-solving skills over the school year helps prepare youngsters for the tests, because many of these tests have become more skill-based than tests of information. If the tests are still information-based or the teacher fears that his students will do poorly, he can take a few weeks before test time to prepare them. In either case, tests need not strangle flexibility or creativity; they can be beaten.

Time and assistance, however, remain as obstacles, preventing teachers from developing their own materials and making the curricular decisions I spoke of earlier. There are, however, compelling reasons for career teachers to squeeze out that twenty-fifth hour in the day and that last ounce of energy to develop and use their lessons and units. If they do not, they will die intellectually. Pride in performance and intellectual stimulation are not encouraged by the organization of the school. In fact, the structure conspires against people thinking, interacting, and growing. To counteract this anti-intellectual cast of the school, a teacher must decide to prepare materials for at least one class (if he is teaching junior or senior high students) or one content area (in his elementary classroom). The next step, if a principal can be persuaded, is teaching a class with a colleague; next is team planning and cross-observations at a departmental or grade level (which, I feel, are just as fruitful and less threatening in the long run than team teaching). Whatever the process, the teacher has to do something to avoid intellectual atrophy.

A teacher, even if the system cannot provide a summer experience or released time during the year, can still prepare materials for at least one class or one segment of the day. Intellectual survival is at stake.

The second approach is one for which a school system must provide time, money, and support. Simply, it is developing a number of ways in which teachers can analyze their own teaching behavior without fear of adverse judgment. Isolation from colleagues continues to characterize teaching. Fantastic as it sounds, the persons who have the largest data bank on teaching behavior are students. It goes untapped for the most part. The only way teachers have of finding out about their techniques and effectiveness is through their own observations, tapping student opinion, and sporadic visits of supervisors and the principal (which only increases blood pressure). Seldom do teachers have a means of getting unbiased feedback about their teaching.

What I suggest is what occurs in various schools around the country: the direct teaching of teachers about how to observe and analyze teaching behavior—interaction analysis, questioning, etc.—linked to opportunities to observe colleagues and be observed by them. What will this do? If done in a climate free of threat, by seeing themselves on videotape, by microteaching, and by using various instruments of analysis, teachers can begin to evaluate specific portions of their repertoire and modify their behavior. Not surprisingly, other issues of attitudes toward children and one's self are raised and dealt with. The trick, of course, is that these methods not be used to rank or judge teachers for purposes of status or salary.

The assumption behind these two approaches is that teachers care and that they want to grow, but they are trapped by the organization of the school, the network of regulations, and the authoritarian cast to the system. Some individual teachers can summon up enough psychic energy to crack out of the trap and, for example, develop materials. Fresh air enters the classroom for a brief moment. But exhaustion ultimately triumphs. Teachers can only do so much given the time and energy they have.

What is needed is a systematic effort at staff development for inner-city teachers that uses approaches which, while dealing with the familiar in content and method, eventually move beyond them. Such approaches can unlock doors and let in the winds of self-examination.

It is a frail hook to hang a hope upon. Will staff development—these approaches and others—upgrade the performance of teachers and thereby make a difference in the lives of inner-city children? I think so. Will school systems move in this direction with dispatch? I doubt it.

BLACK CHILDREN AND DESEGREGATION: RESEARCH PERSPECTIVES

Meyer Weinberg

Meyer Weinberg discusses research perspectives on black children and desegregation, pointing out that there is probably more interracial interaction in the public schools than in any other institution besides factory and workshop, yet the number of children attending segregated schools continues to grow. With the number of children attending desegregated schools also rising substantially, researchers have had plentiful opportunities to examine the impact of the interracial experience on black children.

Weinberg examines a number of studies which deal with the consequences of desegregation on the aspirations and self-concepts of black children. While there is a good deal of conventional wisdom about how the black child's sense of worth, his self-concept, and aspirations are affected, there are altogether too few empirical studies of actual classroom situations. Several studies are reported which have implications for school systems and school personnel involved in arranging the conditions for desegregation and for the integration which must be provided for, once racial balance is achieved. Beyond simple exposure to children of another race, there is a need for positive interaction, aimed at enhancing self-respect and respect for others. Weinberg finds many mistaken efforts to substitute self-enhancement for substantive academic achievement in desegregated situations. He believes that the two are related but not interchangeable.

Most classroom- and school-based research deals with desegregation in which black students joined previously all-white classes; seldom is the reverse true. Several researchers report on the interaction between white and black students and the impact on the desegregators. Often, comparisons are made between blacks who participated in desegregation and those who did not in terms of perceptions of school and their white peers. Blacks do not necessarily conform to the pressures of white influence in an interracial learning situation, although the amount of conformity seems to depend on the racial balance which exists. Contact alone seems not to affect prejudice and biases; the qualitative nature of these contacts must be examined.

A third area on which Weinberg reports research is the impact of the teacher on the adjustment of black students in the desegregation process. He finds relatively little rigorous research in this very crucial area. Teacher attitude is particularly critical in its affect on the classroom atmosphere and the expectations for achievement. In many instances, black students have their potential underestimated. Student relations, as might be expected, have been marked by both violence and tolerance, with students generally more "liberal" than their parents.

Weinberg interprets the research to indicate that black children in desegregated classrooms have maintained and strengthened their life aspirations, and increased their self-respect and self-understanding. In general, "the fate of the black child in the desegregated classroom is one of promise and fulfillment." However, unless the school, by working with all personnel in the community as well as the classroom, takes affirmative action, the positive aspects of desegregation will not be fully realized.

Meyer Weinberg is Editor of Integrated Education *and Coordinator of Innovation and Master Planning at Chicago City College.*

BLACK CHILDREN AND DESEGREGATION: RESEARCH PERSPECTIVES*

Meyer Weinberg

Aside from the factory and workshop, the American school is the locale of more interracial interaction than any other American institution. Since 1954, the number of children attending desegregated schools has risen substantially. At present, one-seventh of all elementary and secondary students, or about seven million children, are enrolled in such schools. This is far more than at any previous time; and the numbers are growing. Indeed, the fury of segregation sentiment is stoked by the increasing reality of desegregation; the stridence of this sentiment should not be mistaken for self-confidence—to the contrary. Least of all, however, is this cause for self-satisfaction by proponents of desegregated schools. The number of children in segregated schools continues to grow.

During the past five years, the rising trend of desegregation has supplied researchers with plentiful opportunities for significant work. Although researchers have responded to a degree, the dynamics of the desegregated classroom lie largely beyond the ken of American social science. (It is small comfort to realize that the dynamics of the segregated classroom are also a mystery to social science.)

What is the fate of the black child in a desegregated classroom? Is the interracial experience simply another message to him that he must shed his blackness if he is to succeed? Or, does his blackness thrive as he experiences for the first time a pluralism based on equality? How are his sense of worth, his self-conception, and his aspirations affected, if at all, by the racial character of the classroom? Common sense answers to these questions abound. A number are simple-minded deductions, based on irrelevant analogies. Extremely few are based on an examination of empirical studies into actual classroom situations.

These studies, by and large, lend strong support to a view that black children often make the interracial classroom an occasion for self-discovery and growth. Notable, also, is their ability to combine

*Based on material in Meyer Weinberg, *Desegregation Research, An Appraisal*, 2nd ed. (Bloomington, Ind.: Phi Delta Kappan, 1970), Chaps. 3 and 4.

acceptance of self with a more realistic and non-antagonistic assessment of white children.

Aspirations and Self-Concepts of Black Students

Let us examine first a series of studies that bear on aspirations of black youngsters. Blake (1960) studied level of aspiration in a suburban area near a large midwestern city. He matched three groups of students on socioeconomic status, IQ, and achievement:

Group W: 59 white students from integrated high schools
Group NI: 59 Negro students from integrated high schools
Group NS: 59 Negro students from segregated high schools

In the integrated schools, Negroes were a minority but the schools were not transitional to Negro. The school administrators were reputedly fair to Negro children. Blake set out to test four hypotheses:

1. On the average, Negro pupils will have higher levels of aspiration than those of their white counterparts in the mixed school situation.
2. There will be greater variability in the aspirations of the minority groups in the segregated school system than in the mixed school system.
3. The Negro pupils in the mixed school sample will show a higher average level of aspiration than the Negroes in the segregated school sample.
4. The average aspiration will be approximately the same for whites and the segregated school group, but there will be greater variability in the segregated Negro group. (pp. 27–28)

Let us now examine the findings. Negro students in integrated schools did set higher aspirational levels than did their white fellow students. The first hypothesis was thus supported. On the other hand, the second hypothesis was rejected: Negro students in the segregated schools did not set a wider range of aspirational levels than both other groups; indeed, they set fewer low aspiration levels than either Negroes or whites in integrated schools. The third hypothesis was also rejected: Negroes in the integrated schools failed to set higher average aspirational levels than Negroes in segregated schools. Finally, the fourth hypothesis was rejected, inasmuch as segregated Negro students had higher average levels of aspiration than did whites in integrated schools. The segregated Negro students were the highest aspiring of all three groups.

Blake interprets the high aspirations of segregated Negroes as a defensive measure whereby the student attempts to maintain his self-esteem. To set a low goal might be interpreted by others as an admission of lower self-esteem. It is not desegregation, but segregation, in Blake's opinion, that threatens the Negro's self-esteem: "The more rigidly segregated total environment is much more constantly devaluing to the Negro" (p. 69). Blake rejects an alternative explanation which holds that because the segregated school is a protective environment against the harsh reality of discrimination, Negro children find it "safer to set high goals with or without expecting to attain them" (p. 71).

Whatever the explanation, two points should be kept in mind. First, that integrated Negro students of like intelligence, socioeconomic status, and achievement set higher aspirational levels than did their white counterparts. Second, despite the matching, the segregated Negro children responded defensively. They were, in other words, not able to accept themselves as realistically as did the integrated Negro students.

In 1960 Wilson studied the social aspects of aspirations in the public schools of Berkeley, California. He had three aims: "to determine the extent of the differences in social composition between the elementary schools, to confirm the relationship between familial background and academic achievement and aspirations, but, particularly, to investigate how the differing school milieux might modify this relationship" (p. 19).

Wilson found, as expected, that children of higher social status achieved more than did children of lower status. More interestingly, however, he also found that children from roughly similar social backgrounds achieved along a wide range. A key to these discrepancies turned out to be what might be called the social geography of the Berkeley schools: families of the highest social status were concentrated in the Hills; of the next highest, in the Foothills, and of the lowest, in the Flats. At the same time, each geographical area also contained some families of every social group. In speaking of academic achievement, Wilson reports: "The children of professionals in the Foothills attained a poorer average than their compeers in the Hills; the children of manual workers in the Foothills, almost equalling the white-collar group in the same schools, were far superior to those in the Flats" (p. 49).

Thus, academic achievement was found to depend not on broad social status affiliation but on the social climate of the school. Children of the same social background achieved more if they attended a higher-status school. This held for children of every social status. At the same time, Wilson discovered that teachers tended to allocate school marks according to social-class criteria. In lower-status schools, where teachers employed lower academic standards, children of high status received as many A's and B's, for example, as did their social counterparts in upper-status schools.

When it comes to aspirations, according to Wilson, social status factors do not operate in as clear-cut a manner. In fact, in the Flats, where they are a majority, more Negroes have high aspirations than in the Foothills, where they are a minority. School children, however, tend to adopt the aspirations of their peers. In the Flats, each child has much more contact with other children who do not aspire to college, for example. And the non-college aspirants make up a very cohesive group. "Relatively, the terminal students are the social leaders in the lower socioeconomic strata. They gain social support from their peers, and, in turn, set the pace for them, without adopting the standards of success prevalent in the wider community of adults" (p. 67). In the Hills, more children are isolates, whose very isolation protects their high aspirations from the corrosive effect of low-achievers.

Wilson views the segregation of Negroes in Berkeley schools from the standpoint of constructive group functioning. The presence of high aspirations among lower-class Negroes demonstrates "that a segregated social minority can generate and maintain higher hopes than when integrated. It can develop its indigenous leadership, and is not demoralized by continuous tokens of their imposed inferiority" (p. 68).

Clearly, a fundamental conflict exists between Blake's and Wilson's interpretations of the psychological content of segregation. Blake regarded segregation as "constantly devaluing to the Negro," whereas Wilson states that segregation prevents demoralization of the segregated. A crucial question remains: Is the sense of "imposed inferiority" more intense under segregation than under integration? The weight of the evidence probably supports the view that segregation is more destructive.

Veroff and Peele (1969) studied some of the consequences of closing a predominantly Negro elementary school and transferring its students to six receiving schools. Then children were compared with a similar group who attended a predominantly Negro school. After a year of desegregation, the transferred Negro children had acquired "consistently higher autonomous achievement motivation scores" than Negro boys in the non-transferred group. Desegregation seemed to have moderated the "unrealistically high aspirations of the Negro boys" (p. 87), while at the same time having given rise to a greater self-confidence. The researchers declare:

To guard against defensive overaspiration in children a desegregation program has to juggle two paradoxical factors. It first must avoid placing Negro or white children in positions in schools that make them feel a salient "minority" status. It must also provide contact with children whose background represents a higher status than their own. All of this suggests the desirability of a school desegregation program that promotes a thorough intermixing of children of different races and social classes. (pp. 89–90)

Durig (1967) explored the possible interrelations of occupational choice and social-class background or neighborhood. He studied Negro and white students in three Indianapolis, Indiana, high schools. He found that occupational aspirations of white boys were related not to neighborhood but to the prestige level of their fathers' occupation. For Negro boys, however, aspirations exceeded the prestige level of fathers' occupations. Why was this so? Durig speculated that the reason lay in the integration of the school and the neighborhood in which the Negroes in the sample studied and resided. Referring to the Negro students, Durig explained: "In their striving toward emancipation they compare themselves with members of the dominant group. This comparison might motivate them to emulate the occupational aspirations as well as the values of the dominant group. This motivation is undoubtedly increased among Negroes in an integrated neighborhood" (p. 95). (It should be noted that most of the white students in the integrated school came from white-collar families.)

From these and other studies, one may conclude that the interracial classroom has the potentiality of teaching black children to add an element of realism to already-high aspirations.

Let us now proceed to the area of self-concept. "Other things being equal," wrote DuBois in 1935, "the mixed school is the broader, more natural basis for the education of all youth. It gives wider contacts; it inspires greater self-confidence; and suppresses the inferiority complex" (p. 335). Today, we might say more simply that in the integrated school, children develop sounder self-concepts.

Meketon (1966) studied the impact of desegregation upon the self-esteem of Negro children. Eighty-nine fifth- and sixth-grade Negro students were located in three schools, as follows:

School	*Total Enrollment*	*Percentage Negro*	*Number of Negroes in Sample*
School A	821	100	29
School B	416	30	29
School C	586	22	31

Students were matched comprehensively; a control group for children in School A was also matched. It is important to note here that schools

B and C had desegregated under very different circumstances. In B, desegregation had taken place on administrative initiative; no demonstrations or public pressure had come from the organized Negro community. In C, however, desegregation had come as a direct consequence of prolonged and bitter public controversy, involving debates and demonstrations by the Negro community. School A was, of course, still segregated, as shown above.

Two principal hypotheses were entertained:

1. The Negro child's performance will be adversely affected by the process of school integration.
2. Forced competition with a group considered to be "superior" will affect the child's feelings of self-esteem in a negative fashion (pp. 1–2).

The findings contradicted both hypotheses. The predicted significant differences did not appear in the data. Various other hypotheses and sub-hypotheses fared differently. As between School A and School B, children at the former—i.e., segregated—school scored significantly higher on the Self Subtest, a partial test of self-esteem. On the other hand, Negro children at the peacefully desegregated School B did not have significantly higher self-esteem scores than children at the tumultuously desegregated School C. Indeed, children at the latter school had significantly higher self-esteem scores than children at School A. Teachers at all three schools were asked to make certain judgments about the children. Meketon reports: "School C teachers evaluated their students as possessing higher levels of self-esteem than did either of the other two schools, and in Schools A and B, teachers found more evidence of defensive behavior than did teachers in School C" (pp. 67–68).

Why did Negro students at School C hold up so well? Meketon suggests that the explanation lies with the salience of family and home for these particular children. Among the factors contributing to the high morale of School C children were:

The support and sympathy of a close-knit Negro community, national encouragement represented by legal counsel from NAACP, and Supreme Court decisions. Negro community morale, together with the obvious fact that integration had been accomplished to a large extent on their own [parents'] terms, must have served as a source of encouragement to the children. Victories for Negroes in their exchanges with whites are infrequent. (p. 79)

Several Negro teachers worked in School C, and they proved a valued refuge for the desegregated Negro children. In School B, on the other hand, the entire community support aspect was absent. Also, not a single Negro teacher worked in School B.

Student anxiety, which Meketon had originally thought would undo the desegregated child, did not have this consequence. "The child," observed Meketon, "is remarkably adaptable and flexible, and given the right circumstances can overcome many of the detrimental aspects of integration" (p. 90). Parental support, she adds, is crucial: "Parental understanding and consideration when the child fails scholastically in his competition with his white peers or meets with rebuffs will help counteract the child's feelings of guilt and inferiority" (p. 91).

In Florida, Negro students who desegregated a high school experienced a drop in self-concept as compared with Negro students who remained in the segregated school. Several special factors may have operated to help bring about this unusual feature of a desegregated situation. A great deal of conflict continued between Negro and white students, with non-acceptance of the Negro the rule. The whole integration experience in the community was "an anxiety-producing phenomenon." Academically, the Negro students were having a very difficult time of it. A number of the subjects were militants whose first interest was trailblazing. Bienvenu (1968) reported that guidance counselors said that in the second year the entrants were students "who performed on a higher academic level and whose incentive to integrate was to avail themselves of better educational opportunities" (p. 52).

Lessing (1969) studied certain aspects of ego-functioning of Negro and white eighth- and eleventh-graders in three suburbs of Chicago; the schools were integrated. She sought possible implications for academic achievement. In the first phase of the study it appeared that Negro children were significantly less willing to delay immediate gratification and were thus less able to study and learn. When, however, Lessing controlled the effects of IQ, this apparent racial difference in gratification-delay disappeared. Lessing believes the Coleman Report overestimated the achievement-effect of fate-control for Negro students for the same reason: IQ was not controlled (p. 163). It is intelligence, rather than fate-control or gratification-delay, that is the principal avenue to academic achievement. For this reason, Lessing concludes, remedial programs must have a cognitive focus rather than one aimed primarily at certain ego-functions. She acknowledges, of course, the ultimate interdependence of all the factors.

All in all, then, the evidence suggests that black children need not succumb to anti-Negro pressures and, given family support, may well come through an outwardly destructive desegregation with their self-concept unimpaired.

What are the interrelationships between the black child's self-concept and his attitude toward white classmates? Singer (1966) compared white and Negro fifth-graders to determine the effect of segregation and desegregation on interracial attitudes. Her general hypothesis follows:

> A differential cognitive structure (the ability to maintain several attitudes and opinions simultaneously concerning another individual who is a member of the outgroup) and more positive attitudes, as a function of proximity and intelligence, should be found for children in the integrated school concerning their attitudes towards Negroes, when compared to the less positive attitudes toward Negroes held by the white child in a school where there is no contact with Negroes. (p. 19)

Three schools were selected for the test: (1) a High Exposure School (HES), whose fifth-grade student body was 60 per cent white and in which extensive interracial contact was evident; (2) two Low Exposure Schools (LES), one whose fifth-grade student body was all-white, and the other whose fifth-grade enrollment was 15 per cent white. While IQ scores were similar for the two schools, the white students were primarily middle class, the Negroes lower income.

The white children in the HES consistently scored lower on social distance toward Negroes. In accounting for white desire to have social contact with Negroes, Singer found exposure to be more important than either intelligence or sex. Unexpectedly, it did not appear that the brighter children were less prejudiced. Girls were, in general, less prejudiced than boys.

If Negro exposure to whites led to less anti-white prejudice, how did it affect Negro self-concepts? Singer administered certain drawing tests to all children. Twenty-four Negro children colored the face of a figure supposed to be a self-portrait; not a single white child did so. More significant, perhaps, is the fact that 18 of the 24 were in the HES. "In other words," observed Singer, "the Negro children who had greater contact with white children showed a tendency to differentiate themselves and assert their identity more clearly" (p. 101).

Generally speaking, Negro children in the HES had less regard for whites as academic achievers than did Negro children in the LES. As Singer comments, "the segregated Negro may see the white world as one of success and his own world as one of failure" (p. 105). (This observation is supported by the research of Blake and Haggstrom (1963); Meketon's work is also relevant.) The bright Negro girl in the HES "can conceive of herself as achieving *more* than a white child, and turns to her own group rather than to whites for socialization" (p. 108). Under integration, then, the Negro child is able "to differentiate himself without anxiety" (p. 109). On the other hand, Negro children in the LES "were less accepting of their skin color, saw themselves as poorer achievers, and developed negative attitudes toward various nonwhite groups" (pp. 113–114).

Children were not merely "exposed" to one another; they interacted with each other. True, white children usually rated Negro children as "aggressive" on tests; but this was fact, not prejudice. Despite this awareness, white children in the HES still were more willing to associate with Negroes than were white children in the LES. These latter white children, in fact, tended on tests to deny the existence of Negro aggression. As Singer noted: "Whites with no contact perceived the Negro in a distorted manner, giving him intellectual credit, but refusing to associate with him" (p. 114). In so doing, we may add, they exhibited their mastery of a cultural pattern which is characterized pejoratively as "white liberal." This pattern, it should be noted, arises in a context of non-association.

It may be of some interest to examine the relationship of race consciousness and attitude toward persons of another race with regard to adults. Noel (1966) studied this relationship, using 515 adult Negroes as his subjects. The subjects were divided into two classifications, with reference to ethnic identification: (1) *Identifiers,* or those who had a positive identification with Negroes as a group, and (2) *Disparagers,* those who had a negative identification. Noel found that "Negroes who are militantly identified with the minority group are consistently more favorably inclined toward integration, both in attitude and action, than are Negroes who disparage the in-group" (p. 5). In other words, those who felt *most Negro* were likely to be least anti-white. Ethnic consciousness need not necessarily become ethnocentrism.

Noel explored the relationship of ethnic identification to "defensive insulation." Respondents who accepted the following proposition were classed as believers in defensive insulation: "It is best to stay away from white people; then you will avoid all embarrassing situations." Table 1 reports the data.

TABLE 1. Ethnic Identification and Defensive Insulation

Believe in Defensive Insulation	Identifiers (N=229)	Ambivalents (N=180)	Disparagers (N=106)
Yes	16%	28%	56%
No	84	72	44

This highly significant difference (beyond the .001 level) points up the socially constructive function of ethnic consciousness. What Noel calls "positive group identification" is precisely what Singer described as Negro children "differentiating themselves." (See, also, Marx (1967) on self-image and out-group hostility.)

Morland (1969) viewed the subject from an international perspective. He conducted a comparative study of race awareness among 450 Hong Kong Chinese and Negro and white American children, ranging in age from four to six years. While both Hong Kong and the United States are multiracial societies, in the former, the Chinese are of parallel, not subordinate, status to that of the British. In the U.S., of course, the Negroes and whites are in a subordinate-superordinate power relationship. Morland set out to discover whether racial awareness of children responded to these differences. "The great majority of respondents," according to Morland, "accepted both their own and the other race" (p. 366). Negro children, while tending to accept their race, also showed more conflict over race-identity. The Chinese children were more self-accepting and less stressful about the matter. This, Morland held, was to be expected, inasmuch as "in such a society there is no dominant race to maintain its superior position and no subordinate race to show unconscious preference for and identification with the dominant race" (p. 371). To Morland, the study suggested that once American society changes so that Negroes cease being subordinate, "the racial preference and racial self-identification of Negro children will change" (p. 374).

Thus, both domestically and internationally, evidence supports the interaction of self-respect and respect for others, across racial lines.

While the study of self-concept is proceeding, many mistaken attempts to apply the new knowledge have been made. One of the most widespread—and therefore one of the most serious—is the effort to substitute self-enhancement for substantive academic achievement. The two, to be sure, are hardly unrelated. But they are not interchangeable.

Guggenheim (1969) studied self-esteem among children in Harlem schools. He reported that low self-esteem appeared not to be a problem. Then he proceeded to make an important practical application of his findings:

> The results of this study certainly raise a question concerning the validity of pre-kindergarten and elementary school programs for disadvantaged Negro children that have as a primary goal the raising of self-esteem. . . . Strong evidence from this and other studies . . . indicates . . . that many disadvantaged Negro children's school problems center around low achievement and not low self-esteem. (p. 70)

Coopersmith (1968) takes a step beyond:

> It may be that pride evocation is a rapid procedure for gaining esteem, and if so, may well serve as a first step in programs to increase initiative and motivation. However, unless esteem is subsequently related to skills, performance, etc., the motivation aroused may be socially unproductive. (p. 15)

Some time ago, Erikson (1964) explored this question with great wisdom. Two aspects of the general subject of identity are of interest here: (1) its substantive content and (2) its social-psychological dimensions. Both are illustrated by the following statements by Erikson.

> In this, children cannot be fooled by empty praise and condescending encouragement. They may have to accept artificial bolstering of their self-esteem in lieu of something better, but what I call their accruing ego identity gains real strength only from wholehearted and consistent recognition of real accomplishment, that is, achievement that has meaning in their culture. (p. 32)

And further:

> Identity formation goes beyond the process of identifying oneself with ideal others in a one-way fashion; it is a process based on a heightened cognitive and emotional capacity to let oneself be identified by concrete persons as a circumscribed individual in relation to a predictable universe which transcends the family. (p. 33)

As Erikson observed, "empty praise and condescending encouragement" have no real relationship to identity-formation. One can do this only to children whom one disrespects. Without serious attention to cognitive development, we are left with hardly more than esteem-uplift. Undoubtedly, one of the advantages of such programs is their low cost—in money, that is.

Interaction of Black and White Students

Thus far, we have examined the interracial classroom in terms of development of self-concept by black children. In addition, we were interested in noting the relationship of self-concept to interracial attitudes. Let us proceed now to a more concrete classroom level and review studies of day-to-day interaction of black and white students. In nearly all the cases, black students were the outsiders joining classrooms that had heretofore been all-white.

Chesler and Segal (1967) made a comprehensive study of desegregation in Alabama. Their interviewers—all Negro college students—talked during June–August, 1966, with a total of 217 Negro students who had attended a white junior high or high school in Alabama during the 1965–1966 school year. This number was equal to over 40 per cent of the entire population of Negro junior and senior high students attending desegregated public schools in Alabama in 1965–1966 (p. 15). A control group of 75 Negro students was established; these were persons who lived near a desegregator but who, for one reason or another, had not transferred to the white school. Thirty-nine white teachers who had taught in the desegregated schools were also interviewed. The desegregators were extremely apprehensive about what reception they would meet in the white school: "Over one-fourth of the Negro students went to school expecting to be beaten or harmed physically. . . . Another 52 per cent felt 'uneasy' or 'worried,' but not actually scared" (p. 28). (These fears were realistic. In Alba, Alabama, where two Negro children had desegregated the town's high school, two separate bomb explosions occurred. See, *Integrated Education,* 1966, p. 6.) Chesler and Segal summarize the students' actual experience: "Quite clearly, Negro students experienced considerable indifference and rejection, and often physical and emotional brutality, when they entered white schools" (p. 36). Yet, 15 per cent of the desegregators reported "positive reactions" and 74 per cent said some whites had acted in a friendly way. Nearly half (48 per cent) said they belonged to an interracial school club (pp. 31 and 35).

Chesler and Segal compared the desegregators with the control group of non-desegregators. There was no significant difference between the educational levels of the two groups of parents. While both groups of students had the same educational aspirations, the desegregators had significantly higher expectations (80 per cent vs. 65 per cent) of attending college. Most significant for the study, the researchers reported that "desegregators seem to be less negatively prejudiced against whites, and more actively concerned about change and their efforts in change roles" (p. 60). This finding is clearly in line with those of Singer, Haggstrom, and Blake.

Had the desegregators' perceptions of white students changed? As the researchers report: "It is clear that before entering the white school Negro youngsters had an unrealistically low estimate of their abilities in relation to white students" (p. 80). But experience is, at times, a great teacher. When desegregators were asked whether, before transferring, they thought white students would be smarter, 63 per cent said, "Yes." Only 22 per cent still thought so after desegregation. This was a highly significant change. Incidentally, over three quarters of the desegregators reported that the white students turned out to be noisier and less well-behaved than they had expected.

Contacts with whites outside class were reported by a majority of desegregators; three-quarters of the groups regarded at least some of the white students as friends. Did they trust whites more or less since desegregation? Thirty-seven per cent said "more," but 41 per cent said "less."

How had the desegregators fared in academic achievement? No test scores or school records were available, and so self-reports of grades were recorded. Table 2 summarizes the results for desegregators and non-desegregators. What appears to have been a disastrous change for the worse is probably the very opposite. As Chesler and Segal report: "Overall, 83 per cent of the desegregators unequivocally said they gained a lot from being in the white school, and the rest felt they made gains although they had been severely or moderately tempered by sacrifices" (p. 85).

TABLE 2. Self-Report of Change in Grades During Two School Years in Desegregator and Control Population

Change	Desegregators (N=197)	Control (N=275)
Grades increased	11.3%	26.6%
Grades remained unchanged	28.2	49.3
Grades declined	60.5	24.0

The Chesler-Segal study is rare for its locale, exemplary for its modest aims, and excellent for the rigorous care with which it was carried out. Its findings are rich in implications for desegregation, North and South.

Do Negro children tend to conform to the pressures of white influence when in an interracial learning situation? Janney and associates (1969) studied 80 Negro and white children in the Wichita, Kansas, schools. Unexpectedly, they found that Negroes did not conform any more than whites. The researchers explained the outcome as resulting from the integrated nature of the group; most earlier studies had occurred in a more segregated context. Mock (1968) studied conformity among 280 Negro and white fourth-, fifth-, and sixth-graders in the Berkeley schools in 1965, when these were still largely segregated. Negro children were high conformers, Mock reported: "The more whites there were in the group, the more the Negroes conformed. The more Negroes in the group, the less the whites conformed" (pp. 75–76). High credence was given to information derived from the group with greater prestige. "As the balance of relative power and self-esteem between the races alters," Mock comments, "experimental results of quite a different sort could easily be obtained" (p. 124).

In Daytona Beach, Florida, Schneider (1968) studied conforming behavior in 192 Negro and white seventh- and eighth-graders. Subjects were given several experimental tasks to perform under four grouping arrangements. No significant difference in conformance was found between Negro and white groups. White subjects conformed more in the face of unanimous opposition when voiced by blacks. Negro subjects did not experience a similar effect. A good deal of interracial antagonism existed within the school; on social distance tests Negro children were considerably more accepting than white children. Schneider observed: "An ominous outlook was reflected in the behavior of the white children. The so-called white racism of America was evident in the white children's hostile attitudes toward Negroes and in their disrespect for their Negro peers as sources of influence." Yet, "the Negro children did not buckle under to the influence of their white peers" (p. 55). Schneider failed to find, contrary to some other studies, that Negro children became more anxious after experiencing opposition of their white peers.

A related investigation was conducted by O'Connor (1967) in two desegregated schools in Gainesville, Florida. He studied the degree to which Negro and white children, seven years old and in first grade, would imitate adult and peer models in two experimental tasks. Negro children, he found, did not imitate white peer models more than they imitated Negro peer models. Instead, they imitated Negro peer models more than white children imitated white peer models. Thus, once more, conformity was found not to be especially salient among Negro children.

The negative impact of poor student relations is evident in Moorefield's (1967) study of Kansas City. He found, contrary to most experience, that desegregation did not result in improved academic achievement of the black children. Some light on that outcome might be shed by an examination of social interaction inside the classroom. Nine out of ten Negro parents stated that "positive relationships" existed between their bused-in children and those in the receiving school. Sociometric data showed, however, that three-quarters of the bused-in Negro children were rated low-acceptance by the children regularly in attendance in the receiving schools (p. 157). Two-thirds of the bused-in children were regarded as "aggressive" by the regular students. Those Negro children who were accepted by white children generally had higher academic self-concepts than the other Negro children.

Thirty-eight per cent of the teachers who taught in classes having bused-in children indicated to Moorefield a "non-acceptance of busing" (p. 81). Few if any teaching adaptations were made in the classroom.

> Thirty of the forty-two teachers . . . in this study said that having the bused-in children in their rooms did not cause them to alter or adapt their teaching or cause them to do anything in a different way in their teaching methods or techniques. . . . The other twelve teachers indicated that the principal difference with the presence of the transported-in pupils was that they had to slow down and could not cover as much material as previously. (p. 192)

In assessing the desegregation experience, teachers seemed most concerned about the academic aptitude and achievement of the transported children.

In the South Carolina study by McWhirt (1967), it was found at the end of a year of desegregation that "interracial contact was conducive in bringing about changes in the attitudes of the Negro students in the integrated school. . . . The highly favorable self-concept rating of the Negro students indicates that they did not submit to self-depreciation in order to gain acceptance from whites" (p. 41). White children did not experience any lessening of anti-Negro prejudice. Bienvenu (1968) found in a Florida high school that lack of acceptance by white students as well as academic difficulties helped make desegregation an anxiety-producing experience. In Delaware, Harootunian and Morse (1968) found that Negro students in segregated schools had the highest anxiety levels. No simple statement can be made about the effect of desegregation on anxiety. According to Epps (1970), the facts that lower-class children display more anxiety than middle-class children and Negro children generally display more than white children are not at all connected with segregation or desegregation.

In the Deep South, social relations between black and white students are more often "correct" than anything else. An Office of Civil Rights, HEW study, conducted during the spring of 1969, in five Southern states, reported that extracurricular activities were open to all in the desegregated schools but that "Negro students often indicated their resentment at losing their leadership positions on transferring to the formerly-white school" (p. 47). Further, the OCR study noted: "Negro students reported considerable insecurity concerning social activities at the desegregated school. . . . In most of the high schools visited, it was noted by black and white students that the races tended to be separate in the cafeterias, assembly halls, on the school ground, even in classes where seating was optional" (p. 48). Where numbers of Negro students were fairly large, they experienced less insecurity. Where white students were a minority in formerly all-black schools, they exhibited the same "minority" characteristics. (See also, Ten Houten, 1956.)

One of the most instructive studies in this entire area was made among black youth, two-thirds of whom reported they had never attended schools with whites. McDowell (1967) studied the willingness of 582 Negro youths, aged sixteen to nineteen, in the District of Columbia, to associate with whites. As a whole, they expressed a very high readiness to do so. The 8 per cent who were attending schools were more willing than were the 20 per cent who had dropped out of school. McDowell found: "The degree of voluntary, informal associations that Negro youth have had with their white fellow students is the one variable that we have examined whose influence on willingness to associate is both strong, unambiguous, and statistically reliable. This is true with regard to social contacts in school but even more so with regard to social contacts out of school" (p. 82). To the researcher, informality of social contact signalled interaction on a more human level. "Without these voluntary, informal dealings," noted McDowell, "in-school contacts are a ritual, a temporary fiction in which both Negro and white participants concur, until they depart the confines of the school building for the 'real life' outside" (p. 72).

Fewer than a third of the boys had attended a predominantly white school or one with equal numbers of whites and blacks. Many fewer had experienced informal social contacts with white boys. It was precisely these Negro students who seemed especially prepared for more extensive contacts in other areas of social life. (See also, Levine and Fiddmont, 1969.)

What criterion did Negro boys employ in selecting whites with whom they sought to socialize? "By far the most frequent criterion in judging whites," according to McDowell, "is how those whites judge Negroes" (p. 93). She explained that in any stratification system a social subordinate generally pays "close attention to the clues of his superior" (p. 114). In the studies of conforming behavior that were reviewed earlier in this paper, this factor of superordination and subordination was critical. If its force was overcome, it was far from a mere accident. This same inequality of status, McDowell notes, precludes, strictly speaking, emergence of Negro *prejudice.* The Negro is ordinarily not in a position to enforce his ethnic antipathies nor is he accustomed to initiate exclusion. McDowell stresses that "interracial contact is not rejected per se [by Negroes], but [only] when it involves a greater risk of non-acceptance by whites" (p. 117).

One is reminded of Morland's point that social interaction between Negro and white in racist America will become more humanizing when notions of racial superordination and subordination disappear. McDowell's research is significant for its sensitivity to the quality of social interaction and for its awareness of status factors in interracial relations.

Impact of the Teacher in the Desegregation Process

A final area of investigation is the impact of the teacher on adjustment by black students in the desegregation process. Although this would seem to be a crucial area for study, surprisingly little rigorous inquiry has occurred. In the Chesler-Segal (1967) study of Alabama, discussed earlier, the role of teachers was examined in two respects: (1) its relation to classroom atmosphere, and (2) its expectancy or non-expectancy of achievement by the Negro desegregators. Although three-quarters of the desegregators regarded their white teachers as fair-minded, most teachers permitted white students to establish the tone of the classroom. This laissez-faire attitude of the teachers increased tensions. Where teachers were seen as fair-minded, the white students in the classroom were generally also so regarded. Thus, the classroom atmosphere pretty well reflected the leadership (or lack of it) shown by teachers. Some teachers were cruel to the Negro students: "About one third of the descriptions of unfair behavior identified teachers who called students 'nigger,' or had . . . mispronounced 'Negro.' More than another third of such unfair reports noted that students felt they were singled out by their teachers or mistreated . . ." (p. 42).

Teachers at first underestimated the academic ability of the Negro students: "Only 75 per cent of the teachers reported that before the desegregators entered their classes they did not think the Negro students would be as smart as the white students. By the end of the year or two of desegregation, however, half of that 75 per cent had changed their minds. . ." (p. 78). Desegregation was an important experience of discovery by many people. Many desegregators found they could do as well as white students; many teachers increased their respect for the abilities of Negro students. (One wonders how the white students felt about all this; but, unfortunately, the Chesler-Segal team was unable to interview them.)

Boney (1967) reports on Negro social style on white campuses. Reporting from a Northern university, Boney observes: "Non-white students tend to assign a disproportionate amount of importance to the evaluations of whites with reference to their role expectations. Docile and submissive behaviors in racially integrated learning situations are expected and rewarded by many white teachers" (pp. 318–319).

In virtually none of the above studies of desegregation is there any indication that special teaching or curricular adaptations were made. When Baltimore's schools underwent their initial desegregation in 1955, for example, the school administration held that "special 'preparation' of teachers for integrated schools was unnecessary, and would probably do more harm than good by calling attention to differences when teachers should think of likenesses" (Pancoast, 1956, p. 103). Such a view was wholly consistent with common sense and, since virtually no large-scale desegregation projects had occurred anywhere to show otherwise, very possibly justified. Since then, however, a good deal of experience has been accumulated. Repeated studies have shown the importance of deliberate classroom changes that are required for effective desegregation.

Amos (1952) studied ninth-graders in three integrated schools in Flint, Michigan. Both Negro and white students felt rejected by their teachers, although the white students thought their Negro classmates were being accepted. Amos reported a difference between the expressed attitudes of the teachers toward Negro students and the way the Negro students perceived their teachers' behavior.

Edwards (1966) analyzed the records of a series of seminars conducted by teachers of disadvantaged children. The seminars were held in the hope of developing better attitudes and thus becoming better teachers; panels met from fifteen to twenty times. Edwards reported that: (1) the panels were never clear as to their goals; (2) "most of the conversation seemed superficial and at times banal" and (3) successful teachers were not those with the "best" attitudes but those who had worked out "classroom techniques and procedures that are successful in the sense of keeping teacher and students, hence administrators and parents, reasonably content with the classroom situation" (p. 85).

Wilcox (1967) has suggested that the ghetto system of school and community life creates the groundwork for not educating the children of the ghetto: "Teachers can legitimately fail to teach and students can legitimately fail to learn. The non-achievement of the student has no bearing on the professional fortunes of the teachers; the non-achievement of the students is viewed as a mere fulfillment of the self-fulfillment prophecy" (p. 374). A more recent declaration by the HEW Urban Education Task Force (1970) has made a similar point: "By and large, the [school] system has expected the [inner-city] student to be a failure, and unaware of its failure has succeeded in creating the student in its own image" (p. E52). Empirical tests of the above view are not very numerous and no full test of it has yet been made.

Student Relations under Desegregation

Student relations under desegregation have been marked by toleration, for the most part, and, less prominently, by both violence and positive respect. In many more cases than one would imagine, interracial friendships have developed. The old saw about students being more "liberal" that their parents is quite true, according to various studies. Whether in Syracuse or Detroit, students of the most varied social circumstances have learned to cooperate—to their mutual benefit. Very few studies afford insights into the behavior of white students under desegregation.

Most administrative planning for desegregation has concerned political and (white) community problems; very little has dwelt on changes in classroom and curriculum. Until very recently, it appeared that teachers attended to the single most important change in the classroom—they made the Negro children feel welcome. This is far from saying that interracial classrooms are typically operating at, or even near, the maximum benefit to Negro and white children. Reports of desegregation in Deep South schools during the spring of 1970 bespoke a widespread failure of teachers and administrators to contribute toward a productive learning atmosphere in their newly desegregated classrooms.

In Summary

To sum up, black children in desegregated classrooms have maintained and strengthened their life aspirations. They have, as a rule, augmented their self-concept, as greater self-knowledge enables them to see their abilities and potentialities through the fog of racial smokescreens. Greater self-understanding and an enlarged sense of purpose lead to a readier acceptance of white peers. The most enduring sense of identity rests on genuine accomplishment rather than on an empty ritual of abstract encouragement.

In the real world of the classroom, both black and white children navigate a careful journey between the narrow straits of community sentiment and elementary human decency. The pressures upon black children, especially, range from simple unfamiliarity to bombings and beatings. Nevertheless, the black children show increasingly a willingness to try the new way. They are not, however, superhuman. Incessant opposition takes its toll. It is the teacher and principal who can make the critical difference. Evidence suggests that their failure to lead too often permits destructive influences to take command.

In conclusion, let us return to our initial concern. The fate of the black child in the desegregated classroom is one of promise and fulfillment. He does not need to bargain away his identity as the price of an education. If black children have at times, however, experienced the opposite, then it is not desegregation that is at fault. The school is most readily in command of just those factors that threaten the stability of the desegregated classroom: preparations before actual desegregation, teacher-training, and working with parents and children, for example.

The desegregation option is consistent with a concern for blackness—so long as it remains a real alternative, genuinely available. The great bulk of research suggests that ethnic identity can thrive only where children are free to be themselves. In a racist social order, the desegregated classroom would seem to be one of the few such places.

References

Amos, R. T. "The Accuracy of Negro and White Children's Predictions of Teachers' Attitudes toward Negro Students," *Journal of Negro Education,* 21 (Spring 1952), 125–135.

Bienvenu, M. J. Effects of School Integration on the Self-Concept and Anxiety of Lower-Class, Negro Adolescent Males. Doctoral Dissertation, Florida State University, 1968. (University Microfilms Order No. 68–11, 671)

Blake, E., Jr. A Comparison of Intraracial and Interracial Levels of Aspiration. Doctoral Dissertation, University of Illinois, 1960. (University Microfilms Order No. 60–1616)

Boney, J. D. "Some Dynamics of Disadvantaged Students in Learning Situations," *Journal of Negro Education,* 36 (Summer 1967), 315–319.

Chesler, M. A. and P. Segal. *Characteristics of Negro Students Attending Previously All-White Schools in the Deep South.* Ann Arbor, Mich.: Institute for Social Research, University of Michigan, 1967.

Coopersmith, S. *Psychosocial Deprivation and the Development of Self-Esteem: Comments and Recommendations.* Bethesda, Md.: National Institute of Child Health and Human Development, 1968.

DuBois, W. E. B. "Does the Negro Need Separate Schools?" *Journal of Negro Education,* 4 (July 1935), 328–335.

Durig, R. D. A Study of Social Status and Occupational Choice among High School Students. Doctoral Dissertation, Indiana University, 1967. (University Microfilms Order No. 68–2283)

Edwards, T. B. "Teacher Attitudes and Cultural Differentiation," *Journal of Experimental Education,* 35 (Winter 1966), 80–92.

Erikson, E. "A Memorandum on Identity and Negro Youth," *Journal of Social Issues,* 20 (1964), 29–42.

Epps, E. G. "Interpersonal Relations and Motivation: Implications for Teachers of Disadvantaged Children," *Journal of Negro Education,* 39 (1970), 14–25.

Guggenheim, F. "Self-Esteem and Achievement Expectations for White and Negro Children," *Journal of Projective Techniques and Personality Assessment,* 33 (1969), 63–71.

Haggstrom, W. C. "Segregation, Desegregation and Negro Personality," *Integrated Education,* 1 (October-November 1963), 19–23.

Harootunian, B. and R. Morse. *Characteristics of Negro and White High School Students Prior to Desegregation. A study of Negro Student's Freedom of Choice,* September, 1968 (ERIC # ED024745).

Integrated Education, 4 (April-May 1966), 6.

Janney, F., S. Mallory, R. Rossitto, and J. Simon. "Conformity as a Function of Race and Age," *Psychological Reports,* 25 (1969), 591–597.

Lessing, E. L. "Racial Differences in Indices of Ego Functioning Relevant to Academic Achievement," *Journal of Genetic Psychology,* 115 (1969), 153–167.

Levine, D. U. and N. S. Fiddmont. "Integration Is Up to Date in Kansas City," *Integrated Education,* 7 (1969), 3–16.

Marx, G. *Protest and Prejudice: A Study of Belief in the Black Community.* New York: Harper and Row, 1967.

McDowell, S. F. The Willingness of Negro Youths to Associate with Whites. Doctoral Dissertation, University of Chicago, 1967.

McWhirt, R. A. The Effects of Desegregation on Prejudice, Academic Aspiration, and the Self-Concept of Tenth Grade Students. Doctoral Dissertation, University of South Carolina, 1967. (University Microfilms Order No. 67–15,568)

Meketon, B. F. The Effects of Integration upon the Negro Child's Response to Various Tasks and upon His Level of Self-Esteem. Doctoral Dissertation, University of Kentucky, 1966.

Mock, R. L. The Relationship among Children between Conformity and the Racial Composition of Small Quasi-Groups. Doctoral Dissertation, University of California, Berkeley, 1968. (University Microfilms Order No. 69–3658)

Moorefield, T. E. The Busing of Minority Group Children in a Big City School System. Doctoral Dissertation, University of Chicago, 1967.

Morland, J. K. "Race Awareness among American and Hong Kong Chinese Children," *American Journal of Sociology,* 75 (1969), 360–373.

Noel, D. L. "Minority Group Identification and Societal Integration." Paper presented at Annual Meeting of American Sociological Association, 1966.

O'Connor, A. L., III. The Relationship of Imitation to Intelligence and Scholastic Achievement of Negro and White First Grade Pupils in Integrated Classes. Doctoral Dissertation, University of Florida, 1967. (University Microfilms Order No. 68–13,023)

Pancoast, E. *The Report of a Study on Desegration in the Baltimore City Schools.* Baltimore: Maryland Commission on Interracial Problems and Relations, 1956.

Schneider, F. W. Differences between Negro and White School Children in

Conforming Behavior. Doctoral Dissertation, University of Florida, 1968. (University Microfilms Order No. 69–17,040)

Singer, D. G. Interracial Attitudes of Negro and White Fifth Grade Children in Segregated and Unsegregated Schools. Doctoral Dissertation, Columbia University, 1966. (University Microfilms Order No. 67–2836)

Ten Houten, W. D. Socialization, Race and the American High School. Doctoral Dissertation, Michigan State University, 1956. (University Microfilms Order No. 66–444)

Urban Education Task Force, Department of Health, Education and Welfare. "Report on Urban Education," *Congressional Record,* January 20, 1970, pp. E21–E78.

Veroff, J., and Peele, S. "Initial Effects of Desegregation on the Achievement Motivation of Negro Elementary School Children," *Journal of Social Issues,* 25 (1969), 82–93.

Weinberg, M. *Desegregation Research: An Appraisal,* 2nd ed. Bloomington, Ind.: Phi Delta Kappa, 1970.

Wilcox, P. R. "Teacher Attitudes and Student Achievement," *Teachers College Record,* 68 (1966–67), 371–379.

Wilson, A. B. "Residential Segregation of Social Classes and Aspiration of High School Boys," *American Sociological Review,* 24 (December 1959), 836–845.

———. The Effect of Residential Segregation upon Educational Achievement and Aspirations. Doctoral Dissertation, University of California, Berkeley, 1960.

GUIDANCE IN THE URBAN SETTING

Edmund W. Gordon

Edmund W. Gordon writes of guidance in broad terms, including "all those professional activities directed at the facilitation of decision-making and development." Applied to the urban setting in recent years, the term has come to mean a concern with the problems of poor and minority group students. Gordon observes that the characteristics of disadvantaged populations do not really define the particular group. They are simply characteristics found with high frequency in particular populations but which may be found in any segment of the population. Yet, the high frequency with which certain characteristics are encountered in disadvantaged populations makes it important that these be recognized and identified as potential problem areas.

Among the characteristics Gordon sees as potential problem areas are: contradictory attitudes toward self, a higher incidence of a utilitarian or materialistic attitude, a lower level of aspiration or motivation, and a reduced attention span. While we have gained increased understanding of differences in learning styles, modes of perception, and temperamental traits, we seem not to have taken these into account in educational planning designed to deal with individual and group differences. In addition, the way the school arranges conditions for learning may not reflect what is known about the wide range of variation in behavioral adaptations. Gordon argues that educators have not identified the potential strengths of disadvantaged children and used them effectively in the educational development of youngsters.

Gordon discusses a number of guidance functions that seem important for the disadvantaged—functions which are equally appropriate for all youngsters. In fact, he points out, as we better understand and act on problems related to the disadvantaged, we can make considerable progress in upgrading education for all.

Gordon suggests that the guidance function begin with appraisal—a psycho-educational, qualitative appraisal of behavioral functioning, leading to an educational prescription, and a qualitative analysis of the environment in which the learner functions. With these two aspects of appraisal, it is possible to begin prescribing a proper learning treatment—

that is, matching the learner's characteristics and those of the learning situation for more efficient learning. A central guidance function, Gordon maintains, is understanding the way in which a learner functions and planning the ways in which learning experiences can be implemented for each youngster.

Another guidance function is the provision of psychological, social, and material support for individual development. Counsellors have done a fairly good job at provision of psychological support but have not done as well in providing social support "through the way in which the student is exposed to other people, and the way in which he experiences interactions with others." Material support requires assisting with provision of the resources needed for survival —ranging from food supplements, to pocket money, to clothing, and so on.

Still another guidance concern is that of orientation and interpretation, providing educational, occupational, economic, and political information and understanding. A neglected area of orientation, Gordon observes, is what he calls "values interpretation"—the bridging of gaps between the values that are peculiar to them, the values that society professes, and the values needed "to make it" in society. Often, in protecting the mores of society, we have ignored the values and practices of the individual student.

Guidance people should be more concerned with socialization and politicalization of disadvantaged youngsters. Socialization involves learning how to survive, to comply, to conform; politicalization involves learning to get what one needs from the system. Gordon suggests that disadvantaged youngsters need to learn how to manipulate the system to get from it what they need. If, as Coleman suggests, there is a close relationship between achievement and the individual's sense of fate control, these two areas can contribute to developing such a sense of power to influence one's future.

Finally, Gordon proposes that the guidance function include pupil advocacy or protection of student's interests, and assistance with role definition and role choice. Performance of these functions for the urban disadvantaged student will upgrade life for them and, in addition, will advance guidance and education for all children.

Edmund W. Gordon is Professor of Education and Director of the Division of Health Services, Sciences, and Education at Teachers College, Columbia University.

GUIDANCE IN THE URBAN SETTING

Edmund W. Gordon

In education, the term "guidance service" can best be regarded as referring to those professional activities directed at the facilitation of decision-making and development. If we are talking about school-age youngsters, we would add, in children and youth, but the term, of course, could apply to decision-making and development at any stage. When these processes are applied to urban youth, we could drop the term "urban youth" and simply talk about guidance in general, since, as we certainly know by now, "urban youth" is a very broad term and includes a wide variety of youngsters. However, in the past few years we have come to think of this term as referring more specifically to poor children, to minority group children, to children who have come to be congregated in the centers of our cities, so that "guidance in the urban setting" might be assumed to concern the problems of the groups that some call "disadvantaged," "poor," or "minority." Whatever term is used, we know that we are talking about poor, black, Puerto Rican, Mexican-American, American Indian, or other minority group children.

Characteristics of the Disadvantaged Populations

Generally, in developing such a topic we find it necessary to say something about who the youngsters are in terms of their characteristics. We can review some of these characteristics here, keeping in mind that these are not characteristics that clearly define this particular group of youngsters; they are characteristics that are encountered with high frequency in particular populations, but which may be encountered in any segment of the population. Some years ago a British team of psychologists, the Clarkes, looked at behavior disorders in school-age youngsters and compared these to behavior disorders seen in youngsters in an institutionalized population. They came up with a list as wide in range for the school-age kids as for the hospitalized kids. In other words, anything from thumb-sucking, nail-biting, and stomach cramps, to nightmares, or even delusions, occurred in both of these groups of youngsters. The difference was that when these characteristics were ordered in relation to what we generally regard as their severity, moving downward from least severe to most severe, the school-age children tended to cluster around the top and the institutional youngsters tended to cluster around the bottom. But, in both of these populations the total list and total range of disorders were fairly similar; it was the frequency with which the more severe disorders occurred that distinguished the institutionalized group from the non-institutionalized group.

Much the same kind of distribution can be found when we talk about the characteristics of poor or black or disadvantaged children. A whole list of characteristics can be found, but we tend, of course, to focus on those that are assumed to have some deleterious effect on learning. We find the full range appropriate to white middle-class, upper-class, or black lower-class children. We find that the range is appropriate to all groups, but the frequency with which they are encountered in the disadvantaged population is greater. What is important is that the frequency is high enough for us to identify these characteristics as potential problem areas with which we must be concerned.

Among the characteristics which constitute problem areas is one involving contradictory attitudes toward self. It has been described in any number of ways in the literature on the disadvantaged, but can best be referred to as a problem in self-concept: basically that youngsters who occupy a disadvantaged position in the society tend to have a higher incidence of problems of self-concept than do youngsters who are in more privileged circumstances. This does not mean there are not problems of self-concept in more privileged individuals.

The problem of self-concept may be reflected in a depressed or an exaggerated sense of one's own place and role in the society. It has frequently been described as being reflected in a sense of powerlessness to influence one's destiny. Some investigators have related self-concept to the child's perception of those models with whom he identifies. Given the disorganized and depressed quality of many aspects of the environments in which these children live, it is generally considered that their view of self is more likely to be inadequate and negative than adequate and positive.

Secondly, there is a higher incidence of a utilitarian or materialistic attitude in the disadvantaged group than in the more privileged group. That is, the disadvantaged tend to view education, or any experience, in the context of its utility—what can it do for me? This probably is an aspect of behavior which is more obvious in these youngsters rather than an aspect which is absent in one group of youngsters and present in another. The fact is, utilitarian and materialistic attitudes are endemic to our society. However, children in more privileged circumstances are called upon to make fewer sacrifices with respect to the satisfaction of basic material needs than are poor children. For example, few middle-class high school seniors are required to do without desired clothing, automobiles, or opportunities to participate in a social life which requires ready pocket money in order to complete school, whereas the poor youngster must do without these and many other material accoutrements unless he drops out of school and goes to work. Thus, it can be argued that any difference in the manifestation of this materialistic or utilitarian attitude on the part of different classes is not so much a difference of degree as one in the conditions under which that attitude is called into play by circumstances.

Disadvantaged children also show a low level of aspiration or motivation relative to academics or academic products, as well as in relation to some social norms. These youngsters are not as readily involved in some of the traditional tasks of academia as are youngsters who have grown up in circumstances where higher value has been placed on this behavior dimension. In a number of studies where the extent of the learning task has been modified to more greatly reflect interests central to disadvantaged children, their aspirational and motivational patterns are reported to have been changed. In the absence of such adaptation of material, they show lower-level academic task orientation and variable levels of general task involvement. To put it much more simply, the attention span, the ability to concentrate on many of the things that the school thinks are important, is somewhat reduced. Some people suggest that this is because of the impinging of a number of other interests rather than a problem of inability to attend or to concentrate, since in matters that have high interest for these children there seems to be no diminution in attention span. When they are confronted with academic and some of the norm-based demands of the broader society, attention and task involvement seem to be depressed.

In recent years we have gained increased appreciation for differences in learning styles, modes of perception, perceptual habits, and temperamental traits, some of which do not complement the emphases that are peculiar to the academic setting. Increasingly, research evidence points to the fact that our general neglect of a sophisticated concern for individual and group differences may be having a deleterious effect upon educational productivity. We know that differences in temperamental traits can be identified in children as early as the third month of life. We knew that there are individual and group differences, probably culturally based, in the facility with which learning proceeds from concrete as opposed to abstract experiences. We know that there are cultural group differences in perceptual habit patterns (the way in which children listen or look). We also know that the organization of learning experiences in the schools does not reflect what we do know about the wide range of variation in behavioral adaptations in the children served. Thus, the style that a disadvantaged child uses in approaching a learning task may not be the style that we have become accustomed to seeing in youngsters in school.

Also, there are marked sociocultural patterns in the conditions of life for these youngsters which tend to be non-complementary to traditional standards in academic achievement and social stability. These include hypermobility, family instability, distorted model relationships, economic insufficiency, housing inadequacy, repeated subjugation to discriminatory treatment as well as forced separation from many of the main channels of our society.

Some years ago when many of us were just beginning to talk about the education of the disadvantaged as a major problem area, Riessman (1963) identified some positive characteristics in this population. Since that time, others have focused on these and have even suggested that it might be possible to build learning experiences around such factors as selective motivation, selective creativity, and selective proficiency. In other words, these youngsters are not unmotivated in every area, they do not show lack of creativity in every area, they do not show uniform lack of proficiency—in fact, there are many areas in which they are highly creative, highly proficient, and highly motivated. One of the tasks of education is to identify these strengths and to use them in the educational development of youngsters.

Despite the difficulties in symbolic representation, there are fairly complex processes of symbolization in the disadvantaged population. These processes can be observed especially in the in-group language forms. With respect to the slang or dialects used by some of these groups, one observes that although they do not follow the structure of standard English, they are not correctly described as non-complex language forms; they *are* complex. They have relatively little utility, however, in formal learning situations where the only accepted form is standard English.

In addition, these children do have functional computational skills. They can solve arithmetical and other problems when necessary to their survival in the street culture, in the cultures in which they live. They also show accuracy of perception and accuracy of generalization about some social, psychological, and physical phenomena. If one wants to know about the values of people in the streets of Harlem, the best people to talk to are some of the kids who roam those streets. They have very good insights into many areas—for example, a very high degree of appreciation for the subtle differences between the cop you can get along with and the cop you can not trust.

It is incorrect to assume that perception in social situations and capacity to generalize is absent in them. It is more a problem of refinement of these qualities in the areas with which academics are most concerned. They have the capacity for meaningful and loyal personal relationships, the capacity for resourcefulness in the pursuit of self-determined goals. When one watches a group of these youngsters as they pursue tasks or goals that are important to them, one finds a tenacity, a degree of creativity, and considerable ingenuity that would be very valuable if we could but capture them and channel them into academic pursuits.

Guidance Functions for the Disadvantaged

With a group of youngsters who have these and other characteristics, and for whom school has been relatively unsuccessful, there are a number of guidance functions that become important, maybe even more important for them than for other youngsters. But when these functions are considered carefully, it is possible to conclude, as indeed I have, that they are not simply appropriate for this population alone; they are probably equally appropriate for any population of youngsters. In fact, one of the values of studying this particular area is that as we begin to solve these kinds of problems we will make considerable progress in the improvement of education in general—in the same way as, in the field of medicine, for example, much recent progress has been a result of the concentration of medical research on pathology, on the problems of public health and disease. Many of the solutions we may find from the study of these youngsters who are not "making it" in the system—atypical learners, if you want to call them that—will be entirely appropriate to the improvement of education for all people. One other qualifying statement: I view guidance very broadly. Counseling is only one aspect of guidance, and, from my biased position, probably the least important.

The first of these guidance functions is something that I call "psycho-educational appraisal." By this, I mean the responsibility of persons who would facilitate the development of others to begin with a qualitative appraisal of behavioral function. Qualitative as opposed to quantitative assessment is stressed. In the past fifty years, we have made enormous progress in the quantification of behavior. We can measure some aspects of intellectual function fairly accurately, and there is no question about the predictive value of these measures in certain situations. If one wants to know how a youngster will progress through the public schools in this country, there is no better predictor than, say, the Stanford-Binet or the Wechsler Intelligence Scale for Children. The one competing indicator is social class. Family income and school achievement are very highly correlated. With respect to measurement, we can certainly depend upon these quantitative scores of intellectual function to predict what people will do in fairly standard educational treatments. (I do not suggest that we can make an absolute prediction or that there is a one-to-one relationship since many factors interfere; but we do know enough about the measurement of intelligence to be able to make reasonably good predictions from that quantitative data.) However, what these tests do not predict is what students will do in non-standard treatment situations. If we can vary the treatments sufficiently, and they can, in fact, be varied greatly, then it is hard to predict from an IQ test score what the achievement will be.

I suggest here that part of this first basic guidance task is the development of a greater concern for qualitative as opposed to quantitative appraisal of intellectual and social functions. This emphasis on qualitative appraisal leads to what I call *educational prescription* rather than *diagnostic classification.* Psychological test scores tend to show what the child's teacher already knows: that this youngster is "relatively bright," or "relatively dull," or "about average." In the traditional reporting of these scores, there is little specific indication as to where to go in educational treatment. But a report which indicates that this youngster responds to specific types of stimuli; is likely to be turned off by certain kinds of learning experiences, will, if the learning experiences are put in a certain form, move ahead rapidly; and is, under certain kinds of conditions, retarded in his functioning—these kinds of specifications can be used in planning the day-to-day educational intervention. These descriptions of behavior will be more useful than a reported score of 90, 80, or 110. A quantitative classification indicates a position the child holds relative to other children, but does not tell much about the specific operations required to facilitate his learning. So the first aspect of this concern for psychoeducational appraisal is the qualitative appraisal of the functioning of the individual.

A second aspect is the qualitative analysis of the environment in which he functions, an area of measurement which, unfortunately, has been grossly neglected in our society. We have focused on measurements of individuals but have not turned to the measurement of the learning environments in which individuals function. I am beginning to believe, and the work of J. McVicker Hunt (1961) would support this belief, that, given relatively controlled variation with respect to basic intellectual functions, the learning environment may be the more crucial determinant of intellectual achievement. In other words, if one can manipulate the conditions under which learning occurs, one may compensate for or retard the impact of the basic intellectual patterns. If we look at the people who succeed and fail in the society, we find that all of those who succeed are not the brightest people in the world, and all of those who fail are not the dumbest. Something else intervenes, and much of the intervening process may be better appreciated through a qualitative analysis of the learning environment.

With these two aspects of appraisal, we are then prepared to think about prescribing the learning treatment, that is, matching the characteristics of the learner and the characteristics of the learning situation, which together should make for more efficient learning. I suggest that this is an essential function of guidance, more important than the interpersonal relationship between a counselee and a counselor—responsibility for understanding the way in which learning occurs in this youngster, and helping to plan the ways in which these learning experiences can be implemented. Given new techniques and new concern for qualitative analysis of the student's behavior, the guidance specialist can identify patterns and define the dominant cognitive style, the level of achievement, the rate at which the student learns, and what facilitates or retards learning for him. The specialist can then translate these into formulae for methods which suit the particular needs of the child. This approach is reflected in the important work now being done on individually prescribed instruction and may prove to be the dominant educational practice in future years.

A third area of concern is the provision of support for development, and this grows out of a respectful concern for the conditions under which learning occurs. This support can be divided into three areas: psychological, social, and material. Guidance has been reasonably good for some of those youngsters that we reach through the provisional psychological support; that is, with a youngster who is having difficulty or is fortunate enough to see the counselor before getting into difficulty, we do a reasonably good job of hand-holding. We can tell people not to feel bad about certain kinds of experiences, we can tell them what to expect, we can give them the moral support that they need in difficult or challenging situations. Where we have not moved as rapidly as our technology would permit us is in the provision of social support. The whole field of group dynamics (more popularly known as sensitivity training), a field concerned with the application of social psychology to human organization and human behavior change, is one that we in education have not taken adequate advantage of. Few of us as teachers are prepared in any sophisticated way to manipulate grouping and group interaction to support or facilitate learning and development for youngsters. We still handle this in very crude ways although the technology for it is relatively advanced. What is required is the provision of social support through the way in which the student is exposed to other people, and the way in which he experiences interactions with others, whether these be pupil-pupil or pupil-teacher interactions, individual or group interactions.

The last aspect, material support, is one that we have certainly known about for a long time, but, under the impact of psychoanalysis, have moved away from. This is simple material support for development and learning. When social work first developed in this country, old-fashioned social workers went out trying to see what they could do to supplement the meagre resources of families that were having difficulty, to try to bring these resources up to a level that was essential for their survival and to provide for youngsters the things, the physical supports, that they needed for schooling. In the large number of educational programs that have developed for disadvantaged youngsters, few have placed any heavy concentration on a thing as simple as food supplements. Many of us have been shocked to learn that, even in this country, there are people who are starving. Yet, even before one reaches the level of starvation, there is a degree of food deprivation which seriously endangers normal functioning. We know that there are many children who sit in school day after day with inadequate nourishment, who are not starving, but are less efficient learners than they might be because they simply do not have the nutritional support for learning.

It is certainly much more obvious when youngsters do not have the clothing that permits them to come to school. What may not be so obvious, however, is the youngster who lacks, not the bare minimum, but the second and third level supports: the high school youngster who is turned off from some crucial aspects of the academic learning experience because he does not have the pocket money that permits him to participate in an apparently unrelated social event. For him, this may be the bridge to the more formal academic learning experience. Guidance people have to be concerned with these three levels of support for development and learning: psychological, social, and material.

The fourth area of concern in guidance is orientation and interpretation. This runs the gamut from educational, occupational, social, and economic information, to an area which must be regarded as equally important, and that is political information.

First, there is the long-recognized field concerned with providing educational information for youngsters. Most guidance people can provide the educational information necessary to make it through the usual paths that youngsters follow in our school; they can tell a student what it takes to get into college and they can tell him what courses he needs to prepare for certain kinds of jobs. This is the kind of educational or occupational information we are reasonably good at providing. However, we have not yet moved fully into the whole area of providing social information. Perhaps when it comes to the interpretation of the rules of society, what is expected of one, we are reasonably useful. But, if we look at the ways in which today's youngsters, privileged and underprivileged, are tuning out of the society, it suggests that as parents or as teachers or as guidance people we have lost contact and that the communications have broken down in the interpretation and understanding of social information, information about "me as a being" in relation to other people and the processes of the society. At the economic level our information has focused primarily on occupational and vocational information: what do you need to get this out of the economy, or to get this kind of job, which will support you in such and such a way? We are not doing a very good job of helping youngsters understand what I like to think of as the political economy of the society—the relationships between politics and economics. We are now being awakened to the importance of political economic information. Looking at the problems of finance for public education or looking at the problems of the internal dynamics of public school administration, I am convinced that political information and the political economy of education may be as important, if not more important, than some of the more strictly pedagogical issues with which many of us have been preoccupied. Certainly one can have the technical answers, but without the political power or political know-how to get them implemented, he is as bad off as if he did not have them at all.

Another neglected aspect in this area of orientation and interpretation is what I call values interpretation. Here we manage to get ourselves into a bit of trouble because, as a guidance specialist, I am likely to communicate my values when the task really is to help youngsters bridge the gaps between the values that are peculiar to their own circumstances, the values that the society professes to believe in, and the values which are perhaps essential to making it in the society. These three do differ. We have focused much too sharply on the protection of mores of the society and the values that we profess to believe in, ignoring the values and practices that the youngster brings and his perception of the differences between the values that society professes and those it practices.

Socialization and Politicization

This leads us into a concern with socialization and politicalization as functions of guidance people—socialization meaning learning how to survive, how to comply, how to conform. This is what I mean by helping youngsters to understand the values that the society professes to live by. One learns, and it is difficult not to be cynical, how to pay lip service to these values so that you can get along in the society. But another aspect that I think we have not helped youngsters deal with is their politicalization; that is, learning to get what you need out of the system. Disadvantaged children somehow have to learn to manipulate the system in a way that allows them to get from it what they need, just as we more privileged people manipulate the system to get what we need. I do not use manipulate in an entirely negative sense. Manipulate means to operate, to turn, to twist, to adjust, to use. It can have positive as well as negative meanings. Referring to my concern earlier with the importance of political power, I think one of the most essential things that guidance people can do for young people these days is to teach them respect for the political power that is vested in them and how to use it. I hope that they can be shown how to use it in the best interests of the total society, but I suspect that if they do not first learn how to use it in their own individual best interests, they will not be able to extend that technique further to the broader society. Just as, if we do not help youngsters to respect themselves, it is hard to help them learn respect for others in their larger group interactions.

There have been important research developments which support this suggestion of the importance of politicalization. These analyses have shown that, of all the variables considered to be associated with success for the student, two are of striking importance: one is reflected in the relationship between achievement and the individual's sense of power to influence his future, and the other is suggested by the relationship between achievement and participation in resistance movements. Coleman has reported that, for youngsters with a sense of capacity to influence their lives, this feeling outweighed all other factors except the impact of their home background in determining their school achievement. An example of the importance of the second variable has been provided by Robert Coles (1967), who reported an association between participation in civil rights activities by black students in the South and their school adjustment. Similarly, Bettelheim (1960), in studies of concentration camp behavior, found superior emotional adjustment among those members involved in some resistance activities. We can also cite the notable success of the Black Muslim movement in this country in rehabilitating some of the most disorganized and depressed young blacks, largely through helping them to identify themselves as resisters of white oppression. Mobilization of one's energies and resources in a purposeful assertion of self appears to be a powerful instrument for positive behavior change.

The last two areas I would include concern the function of guidance persons in the protection of the best interests of youngsters, something I call pupil advocacy, or, to use a legal term, the guidance person as an ombudsman. He should be the protector of the best interests of the youngster. One might use for an example the role and function of an architect who is working for someone who wants a building constructed. He sits down with his client, helps him to decide the nature of the building he wants, what purposes it must serve, and what goals are involved. Once these have been identified, the next step is to translate these goals and purposes into a plan, or a blueprint. Then it is necessary to find the people who are actually going to construct the building, and the architect helps to do this. He gets these people under contract, but his job does not stop there. He stands by while the construction is going on and, at every point, checks to see whether or not it is being properly done. He is responsible for quality control. Think what would happen if there were people operating in the public schools now who at every point in the development of every youngster were insuring that the proper pieces got in, the proper experiences were there, the proper achievements were arrived at, that the youngster had developed the kind of foundation which was necessary to support the developing superstructure.

This is the role of guidance people in the protection of the best interests of youngsters: pupil advocacy, the pupil ombudsman. This, incidentally, does not involve the guidance person in a large amount of personal counseling but in a large amount of consultation with a wide variety of people: consultation with school administrators about the organizational structure of the school, consultation with teachers about the learning needs and the learning experiences that are likely to be most appropriate for this youngster, consultation with parents and community people, consultation with other youngsters who may need to be organized in certain ways to provide certain kinds of experiences or a supporting climate.

Finally, the last of these guidance functions is the counseling that has to do with role choice. In this counseling role, the guidance counselor helps the young person to face the questions: Who am I? What can I become? How can I become it? I do not think that we should be involved with the treatment of psychopathology; we are not prepared for it, nor do we have the time. Those of us who let ourselves become the troubleshooters for the school, trying to handle the disturbed or disturbing youngsters, are doing the field and those youngsters a disservice, because few of us are trained to function in that way. Our counseling functions have to do with role determination, role choice, and the discovery of answers to questions related to role identification and role achievement.

Counseling in the guidance area, I believe, should be generally limited to this function and should involve a small proportion of the counselor's time. I would say that most of his time, particularly with a disadvantaged population, should be devoted to the other categories of work mentioned above.

In Summary

A comprehensive program of guidance for the urban disadvantaged student would involve the specialist in these several kinds of activities: *appraisal,* a qualitative rather than quantitative analysis of individual functioning and environment; *prescription,* the planning and design of appropriate learning experiences; *support,* for development and learning, psychological, social, and material; *orientation and interpretation* with respect to a wide variety of kinds of information and values; *socialization,* the development of appreciation for what it takes to survive in the society; and also, as important, if not more so, *politicalization,* learning how to get what one needs from the system; *pupil advocacy,* the protection of the best interests of the pupil; and finally, *counseling* relative to role choice and implementation. To the extent that we, as guidance specialists, can perform all these functions effectively for the urban disadvantaged child, not only will life for these children be greatly improved but guidance and education for all children will be significantly advanced.

References

Bettelheim, B. *The Informed Heart: Autonomy in a Mass Age.* Glencoe, Ill.: The Free Press, 1960.

Coles, R. *Children of Crisis: A Study of Courage and Fear.* Boston: Little, Brown and Co., 1967.

Hunt, J. McV. *Intelligence and Experience.* New York: Ronald Press, 1961.

Riessman, F. "The Culturally Deprived Child: A New View," in *Programs for the Educationally Disadvantaged.* Washington, D.C.: U.S. Government Printing Office, 1963. Pp. 3–10.

THE LIFE SKILLS PROGRAM—STRUCTURED COUNSELING FOR THE DISADVANTAGED

Winthrop R. Adkins

Winthrop R. Adkins draws on his experience with Training Resources for Youth, Inc. (TRY) in helping disadvantaged students "learn the life skills—the psychological and social skills for mastering the interrelated problems in living encountered in training, on the job, in the home, and in the community." Although there is agreement that counseling programs for disadvantaged have not been particularly successful, numerous explanations for these failures have been advanced. Adkins sees the reliance on non-structured discussion methods in individual and group counseling situations as having serious limitations.

Adkins and his associates made a number of observations of the inadequacies of traditional individual and group counseling sessions with black disadvantaged adolescents in a vocational training program. Adkins studied and categorized the common problems of the trainees, analyzed their problem-solving style preferences, and designed what was to become a curriculum for counseling. The design requirements for the program included these: (a) it should be life-problem-centered and easily adapted to a variety of problems of living and working in the city; (b) it should build on knowledge and skills already possessed and provide a means for improving problem-solving skills; and (c) it should take advantage of existing peer relations by maximizing group activities in areas of common concern while providing for individual needs.

What emerged was the development of a Life Skills program which Adkins describes in some detail. From an analysis of current counseling problems and a study of major psychological and social skills needs for employment and personal development, some fifty common life problems were identified. These were clustered into five major headings: (a) Developing Oneself and Relating to Others; (b) Managing a Career; (c) Managing Home and Family Responsibilities; (d) Managing Leisure Time; and (e) Exercising Community Rights, Opportunities, and Responsibilities. Curriculum units have been designed for each of the life problems. The Life Skills curriculum is designed for small groups of ten trainees who are enrolled in basic education, vocational education, or on-the-job training programs. A four-stage model—stimulus, evocation, objective inquiry, and application—is used for sequencing Life Skills learning, with stages designed to enhance motivation, demonstrate the value of past learning, guide further exploration, and apply knowledge usefully. Each of these stages is illustrated by Adkins, who continues to develop and refine the program by testing it with different populations in various contexts.

Winthrop R. Adkins is Associate Professor of Psychology and Education at Teachers College, Columbia University.

THE LIFE SKILLS PROGRAM—STRUCTURED COUNSELING FOR THE DISADVANTAGED*

Winthrop R. Adkins

The multiple problems of disadvantaged adolescents and adults, which make it difficult for them to take full advantage of emerging training and employment opportunities, have been frequently described (Harrington, 1962; Riessman, 1962; J. E. Gordon, 1969). Some progress has been made in devising meaningful programs to teach vocational and basic reading and mathematics skills (U.S. Dept. of Labor, 1969). There has not, however, been a concomitant advance in finding ways to help disadvantaged students and workers learn the life skills—the psychological and social skills for mastering the interrelated problems in living encountered in training, on the job, in the home, and in the community.

Although virtually every training and employment program for the disadvantaged has employed counselors to help students and workers deal more effectively with their problems in living, the relatively high percentage of premature terminations attributable to various psycho-social problems (U.S. Bureau of the Budget, 1969) attests to the fact that counseling programs are not yet coping effectively enough with the needs of disadvantaged clients. One reason why counselors have not been more successful is that the personal problems faced by their clients are numerous and complex. Another is that counselors often lack appropriate preparation and experience, and understanding of their clients (Trueblood, 1960; E. W. Gordon, 1964). However, perhaps an even more basic reason is that, lacking more effective tools, counselors have relied heavily on non-structured discussion methods in individual or group counseling as the primary means for helping them resolve their difficulties and make appropriate plans.

*The Life Skills Program was initially developed by the author with the assistance of Robert Wolsch and Sidney Rosenberg, formerly at Training Resources for Youth, Inc., Brooklyn, New York. This chapter is reprinted from the Personnel and Guidance Journal, (October 1970) 49:108-116, with permission of the American Personnel and Guidance Association.

The traditional counseling interview, and even modern sensitivity training methods, structured by the client's problems as they unfold and the techniques of the counselor, were developed primarily with middle-class clients coming from highly organized communities, who could be presumed to possess a reasonable amount of knowledge of and familiarity with the resources and demands of their environment (Strodtbeck, 1964). The disadvantaged client, however, frequently comes from a disorganized community, has few dependable family, school, and community resources, and has had little opportunity to learn about his interests and abilities and the requirements of training and employment. There are distinct limits to how effective nonstructured discussion can be as a means of helping him to acquire the considerable new experience, knowledge, and skill necessary to cope with his problems and make meaningful choices, as Amos and Grambs (1969) suggest.

A Need for New Methods

A number of observations of traditional individual and group counseling sessions with black disadvantaged adolescents bear this out. It was found in a vocational training program (Adkins and Wynne, 1966) that:

1. Trainees found it difficult to sustain focused discussion on any one topic, and, instead, kept flitting from problem to problem with insufficient attention or effort on any one. When counselors helped to structure their sessions with pre-prepared leads, materials, and exercises on specific, common personal problems, trainees were able to focus effectively, make progress, and attend to their other training tasks.

2. Group discussion frequently revealed a great deal of shared ignorance. Patently false concepts and facts were uncontested by all but the counselor. The group appeared to have little access to new knowledge which would challenge their misconceptions about important areas of their lives. The counselor's efforts to get them to collect evidence which called into question their own facts and assumptions were quite successful.

3. Counselors reported that the majority of their clients had very similar problems and that they noticed a great deal of repetition in their own behavior in working with different clients and different groups. It was apparent that a more efficient way of handling these common problems would be desirable.

4. Most of the "emotional" problems of trainees had large cognitive and intellectual components and, in effect, were largely problems of not having sound knowledge, sufficient facts and categories

to define them, information about resources, and the ability to frame alternative courses of action. Frustration over an accumulation of unresolved problems produced negative emotions such as fear, guilt, and anger, which cumulatively led to patterns of withdrawal, apathy, aggressive acting-out, or feelings of alienation. Yet when problems were analyzed into tasks, rather than dealt with holistically, trainees experienced needed success in dealing with them, which had the effect of supplanting negative emotional reactions with positive ones and encouraging renewed attack on other problems.

5. Words and concepts used by clients and counselors, even black counselors, were not based on common experiential referents. Lacking common experiences, words simply meant different things. Trainees appeared to be eager for experiences in which they could see, hear, and otherwise sense new activities, settings, and tasks. They seemed to trust knowledge gained through direct experience and mistrust ideas expressed verbally or in writing unless related to their experiences.

6. Many of the trainees acted as if "talk is cheap" and either saw group sessions as stages on which to perform or became apathetic with prolonged discussion unless it led to action. When talk was either a prelude to action or a reflection of past action, focused interest remained high and trainees seemed to benefit.

7. Like most adolescents, trainees had effective and rewarding relationships with their peers and responded well to peer-group learning activities. They seemed most open to learning if the peer group and the counselor encouraged them to express their own ideas about the issue or task at hand and appeared to value what they knew.

These observations suggested that a different kind of counseling program could be designed which would help disadvantaged clients minimize their weaknesses and take full advantage of their strengths. Could we not collect and categorize the common problems of trainees and deal with them more efficiently? Could we not take advantage of their preference for solving problems and for obtaining knowledge inductively from experience and gradually introduce them to other means of learning about themselves and their opportunities? Could we not, in effect, reach our counseling goals more effectively if we considered the problems of our trainees our curriculum, and employed a variety of teaching as well as counseling methods? Why not a curriculum for counseling?

Design Requirements

On the basis of these and other observations it was felt that the program should meet the following design requirements:

1. It should be life-problem-centered and be capable of adaptation to a wide variety of problems related to living and working in the city.

2. It should build upon the knowledge and skills they already possess and provide a means for improving problem-solving skills while demonstrating the utility of new knowledge gained by reading, study, and research, as well as by experience and discussion.

3. It should take advantage of their good peer relations by maximizing group activities in areas of common concern and yet provide for individual needs through individual counseling.

These initial observations and design requirements for a structured counseling program led to the development of the initial version of a Life Skills program at Training Resources for Youth (Adkins et al., 1965), a large, comprehensive, experimental training project for disadvantaged adolescents living in the Bedford-Stuyvesant section of Brooklyn. In the succeeding years the author has continued the development of Life Skills concepts and operations with black, white, and Indian populations both in the U.S. and Canada (Adkins and Rosenberg, 1969). The process of curriculum design and the learning model herein described represent the most recent version of that development.

The Design of a Problem-Centered Curriculum

The syllabus for the Life Skills curriculum is based on the problems the trainee target population is currently facing and those it will encounter as it progresses through training to actual employment. The problems for the most recent syllabus were collected by working with counselors and other staff familiar with disadvantaged clients to make a crude task analysis of current counseling problems and the major psychological and social skill requirements of employment and personal development in the context of work, family, and community. Numerous individual problems resulting from this were then analyzed, combined, and categorized into some fifty common life problems, which were in turn clustered together under five major track headings representing composite objectives. These are: Developing Oneself and Relating to Others; Managing a Career; Managing Home and Family Responsibilities; Managing Leisure Time; and Exercising Community Rights, Opportunities, and Responsibilities. The life problems provide the basis for the design of curriculum units. The representative curriculum unit headings in Table 1 illustrate the range of simple and complex problems which must be resolved in order to demonstrate competence on a given curriculum track. Because the curriculum is developed from the actual problems faced by trainees,

TABLE 1. Major Curriculum Tracks and Representative Units

Tracks	Representative Units
1. Developing Oneself and Relating to Others	Dealing with Parental Rejection; Identifying One's Interests and Abilities; Proper Diet
2. Managing a Career	Interviews, Tests, and Application Blanks; Relating to One's Boss; Paycheck Deductions
3. Managing Home and Family Responsibilities	Becoming a Father; Meeting Needs of Wives; Budgeting and Buying
4. Managing Leisure Time	Planning One's Time; Changing Mood and Pace through Recreation; Participative vs. Spectator Activities
5. Exercising Community Rights, Opportunities, and Responsibilities	How Organizations Function; Dealing with Discrimination; Finding One's Way Around the City

motivation is greatly enhanced and the dangers of irrelevance and designer bias are greatly reduced.

The Life Skills curriculum is designed to be used in small groups of about ten trainees who are concurrently enrolled in basic education, vocational education, or on-the-job training programs. It is followed up by regular individual counseling sessions. Trainees spend about two hours each day in the Life Skills program. Each Life Skills group is led by a specially trained Life Skills Counselor who is thoroughly familiar with the trainees and the instructional and counseling requirements of the learning model.

The Structured Four-Stage Model

Effective counselors and teachers engage in a number of different processes in implementing their goal. If these processes were made explicit, they could define a series of distinct sequential roles for learners and educators which would help to clarify the expected behavior of both and could be relatively easily learned. The four stages of the model through which a Life Skills learning sequence progresses —stimulus, evocation, objective inquiry, and application—are designed explicitly to enhance motivation, to demonstrate the value of past learning, to guide exploration, and to apply knowledge usefully. In addition they provide a model for problem-solving. Each lesson is planned on the basis of the four stages. The goal is to increase self-knowledge and knowledge about how to cope with one's environment and to facilitate planning and action based on this greater knowledge. A fundamental notion is that experience followed by reflection, followed by goal-setting, followed by further exploration, reflection, and

Figure 1. Overview of the Four-Stage Life Skills Model

	STIMULUS	EVOCATION
OBJECTIVES	—focus attention of group —stimulate group to respond	—evoke responses from all group members —demonstrate knowledge already acquired and dignify the learner —enhance group rapport —categorize group knowledge —raise curiosity
ROLE OF LIFE SKILLS COUNSELOR*	stimulator —prepare and present stimulus	evocateur —ask questions and lead discussion to elicit what group already knows —record group responses —help group categorize knowledge and raise questions
ROLE OF LEARNER	—respond to stimulus	—discuss what each knows and feels about problem
MATERIALS FOR LESSONS	—films, clippings, pictures, stories, experiences with high emotional impact	—blackboard, tape recorder, mimeographed materials
DURATION	—until discussion starts	—as long as group can still produce ideas and is interested

*in addition to the above, conducts regular individual

so forth, in the process of implementing goals, is an effective means for encouraging self-induced behavioral change. The four-stage model, described in Figure 1, which was adapted from the work of Wolsch (1969) and revised with the assistance of Rosenberg (Adkins and Rosenberg, 1969), indicates how this is accomplished.

Stage I: Stimulus

The Life Skills learning sequence begins with a provocative classroom encounter with a selected problem. As the name implies, the objective is to stimulate the interest of the learners in a common topic and thus to create readiness for group discussion. A second purpose is to provide immediate content for initiating discussion. The Life

Figure 1. Overview of the Four-Stage Life Skills Model

OBJECTIVE INQUIRY	APPLICATION
—aid inquiry into what is known by others —help find and use resources —help discover new sources of knowledge —help test current assumptions about knowledge	—apply knowledge to aspects of problems to acquire skills —broaden experience —feel success in coping effectively
resource person —suggest sources of knowledge —provide resources —assist learners in using resources and making presentations —conduct discussions to assimilate what is learned	shaper and coach —help define and select problem —provide initial projects —help learners to frame and carry out own projects
—make inquiries to obtain knowledge using multimedia kit —present findings to group	—define, select, and carry out individual, team, and group projects
—multimedia kit of pamphlets, films, recordings, suggested trips	—selected prepared projects and suggested project types
—as long as group wants to know what others know and what is knowable	—as long as project takes or until interest wanes

counseling sessions at various times

Skills Counselor (LSC) selects a highly controversial or emotionally laden aspect of the problem and presents it in the form of a film (either fully presented or stopped at an exciting point), a picture, a tape-recording, or a news clipping, or by telling a story of a particularly pertinent experience. This initial stimulus may be external (from the LSC) or internal (from the group itself). The LSC's main role is to select and plan the stimulus, convene the group, and insure that the stimulus is effectively presented for maximum impact. His enthusiasm and involvement are most important. The desired outcome is that the group will be pensive, agitated, intrigued, or amused and will be ready, even "raring" to talk about the problem they have just experienced. Depending on the unit chosen, the LSC might present a video tape of a black youth being fired from his job, have a trainee describe his feelings about the recent birth of his baby, or show a film depicting a narcotics addict suffering from withdrawal symptoms.

Stage II: Evocation

Once the discussion is initiated, the objective is to evoke (call forth) from each of the group members what he knows about the problem based upon his own experiences. The main intent is to help the trainee become aware of how much he and others already know about the problem and thereby dignify him as a learner. Other purposes are to encourage the free expression of ideas and feelings on a focused topic in a supportive, non-judgmental atmosphere, and to provide a living illustration of basic epistemological issues and the multiple sources of knowledge now being utilized by the group (experiencing, finding out from a self-proclaimed or culture-proclaimed authority, observing, reading, counting, listening, and so on). By judicious questioning, comparing, and reflecting the LSC attempts to keep a lively discussion going about the topic. It is most important that he be receptive and that he set a tone similar to that of brainstorming sessions, by insisting that all have the opportunity to speak and that there be group respect for each person's contribution.

During the discussion the LSC also acts as a recorder of ideas by writing the ideas, words, phrases, or images on the blackboard or a flip chart in the original form in which they are expressed. He may fill boards on all sides of the room as he attempts to exhaust the knowledge of the group on the subject. He liberally dispenses verbal rewards for effort in the manner of an art teacher attempting to get students to express themselves freely on a blank canvass. The blackboard recording tends to give the contributions of the group a semi-permanent status instead of allowing the comments to disappear immediately after utterance. Members feel they have been heard and their ideas have value for subsequent analysis and discussion.

When the boards are filled, the topic is exhausted, or interest begins to lag, the LSC asks the group to identify ideas that "go together" or that are contradictory, or that they agree with or dispute. The intent in this phase of the Evocation Stage is to categorize the output of the discussion and to raise interest in finding out more about the topic in order to follow up associations or resolve contradictions. If the LSC also mimeographs the categorized knowledge of the group and hands it back as "curriculum material," the trainees tend to feel pride in what they as a group know and what they have constructed. Having been given an opportunity to describe what they *know* about a topic, they can psychologically afford to admit what they *do not know*. The novel concept of "I have been a learner" seems to translate into "I am a learner" and leads to curiosity and additional inquiry.

Stage III: Objective Inquiry

Having probed the limits of their own knowledge, the major objective of the next stage is to encourage and assist members of the group to explore a variety of other sources of knowledge about the problem. After identifying major questions of interest and what new knowledge is needed, the group is led to assign its members tasks of obtaining information. The LSC shifts his role from question-asker and recorder to resource person and question-answerer. He assists teams and small groups of learners to make full use of specially prepared multimedia kits, which are cardboard boxes containing preselected films, filmstrips, pamphlets, books, pictures, tests, maps, lists of lectures, addresses of libraries, cards listing suggested field trips to agencies, places of employment, or points of interest, persons to talk with, things to count, subjects to research, and additional sources of information.

Although constructing the multimedia kits in advance is a somewhat time-consuming process, they are extremely useful in minimizing the information search problem for the learner and can be tailor-made for the particular needs of the group. With a small materials development staff, individual items on a whole range of likely problems can be assembled. Curriculum materials and video and audio recordings made by other groups can also be included.

After the teams of learners have found information relevant to their assignment, both outside and inside the classroom, the LSC helps them use it to plan their presentations as experts on a subject before the whole group. Initially the LSC leads the group presentation session. He gradually shifts the responsibility for such sessions to individuals in the group. As groups become more familiar with the process of searching out relevant information, they become less dependent on the multimedia kits and the LSC and discover their own sources of information. In the process of completing their tasks, trainees learn how to operate projectors, find books in the library, plan trips, improve their reading and discussion skills, carry out simple research, take tests, talk with experts such as doctors, lawyers, and employers, interview others, prepare presentations, analyze results, and hopefully think more clearly. The desired outcome is not only that they will obtain useful information about a specific problem, but that they will have a variety of new experiences and learn the basic skills of inquiry and resource identification.

Stage IV: Application

It is not enough to obtain, present, and discuss information, since it is likely to be forgotten if not put to use. The main objective of this stage, therefore, is to demonstrate the utility of knowledge by providing opportunities to apply what has been learned to real life problems, under either real or simulated conditions. The group surveys its accumulated knowledge and selects one or several aspects of the problem it is interested in acting upon. The LSC shifts his role from research person to coach. His main task is to help trainees frame projects they can carry out with some success. If the subject of the unit is selecting an occupation, for example, an appropriate project for an early lesson might be to make an inventory of one's interests and abilities based on information and categories gained in the Evocation and Objective Inquiry stages. If the subject of the unit is "Making Your Emotions Work for You" and the lesson deals with controlling one's anger, the project might be to role-play techniques of re-perception and delayed response learned in the Objective Inquiry Stage in a simulated anger situation. If the subject of the unit is the role of a father in a family, the project might be to tutor a younger child in some skill. If the subject of the unit is presenting oneself effectively to others, the project might be to make a video-tape of a job interview conducted with a cooperating employer using new knowledge about verbal and nonverbal communication. Initial projects should, of course, be relatively simple, but with experience much more complicated projects, such as planning to start a laundromat business, or managing a voter registration campaign, or locating and renting an apartment, can be undertaken. The desirable outcome is that group members will be able to carry out projects which help them to solve their own life problems with minimal help from the LSC.

Flexibility of Operations

When projects are completed, the four-stage model for the learning sequence is recycled. If the next lesson is an extension of the lesson just completed, it is possible that the Stimulus Stage can be eliminated. If the group elects to move on to a different unit, then of course the new lesson begins with a Stimulus Stage as described. The four-stage model can be employed flexibly. Cycling through all four stages may take several sessions or be completed in one session. The sequence of stages can be shifted when appropriate. The stages may be explicitly explained to trainees and adhered to strictly by the group, or they may be used more informally as a guide by the LSC. The units selected may focus on one area in depth, such as gaining employment or coping with problems of health or marriage, or may deal in less depth with a broad range of problems, such as suggested in this article. The problem-centered Life Skills program may form the core of an entire training center curriculum integrated with more conventional classroom treatments of subjects at advanced levels or it may be used on a more limited basis to deal with the most pressing life problems faced by learners at school or at work. In all cases it is recommended that individual counseling be regularly employed to supplement group activities and to facilitate reflection and goal-setting.

There is reason to believe that the Life Skills program may have certain advantages over other didactic and counseling approaches. In developing units one is forced to make an explicit study and analysis of the actual problems trainees are experiencing as they negotiate their social environment and the tasks these imply. These must be stated in terms of specific behavioral objectives. Rigorous thinking is required to identify what will stimulate the trainees, what they are already likely to know, what resources are needed to help them find answers for themselves, and, most important, how they can concretely apply what they have learned in order to realize success and progress in solving problems. Moreover, in conducting a Life Skills lesson the LSC must pay attention to a variety of important aspects of learning which are frequently omitted in many counseling and teaching situations. As a result of these features and the fact the curriculum units themselves are derived from the actual life problems of great import to the trainees, motivation for learning is usually high.

Staff Requirements

The skills of individuals from various fields have been employed in *designing* Life Skills lessons and units. Interestingly enough, staff with counseling backgrounds and without special training can cope very effectively with the Stimulus and Evocation stages, but surprisingly poorly with the Objective Inquiry and Application stages. Teachers tend to be good at thinking about Objective Inquiry, but poor at Evocation and Application. Some of the most provocative Stimulus stages have been suggested by salesmen, and some of the most realistic Application projects designed by job developers and placement specialists.

In *conducting* Life Skills units and lessons, staff with counseling and teaching backgrounds have been most frequently used as LSC's, although there has been some experimentation with paraprofessionals. With special training in the operation of the four stages of the Life Skills model and with practice, LSC's become adept at thinking operationally and conducting lessons. They report that they find the four-stage sequence very helpful in structuring their various roles and preparing for lessons.

Development of the Life Skills program is continuing. The initial program, which was designed to help urban black adolescents in New York City, is now being refined and adapted for use with Indian adults in rural Canada. Second generation programs will explore the implications of the Life Skills approach for other populations, both disadvantaged and middle class, in industrial, educational, and community center contexts.

References

Adkins, W. R. Counseling in the Inner City: Life Skills Education. Paper presented at the American Personnel and Guidance Association Convention in Washington, 1966.

——— and S. Rosenberg. *Theory and Operations of the Life Skills Program.* 1½ hr. video-tape, privately produced, 1969.

——— and P. Sharar. *Training Resources for Youth Proposal. A Comprehensive Operational Plan for a Demonstration-Research Training Center for Disadvantaged Youth.* New York, privately printed, 1965.

——— and J. D. Wynne. *Final Report of the YMCA Youth and Work Project.* Contract 24–64, Department of Labor. New York, privately printed, 1966.

Amos, W. E. and J. Grambs. *Counseling the Disadvantaged Youth.* Englewood Cliffs, N.J.: Prentice-Hall, 1969.

Gordon, E. W. "Counseling Socially Disadvantaged Children," in F. Riessman et al., *Mental Health of the Poor.* Glencoe, Ill.: The Free Press, 1964.

Gordon, J. E. "Counseling the Disadvantaged Boy," in Amos and Grambs, *Counseling the Disadvantaged Youth.*

Harrington, M. *The Other America: Poverty in the U.S.* New York: Macmillan, 1962.

Parsons, F. *Choosing a Vocation.* Boston: Houghton Mifflin, 1909.

Reissman, F. *The Culturally Deprived Child,* New York: Harper & Row, 1962.

Strodtbeck, F. L. "The Hidden Curriculum of the Middle Class Home," in *Urban Education and Cultural Deprivation,* ed. C. W. Hunnicutt. Syracuse, N.Y.: Syracuse University Press, 1964.

Trueblood, D. L. "The Role of the Counselor in the Guidance of Negro Students," *Harvard Educational Review,* 30, 3, (1960), 252–269.

U.S. Bureau of the Budget. *Study of the Programs of the U.S. Office of Economic Opportunity.* Washington, D.C.: U.S. Government Printing Office, 1969.

U.S. Dept. of Labor. *Manpower Report of the President.* Washington, D.C.: U.S. Government Printing Office, 1969.

Wolsch, R. *Poetic Composition in the Elementary School: A Handbook for Teachers.* Doctoral dissertation, Teachers College, Columbia University, 1969.

VOCATIONAL-TECHNICAL EDUCATION NEEDS AND PROGRAMS FOR URBAN SCHOOLS

Grant Venn

Grant Venn examines the provisions of the Vocational Education Amendments of 1968 and points out how this legislation could have a profound affect on more than twenty-five million persons annually, helping to counteract problems of unemployment, discrimination, and social unrest. To Venn, this amended act "is probably the most challenging mandate in the history of federal education legislation, aimed at making occupational preparation an integral part of the educational process below the baccalaureate level." Resources are provided to make it possible for schools to prepare all students for the world of work.

The legislation is comprehensive, providing for in-school youth, for those who have completed or dropped out of school, for the disadvantaged, and for the handicapped. It could remove barriers between the academic, general, and vocational curriculums. The threefold emphases in the new legislation are on (a) vocational education needs of all groups, (b) the educational and manpower priorities in disadvantaged areas with high unemployment rates, and (c) the development of new careers and occupations.

Venn points out that the problem is not lack of jobs or lack of people to fill jobs; the problem is lack of educated and skilled people to fill available jobs, especially in the professional, semi-professional and technical fields.

How the 1968 legislation can bring about the necessary changes in education and training are detailed by Venn, who cites nine provisions for which appropriations are authorized. Now, it is up to schools and communities to prepare meaningful programs which will "spur each person's willingness to learn, make room for his personal capacity to grow, and hold to the promise of reward for his daring to venture."

Grant Venn is Director, AASA-National Academy for School Executives.

VOCATIONAL-TECHNICAL EDUCATION NEEDS AND PROGRAMS FOR URBAN SCHOOLS

Grant Venn

By virtue of size, location, and historical background, each big city or urban area in our country developed its own personality and its own strengths. All, however, have been plagued by the same, almost insurmountable, problems during the past ten or fifteen years. We can begin with problems of transportation, housing, and environmental pollution. Or, we can focus on the people of urban America: the population boom; the impersonality of urban institutions toward social and economic issues affecting citizens; the impact of congestion, juvenile delinquency, and crime on urban residents. We cannot overlook the high rates of unemployment, especially among the youth, the least skilled and educated who migrated from rural communities and small towns, and the handicapped. We also must include the blighted inner cities, where environmental mastery is virtually impossible. Today, some inner cities have a barren quality, gutted by violence and destruction. We might then try to understand the sullen resentment of inner-city minorities toward those who prosper and find some measure of fulfillment in the urban environment.

Doing this, we see that most inner-city residents have been denied the chance there or elsewhere to learn enough to contribute to or share the affluence that surrounds them. Since they are non-contributors, they are unable to reap and enjoy a fair share of this affluence, and urban life for them has become hostile and growth-killing. The one generalization usually applicable is that they cannot gain a foothold in the labor market. They have neither the education, training, nor attitudes needed to get and hold jobs.

Our urban areas have both the manpower and the jobs—an abundance of manpower and thousands of jobs that go begging for *skilled* workers. This paradox underscores the absence of skills and occupational training among the jobless in our cities. It also represents a challenge for schools to become responsive to people's needs. Most educators admit that our present educational system has proved to be less than successful with the poor, with the inner-city and ghetto resident, and with the black people and other minorities. In many respects, our educational system has not responded to technological and social change.

The Vocational Education Amendments of 1968 contain important provisions which, in operation, could affect more than twenty-five million persons a year and indeed become a major weapon to counteract problems of unemployment, discrimination, and social unrest in our large cities. Probably the most challenging mandate in the history of federal education legislation, it is aimed at making occupational preparation an integral part of the educational process below the baccalaureate level. The law provides resources for building into the nation's elementary, secondary, and post-secondary schools the capability to prepare all students for the world of work. Nowhere else can we really focus our resources so effectively.

To become a progressive force in an urban society characterized by social change and technology, the school must change its directions and concepts. It must assume responsibility for not only the middle-class or academic-minded boy and girl who plans to go to college, but also for the slow learner, the underachiever, the youngster who has lost interest in school because it has no relevancy to him or his future, the physically and mentally handicapped, the slum youth, the school dropout, the adult who was "shortchanged" in the system. A "non-reject" philosophy has become a *must!*

This admittedly is a large order, but it can be filled. Virtually our entire population is exposed to the public-school experience. Does it not make sense to strengthen and change the public school system so that it can cultivate our human resources, and provide them the opportunities and incentives for learning and earning, for good living, for growing, and for becoming productive citizens in their environment?

The fact that we are supporting additional projects in our cities to mend or salvage many whom we could not, or did not, reach in public school is an indictment of the basic purposes of American education. Experience shows that remedial efforts for both youth and adults are expensive and often futile. This is why the 1968 vocational education legislation points to and supports some needed changes in purposes for public education.

In its broadest sense, this legislation can help remove the barriers between the academic, general, and vocational curriculums, so that no young person will be denied an opportunity to prepare for the work that suits him as an individual. For the first time, educators and administrators have the opportunity to reach all those most in need of new educational programs and approaches, because funds have been authorized not only to strengthen and expand current programs but to develop new ones that will serve *all* youth and many adults. The legislation emphasizes development of programs for equipping in-school youth, persons who have completed or left high school, and the disadvantaged and handicapped with job attitudes, knowledge, and skills. It is specifically oriented toward reaching those in the ghetto—the potential dropouts.

Although society cannot guarantee every man the fulfillment of his individual quest, it can help him to build a foundation which will not crumble in this fast-changing world. Past goals of education have too often been touted as great hopes, only to end like New Year's resolutions. Educational goals now and in the future will have to be realistic and relevant, linked to what students are expected to know and do. Behavioral tasks that are linked to an entry career job can become an evaluation instrument for measuring the individual's success as well as the institution's quality.

Effecting Change Through Vocational Education Legislation

The emphasis in the new legislation on (1) the vocational education needs of all population groups, (2) the educational and manpower priorities in economically depressed areas and those with high rates of unemployment, and (3) the development of new careers and occupations should encourage school systems to move quickly in planning to serve those whose opportunities for good occupational training have been limited. The law challenges the imagination and ingenuity: programs can be created which bridge the gap between learning and earning and make good the promised value of a high school diploma—"employability." This in itself may encourage students to complete high school and then to undertake technical training or advanced occupational preparation at the post-secondary or adult level.

During a period when we had maximum economic growth, an increasing gross national product, and an unemployment rate below 4 per cent, we just cannot "explain away":

—the nearly 13 per cent of young people between the ages of 16 and 22 who are unemployed;
—the 24 per cent of Negro youth in the same age group who are unemployed;
—the nearly one million boys and girls who drop out of our public schools each year before completing high school;
—the thousands of men and women who lose their jobs every week because of automation.

As we know, lack of jobs in our cities is not the problem. Lack of people to fill the jobs is not the problem. The problem is lack of educated and *skilled* people to fill the jobs. Employment opportunities in the professional, semi-professional, and technical fields continue to increase. Demands in the public service field alone exceed labor supply by five to one. The technological breakthroughs that have been witnessed in the last five years have boosted the demands for trained personnel in scientific research, development, production, and services in all fields of applied science. Today, estimates show that four technicians are needed for each engineer or physical scientist, six to ten for each medical doctor or researcher in the health fields, and four to five for each biological scientist.

How can the 1968 legislation bring about the needed changes?

First, it authorizes appropriations for state grant programs, making it possible to greatly expand vocational education programs and implement new programs throughout the nation. These grants require fifty-fifty matching funds and will assist states in conducting occupational education programs for persons of all ages in all communities. The legislation requires that state plans include programs designed to train persons for career vocations so that such training will be available to all who need or want it.

I am convinced that America wants its schools to help every citizen learn and become a part of society. It can no longer tolerate a system that excludes those who, for some reason, are not learning well at the moment. Our educational system must therefore integrate, rather than separate, vocational and general education at all levels.

Presently, the average person will need to change his occupation four or five times during his life. Because occupations are expected to change rapidly and because workers are expected to change jobs more frequently, people can no longer benefit from simple, specific job skills. They must have a broad basis for a variety of occupations. A person must be trained for clusters of jobs so that he may switch from one job to another as technology advances.

Second, it authorizes special programs for the disadvantaged that require no matching funds. Beginning with fiscal year 1970, the legislation earmarked specific percentages of state allotments for these programs to assure continued training for the handicapped, the dropouts, the unemployed, and other disadvantaged persons. We place a premium on intelligence, on education, on minds and bodies intact, and have long rejected the less capable among us. Yet we know that the unemployment statistics include primarily the handicapped, the underachiever, the uneducated, and minorities. The special programs will open the way for these persons to enter into the mainstream of our society.

Third, it provides for pilot programs and projects. Half of the amount appropriated for this purpose is to be allocated by the Commissioner of Education to pay all or part of the costs of projects that create "a bridge between school and earning a living for young people who are still in school, who have left school either by graduation or dropping out, or who are in post-secondary programs of vocational preparation," and for promoting cooperation between public schools and employers. The remainder of the appropriation may be used by state boards for awarding grants to local educational agencies for full or partial payment of developing and operating exemplary programs.

The whole educational system—the curriculum, the instructional programs, and their relationship to each other—must take into account present and future occupational opportunities for all kinds of people. We need an exploratory occupational education program for all junior high school students. It is during grades seven, eight, and nine that the majority of our young people drop out of school psychologically, if not physically. Many of the approximately ten million boys and girls enrolled in junior high schools in urban areas have little knowledge or understanding of the world of work, or of the career opportunities in various occupations. Even in small towns and rural communities where work is no stranger to young people, knowledge of the occupational spectrum is limited. Through an occupational orientation and guidance program students could become acquainted with the wide variety of job opportunities in business and industry, understand the different skill requirements, and know what compensations jobs offer. We must increase the "options" in our schools.

Efforts should be directed toward providing a base for developing an occupation-oriented program for all students in grades ten to twelve, and a skill-development program for some high school students, which will lead to post-secondary on-the-job or in-school preparation for careers. In this way every student at the secondary level is encouraged to make a tentative occupational choice, and has a means of achieving it. The program must be continuous, with expert counseling and guidance provided whenever a student changes his goal. The program must be flexible enough to permit a crossover from one curriculum to another without penalty.

Job-placement and follow-up services should be made available to high school students. The secondary school now assumes full responsibility for placing baccalaureate-bound students in academic programs that suit their future needs but has avoided the task of initial job placement. More than 80 per cent of our young people enter into the work force without benefit of a four-year-college degree, and high schools must accept responsibility for placing these students in their first job. This service should be extended to dropouts who return to school for vocational training and to persons in post-secondary programs of vocational education. The success of placement programs in the secondary schools will require the involvement of business, industry, and labor, who, in turn, will gain the services of well-educated and well-trained employees.

Fourth, the new legislation authorizes cooperative vocational education programs. This provision adds that needed fourth "R" to education—relevancy. It also encourages a partnership between the schools and the business and industrial community. Cooperative programs offer many advantages to young people who are preparing for job entry. Meaningful work experience is combined with formal education to enable students to acquire job skills and job attitudes. These programs remove the artificial barriers which separate work from education and, by involving educators and employers, create an interaction which reveals the needs and problems of the school and the employer. This leads to the revision of curricula to reflect current trends and requirements in various occupations.

The legislation also encourages the expansion of cooperative work-experience programs. It authorizes funds for obtaining personnel to coordinate the programs and instruct students and also for reimbursing employers for added costs incurred in providing on-the-job training and supervision.

In addition to the cooperative work-experience programs, the legislation has made provisions for work-study programs to encourage *needy* students to remain in school, complete their training, and learn good work habits. The work-study program enables these students to receive wages for part-time work in local educational agencies or public institutions. Student jobs should be obtained through cooperative arrangements between the school and the educational or public agency, so that the work done will be relevant to the student's education and contribute to his employability. Dropouts who have been accepted as full-time students in a vocational education program, as well as unemployed in-school youth in such a program are eligible to participate in work-study programs. All participants must be in good standing and between the ages of 15 and 21.

Fifth, the legislation authorizes funds for consumer and homemaking education. When appropriated, at least one-third of the federal funds will be used in economically depressed areas *or* in areas with high rates of unemployment for programs to assist consumers and help improve home environments and family life.

Sixth, a provision stipulates that from 10 per cent of each state's allotment for vocational education research, the state board must use half for paying 75 per cent of the cost of state research coordination units and 90 per cent of the cost of research grants to colleges and universities, local educational agencies, and other public or private agencies. The remaining half of the 10 per cent of each state's allotment is to be used for research and training projects approved by the Commissioner of Education, especially projects in the development of new careers.

The amendments also include a program of grants whereby the Commissioner may contract with colleges and universities, state boards, and other organizations to promote the development and dissemination of vocational education curriculum materials. In addition, special studies will be made by the Department of Labor to project and determine national, regional, state, and local manpower needs.

Seventh, the legislation authorizes stipends to encourage vocational education personnel to attend leadership development programs at colleges and universities and state programs of inservice training. It promotes the retraining of experienced personnel and the exchange between school and industry of teachers and skilled technicians. It also supports special institutes to familiarize teachers with new curricula. The field of teacher training no longer should be tied down to solely academic certification requirements and other limitations that may prevent schools from obtaining the personnel needed. A major thrust in this area may be the exchange between the school and industry of teachers and skilled technicians, who, after some intensive training, could come into the schools to teach or assist teachers; or teachers could go into the business and industry community on a part-time basis.

Eighth, the law authorizes funds to promote the development of curriculums for new and changing occupations, the preparation and dissemination of curriculum guides, the development and evaluation of new curriculum materials, and the training of personnel in curriculum development.

Ninth, it provides for the construction and operation of residential vocational schools for youths 15 to 21 years of age. The Commissioner may award grants to state boards, colleges and universities, and public education agencies for this purpose. In addition, funds are to be made available to the states for planning, constructing, and operating residential vocational education facilities, with the state's share of the costs set at a minimum of 10 per cent. It authorizes such sums "as may be necessary" for making annual grants to reduce the cost of borrowing for the building of residential schools and dormitories.

All of the programs mentioned must be included in the state plans. Priority is to be given to programs for the disadvantaged and handicapped; for slum youth, dropouts, and post-secondary students; and for developing projects in new and changing occupations.

Providing for Long Range Planning

The 1968 Vocational Education Amendments have strengthened the standards for preparing and approving state plans. The legislation includes new requirements for information in the long-range and annual plans, and for the evaluation of reports. The legislation requires that state plans each year must cover current programs and include those planned for four years ahead. In addition, the state must present its plan to members of the State Advisory Council and then conduct a public hearing for the benefit of the people of the State. In this way a variety of ideas and talents will be brought to bear on the state plan.

The legislation also provides for a National Advisory Council and makes funds available to it and to each State Advisory Council for staff, studies, and other work needed in evaluating and reviewing plans. With this backup, state plans hopefully will become creative instruments for improving vocational education.

The machinery for implementing the Vocational Education Amendments of 1968 is in action. A National Advisory Council on Vocational Education has already held several meetings. Its 21 members include: representatives of labor and management; persons familiar with the administration of state and local vocational education programs, the training of the handicapped, the problems of the disadvantaged, and post-secondary and adult programs; and representatives of the public at large. The Council's chairman is an attorney and a member of the Cleveland, Ohio, Board of Education.

National conferences on each section of the new law have been convened. The conferences have dealt with: *research, exemplary programs, residential facilities,* the *handicapped, consumer and homemaking education, cooperative programs, curriculum development, special needs,* and *state plans*. Nine regional clinics were also conducted. More than one hundred education researchers and representatives of business, industry, and government presented ideas for new approaches in vocational education at the meetings. Specialists and practitioners exchanged information and sought ways to resolve some of the problems of program planning. A draft of the proposed regulations for the 1968 Amendments has already been sent to the states for their use, pending publication in the *Federal Register*.

If educators, with the help of business and industry, fail to solve the explosive problems brought about by social change in our cities, the goal of more time, more comfort, more leisure, and more goods will become a curse rather than a blessing. Our one hope is to change our educational system in a way to spur each person's willingness to learn, make room for his personal capacity to grow, and hold to the promise of reward for his daring to venture.

To translate hope into action, our schools must:

—Become "including in" rather than "selecting out" institutions;
—Make the curricula relevant for each student;
—Provide vocational education and work experience for each high school student so that he may have at least one job-entry skill and know how to get along on the job;
—Assume responsibility for getting graduates, dropouts, and the handicapped a job suited to their capabilities and interest;
—Become involved with the business, industry, and labor community through work-experience programs;
—Teach our affluent and middle-class white students what it means to be black in America; why we have slums; the meaning of equality and citizenship for everyone; and the meaning of justice, tolerance, and compassion.

These are the tasks for our generation. We have very little time for paper programs and lip service. Today's youth will have to rebuild this country, clean up the ghettos, tear out the slums. We must tip the scales in the right direction to build for them and help them to build the future our people *can* have.

Judith P. Ruchkin discusses some of the significant issues involved in current collegiate compensatory efforts. Specifically, she focuses on a review of the current status and curricula of compensatory programs, some of the historical background underlying present efforts, some definitional issues, the need for effective and valid evaluation and research, and some specific proposals for action-research.

Data on various target populations has been sparse and somewhat inaccurate due to collection procedures. Nevertheless, there is hardly any question that non-white minority groups have been seriously under-represented in colleges and universities, two-year or four-year. It has been estimated that half of all black college students are enrolled in "predominantly Negro" colleges. Various approaches—talent searches, special recruitment, scholarships, counseling, and special instructional procedures—have been used to increase college-going among minority groups and to ensure that they will be successful once enrolled. As Ruchkin points out, while many efforts are being made to upgrade educational achievement, little is being done to reach the "inner man" and to come to grips with the feelings of powerlessness, discrimination, and isolation which many college youth from minority groups feel on campus.

SELECTED ISSUES IN COLLEGIATE COMPENSATORY EDUCATION

Judith P. Ruchkin

Compensatory collegiate programs may be viewed as part of the drive for universal opportunity, extending education upward beyond the twelve-year common school. Historically, expansion in public education has come about because of political and social demands rather than research or experimentation. If one looks for research evidence on which to base compensatory collegiate efforts, he finds himself on the same thin base that is found with respect to other compensatory efforts, such as those in the early childhood sphere.

Ruchkin maintains that institutions of higher education probably cannot compensate for the host of societal wrongs historically inflicted on the disadvantaged. Thus, it may be that compensatory efforts should be viewed as "high risk programs" in which the student is granted an opportunity to succeed, with or without special services and assistance. Everybody involved, she points out, "the institution, the faculty, the student, and whoever foots the bill—is engaging in risk-taking, to be sure for a socially, individually, and even economically desired end."

To do more than attract temporary visitors through an open door policy at colleges and universities, Ruchkin suggests that there be greater attention to program evaluation and research. Two major questions requiring attention are: What are appropriate criteria for assessing compensatory programs? And what program components are most successful in achieving criterion measures? Or, put another way, it would be good to know "what works for whom, when, where, and why." Ruchkin concludes her article with a series of suggestions for research proposals, studies which might be undertaken in ongoing programs. What is needed, she maintains, is not a new conception of higher education as much as better delivery and realization of existing promises.

Judith P. Ruchkin is Associate Director of the Office of Laboratory Experiences and member of the faculty of the Department of Secondary Education at the University of Maryland.

SELECTED ISSUES IN COLLEGIATE COMPENSATORY EDUCATION

Judith P. Ruchkin

But, America is not now mature enough to develop a truly democratic educational system. The experience since May 17, 1954; the mockeries of evasion, tokenism, the spreading of segregation in the North—all of these have convinced me that America is suffering from a serious form of moral dry rot, and is willing to sacrifice children for an alternate racism if their skin is brown or black. (Clark, 1967, p. 202)

Whether the above societal indictment issued in 1967 is accepted wholly or in part, the burden of proof rests with those who still claim to have both the moral commitment and the technical knowledge to create an open society which will include all those long barred from full participating membership. Against this moral and political context, an examination of current collegiate compensatory efforts becomes particularly relevant. The rationale, design, implementation, and evaluation of such programs raise fundamentally moral questions, and may serve to recast universalistic, liberal educational philosophy into a more particularistic mold (see Fein, 1970). However, this exploration will focus on the more ordinary issues of (1) the current status and curricula of compensatory programs, (2) some historical background, (3) some definitional issues, (4) the need for evaluation and research, and (5) some specific action-research proposals. Such a pragmatic approach recognizes the need for an in-depth and direct examination of changing social and educational philosophies, and hopes that some directions may be discernible in existing programs and practices.

Current Status and Curricula

Any review of the status of collegiate compensatory programs needs to be qualified by pointing out the paucity of accurate, basic, demographic data collected either by institutions or on a more uniform basis. Many colleges have not identified students by race and, therefore, lack the means to gather such information; in some instances, they were legally barred from collecting such data. Therefore, until the results of the 1970 census and a series of other surveys and studies in progress (such as those by the American Council on Education, the College Entrance Examination Board, and NSSFNS, the National Scholarship Service and Fund for Negro Students) become available, previous estimates of varying degrees of reliability will have to serve. Currently available data on black students are confounded by the joining of data from two-year and four-year colleges as well as part-time and full-time enrollments. Furthermore, statistics on Mexican-Americans, Puerto Ricans, American Indians, and other minorities are especially subject to all of the aforementioned problems and are exacerbated by sample size.

With all these limitations in mind, it may still be useful to note that according to one estimate, among the 8.3 million college students enrolled in colleges and universities during 1969–1970, slightly over 8 million were classified as white; 275,000 as Negro; and 55,000 as other non-white (Clift, 1969). Another estimate suggests that between 5 and 6 per cent of all college and university students are black, whereas the black college-age population constitutes 12 per cent of that age group. It is further asserted that between 40 and 50 per cent of these students are enrolled in what are euphemistically termed "predominantly Negro" colleges (Bayer and Boruch, 1969). However, it needs to be recognized that many minority students do not have a need for compensatory programs although they belong to groups which have been under-represented in higher education and are identified as "clearly below national averages on economic and educational indices" (Kendrick and Thomas, 1970, p. 151).

A variety of organizations and approaches have been attempted for this target population. Starting with programs of talent search, special recruitment, scholarships, and counseling, provided by such groups as NSSFNS, the National Achievement Scholarship Program of the National Merit Corporation, and the United Scholarship Service for Spanish-Americans and American Indians among others (McKendall, 1965), the effort has recently encompassed "non-traditional" students, for whom special support practices and/or programs have been instituted. These efforts may include any, all, or a combination of the following: intensive orientation to the institution, personal counseling, special courses, small-group instruction, video-taped lessons, programmed instruction, a personalized teaching approach, tutorial assistance, financial aid, free transportation, free lunches, legal assistance, part-time employment, and a special institutional "home base" (Williams, 1969). Beyond these "additional services," there are a series of "alterations" or revisions of academic procedures in such areas as: grading, transfer, probation, disqualification, prerequisites, registration, credits, scheduling, community-based courses and seminars, as well as vastly expanded ethnic heritage studies (Berg and Axtell, 1968).

It may be that: "The university has exhibited the most inertia, the least inventiveness, and the most contempt for pedagogical innovation of all echelons of the American educational system (Bressler, 1967, p. 261). Nevertheless, these additions and alterations indicate that higher education is not totally bereft of adaptability. Neither is the picture one of unalloyed optimism, since the surveys completed to date indicate that only a small percentages of institutions are addressing themselves to the problems of "high risk" students in any concentrated fashion (Egerton, 1968; Gordon and Wilkerson, 1966). Several institutions which have reported new practices with enthusiasm, such as San Francisco State's Experimental College, the College Readiness Program at the College of San Mateo, Antioch, Wesleyan, and Cornell, seem to have suffered financial and other institutional reverses.

Whether the unusual program at the Experiment in Higher Education at Southern Illinois University will be similarly affected is not clear, but, in any case its curriculum merits a brief discussion. A unified program in social sciences—humanities and the natural sciences, reminiscent of the core curriculum, was buttressed by individual and small-group instruction in reading, writing, and speaking for an initial group of 100 students, of whom 74 continued into the second year. Lectures, seminars, and small-group discussions were planned and directed by students, with workshops and skills clinics utilizing programmed materials, video-tape replays, and with tutoring and personal support provided by a diverse group of successful minority role models. In addition, conventional courses were also available on a regular grading basis, as well as a curriculum related work-study experience with grades being awarded for blocks of courses.

Although the outward characteristics of students enrolled in collegiate compensatory programs have been delineated both in scholarly and journalistic fashion, accounts of the inner man with whom the curriculum must ultimately connect are less often found. The following excerpt is a rare attempt to view the collegiate situation from the vantage point of the student, who is not always the first to be considered in the selection and planning of learning engagements intended for his development.

In most universities, black and other minority group students have recently been admitted in token numbers and scattered throughout the campus, diluting their already scarce numbers and creating a terrifying, demanding, and extraordinarily lonely experience for individuals accustomed to living in a largely black world, though often not by choice. The feelings of powerlessness experienced by all university students are exacerbated among these black students. They often see themselves as token integrators carrying the burdens of cultural representatives and translators to an enthusiastic but not too understanding audience. Thus black as well as other minority group students are pressed to unite with others of their own group. Regarding integration as a goal not taken seriously by whites at these institutions and achieved at too high a cost, these young blacks identify with the stronger forces in the black community that advocate separation and promote black nationalism. (Gordon, 1969, p. 13)

It is also illuminating to compare a current student curricular prescription with earlier progressive, tradition-based recommendations. The president of the Student Council of the College of Liberal Arts for 1967–68 at Howard University defined her ideas about the preferred characteristics of higher education:

adequate higher education must provide the student with a keen and responsible understanding of himself as part of a particular group, as a citizen of a country, and as a participant in a world society. Adequate higher education must train the student to respect the individual and the group. Adequate higher education must train the student to examine all issues and to explore further only those which logically belong within the student's developing disciplined whole. Adequate higher education must allow the student to discover, through actual research, trial and error, or discussion the "truths" about human existence. And finally, adequate higher education must prepare the student for the economic and spiritual maintenance of himself, and perhaps a family as a result of the educational process. (Stermbridge, 1968, p. 317)

There is a striking similarity between this statement and the successful curriculum for the disadvantaged as outlined by two educationist faculty members who drew upon an illustrious tradition. They assert that there is a need for inclusion of understandings, processes, concepts, attitudes, values, and feelings within the curriculum. The student needs an:

understanding of his own and other cultures; attitudes of citizenship; sound personal health habits; a feeling of the place of adolescents in society; an understanding of ethical concepts of American society; an appreciation of the potential worth to American society of varied ethnic and racial groups, immigrant and in-migrant alike; an understanding of the world of work and the requirements for finding and retaining a job, the meaning of mobility, and the dependence of employment on continuing education, both formal and informal; an orientation to the leisure resources of the urban community. (Passow and Elliott, 1968, pp. 13–14)

That this emphasis on "persistent life situations" is characterized neither by novelty nor by frequent and widespread adoption by the public school, or at the post-secondary level, does not diminish its potential for effective application in the current period. It may also meet the criterion of fresh approaches so sorely needed in collegiate compensatory programs. An honest execution of such a curricular design would eliminate programs in which: "students with difficulties in reading, writing, and speaking Standard English may be flunked, or they may be put into a remedial program based on a philosophy of stamping out ghetto dialect" (Furniss, 1969, p. 365). Instead, it would offer recognition of individual and group uniquenesses as well as universal commonalities.

Historical Background

Scarcely a century ago, universal public education was being vehemently debated at the same time that it was beginning to be implemented. Many of the issues of ability, or capacity, and appropriate curricula now raised about access to higher education were posed then with respect to public school education. It may also be useful to recall that there was a differential regional pattern in adopting this nineteenth-century educational innovation. If passage of compulsory attendance laws may be used as a criterion of diffusion, it appears that moving from the North to the South took a considerable period of time. Massachusetts was first to adopt such laws, in 1852, while Mississippi, the last, adopted them in 1918 (Cremin, 1961, p. 127).

Similarly, access to post-secondary education, sanctioned and begun to be implemented in only a handful of states during the 1960's contains a differential regional pattern, with the innovators being on the West Coast and the comparatively late adopters in the East. While extension of full opportunity in higher education may prove to be a passing fad, the historical and political trends appear otherwise. It may be speculated that with the possible extension of suffrage to eighteen-year-olds, coupled with the awesomely difficult questions of political participation in an increasingly complex post-industrial democracy, higher education will be viewed not only as a device for mobility and credentialling, but as necessary for intelligent citizenship in exercising conscious value choice. Or, from a slightly different perspective:

> The roots of higher education lie deep within the needs and aspirations of entire populations. The range of forces that determine the demand for education, regulate access to it, and define the values that maintain it, reflects some of the deepest values of the surrounding culture. (Thresher, 1966, p. 5)

Compensatory collegiate programs, especially when cast as part of universal opportunity for higher education, may signal a rebirth of an earlier progressive tradition in education, since they provide a steady, upward extension of educational opportunity. Compensatory programs also include such characteristics of the progressive era as the expansion and reorganization of curriculum on all levels, more variation and flexibility in grouping of students, more informal classrooms, a greater variety of learning materials available, and a change in administrative relationships (Cremin, 1961).

Looking retrospectively, two additional historical strands appear to be intertwined in the evolution of compensatory collegiate programs. The first encompasses the increasing opportunities for all minority youth to gain access to college education and can be viewed with some optimism based on the increasing numbers and rising percentages of minority group enrollment throughout the country. The second is the more recent experience with compensatory programs of early childhood education, to which the current collegiate efforts bear striking and disquieting resemblance.

The first strand includes the higher education aspects of the civil rights struggle and is tied to the previously discussed expanded higher educational opportunities. Prior to the Civil War, the education of isolated Indian and Negro students had been reported by a few institutions, such as Dartmouth and Oberlin. However, the advent of higher educational opportunity for Negro students really began with the post-Civil War establishment of Negro colleges, both public and private, sectarian and nonsectarian. Despite the considerable legal and personal efforts to make integrated higher education a reality, the majority of black students in the United States continue to be educated at these colleges, whose worth, mission, financing, and authority are frequently questioned and are certainly uneven qualitatively.

Two additional landmarks need to be included in this chronological sketch: the 1947 Report of the President's Commission on Higher Education, which first brought universal higher education to general public attention, and the formation, in the following year, of the National Scholarship and Service Fund for Negro Students, which not only has been the initiator of the talent search activities during the 1950's and 1960's, but has also served as a model for other minority talent search efforts (McGrath, 1966). NSSFNS assistance has enabled students to take advantage of legal access to state universities made possible by 1963 legal decisions. These institutions appear presently to include only 2 per cent black students in their enrollment. However, data provided in a recent study indicated that the percentage of black students enrolled as freshmen was 45 per cent, in contrast to the 30 per cent of *all* undergraduates who were first-year students. This appears to suggest that black enrollment at predominantely white state universities, as at private institutions, has increased considerably, starting with the 1968–1969 academic year (Edgerton, 1969).

Lest one be too easily impressed by such signs of progress, it is well to reflect upon the recent experience with early childhood compensatory efforts, also much touted for the increase in numbers of children served in summer as well as year-round Head Start programs. A discouraging aspect of the current collegiate practices and programs is the resemblance these programs bear to these early childhood and other compensatory efforts, so numerous and popular in the early 1960's, but so woefully lacking in measurable academic achievement to date. Both the process of design and implementation and the strategies employed possess similarities in leadership, volunteer staffing, time, scheduling, and grouping, while the curriculum tends to remain traditional high school and college fare offered to many previous generations of students without noticeable benefits. The questions raised about the effect of supplementary programs for public school students—often consisting of 3–5 P.M. after-school study centers, focusing on the same material, with the same methods, and usually involving the same students and teachers who are already thoroughly disenchanted with both the program and one another—are a clear and present danger for collegiate efforts. Segregated as the American education system is, in more ways than one, the collegiate compensatory efforts have been undertaken largely by people with college or secondary school experience, whose professional concern has not included familiarity with early childhood efforts. Yet, if what is here perceived as a *deja vu* quality in these college programs is not to become even more evident, far more thoroughgoing curricular examination and planning are indicated than are currently practiced. To have traveled down the road of altering the child by merely tinkering with the program and leaving the institution intact may be forgiven on the grounds of genuine ignorance, but to travel down the same road a second time is not so readily squared with professional responsibility or standards.

From a historical perspective, it is apparent that prior expansion in public education was an outcome of social and political demands, not a result of either educational research or small-scale demonstration projects designed to test the efficacy of universal public education. Clearly, research evidence on such questions could not be examined, because neither controlled experimentation nor *post-hoc* designs were applied to such issues at the time. Thus, it may appear unfair that, when, in the current era, the issue of extending higher education to minorities is raised, a loud cry is heard for demonstrated worth and effectiveness, a cry which did not characterize previous extensions of public education. There is no adequate response to this charge, especially when it comes from previously dispossessed and disinherited members of society, for whom higher education still appears to be the most responsive and quickest path to social mobility.

However, any historical view needs to recognize the tremendous outpouring of billions of dollars in public funds and the relatively new, but considerable, expertise now being applied to assessing previously established as well as newly designed programs on all levels of education, from infancy to old age. While it may be that the call for demonstrated worth and hard data comes from those who prefer the status quo in higher education, it is more likely that such a desire stems from a commitment to effective higher education for as many students as possible and the general recognition of need for change in academic institutions.

Some Definitional Issues

It may be somewhat enlightening to recall the various words, phrases, and acronyms that have come into use during the past decade to describe collegiate programs for poor and otherwise handicapped students. EOP (Educational Opportunity Program), Full Opportunity Program, Open Enrollment, "pre-bac," "prematriculant," SEEK (Search for Education, Elevation, and Knowledge), "calculated risk," "risk-gamble," "college readiness," "probationary," "special," "developmental," "low achiever," "ineffective student," "conditioned," "underprivileged," and "disadvantaged" are among the terms often used to describe collegiate compensatory programs and clients. It is well to remember that "as used in higher education, the term disadvantaged is vague and increasingly unacceptable to those deemed disadvantaged by others" (Kendrick and Thomas, 1970, p. 151).

There are problems with the term "compensatory;" it is unsatisfactory from many points of view. Although the college student may be a more logical target for a "compensatory" program, with the meaning that Bernstein considers inappropriate when applied to preschoolers not yet educated, there are difficulties with this use as well. While societal compensation for the wrongs of slavery or other injustices seems appropriate, individual institutions, faculty members, or students can neither grant nor be the recipients of compensation for a host of prior, multi-faceted, societal wrongs subsumed under "disadvantaged." To call collegiate tutoring, financial aid, modified or special curricula, or extended time for graduation a "compensatory program" implies a promise that the institution offering such a program can, in fact, make up for a whole host of individual and generational abuses, injustices, and inequalities. Such promises, while personally and even politically understandable, especially in racially tense situations, may also prove to be educationally questionable, if not dishonest. Colleges, by and large, have not attempted, except in rare instances, to develop comprehensive programs and social services. Whether they wish to do so, and whether they know how to do so, is an open question—full opportunity, open enrollment, and EOP to the contrary notwithstanding.

Thus, it may be far more accurate—although no more palatable—for students to know that they are as they are in fact—part of a "high risk" program. Not least in that risk are the tenuous relationships of such programs to parent institutions and sources of funding. The burden of such risk is, of course, distributed among the student, the institution, and its supporters. The student comes and is, in many instances, merely granted an opportunity to try for a period of time, with no special assistance from his institution. Or, as in a majority of cases, he is provided special services in the form of tutoring, remedial courses, lighter course schedules, special programs of studies, and the like. It is these efforts that especially require being labelled "high risk," since evaluation, of the overall effort or of its component parts, is almost uniformly lacking. Everybody involved—the institution, the faculty, the student, and whoever foots the bill—is engaging in risk-taking, to be sure for a socially, individually, and even economically desired end.

Need for Evaluation and Research

It seems, therefore, both fitting and essential that concurrent with the initiation of open admissions and of the Full Opportunity Program of the State of New York there be an "open" and "full" investigation of those aspects of collegiate compensatory programs which do result in measurable personal, academic, or economic gains. To open the door may be hospitable, and is here supported, but in order to do more than attract temporary visitors, far more serious attention to institutional—rather than merely student—functioning than is presently practiced seems warranted. As Gordon (1967) has put it:

> Although the careful assessment of students' performances is frequent and practically universal on all levels of American education, the careful appraisal of educational programs is rare. It is not surprising, therefore, that very few of the compensatory programs in higher education have been systematically evaluated. (p. 35)

What seems to be needed is an application of the much touted research expertise (often so competently applied in the service of other societal and personal goals) to the examination and, hopefully, the solution of the educational issues central both to the academy and the society of which it is now an ever more significant portion. That academicians are especially well qualified to do research on the academy, using a variety of qualitative and quantitative techniques, does not, of course, make them any more likely to want to engage in such practices than are the plumbers, surgeons, postal workers, and carpenters eager to protect their craft from outsiders. However, the individual and societal interest is now too great, the economic support base too small, and the attack from high political places too frequent to permit neglect of the internal functioning of the academy. Furthermore, if those charged with leadership of the academy refuse to assume this particular burden, others far less sympathetic to its basic mission appear ready to undertake the task.

Higher education in America serves as a model for much of what precedes it. The university scholars, who have frequently criticized the public school establishment for being unresponsive to students and changing societal needs, now have an opportunity to demonstrate that when the opportunity arises they can devise effective programs within their jurisdiction. In the process of devising viable compensatory programs, the academicians may even discover some allies on their own campuses among the lowly educationists, which might have positive and unanticipated effects on the programs themselves, as well as upon institutional cohesiveness, adaptation, and change. In fact, the potential for curricular reform opened up by the arrival of the non-traditional student may have come none too soon, in view of the current disaffection with collegiate programs articulated by some of the traditional clientele (Todd, 1970). It is none too soon, then, to begin investigations that will address themselves to two major questions: (1) What specific criteria may be used to assess a compensatory program? and (2) Which program components are most successful in achieving highest criterion measures?

All things being equal, it would be preferable to base programs on facts rather than folklore, that is, on better informed guesses and more clearly stated objectives. It is fortunate that prior experience in evaluating early childhood efforts has revealed the difficulties in identifying significant program components contributing to success. This should again serve as a warning to those who design and evaluate collegiate programs not to make the same mistake twice, either in planning or evaluating programs. Moreover,

> there are many reasons for withholding judgments about the nature and content of colleges' impacts. Questions of testing procedure arise. Problems of student selection—both among different colleges and among students

within a particular college—must be examined. College impacts have not been documented directly but only inferred from observed freshman-senior differences. We must look into the ways in which average, or net, changes obscure the actual process by which different students adapt in different ways to their college environments. (Feldman and Newcomb, 1969, pp. 48–49)

The difficult but basic curricular and research question is still: What works for whom, when, where, and why?

Some Specific Action—Research Proposals

As educators and taxpayers, we wish to maximize productive experiences and minimize failure. Since most municipalities are on the verge of bankruptcy, it further behooves us to recommend those instructional approaches which will yield the greatest benefit per cost expended. Prior to the entrenchment of a whole new support system and its personnel, we need to know which treatment yields the most in both individual and societal terms.

In addition to existing and proposed reviews and analyses of the literature on collegiate programs aimed at the disadvantaged, there is a need to examine program specifics that have been developed since the mid-1960's. Such an exploration would be most useful if it focused on identifying successful curricular and organizational components as well as on possible matching of students with a variety of program options. Initially, such studies would be descriptive, although opportunities for testing of hypotheses via altered program design or components seem likely. In order for such studies to be conducted with maximum benefit to a widening clientele and serve as guides to the development of curricular policy, a clearinghouse, or data bank, would be useful. No new vehicle is proposed here; rather what is suggested is that one of the existing regional education research information centers (ERIC) be broadened to encompass systematic, periodic, and detailed data on a variety of programs now extant. Such national collegiate program monitoring may well turn out to be a massive undertaking requiring diverse talents as well as electronic data-processing capacity.

However, it may be worth a great deal in human, social, political, and economic terms to develop such strategies for program analysis in view of the vast current expansion in collegiate programs which started in the Fall of 1970 with the City University open admission plan in New York. Just to monitor that effort so as to make informed revisions as the program progresses requires ready access to an array of program and population data. It would be well if a small portion of the open admission funds and a number of faculty whose research expertise is currently being utilized in the evaluation of a range of public school education projects were actively involved in formative, if not summative, evaluation of the open admission experiences. It is hoped that this opportunity for properly conceiving and designing longitudinal studies will be used at the start, rather than bemoaned after the fact, in hastily assembled *post-hoc* designs. Opportunities now exist for gathering data on student expectancies, demographic characteristics, prior preparation, career choice, peer associations, and the like, previously identified as significant variables in achievement and attitude studies (Feldman and Newcomb, 1969). There is a similar opportunity to generate naturally-occurring matched groups for program treatment purposes using the comparative accomplishments of SEEK and open admission enrollees. This may be quite fruitful inasmuch as the former includes a stipend among its services, while the latter does not.

It is educationally urgent that various program options available both locally and nationally receive critical, built-in assessment. At the very least, it is callous to provide a series of treatments—non-credit remedial courses, tutorial sessions, stipends, work-study, and individual counseling—without identifying the appropriateness and value of each for particular individuals. Enough information is already available on the basis of existing programs to formulate some basic questions regarding various program components and their interaction with student socioeconomic status, institutional affluence, and peer influences.

There is increasing evidence that the unexamined folklore of higher education is no more useful as a guide to program and practice than are the myths of public education to conducting successful programs for all students. The recent and ongoing study of effects of institutional quality on student achievement conducted by the American Council on Education calls into question some of the common assumptions about the relationships. It found that, among a highly selective group of college students:

> Even when the bias resulting from differential student inputs was not controlled, college characteristics accounted for only 20 per cent of the variance in social science achievement and about 10 per cent of the variance in achievement in humanities and natural science. When student input differences were controlled, the contribution of college characteristics shrank to only about 5 per cent of variance in achievement. The substantial contribution of the student input, on the other hand, was only moderately reduced (from about 40 to 30 per cent) if the college characteristics were first controlled. (Astin, 1968, p. 667)

Another proposal might be to utilize both the design and the data collected in the above effort in an investigation of institutional impact upon disadvantaged students. Such a study would need to include more output measures, however, than the single Graduate Record Examination, as criterion. For example, grade-point averages, graduation, retention, and vocational, military or other training pursued are among the more obvious criterion measures that would be useful for designing, revising, and implementing collegiate compensatory programs. In addition, the study proposed would draw upon a more general population than does the National Merit Scholarship Qualifying Examination and would, therefore, shed more light on the question of differential institutional impact upon differing groups of students, which remains far from completely answered.

The following action-research proposals are offered in the hope that they will further the goal of developing practices based on more adequate knowledge. Thus, not all the proposals involve program action, nor do they call for directing the bulk of scarce resources for the disadvantaged into research, which would serve to postpone social action. Rather, they attempt to combine the possibilities inherent in existing and projected programs with the contributions of research methodology in order to effect improvement in both practice and theory. To this end it is proposed that:

1. A detailed description of specific program components be developed to encompass all the collegiate compensatory efforts in existence. (This is seen as precursor to program simulation to aid in designing new programs. It might also enable the preparation of a checklist of program characteristics for use in more conventional design process.)
2. A national computerized data pool be established to explore significant institutional, program, and student variables on a longitudinal basis. This might serve to test the influence of socioeconomic status, sense of control, institutional affluence, and peer association upon student achievement in both intellective and non-intellective areas.
3. The creation of voluntary action-research consortia for trying out specific practices on naturally-occurring matched groups of students or on groups randomly assigned to various approaches wherever feasible. (The City University of New York Open Admission Plan already has this potential with respect to the stipend-differentiated SEEK program.)
4. A student-selected motivation-based effort, in which increase in individual choice among program and general college offerings is tied to improvement in grade-point average, or

other indices. While the administrative problem of such a design may be formidable, the success of behavioral reinforcement programs may outweigh such considerations.

5. The use of both qualitative and quantitive techniques to assess system and sub-system responses to the initiation of compensatory programs, focusing particularly on the nature and characteristics of efforts which survive transplantation from a pilot stage.

Expanding opportunities for higher education presents a challenge to all the participant learners in the process, be they students, faculty, or administrators. The expanding enrollment may be a new challenge and does require attention to hard data on completion, grade-point averages, retention, transfer, and the like, but its core has living, human substance. The challenge is to encompass Whitehead's aims of education as well as Mager's behavioral objectives. For such a union, it may be helpful to consider the observations of humanist novelist-critic Leonard Kriegel (1968), writing about his experiences in teaching English to a group of pre-baccalaureate students, which serve as a reminder of the fundamentals, sometimes obscured in the press of social, political, and economic concerns. He wrote:

> The City College of New York, which built its reputation as one of the country's finest undergraduate institutions by serving residents of other ghettos, stands in the heart of Harlem. But it protects itself from Harlem with a wall built out of "academic standards." What is so hopeful about the Pre-Bac Program is that it has already dented that wall. And it promises to break it down. I do not know what percentage of my students will emerge with degrees from the College, I no longer particularly care. "You've got to understand," a student said to me just before the term ended, "when I came to this school, I figured that if I could get one year . . . just one year . . . of Whitey's college, I would be changed. And, you know, I am. Man, they made me hungry. And it's not the money any more. I want it all. Even to be a poet. Man, I want that too." (p. 273)

It is exceedingly fortunate that there are such individuals among the students who choose to enter collegiate compensatory programs. And, until such time that programs are carefully and widely tested, collegiate efforts will need to continue to place their trust in such individual student and faculty initiative, interest, and commitment. However, with the advent of open admissions, instead of devoting energies to selecting entering students who will most closely resemble outgoing graduates, institutions might address themselves to selecting faculty to teach in such programs. This would require major reordering of internal priorities and rewards so as to place curriculum and teaching first. In addition, testing programs, so often used currently for purposes of inter- and intra-group comparison, will need to be used for individual appraisal and learning prescription and be allied to the host of technological support systems on the horizon. Accompanying such reordering of institutional priorities and procedures is the need to establish categories and measures of institutional impact, in addition to the more traditional achievement criteria. Persistence in learning, value of subject to student, confidence to learn, and task involvement may be areas for development of new criteria and observational techniques. That is, beyond the questions of access lie the fundamental educational issues of individual appraisal, program placement, informed choice, transition, and instruction.

The move toward universal higher education is not based on such curricular considerations. It is frankly political in origin and intent, which renders it very much a part of the American tradition of piecemeal curriculum building in response to community pressures. It would be naive to ignore these political sources, just as it would be to neglect the restricted options of those without college credentials.

In this connection, it may be well to recall previous historical efforts to extend educational opportunities to the unlettered scions of the nineteenth-century British aristocracy. McGrath (1966) has observed that:

> stupidity was no bar to a university education—not when the parents of the stupid young man controlled the universities and regarded their prime function to be doing something for their young people. Every young aristocrat was to be taught something that was useful to him, in the sense that it enabled him to enjoy life and to participate as a full member of his class. If he could not be taught to enjoy books then he could be taught riding; in any case he could be taught how to speak, and what to say on most occasions, and thus to take his place in his society. (p. 44)

The continuing existence of such prior educational models as Oxford and Cambridge, which managed to combine a variety of functions, serves to offer hope in the present era of open admission and fusion of roles. The university needs to develop parallel arrangements for prospective scholars, community-service-oriented students, politically inclined activists, and career seekers, as well as the uncommitted, and provide for individual and group interchanges in diverse collaborative learning situations. It is quite possible for multiversities to encompass a variety of students with a variety of goals and to attempt the much-needed task of social bonding no longer uniformly possible in conflict-torn and segregated high schools.

Prophets of doom may take cognizance of a recent *New York Times* headline which read: "More Top Students Applying at City University Despite 'Open Door'" (June 14, 1970, p. 4).

It is also important to note the increasing number of adults seeking retraining, or even college experience per se, and to recognize the significance of a multi-age group for both educational and social bonding purposes. An intelligent, rather than a panicky, political response would note the potential for perspective, diversity, balance, civility, and a more just order inherent in such a microcosmic clientele. While it may also be desirable to create new St. John's-style colleges, or experimental colleges as proposed by Hutchins (1970) these may prove to be nostalgic rather than contemporary proposals. What is needed is not so much a new conception of higher education to accompany the enlarged clientele as delivery on the promises of liberal education: reason and knowledge coupled with compassion and respect for the individual learner, be he an adolescent or an adult, traditional or non-traditional student or faculty member.

References

Astin, A. W. "Undergraduate Achievement and Institutional 'Excellence'," *Science,* 161 (August 16, 1968), 661–668.

Bayer, A. E. and R. F. Boruch. "Black and White Freshman Entering Four-Year Colleges," *Educational Record,* 50, 4 (Fall 1969), 371–387.

Berg, E. and D. Axtell. "Programs for Disadvantaged Students in the California Community Colleges." Oakland, Calif.: Peralta College District, 1968.

Bressler, M. "White Colleges and Negro Higher Education," *The Journal of Negro Education,* 36 (Summer 1967), 258–265.

Clark, K. B. "Higher Education for Negroes: Challenges and Prospects," *The Journal of Negro Education,* 36 (Summer 1967), 196–203.

Clift, V. A. "Higher Education of Minority Groups in the United States," *The Journal of Negro Education,* 38 (Summer 1969), 291–302.

Cremin, L. A. *The Transformation of the School.* New York: Alfred A. Knopf, 1961.

Edgerton, J. "High Risk," *Southern Education Report,* 3, 7 (March 1968), 3–14.

———. "High Risk: Five Looks," *Southern Education Report,* 3, 8 (April 1968), 25–36.

———. "Almost All-White," *Southern Education Report,* 4, 9 (May 1969), 2–17.

Fein, L. "The Limits of Liberalism," *The Saturday Review,* June 20, 1970, pp. 83–96.

Feldman, K. A. and T. M. Newcomb. *The Impact of College on Students.* San Francisco: Jossey-Bass, Inc., 1969.

Furniss, W. T. "Racial Minorities and Curriculum Change," *Educational Record,* 50, 21 (Fall 1969), 360–370.

Gordon, E. W. "Relevance or Revolt," *Perspectives on Education,* 3, 1 (Fall 1969), 10–16.

———. "The Higher Education of the Disadvantaged," in *New Dimensions in Higher Education,* No. 28. Washington, D.C.: U.S. Office of Education, April 1967.

——— and D. A. Wilkerson. *Compensatory Education for the Disadvantaged.* New York: College Entrance Examination Board, 1966.

Hutchins, R. M. "Manhood and the Liberal Arts," *The Urban Review,* 4, 3 (May 1970), 3–5.

Kendrick, S. A. and C. L. Thomas. "Transition from School to College," *Review of Educational Research,* 40, 1 (February 1970), 151–179.

Kriegel, L. "Headstart for College," *The Nation,* 206 (February 26, 1968), 273.

McGrath, E. J. *Universal Higher Education.* New York: McGraw-Hill Book Company, 1966.

McKendall, B. W., Jr. "Breaking the Barriers of Cultural Disadvantage and Curriculum Imbalance," *Phi Delta Kappan,* 46, 7 (March 1965), 307–311.

Passow, A. H. and D. L. Elliott. "The Nature and Needs of the Educationally Disadvantaged," in *Developing Programs for the Educationally Disadvantaged,* ed. A. Harry Passow. New York: Teachers College Press, 1968. Pp. 3–19.

Stembridge, B. P. "A Student's Appraisal of the Adequacy of Higher Education for Black Americans," *The Journal of Negro Education,* 37 (Summer 1968), 316–322.

Thresher, B. A. *College Admissions and the Public Interest.* New York: College Entrance Examination Board, 1966.

Todd, R. "Voices of Harvard '70," *The New York Times Magazine,* June 7, 1970, pp. 26+.

Williams, R. "What Are We Learning from Current Programs for Disadvantaged Students?" *Journal of Higher Education,* 40, 4 (April 1969), 274–285.

PROJECT UNIQUE: INTEGRATED QUALITY URBAN-SUBURBAN EDUCATION

William C. Young

William C. Young describes the planning and development of a variety of efforts to provide integrated quality education for the children of Rochester, New York. Stunned by widespread rioting in the city's ghettos in the summer of 1964, officials of public and private schools, the local university, and the state education department pooled their talents in planning ways of improving education and the quality of communal life. These persons were augmented by representatives from a variety of agencies and community groups. Project UNIQUE (United Now for Integrated Quality Urban-Suburban Education) was created by the planning committee, which also established two groups to insure continued cooperation on the part of these diverse agencies—SPAN (School Parent Advisors for the Neighborhood) and the Community Resources Council. It was the decision of the planning committee to design a new school rather than place its hopes in compensatory and remedial programs. It was also the decision of the group to act as soon as possible rather than continue to conduct surveys and studies.

The Center for Cooperative Action in Urban Education was created as a semi-autonomous unit of the city school district, free to explore new approaches to persistent problems, to bridge the gap between theory and practice, and to establish a set of priorities distinguishing between needs and wants. The Center provided an avenue for building working partnerships between the schools and industrial and mercantile establishments. The basic operational philosophy for project UNIQUE was set forth in January 1968 and included a set of beliefs "that children from different educational, cultural, racial and ethnic backgrounds can learn effectively together."

The World of Inquiry School was set up as a demonstration of the ethnic, economic, racial, geographic, and achievement mix that is found in the city itself. The school has a "unique administrative structure, a more manageable pupil-teacher ratio, an innovative utilization of teaching and supportive staff, and maximum self-determination and freedom for its pupils." The school uses resource persons from the entire community. It draws its pupil population from the inner city, the city fringes, and the suburbs; there is a bal-

anced mixture of races and ethnic groups, of socioeconomic groups, and of boys and girls. The students are grouped into family units, each of which is multi-aged, and the program is non-graded. The inquiry method is used extensively, and each child follows a curriculum that is designed for him specifically. Young describes the program, the way professional and non-professional staff members are deployed, and the program aims and objectives. The World of Inquiry School was designed to serve as a center for innovation and demonstration for the entire area, and there is some evidence that it has succeeded.

Young also describes the Urban-Suburban Transfer Program, which represented a small step in overcoming racial isolation found in Rochester and its suburbs, no one of which is more than fifteen miles from the city center. In 1969, 440 city pupils were enrolled in fifteen suburban public and non-public schools. Almost two thousand pupils from ten racially imbalanced schools were attending schools outside their neighborhood areas. And, one inner-city school had in excess of 200 white children from the outer city—all of them transported on a voluntary basis. The inclusion of non-public schools in the transfer program has served to underscore the fact that racial isolation is a community-wide problem. A group known as SURE (Student Union for Racial Equality) has attempted to increase communication among various groups. Data indicate that the program has made a difference for both black and white students involved.

A small but significant breakthrough was made by suburban West Irondequoit, which decided that a 99 per cent white school was as racially isolated as one which was 99 per cent black. It represented a step toward recognition that racial balance could only be achieved by a metropolitan attack on the problem. Even this arrangement, involving a maximum of 74 inner-city pupils, did not have easy sailing, as Young points out. The magnet school concept exemplified by the World of Inquiry School and urban-suburban cooperation are first steps toward tackling the complex problem of urban education.

William C. Young is Acting Assistant Commissioner for Equal Educational Opportunity.

PROJECT UNIQUE: INTEGRATED QUALITY URBAN-SUBURBAN EDUCATION

William C. Young

The tranquility that characterized life in provincial Rochester, New York, was shattered in the summer of 1964 by widespread rioting in the ghetto areas of the central city. After decades of neglect, angry residents vented their emotions and frustrations in an outburst of destruction without precedent in the city's history. Restoration of order required the combined efforts of law enforcement officers from Rochester, Monroe County (Rochester and its suburbs), and the State of New York, plus a contingent from the National Guard.

The Way It Was

Between 1954 and 1964, the black population of Rochester rose from 7,500 to over 35,000. Some remained after making the journey North as migrant farm workers, while others came directly to the city in search of a better life. Some were successful in finding what they came in search of, but many found frustration and failure. The crime, though, is that those who were frustrated were invariably invisible—unnoticed by those in leadership positions in business, in industry, and in politics; and only statistically noticed in education and welfare.

Education recognized the gradual darkening of its schools, but did nothing except record the trend in its statistical reports. There was neither enough sensitivity nor enough insight among its leadership to realize that the school system was dealing with a new clientele that required a new program.

Welfare personnel noticed an increase in their clients. The new "immigrants" were unskilled farm workers. Unlike many of the skilled artisans who came from Western Europe to search for jobs, the agricultural workers who left the rural South were ill-prepared to operate the complex automatic machines in the plants of the industrial giants. Regrettably, the welfare agency only noted the change in statistics and did little, if anything, to redesign its services to care for its new clients with their unique problems.

Throughout recent history, the American city has truly been the melting pot; the meshing of a *potpourri* of cultures; the training ground for democratic citizenship in this land of opportunity. However, over the past several decades the cities have been going through a "sorting out process," which has created cleavages along certain economic and social fault lines and produced very clear-cut enclaves within metropolitan boundaries. The disaffection was not with the sorting out process per se, but rather with the fact that this arrangement permitted quality education and failure to exist within the same general geographic area.

Government at all levels lacked the knowledge and will to see or respond to the needs of its newly arrived citizens. It was too naive, too unimaginative to develop or use the leadership that was available within the group. It was insensitive and sluggish, and when it did act, it was often inept. This reaction represented a departure from established practice in the American city. The city was traditionally the melting pot for immigrants who were eventually assimilated into the mainstream of American culture. The most recent arrivals, the blacks from the South, poor whites from the hills, and the Spanish-speaking from Puerto Rico and the Southwest, looked in vain for the melting pot that would enable them to become a part of American society. Their explosive reaction was a response to a society that denied them the opportunities that were so freely given to other immigrants.

We still need a training ground for the type of democratic citizenship this country must have if it is to move away from its collision course with disaster, which many, including the President's Commission on Civil Disorder, have predicted. Those who dedicated themselves to spreading good will and better interpersonal and intercultural understanding were the first to admit the difficulty of achieving this goal. However, they found it repugnant to believe that one absorbs the tenets of democracy simply by being born within the confines of a democratic country, and they wanted to teach democracy in a dynamic and real setting. The community espoused this new concept but did not practice it. So the community exploded. How could it have done otherwise when urban children were being educated in antiquated buildings located in the shadows of gleaming new office buildings, banks, and retail stores? This contrast vividly points out the order of priority in our affluent society. While schools, the acknowledged instruments of upward mobility, were compelled to function with inadequate budgets, the private sector was devoting its funds to underground garages, well-appointed offices, and steam-heated sidewalks.

The Action

Among the many responses to the rioting was a planning conference called by the Superintendent of Schools, Herman R. Goldberg, who sought assistance from schools of education in public and private colleges and universities. Unfortunately, urban educators are disenchanted with the resources available in many schools of education. Goldberg was more fortunate. William A. Fullagar, Dean of the School of Education at the University of Rochester, assigned Dr. Dean Corrigan to work full-time with the superintendent and his staff to design programs that would seek solutions to the problems which faced Rochester in the wake of the riots. Norman Kurland and his staff in the newly formed Center on Innovation of the New York State Education Department also participated in the initial planning.

A major step in the planning of Project UNIQUE was the creation of the Community Resources Workshop during the summer of 1966. The participants were representatives of public and parochial schools and many segments of the urban community. Large and small group sessions were organized to encourage discussion and to develop a climate conducive to the sharing of ideas and free exchange of opinion. Out of these sessions came many approaches to the solution of the problems of urban education.

Federal Funding: A New Concept

The availability of federal funds for experimentation and innovation in public schools is a recent development. Title III of the Elementary and Secondary Education Act of 1965 came along at an appropriate time and provided financing for experimentation, innovation, and exemplary programs. A common criticism, voiced with increasing frequency, about the use of federal funds in both elementary and secondary education was that except for a few isolated school systems nothing really "new" was being attempted. Large sums were being expended for remedial reading teachers, tutors, educational hardware, expanded guidance services, and other forms of compensatory education, but methods of instruction remained basically unchanged, and very little was being done to change the whole educational system. The combination of a creative planning task force and a source of funds through Title III permitted a bold adventure in education—Project UNIQUE (United Now for Integrated Quality Urban-Suburban Education).

The Need for Change

Control of the educational establishment has frequently rested in the hands of certified professional educators who contend that they know what should be done and how best to do it. Those who initially conceived Project UNIQUE recognized the great potential contribution of business, industry, higher education, the social and cultural agencies, the civil rights groups, labor, and other agencies in the community, and the planning committee reflected this diversity. To assure the continued participation and involvement of these agencies in the operation of Project UNIQUE, two components, SPAN (School Parent Advisors for the Neighborhood) and the Community Resources Council, were created.

It is interesting to note that the same educators who suggest that increased parental interest in education will improve student performance will also supply a list of the hazards of parent involvement through a neighborhood advisory board or some other structure. Fear of extensive community participation in public education is now reaching paranoid proportions among both administrators and teachers, and, were it not for the community representatives on the planning committee, the community involvement components probably would not have survived.

Involvement of community representatives also assured new thinking by educators. Educators invariably contended that their effectiveness was limited by inadequate resources: inadequate financing was the only serious barrier to success in education. Although additional funds were undoubtedly needed, there was little factual evidence to support the contention that increased budgests alone would solve the basic educational problems that confronted most urban schools. Regrettably, little was said of the massive resistance to change that was indigenous to the educational establishment.

The planning committee took the position that to pour federal funds into schools to continue and to expand unsuccessful educational practices was to reward failure with a subsidy. Lamentably, the size of the grant would likely have a high positive correlation with the scope of past failure. Those schools getting the poorest results were in a position to demonstrate the most urgent need for federal funds. Their applications, supported by elaborate charts and statistics, were actually testimonials to failure, but tended to be interpreted as "objective" evidence of past underfinancing. Simply to grant aid to those schools might be likened to the use of a patent medicine as a substitute for major surgery. The patient may temporarily enjoy the feeling of comfort that comes from knowing that "something is being done." When the effects of the palliative are gone, however, the basic cause of malfunction remains. The planning committee decided, rather than put its hopes in compensatory programs of remediation, to design a new school.

The committee continually emphasized the need for change, and the federal government recognized that need. To encourage development of new and different techniques and practices, Title III of the Elementary and Secondary Education Act of 1965 (ESEA) set aside a sum of money for what industry usually calls "research and development." A local district or a consortium of local districts needs a research and development unit with enough autonomy to function independently of the established bureauracy. It is unrealistic to expect the entrenched bureaucracy to create programs that might discredit traditional practices or raise questions about their efficacy. This is especially so if the same persons were responsible for initiating the ineffective program in the first place. Self-destruction or criticism is rarely popular and seldom practiced!

The committee was crystal clear about its observation that children in the central cities were not learning at a level of competence satisfactory to anybody. To absolve the professional educator and to attribute all the cause of failure to the children would have been unrealistic and unfair to inner-city pupils. The committee acknowledged that the low achievement syndrome is a phenomenon peculiar to the central parts of metropolitan areas and that it is related to massive poverty, recent migration, unresponsive government, lack of sophistication in manipulation of the system, and the absence of other similar skills. Since it was likely that for the foreseeable future the ghetto would remain basically unchanged, this meant that there had to be an increase in experimentation in inner-city education, including new administrative organization structures.

If change were indeed the answer to failure, then reexamination of the composition of the high-failure school was in order. The committee strongly supported integration and redistribution of children to reflect a cross section of the population. Consideration was given to a variety of administrative devices, including educational parks, a 3-3-3-3 system, open enrollment, two-way busing, and others. It decided that where integrated schools existed, every effort had to be exerted to maintain racial balance. Where racial imbalance existed, all available devices had to be utilized to dissolve it. Where such racial imbalance could not be corrected immediately, all the resources of the larger community had to be brought to bear to assure equal educational achievement, even if it meant giving a disproportionate share of the resources to those schools that had large numbers of children with low achievement. The planning committee concluded that delay was an extravagant luxury and that detailed surveys and studies could no longer be substituted for action.

In July 1965, Dr. Elliot S. Shapiro was appointed Project Director and a staff was employed to assist him. Parent-teacher groups, faculty groups, and church, civic, industrial, and civil rights groups were among those with whom the staff discussed the planning. Opinions were solicited, both formally and informally, in an attempt to assess community knowledge, interest, and feelings. These discussions and interviews were designed to create a community atmosphere that would accept and support quality, integrated education.

The Center for Cooperative Action in Urban Education

The Center for Cooperative Action in Urban Education was created by people who were convinced that the ills of public education were neither inevitable nor beyond solution. They cited the need for a semi-autonomous unit that was part of the city school district, but able to chart an independent course, whose direction could be altered in accordance with the changing needs of the community. Since it would not be burdened with the task of operating and maintaining a school system, the Center would be free to explore new approaches to persistent problems. It would act as a benign irritant to the establishment, making resistance to change less comfortable, but not oppressively painful. The Center would help to bridge the gap between theory and practice, and to establish a system of priorities that reflected the distinction between needs and wants. With no commitment to the past, the Center could urge abandonment of unsuccessful practices with less reticence than those who were initially responsible for those practices. Viability, rather than venerability, would be the criterion for acceptance and retention; pragmatism would be substituted for traditionalism.

Creation of the Center would enable its staff to develop close personal relationships with individuals and organizations in the central city who felt estranged from the school system. Unencumbered by past misunderstanding, conflict, and hostile confrontations, the Center could request, and receive, a hearing with parents and community groups as well as with professionals. Dialogue would replace silence. Mutual trust would dilute the massive suspicion that had weakened the lines of communication between professional educators and inner-city residents.

In the absence of fixed employment regulations and precise, comprehensive job descriptions, the Center could expand the use of paraprofessionals selected from the indigenous population. The new positions would do more than create jobs: the adults employed would find a vehicle for active participation in the educational process and an unprecedented opportunity to influence the goals, structure, and practices of public education.

Geographically, there were no boundaries to separate the business community from public education. The close proximity of mercantile and industrial establishments to public school buildings was the rule rather than the exception in Rochester. Regrettably, the close physical relationship had not produced a working partnership. Although manufacturing in Rochester provides the city with a high concentration of technically trained personnel, this reservoir of talent was not used widely in public education. The need for diverting a portion of these skills into public education was recognized by the Center sponsors, who visualized the use of business and industrial employees as part of the instructional organization in order to reduce the classroom teacher's dependence on textbooks and other learning materials.

Financially, the extension of moral responsibility for society's ills to business and industry created the possibility of new sources of revenue for public education. Grants to a Center engaged in educational research and innovation would enable the private sector to indicate, in a positive fashion, its acceptance of this new rule in the community. Philanthropic foundations that might be reluctant to contribute to the direct support of a school district could be asked to subsidize educational experimentation and innovation. The Center would combine the new fiscal resources with relatively unused available corporate talent and establish a sound, working, productive relationship between the private and the public sector. The Title III operational grant from the federal government in 1967 made it possible to test the validity of these considerations under operational conditions.

When Dr. Shapiro resigned in August 1967 to return to the New York City school system, William C. Young was appointed Director, and implementation of the final plan, with its nine components, was begun and has continued under his leadership and direction.

The basic operational philosophy for Project UNIQUE was formulated and published in the January, 1968, *Project UNIQUE Newsletter:*

> We believe that we are approaching a threshold of change in American society generally and in American education in particular. We believe that there are members in all echelons of our society who are demanding now, and will continue to demand, greater assimilation and integration of people of all racial, economic, ethnic, and educational backgrounds. We believe that this demand for integration and assimilation stems from a desire to guarantee equal educational opportunity and a fuller appreciation of the social spectrum of all America's children.
>
> We believe that society owes to each child an unrestricted opportunity to develop his talents to the maximum; we believe that our staff, both teaching and supportive, has the responsibility to employ all of its capacity to develop the skill of the children. To this end we believe that each child must be permitted to progress at a rate as comfortable for him as the limits of staff, materials, and teaching aids will permit. We hope to constantly expand those limits. We also hold that the freedom of the individual child to inquire into areas and questions which interest him is fundamental and

should not be infringed upon, regardless of planned curricula. We are convinced that learning founded on interest is the most permanent and the most productive. Our staff will be ready to encourage and assist the inquisitive pupil and to provide ample opportunity for diversified investigations. We believe that children of various ages should be permitted extensive interaction, in order to assist each other, and to learn from each other.

We believe that open discussion of racial, economic, ethnic, and educational similarities and differences is healthy and should be encouraged; we expect it to reveal that in the past the differences have been too strongly drawn and the similarities too often overlooked.

We believe that the task of the school must be extended to serve our disadvantaged pre-kindergarten children and their families, and to assist dropouts and high school graduates with remedial and post-secondary training.

We believe that better communication is needed between the school and the community; that someone must be available who will interpret the functions and objectives of the school and make the schools more sensitive to the needs, and more responsive to the desires, of the community.

We believe that our community has resources which can make valuable contributions to the education of all children. In many instances the abilities of the children have not been developed. We wish to encourage greater interaction between the realms of business, industry, government, social service, and art and that of education; among their practitioners, students, and teachers; in order to lessen the gap between the world of learning and the world of work.

We believe that technology has a tremendous contribution to make to education. And we believe that if this contribution is made with sufficient care by all concerned, it will prove invaluable in permitting the increased interaction of teacher and student as individuals. We consider this interaction central to the evolution of a more humanistic society.

We believe that the attitude of the teacher is a vital component in the learning process and that his hopes and expectations for the learner directly affect pupil achievement. To this end we support pre-service and in-service training of teachers that emphasizes attitudinal change.

We believe that we have the responsibility for increasing public understanding and support for quality education; that our Downtown Satellite School, with its daily demonstrations for the public, contributes to greater understanding of the need for education and that it will result in greater public support for education.

We believe that our responsibilitiy in Project UNIQUE is to show that children from different educational, cultural, racial and ethnic backgrounds can learn effectively together. Among the prerequisites for achieving this goal are: (1) a different administrative structure, (2) a decrease in class size, and (3) utilization of the teaching and supportive staff in a manner that is different from that which is usually found in many schools. Our major responsibility then is to show what changes in schools are needed in order to make quality integrated education a viable reality.

The accomplishments in trying to implement this philosophy have been encouraging if not uniformly excellent. The various components are described below.

The World of Inquiry School

The World of Inquiry School is a demonstration of the geographic, ethnic, economic, racial, and achievement mix that is a virtual image of the urban microcosm. To assure maximum academic, social, and psychological achievement, the World of Inquiry School operates under a unique administrative structure—a more manageable pupil-teacher ratio, an innovative utilization of teaching and supportive staff, and maximum self-determination and freedom for its pupils. It utilizes the talents of inspiring, though non-certified, resource persons from the community. The school is completely non-graded, and each pupil is permitted to progress at a rate comfortable for himself (which is really all that one could expect). Individualization of instruction is possible because there is a copious supply of resources, both human and material.

The school draws pupils from all geographic areas—the inner city, the city fringes, and the suburbs. Sixty-one per cent of the pupils are white, thirty-two per cent Negro, three per cent Puerto Rican, and four per cent a mixture of other racial and ethnic groups. There is an equal distribution of boys and girls, who range in age from three to eleven. There is a range in family income from under $3,000 to over $40,000 per year.

The children are grouped into "family units." Each family unit is multi-aged, thus more closely reflecting a true family. To group children simply because they are the same age is artificial, and does not represent any natural grouping. While this might be a minor concern, we are trying to utilize every semblance of a natural setting in a concerted effort to increase achievement. In such a setting, children help each other and are themselves helped in the process. They learn to share and to be compassionate. To help someone else induces the child to review and reinforce what he already knows about the materials being discussed.

The inquiry or discovery method is utilized extensively. Teachers are cautious about making group assignments. Each child follows an individual curriculum that is designed for him. With the help of his teacher, the child makes his schedule. He decides where he wants to go and how much time he wants to stay there. He has a chance to satisfy his curiosity.

The school is organized around the family rooms. There are an early childhood unit with three- and four-year-olds, several primary units with ages ranging from 5 through 8, intermediate units with ages 8 through 11, and also primary through intermediate units with children ages 5 through 11. In addition to the family units, there are interest centers in science, health, physical education, art, music, library and material resources, social studies, and educational technology. Each center is staffed by a certified teacher, along with a teacher's aide and highly competent resource persons from the community. The interest center staff is available to any child who wants to spend some time in that center.

The *family room* teachers are primarily responsible for basic instruction in language arts and number skills. They individualize instruction and keep records of each pupil's progress in the major subject area. Preparation of a single lesson or assignment for use with the entire group is unlikely. Among the innovations introduced is the use of "adjunct" faculty members. These are talented though noncertified teachers from the community, who make a great contribution to the educational program.

The family room teachers work in a cooperative relationship with all staff members and diagnose and prescribe for the individual needs of the pupils. They have responsibility for individual and group pupil planning and guidance. The family room teachers arrange for parent conferences to discuss and evaluate individual pupil growth and progress. At a conference, materials related to a child's work or social development are discussed with the parent. The family room teachers may also arrange for other specialists to be involved.

General Behavioral Objectives

The general behavioral objectives of the World of Inquiry School have been outlined as follows:

The child will demonstrate skills in:

A. Effectively using and caring for instructional resources and media.
B. Self-direction and self-discipline within a free environment.
C. Reading, writing, and arithmetic on standardized tests.
D. Knowledge, thinking, and understanding in areas and in ways specified by the teaching staff.
E. Inquiry by
   defining and selecting areas of interest;
   successfully completing some small tasks within these areas;
   devising his own strategies for solving problems;
   testing his hypotheses against reality;
   experimenting and trying new approaches to reach a desired goal;
   applying acquired skills to the solution of new problems, and discovering new ways to apply acquired skills.

The child will demonstrate an attitude of:

A. Interest in learning by
high attendance records;
participating in an increasing variety of experiences and content areas;
continuously progressing in skill development;
carrying on his learning activities outside of school.

B. Love for himself by
accepting and freely expressing emotions in socially acceptable ways;
resolving and/or coping with certain frustrations and difficulties;
seeking help when necessary;
attempting tasks beyond his immediate ability but not beyond his possible reach;
independently selecting and rejecting experiences as part of his learning activity.

C. Love for others by
working with and aiding others regardless of differences;
meeting, seeing, and interacting with persons in the community;
seeking information and experiences related to other cultures;
listening to and utilizing the ideas of others.

The teacher will enable the child to achieve the objectives
by providing a variety of experiences and a free environment;
by diagnosing his needs and achievements and suggesting alternate activities;
by interacting positively with the child, the parents, and the community; explaining and assisting the individual to understand our program.

These general objectives are refined and applied to specific areas, as will be discussed below.

Instructional Program

Children move freely throughout the school, from family room to interest areas and back again, both individually and in groups, to participate in a variety of activities. The behavioral objectives of the various interest areas are as follows:

Art interest area

The objectives of the art program are as follows:

To stimulate through art an appetite for creativity as an enriching, integral part of the life of every human being.

To recognize that art on the elementary school level primarily provides opportunities for independent thinking and that the end product is only secondary.

To promote the sense of freedom with which every young child participates in art—unless stifled by the restrictive influences of adults, engendered by a lack of understanding of the child's point of view.

To encourage potentially artistic students to work in-depth in the areas of their selection.

To develop sensitive consumers of art.

Technology interest area

The objectives of the program are as follows:

Pupils are acquainted with a variety of raw products, processes, tools, and materials, thereby building an appreciation for the skill, ingenuity, patience, and time required to produce a finished product.

Pupils are given an objective media for expressing purposeful ideas and helped to discover and to develop natural abilities.

Pupils are placed in a natural social situation through which certain character traits can be observed and developed.

Pupils are provided with worthwhile manipulative activities.

The pupils are able to work on additional projects of their own choice in any of the following areas:

woodworking	graphic arts	photography
ceramics	plastics	power
metals	electricity	welding

The prerequisite for individual projects is that each pupil should have a plan before attempting a project in any area of the shop.

The classroom teacher utilizes technology in order to:

add dimension to learning situations.

stimulate purposeful reading and accurate observation and encourage individual and group research.

add variety and interest to classwork.

provide an opportunity to apply principles of construction and design and to develop and encourage creativity.

provide additional channels to retention.

Health interest area

The nurse-teacher:

provides first aid if necessary in case of accident or emergency.

provides services to teachers, recognizing health problems which may affect learning, socialization, etc.

work with parents concerning children's health needs at all levels.

works with children's discussion groups, centered around their interests, inquiries, and questions concerning their full health.

provides materials, books, films, etc., so that children may become concerned about good health and will be better able to become more responsible for their health needs.

Social studies program

Social studies is the study of people and their interaction. It includes what is often divided into sociology, economics, geography, psychology, anthropology, government, history, and civics. The social studies program is designed to prepare students to meet in a responsible manner the challenges of an increasingly urban and culturally diverse environment. Since students are constantly engaged in social interaction, social learning takes place continually in all parts of the school. All family unit groups spend some time working with social studies skills and concepts.

Individuals and groups come to the Social Studies Interest Area to explore particular topics and activities. While this room serves as a base, most of the group activities take place elsewhere in the school (particularly the library and conference room), and on field trips in the Rochester community. Community resources are used extensively in an effort to be where the action is.

Social studies activities emphasize observation, organization of information, recognition of relationships (interdependence, casualty, etc.), generalization, application of generalizations, map skills, research skills, basic knowledge of concepts and facts, value clarification, appreciation of cultural diversity, and understanding of motivation of self and others. Basic concepts and skills are developed.

Science program

The science program involves the family room as well as the interest center. The family room is the place where the interest should initiate. The science interest center serves as a supplement to the learning that takes place in the family room. Units have been taught in the family room on such topics as earthworms, batteries and bulbs, mold gardens, and kitchen physics. Each child is equipped with his own materials. Units provide instant success for children and feedback for teachers to evaluate and coordinate the efforts of each individual child. They are indeed a far cry from the traditional lecture-book oriented science materials. They also function as a springboard to participation in the science interest center, a resource center where children can come and continue their classroom experiences, delve into previous work in depth, or explore new areas using more sophisticated equipment.

The science interest center differs markedly from the ordinary science room in a traditional school. It has a non-regimented atmosphere in which very few or very many children may be working at any one time and in which students representing the entire spectrum of age may be working together at any one time. The physical layout of the center may vary from week to week depending on its utilization. At present it is broken up into several centers, which include the conference center, the zoo, the physics center, and the botany-geology center.

As children enter the science lab on a non-scheduled basis, they are free to experiment in any one of these centers, and they are only limited by the materials available in the room at the time they wish to work there. More generally, the role of science is less to train young children to function as scientists than to open up ways of getting at information and solving problems in all other aspects of their learning.

Racial Attitudes in the School

The school has a Resource Associate in Intercultural Understanding whose primary function is to provide opportunity for interaction to improve racial attitudes on the part of whites and non-whites. A second function is to provide opportunities for interaction and activities which will improve the students' self-images. The resource associate does this by working with children directly and with the staff.

Positive and accepting racial attitudes are an established fact at the World of Inquiry School. In questionnaires returned by parents, not one person indicated anything but positive feelings toward integration. Some sample excerpts indicate the general feelings expressed:

Parents of 11-year-old: As a family group we have always been committed to integration. We like the World of Inquiry School set-up, because every youngster comes to the school on an equal basis and the school is not a home base for any particular group. Although I consider our home environment excellent for understanding of all people, I do believe the school environment played a very important part in helping my child come to her own conclusion!
Parents of 10-year-old: Although we are in favor of integration, it was not a major reason for sending our son to this school. He had been in one of the receiving schools under the open enrollment plan, so I guess we felt he was in an integrated school. However, this is so completely different and so very much better. The friendships formed at this school are completely natural because there are no neighborhood cliques. Also the children see and know an integrated staff. My child has been involved in discussions of civil rights and ghetto problems and has learned much more than he would have discussing these areas with an "all-white" group.
Parents of 7-year-old: We feel that every school in the country should be integrated so that all our students can learn to live in a multi-racial world.
8-year-old: Being in for the second year, I have not given much thought to this aspect of the school in quite some time. It seems the natural and only way.

The Community Resources Council

The Community Resources Council involves both people and things. Any person or organization who wishes to make a contribution to the educational experience of pupils may become a member. Some contribute money, some talent, some materials, and some psychic support. They are persons and organizations in the community upon whom one can depend for the support needed to carry out this educational program.

Acceptance and Success of the World of Inquiry School

All of the available evidence clearly indicates that the World of Inquiry School is one of the innovative programs that should be made a permanent part of the school system. Faculty members, aides, parents, children, and the administrative staff—everyone who is directly involved with the school—have expressed strong support for its continuance. This strong support is reflected in these statements by parents:

—Our child has always looked forward to school. His kindergarten experience last year was very happy. He was delighted to be going to a new school and could hardly wait for that first bus trip. He has anticipated each day just as eagerly as the first, and we are amazed that his enthusiasm has remained so high. He sets his alarm clock faithfully every evening and gets up each morning before the rest of us are awake. He is ready for school an hour and a half before his bus arrives. Not once have we had to urge him to prepare for school. He comes home with a detailed account of his day and has obviously learned a great many things.

—The World of Inquiry School has opened up a whole new life for our children. Instead of the usual Monday morning blues, the children get up eager for school. The one most important overall attitude of both children is the sense of freedom they both experience and express. Another predominant attitude is the sense the children seem to have that the teachers are co-workers and people to be enjoyed, rather than the glowering authority figure which teachers had seemed to be to them before.

—In summary, I should like to say that Dan is full of the spirit of inquiry and joy in life and learning, and if the school can preserve this through grade school, his father and I shall consider this a precious thing indeed.

—My husband and I can see a big improvement in our daughter since she has been attending the School of Inquiry. Her attitude toward school is changing and she isn't as nervous as she was at the other school. We can see that she is taking an interest in school again. We are happy about the whole situation.

—The problem we had with Sally was her dislike of school. She got good grades, was liked by fellow students and teachers, yet each morning she protested going to school. When I read of the World of Inquiry School I felt this might be the answer for Sally. Perhaps there was too much regimentation and not enough stimulation in regular school. Fortunately, this proved true. Since Sally has been in the World of Inquiry School, she is very content. When I asked her if she wanted to return to No. X School, she said, "Never, never, never!"

The following is a typical statement from a teacher:

> The World of Inquiry School is attempting to produce children who can control their environment. The school encourages children to make their own experiments . . . . It is my belief that only in this manner can people be produced who have had the experience that will enable them to deal with the world as it appears to them. Such people, I believe, will be stronger and more capable of controlling their lives . . . . The course of action which I follow sometimes appears erratic, chaotic, and sometimes pointless. If so, it is because that is the nature of the world.

This unanimity is encouraging and refreshing because it manifests itself at a time when division and discord seem to be the main responses to innovation.

The waiting list of pupils for the World of Inquiry School continues to grow, and each addition can be considered a substantive endorsement of the major goal of Project UNIQUE—quality integrated urban-suburban education. The school's neighborhood is metropolitan Rochester, but it is located in the inner city. Externally the building is old; but internally it is new and houses an educational program that could well be the educational prototype for the future.

Standardized test scores reveal a spread along the entire achievement gamut. Teachers also vary, some have had considerable experience prior to their assignment to the World of Inquiry School, while others are in their first year of teaching. Within this mass of contradictions some new, exciting, and promising educational methods are developing.

Responses to questionnaires mailed to parents in November revealed a high degree of pupil enthusiasm for the school program. The return on the first questionnaire was 94 per cent and almost all of the respondents, 98 per cent, indicated that their children go to school eagerly each day. For 51 per cent of the children this reflects a change from their attitude last year. A follow-up questionnaire in February was returned by 91 per cent and the responses were essentially the same.

The enthusiasm exhibited by the children both at home and at school attests to the esteem they have for the World of Inquiry School.

—He came home from school and said, "Y'know, Mom, I'm really worth something!" This from a child whose self-opinion was so scholastically and socially self-destructive at the end of the last school year that we had just about resigned ourselves to his being a high-school dropout (if he made it that long).

—My seven-year-old came home in a state of wonderment. "You know, in this school, if you don't understand, they don't scream at you. They sit down and talk to you and make you understand, and you work out some problems, and if you still don't understand, they still don't scream and nobody ever gets embarrassed." One delightful fact that this child can't get used to is that the pressure is off. She has heard it from the teachers, but she still doesn't believe it. Last year she was afraid to make a mistake.

—Our youngster has become increasingly self-confident over the year. She looks forward to every single day of school. She has developed different relationships with a variety of adults and is more comfortable with adults.

The following quotation from a parent expresses the impact of the World of Inquiry School on other schools in the district as well as on student opinion in some of the area colleges.

—Since the school has started, it has been very obvious that it is a success as far as our child is concerned, as she really enjoyed school and everything that is involved with it. Also we have noticed that the other city schools are beginning to plan programs like the School of Inquiry, so that proves that it is a tremendous school. We have even been involved with students . . . from nearby colleges, and they stated that the program at your school is fabulous and hope that all schools change their programs to the way your school is conducted.

Parent Involvement

Experimentation has not been restricted to the daily educational program. Parent involvement in the operation of the World of Inquiry School might conceivably be the prototype of an advisory committee that could be organized in every school district in the city. The primary concern of parents at the World of Inquiry School is quality integrated education. Because of the diversity of its student body, parent involvement is a vital factor in the development of a feeling of belonging and in de-emphasizing the tendency to consider the school as something totally removed from one's neighborhood. The World of Inquiry School has proved that references to "our school" need not be limited to schools located within the immediate area of the home. In the same way that many colleges have succeeded in obtaining strong support from alumni throughout the state and nation, on a more modest scale the World of Inquiry School, through parent involvement and interest, has succeeded in developing a strong sense of loyalty among those whom it serves.

An indication of the positive attitudes toward the school and education on the part of children and parents is the high percentage of parents who come to the school to act as tour guides, observe classes and special programs, and assist in many ways. There are a number of them who just want to be "a part of the excitement of the school" and appear frequently.

Urban-Suburban Transfer Program

The 1954 decision in the case of *Brown vs. Topeka Board of Education* was the triumphant climax of the campaign against segregation in public schools. In retrospect, the legal destruction of the myth of "separate but equal" schools proved to be merely the introduction to the problem of segregated education. Initially, public attention was primarily directed toward southern states, where dual educational systems were mandated by the legislatures. Prolonged litigation by state officials, generously financed by taxpayer funds, successfully delayed implementation of the court's decision and glacial speed was substituted for "deliberate speed."

Residents of northern urban centers, especially those who lived in the inner city, inspired and encouraged by the assaults against segregation in the South, began to examine the racial composition of the northern ghetto schools. The de facto segregation in the schools in the central city was, in most instances, almost as complete as the segregation that resulted from the de jure procedures in the South. In many instances, the educational differences between segregated inner-city schools and their counterparts in the outer city proved to be even more glaring than those encountered in states with dual educational structures.

Pupil achievement, teacher turnover, physical facilities, and quality of faculty were some of the areas where major differences were easily and accurately identified. Bereft of political power, inner-city residents were ill-equipped to force the power structure to improve the quality of education in the ghetto schools. Since the political process had no real meaning to residents of the ghetto, they resorted to the same vehicle used in the South—the courts. On the basis of legal decisions by state courts that declared de facto segregation unconstitutional, the citizens demanded alterations in the traditional residence requirements that prevented children from attending schools outside their neighborhood.

If this restriction were removed, a variety of devices could be used, it was argued, to reduce segregation in the public schools. Many plans were being considered in Rochester in 1964 when the massive rioting erupted. The widespread destruction had a catalytic effect that hastened implementation of some of the proposals.

The racial statistics for schools in the United States and for those in Monroe County are depressingly similar. Almost 80 per cent of the white students in the United States attend schools that are more than 90 per cent white, and more than 54 per cent of all Negro students attend schools that are more than 90 per cent black. In Monroe County more than 95 per cent of the whites attend schools that have a black enrollment of less than 5 per cent, and 54 per cent of the Negroes are enrolled in schools where more than 70 per cent of the pupils are black. This high degree of racial imbalance is difficult to defend when one examines the population density of the county: no suburb is more than 15 miles from the center of Rochester. This proximity sharply reduces the logistical problems that are frequently associated with urban-suburban transfer programs.

There is little evidence to suggest that racial attitudes in Monroe County are basically different from those found in other areas. Despite the presence of small, isolated pockets of socially conscious citizens, the prevailing point of view seems to be to do nothing about segregated schools. The combined effect of the neighborhood school concept and established housing patterns is to prevent meaningful action in altering racial imbalance in either inner- or outer-city schools. This, in brief, was the environment that contributed directly to the creation of the Urban-Suburban Transfer program.

Toward Racial Balance

This program is based on the conviction that neither an all-white nor an all-black school can provide a realistic climate for children who are being educated for life in a pluralistic society. Unfortunately, that premise is held by a relatively small segment of the population. Affluent whites continue to move from the city to the suburbs, and their places are taken by impoverished blacks and poor whites from rural areas. The effects of this mass migration were, and still are, painfully obvious. Opportunities for pluralistic experiences are sharply decreased as the populations of communities became more homogenized. In an attempt to expand pluralism, the Urban-Suburban Transfer Program was created. It was supported by those who sought to breach the barriers that separated the poor from the affluent, black from white, and city from suburb. "Separate but equal" has proved in practice to be patently absurd, utterly fallacious, and grossly unequal.

Black ghetto schools are presently burdened with serious physical and educational deficiencies. They lack high quality academic performance. Teachers tend to expect less and students communicate their awareness of low expectancy by producing less. In suburban schools, the existence of racially isolated student bodies contributes increased polarization of racial groups. Segregated children are uncomfortable with members of a race with whom they have had either limited contact or no contact.

The objectives of the Urban-Suburban Transfer Program are as follows:

1. To implement and administer programs designed to reduce racial isolation within and outside the City School District of Rochester.
2. To improve the racial attitudes on the part of whites and nonwhites in the sending and receiving schools.
3. To prepare sending and receiving school staffs, children and parents for inter-school transfers.
4. To involve the non-public school in a program to reduce racial isolation.
5. To work with youth and student groups in their efforts to reduce racial isolation.

In 1969, there were 440 city pupils in 15 suburban public and non-public schools. "Non-public" includes parochial, Protestant denominational, and private non-sectarian schools. Within the City School District of Rochester, 1,807 pupils from 10 racially imbalanced schools were attending schools outside their neighborhood area. Although complete racial balance remains a distant goal there is no longer an all-white school nor an all-black school in the City School District.

In response to the criticism that only black children are transported to schools outside the neighborhoods, it is important to note that one inner-city school now has more than 200 white children from the outer city. All of them are transported to the inner city on a voluntary basis, and there are more than 100 white children on the waiting list for admission to this school. The success of this program illustrates how parents and school administrators can work together effectively when they are convinced that a program has merit.

Despite the fact that the percentage of participation is relatively small, there were 2,247 pupils involved in the transfer program and there are long lists of blacks and whites who want to participate. If funds were available, well over 3,000 pupils would be enrolled in transfer programs. Evaluation of any program designed to alter racial attitudes is likely to be at least hazardous. However there is evidence of increased interest in race relations in suburban communities with the program administrator having spoken by invitation to thousands of teachers, parents, and students at conferences, in churches, homes, and schools.

There are many factors that contribute to the success of the Urban-Suburban Transfer Program: (a) the enthusiasm of the leaders, (b) the dedication and interest exhibited by the parents of the children, and (c) a recognition of the need for extensive communication among all who are involved. Teachers, administrators, parents, and pupils in both sending and receiving schools need orientation to the program and continuous support and assistance. The physical transportation of pupils is merely the first, and frequently the easiest, step toward complete and unqualified acceptance.

Inclusion of non-public schools in the program has served to illustrate that racial isolation is a community problem. Acceptance of this extension of the previous limits of moral responsibility by the non-public schools has been encouraging. Although only 91 pupils from the inner city are presently enrolled in non-public suburban schools the departure from established practice is noteworthy.

The creation of SURE (Student Union for Racial Equality) demonstrates the diverse methods utilized by the Urban-Suburban

Transfer Program. This student group has addressed school boards, worked in concert with suburban human relations groups, provided speakers for school assemblies and youth groups, and worked cooperatively with high school and college students in the greater Rochester area.

Although the well publicized "generation gap" has frequently prevented or inhibited discussion between some segments of society, the Circle K Project at the State University at Geneseo proves that productive communication can occur. The Circle K students decided to recruit black applicants for admission to the college and extended invitations to a number of Rochester seniors to visit Geneseo for a weekend. The guests were encouraged to apply for admission and many did. As a result of this effort, the black enrollment more than doubled.

Initiating creative ideas and programs in the area of human relations and obtaining the necessary funds for implementation constitutes an important function of this component. Suburban Title I funds were combined with Title III appropriations from the city school district to finance the Suburban–Urban–Rural Enrichment program. The basic objective was to reduce racial prejudice through intensive development of skills in social awareness. This was accomplished by having junior high students from all of the areas (urban, suburban, and rural) participate in a summer program at Keuka College.

Academically the students began with studies in sketching, painting, printmaking, sculpture, choral singing, and Afro-American heritage. Recreation included field trips and sports. Social awareness was stimulated through discussion groups and weekly student government meetings. Many students spent their weekends in the homes of area residents. This provided another intercultural experience for farmers, teachers, businessmen, and ministers, as well as students.

The statistical evidence, both in terms of numbers involved and the results, strongly supports the urban-suburban experiment. During the 1965–66 school year, 30 inner-city pupils were attending two suburban schools, one private and the other public. The number increased to 146 pupils and four schools in 1966–67. Three new schools and 75 pupils were added in 1967–68. In September 1968, 15 suburban schools accepted 440 inner-city pupils, and in 1969–70 over 600 pupils from the inner city were enrolled in suburban schools. It is important to note that no school has dropped the program although there has been opposition in some communities.

Examination of the racial composition of many city schools reveals the same encouraging trends. In 1963–64, 495 pupils were being bused. The slight decline to 480 in 1964–65 was sharply altered the following year when 876 were transferred to outer-city schools. This number has increased steadily, and in 1969, 2,335 pupils were attending schools outside their neighborhood area.

Impact of the program on pupil achievement was evaluated by the Department of Planning and Research for the Rochester city school district and the summary report concluded that:

1. Negro pupils achieved better when in smaller classes almost completely Negro in enrollment than when in larger classes of this same composition.
2. Negro pupils achieved better when in larger classes that were integrated than when in small classes almost completely Negro in enrollment.
3. With the exception of one grade level, no difference was found between the achievement of those Negroes in integrated classes in an inner-city school and those in several outer-city schools.
4. The white children who voluntarily transferred into an inner-city school and those who remained in their neighborhood school achieved at the same level during the year.
5. Within the same school, Negro pupils achieved better when in integrated classes than when in classes almost completely Negro in enrollment.
6. Negro pupils who transferred out generally did as well as pupils who remained in classes almost completely Negro in their home school.

Personnel from the Brighton Central Schools, a suburban school district that accepted pupils in February, 1967, evaluated their program on several occasions. The summary statement of the 1968 report concluded that the program had succeeded in producing significant improvement in pupil achievement.

Seventy-six per cent of inner-city children are now scoring at the national average or above in reading as compared to 62 per cent in 1967. Sixty-seven per cent have achieved the national average in arithmetic as compared to 51 per cent in 1967.

The composite scores include results in other areas of study in addition to the two skill subjects of reading and arithmetic. Spelling and simple language skills (usage, capitalization, and punctuation) are included in the third-grade tests and work study skills at the fourth-grade level. Sixth-grade students take a complete battery including Social Studies and Science as well as language skills, reading, and vocabulary. Seventy-six per cent of inner-city students in 1968, as compared with 62 per cent in 1967, attained at least the national average in composite score.

Although some of the children made little or no improvement as measured by the standardized tests, the results of the group as a whole are indeed encouraging.

The Urban-Suburban Transfer Program is not a statistical exercise in which children become numbers and groups become totals. Our hope is to alter the present trend toward racial polarization by reducing racial imbalance in the schools. White racism is a formidable barrier to this goal, but there are encouraging signs that this can be overcome. West Irondequoit, a suburb adjacent to Rochester, is an illustration of what can be accomplished by people who are committed to racially balanced schools.

Originally, a school was considered racially imbalanced if its enrollment was more than 50 per cent black. Several members of the Board of Education in West Irondequoit discussed this criterion in an informal fashion while attending an educational conference. They concluded that a school that was 99 per cent white was just as much a victim of racial imbalance as one that was 99 per cent black. After careful review of the legal implications, with the advice and consent of the New York State Education Department and the approval of the boards of education in both communities, the pupil transfer was begun in September, 1965. Although the number was modest—only 24 pupils were involved—the breakthrough was crucial.

Initial reaction in the suburbs was exceedingly antagonistic. Opponents of the program made repeated allusions to the Board's "secrecy." They flatly refused to discuss the merits of the proposal and elected to concentrate their attack on the "method" used. This unwillingness to discuss the advantages and disadvantages of racial isolation for pupils in both West Irondequoit and the inner city permitted the inference that the emphasis on method was used to camouflage the racism that had surfaced. School Board elections after the adoption of the plan resulted in election of three members who campaigned on an anti-busing platform. This trend was partially reversed in March of 1969 when an aroused segment of the community responded to an attempt, by members of the Board, to terminate the program. As a result of strong community action and the active support of the Irondequoit Teachers Association, the motion to abolish was defeated. A majority of the Board voted to permit the 74 inner-city children to continue in the program and deferred action on a plan to add 25 new pupils in September, 1969.

Although it cannot be said that the entire community is now united in support of the Urban-Suburban Transfer Program, there is evidence of a sharp decrease in antagonism toward the program. APT (All Parents Together), a group of inner-city and suburban parents who are directly involved in the plan, deserves special recognition for its effectiveness in communication and its accomplishments in the area of human relations. Expansion of this kind of activity will contribute to the ultimate elimination of racial isolation throughout metropolitan Rochester.

In restructuring the Urban-Suburban Transfer Program consideration will be given to the possibility of having the program assume responsibility for human relations. The need for a human relations specialist has already been indicated by the Rochester Teachers Association and the State Education Department.

More time must be devoted to expanding the participation of non-public and parochial schools in the transfer program. There are many signs of interest, but staff assistance is needed to convert the interest into active involvement. Additional funds must be found to finance tuition and transportation costs. Acceptance of the program and its value are demonstrable facts, but implementation of plans for expansion requires both commitment and funds.

A variety of methods and techniques are needed to guarantee quality integrated education for all. Project UNIQUE has successfully demonstrated the effectiveness of a magnet school—The World of Inquiry School—and urban-suburban cooperation through its Urban-Suburban Transfer Program, but the task has only begun.

TRENDS AND DEVELOPMENTS IN STATE PROGRAMS FOR THE DISADVANTAGED

Irving Ratchik

Irving Ratchik details trends in the New York State Department of Education in developing programs for the disadvantaged. In the first five years of the Elementary and Secondary Education Act of 1965, New York State received over half a billion dollars under the provisions of Title I, ESEA. Ratchik observes a marked positive effect on the schools of the state. Planning for the disadvantaged can now be comprehensive and cohesive, extending from preschool experiences through higher education. Pupils in both public and non-public schools have benefited from such programs. Professional development of staff members has been enhanced through pre- and in-service programs. New instructional materials, personnel, and supportive services have been made possible. And schools have been brought into closer relationships with the communities they are supposed to serve.

Ratchik discusses fourteen areas which seem most significant to him in the development of programs for the disadvantaged. These include: increased accountability, comprehensive planning efforts, community participation and parental involvement in planning and program implementation, development of program planning budgeting systems, long-range planning for the redesigning of education, development of professional and paraprofessional personnel, racial desegregation and integration, development of curriculum and instructional materials, building of shared services programs on regional bases, intensive reading instruction programs, assistance with decentralization of school administration and decision-making, increased federal-state sharing of instructional costs, increased involvement of higher education institutions in programs for community planning and education, and research and dissemination of information concerning the disadvantaged.

Ratchik views education as a major force in the elimination of poverty and sees the State Education Department as a potent force in coordinating efforts toward providing equal educational opportunities for all.

Irving Ratchik is Assistant Commissioner of Education in the New York State Education Department.

TRENDS AND DEVELOPMENTS IN STATE PROGRAMS FOR THE DISADVANTAGED

Irving Ratchik

In the first five years since the Elementary and Secondary Education Act of 1965 was passed, New York State has received, under Title I of the Act, over half a billion dollars. These funds were given to the state for distribution through counties to school districts for special educational programs and services for educationally deprived children residing in pockets of poverty. Amendments to the Act under Public Laws 89-313 and 89-750 provided additional funds for state-operated and supported schools and for children who reside in institutions for neglected and delinquent children. In Title I, ESEA, Congress declared it to be the policy of the United States to provide financial assistance to local educational agencies serving areas with concentrations of children from low-income families in order to expand and improve their educational programs.

In general, Title I, ESEA, has had a marked positive effect on the schools of the state. In considering programs and services for educationally disadvantaged children and youth, new dimensions are possible, as reflected in the following observations:

1. Education of the disadvantaged can now be planned on a continuum beginning with preschool experiences and extending through elementary, secondary, and post-high school years.
2. Education in each school district became more cohesive, in that public and non-public schools were involved in the planning of programs and services for disadvantaged children. (This closeness gained an impetus from the New York State Pupil Evaluation Program, in which pupils in grades 1, 3, 6, and 9 in both public and non-public schools were given the same tests in order to establish baseline data.)
3. Direct immediate benefits were accorded pupils in both public and non-public schools. In the non-public schools, programs included a variety of special services, such as remedial,

therapeutic, welfare, health, and guidance and counseling services.

4. Supplemental special programs and services were made available to physically, mentally, and emotionally handicapped children.
5. Staff members became more cognizant of the learning characteristics of all pupils as they studied the nature and needs of the educationally disadvantaged.
6. Professional development of staff members was accelerated through opportunities for school districts to provide in-service education programs.
7. Schools were able to acquire desirable curriculum materials, personnel, and supportive services to assist the educationally disadvantaged with their learning experiences. This included both additional professionals and paraprofessionals.
8. Broader horizons for the educationally disadvantaged were made possible by cultural enrichment activities.
9. Staffs were brought into closer contact with parents through programs which focused greater attention upon the educationally disadvantaged.
10. Schools were brought into closer relationships with community agencies and higher education institutions in the planning, development, implementation, and evaluation of programs for the educationally disadvantaged.
11. In focusing upon the educationally disadvantaged, staff members acquired a deeper understanding of the community, including socioeconomic and cultural factors, and the community agencies and other resources.

Trends and Developments

Concerning trends and developments in state programs for the disadvantaged, the following fourteen areas, not necessarily in the order of importance, seem most significant:

1. *Increased Accountability.* Availability of financial resources has become tighter due to international and national commitments. Among increased financial resource allocations are those included for defense, education, space, and social services. These, coupled with a variable economy, as reflected by the rate of unemployment, stock market jitters, and the squeeze between higher taxes and the increased demand for funds, are causing many legislators and citizens to look more carefully at expenditures of all kinds. Expenditures for education are being reviewed and questions raised as to whether Title I, ESEA, has made its mark in terms of the funds given for its implementation.

Added to the general problems of the total funds available and demands for sharing of that money have been reports critical of the use of educational funds.

One report entitled *Title I of ESEA: Is It Helping Poor Children?* was issued by the Washington Research Project of the Southern Center for Studies in Public Policy and the NAACP Legal Defense and Educational Funds, Inc. (1969). That report criticized the expenditures of Title I, ESEA, funds and charged that several states had circumvented the primary purpose of the legislation and the appropriation of funds. As an outgrowth of this report and other criticisms, the U.S. Office of Education created an Urban Education Task Force with eleven sections to review different aspects of Title I, ESEA. Its report, *Urban School Crisis: The Problem and Solutions* (HEW Urban Education Task Force, 1970), contains a thorough, intensive analysis of urban education today. It provides information about financial crises, the urban schools, characteristics of the environment, education systems, the student, problems of evaluation, and the federal role in urban education (limits and obligations), and recommendations about future education programs, organization, and funding. It contains a wealth of information about urban education.

The foregoing indicates that there is and will be increased attention given to how educational funds are spent. A significant aspect of this accountability, aside from the fiscal auditing, is the requirement and demand for evaluation. Generally speaking, when asked whether a program has been "successful," the response is in terms of increase in academic achievement. If there has been a gain in reading, the program is successful; if there was no gain in reading, then the program is not as successful. Of course, evaluation is not as simple as this.

There are many factors which determine whether or not a child gains in academic achievement. One of the important variables, especially in the inner city, is mobility. Pre-test and post-test data mean very little with regard to mobility. Other items, such as health, preschool and cultural experiences, stability of the family, adequate diet, clothing, and shelter, are all related to a student's achievement in school. It has long been recognized that parental aspirations and attitudes toward themselves as well as toward their children provide a motivational matrix for children in the learning environment. It is also recognized that school is only one area of learning for a child: what he learns outside of school may be more meaningful to him and more motivational than what he learns in school. We also know from research that teachers' expectations, attitudes, and judgments have a real impact on children's learning and motivation. In the future, there will be increased emphasis on performance and behavioral objectives in evaluation; both the cognitive and affective domains must be interrelated in a unified approach to evaluation, especially in determining the effectiveness of programs for the disadvantaged.

2. *Comprehensive Planning.* In fiscal year 1970, New York State received $170,000,000 under Title I, ESEA, for over 700 districts and an additional $52,000,000 from the State Legislature for its Urban Education programs in the 32 selected cities that have special needs associated with poverty. Administration of the offices of Title I, ESEA, and Urban Education is the responsibility of an Assistant Commissioner whose task it is to bring about more comprehensive planning in programs for the disadvantaged. Conferences have been held with the 32 districts that receive both Title I, ESEA, and Urban Education funds. In addition to programs supported by these two sources of funds, a variety of other programs exists pertaining to the disadvantaged, funded by both the state and federal governments. Just as the Department of Education itself has aimed at comprehensive planning and coordination of programs for the disadvantaged, it has directed a similar effort in the school districts.

3. *Community Participation and Parental Involvement.* As an integral part of comprehensive planning at the local level, it is essential that there be community and parental involvement. In general, comprehensive planning should help bring about greater understanding of the nature and needs of the disadvantaged and the resources available in the planning, development, implementation, and evaluation of those programs. With that objective in mind, the Department is encouraging and requiring the use of local advisory committees. These committees are advisory to the Board of Education and consist of representatives of the schools, the community, various agencies, and parents of the disadvantaged. The function of a local advisory committee is to consider the totality of planning for the disadvantaged.

4. *Program Planning Budgeting System.* Within the last three years, the Department radically changed its method of budget preparation. In its desire to make budgeting more functional, it has instituted the Program Planning Budgeting System (PPBS). There is a PPBS program structure and a table of priorities, with a program organized around four key areas: (a) assisting institutions to overcome their financial crises; (b) equalizing educational opportunity; (c) developing educational manpower; and (d) system improvement, research, and demonstration. The PPBS is a method of determining program and budget planning in conjunction with objectives and the allocations of resources to implement them. Involved also is a study of needs for future years. Just as the Department itself is being geared for the PPBS, so school districts will be planning their programs and budgets in accordance with the functional objectives and priorities, and the

funds available to carry out these objectives. The Department itself is continually evaluating its role with regard to present needs and future directions.

5. *Project Redesign.* The Department of Education staff has listed 19 areas of major concern in education in the state. Three of these concerns which have been considered as having highest significance include: (a) New York City decentralization: (b) *Project Redesign;* and (c) reading. Others include environmental education, narcotics abuse, student activism, and increased funding.

As part of the planning effort, a Mission Task Force was formed to consider the mission of education and of the State Education Department for the future. A program Task Force was formed to consider program planning, development, implementation, and evaluation in meeting educational needs of the future. Out of the Program Task Force emerged the concept known as *Project Redesign.* Its primary purpose is to work with school districts and communities to enable them to consider the process of change; to assist them in determining the kinds of schools they believe will be essential to meet future needs within their community; and to consider how to effect change. As the Department organizes itself for *Project Redesign,* every unit is asked to indicate what inputs it can make to this effort. There have been training sessions with Department staff and consultants to consider the processes of change and how Department staff can assist local school administrators and staffs in understanding and implementing processes of change.

6. *Personnel Development.* A major concern in programs for the disadvantaged is the recruitment, training, and professional development of teachers, supportive staff, and paraprofessionals. Changes have occurred in certification procedures, and there will even be more changes in the future. Teaching performance will be an integral part of certification, with such performance judged less on what one learns in courses and more on how one acts in real-life situations. Greater emphasis will be given to the practical experiences that a perspective teacher has, especially in working with the disadvantaged. In the final analysis, it is the classroom teacher who motivates a child, and how a prospective teacher performs in a real-life situation will become more significant than what formal courses he has passed.

In addition to recruitment, intensified training of teachers, both pre-service and in-service, will emphasize understanding of disadvantagement. Especially pertinent will be the opportunities for teachers to develop professionally and to have the kinds of educational experiences essential in order to maximize the development of disadvantaged boys and girls. The use of paraprofessionals will be increased. One of the spin-offs of programs for the disadvantaged has been a greater understanding of how paraprofessionals can be used effectively. Not only were the paraprofessionals affected by coming into closer contact with students and adults, filling important roles as adult models, and increasing ethnic identification, but many were motivated to further their own education. This resulted in the development of career-ladder programs, where paraprofessionals had the opportunity to progress to higher levels in furthering their education and acquiring saleable skills. Greater understanding between the paraprofessionals and the professionals about their relationships has resulted in mutual benefits. New York State has modified its regulations concerning paraprofessionals so that it is now possible for them to give instruction under the tutelage and supervision of a certified teacher. (Heretofore, paraprofessionals could only engage in non-instructional activities.) In addition, there has been study of differentiated staffing patterns to determine how optimum use of personnel can be obtained.

7. *Racial Desegregation and Integration.* There will be continued emphasis upon racial desegregation and increased integration. Research and development nationally indicate that racial barriers have to be broken down; that an integrated society is a healthy society; and that an understanding of peoples and their aspirations, their needs, their hopes, and their accomplishments is essential in perpetuation of a democratic society. The Department has a racial balance fund that provides money for school districts to foster integration.

The Department is continually conscious of the need to effect integrative activities. In discussions on decentralization, it is argued that community control of local school districts with high concentrations of racial and ethnic groups would lead to separatism. Consequently, there would be less incentive for integration as compared with a press for quality education within the segregated or separatist community. Pragmatically, the basic prerogatives of the local school boards will determine whether open enrollment projects and other activities will be encouraged to foster integration. The Department firmly believes that an integrated educational experience is more beneficial for all groups; that the achievement of whites is not adversely affected, and the achievement of other ethnic and racial groups, especially blacks, is improved. We see a continued emphasis on the development of programs and supportive activities to desegregate the schools and foster integration.

8. *Curriculum Development and Instructional Activities.* Curriculum experiences must continually be evaluated in order to consider their relevancy in the education of the disadvantaged. The life styles of ethnic groups, the heritage, the contributions, and the impact of

present movements in establishing ethnic identifications, especially among the blacks and the Puerto Ricans, as well as the Indians, Mexican-Americans, and Chinese, must be incorporated in curriculum materials.

Several current developments bear watching. Increased use of technology is providing opportunities for individualized instruction. Examples are computer-aided instruction, teaching machines, dial-a-drill programs, talking typewriters, television, and recorders and cassettes. Developments such as the Parkway School in Philadelphia and the Texarkana performance contract concept will undoubtedly be replicated and tested. The Office of Economic Opportunity is now contracting with private companies to determine whether the business sector can improve education of the disadvantaged. The extended school year will be emphasized. Also, there is interest in examining the voucher plan, in which parents are given vouchers and have the opportunity to choose a public or private school for their child. In addition, there will be greater participation by pupils and teachers in decision-making affecting curriculum development and instructional activities.

9. *Shared Services.* In New York State, there is a network of regional centers funded under Title III of the Elementary and Secondary Education Act of 1965. The regional centers work with school districts within the counties. Also, for some time in New York State there have been Boards of Cooperative Educational Services (BOCES), which provide a vehicle for school districts to participate in shared services. The BOCES provide the kinds of services that school districts are not able to support individually on account of size. A school district can become a component member of a BOCES and participate in determination of the kinds of programs and services in which it would like to share. There has long been an emphasis on consolidation of small school districts, especially with the thought that it is more efficient and effective to have school districts of sufficient size to provide the necessary curriculum experiences and opportunities for students on a broader scale. The Department is considering ways of improving the intermediate administrative arrangements. Many activities and services carried out by BOCES and by the regional centers can be performed more effectively on these bases than by a local board.

10. *Reading.* The emphasis on reading is tied up with national and state efforts to erase illiteracy. The Department has a Task Force on Reading. Units in the Department have to indicate how their efforts can be related to this national priority and to the Task Force. Former Commissioner James Allen's *Right-to-Read Program* is an important aspect of Department efforts. Legislation has been proposed for dem-

onstration districts, although it has not yet been passed. Meanwhile, the majority of programs submitted for ESEA Title I funding concern reading.

The Department's Division of Research is developing an instructional objectives and test-item bank in reading. The Division of Research is also conducting an interpretative study in reading and developing a comprehensive achievement monitoring (CAM) capability for assessing the effectiveness of ESEA Title I reading programs.

11. *Decentralization.* The New York City decentralization took effect July 1, 1970. The Department formed a task force and appointed a coordinator for New York City decentralization, gearing itself to determine how to assist in the process, and what resources are available and what resources are needed. The basic concept of decentralization is that parents at the local community level should have control of the resources available for the education of their children and share responsibility for the decisions affecting them. It means the highest degree of community involvement and accountability at the local level. The decentralization processes in New York City could very well be a prototype for cities throughout the country.

Under the Urban Education funding, Community Education Centers (CEC) were founded to involve the school and the community at the local level. Although there were administrative problems in the establishment of the CEC's and conflicts about the role of advisory committees, the concept of involving parents and community agencies is clearly a desirable one and one which will continue to be emphasized.

The Department today is urban oriented. The Big Six, consisting of New York City, Buffalo, Syracuse, Rochester, Albany, and Yonkers, encompasses about 77 per cent of those who are economically disadvantaged and eligible under the programs in the state. From a total federal Title I, ESEA, allocation of $170,000,000, New York City alone receives approximately $117,000,000. From the state Urban Education fund of $52,000,000, New York City receives about $44,000,000. From both programs New York City receives approximately $161,000,000, almost 73 per cent of the total available.

12. *Increased Federal-State Sharing.* The cost of instructional services has gone up each year. Expenditures per pupil for purposes of Public Law 89-10 have risen from $833.40 for 1965–66 to $1,154.13 for 1968–69. At the same time, the number of school budgets that have been defeated within the last several years has increased. School budgets are one of the few areas where taxpayers can have a direct impact. When taxes over which taxpayers have no say are imposed, when the cost of living index is rising, when there is an upward trend of inflation and a decrease in the buying power of the dollar, the

taxpayer is able to give vent to his feelings in only a few ways, one of which is a negative vote on the school budget. As a result, although many individuals profess to want good education for their children, when the pocketbook is pinched, there is a tendency to rationalize why the school budget should not be passed. In order for programs to be carried out that provide equality of educational opportunity and in order to support essential services, money is required. There must be increased contributions on the part of the federal government and the state government toward helping local school districts with the cost of instruction. Local taxing power is considered by many to have reached its limit, and other sources of funds must be forthcoming in order to maintain a sound educational system. Federal-state sharing is more important than ever.

Funding, as well as future parameters of education, will be explored thoroughly in the state's new Commission on the Quality, Cost, and Financing of Education. One of the matters which will be considered is aid to non-public schools. In a recent statement, State Commissioner of Education Ewald Nyquist observed:

> Whatever the final resolution of this knotty problem, the solution must achieve accommodation of at least three principles: the right of every child to a good education; the right of every parent to provide for the religious instruction of his child; the necessity of preserving and strengthening the public school system.

13. *Increased Involvement of Higher Education Facilities.* An important consideration in planning for the disadvantaged is planning on all levels. Consideration must be given to education for the disadvantaged not only in preschool experiences, but also in all levels beyond. Heretofore, education terminated for most students with high school. With the demands of an industrial technology and changing society, the individual has an opportunity and responsibility for life-long learning. The transition between secondary school and the world of work must become smoother. The community colleges and other higher education institutions must become involved in community planning and service. This is especially important in programs for the disadvantaged.

14. *Research and Dissemination.* Pervading all of these areas is the need for carrying out research and disseminating the results of the research. For example, if it is indicated that preschool education is basic to the initial phase of education of the disadvantaged, then such findings must be disseminated on a basis for planning. Information about prototypes and exemplary models should be disseminated for the purpose of replication in order that desirable projects and activities

can be considered by other school districts. There will be much emphasis on the practical aspects of research and how research findings can be implemented more effectively in the classroom. Also, there will be greater emphasis on communicating what works and the factors involved in the programs that make them work.

In summary, the preceding fourteen items are related significantly to education of the disadvantaged. Education is a major force in the elimination of poverty and the Department has given its highest priority to emphasizing equal educational opportunity for all children and youth in the State of New York.

References

HEW Urban Education Task Force. *Urban School Crisis: The Problem and Solutions.* Washington, D.C.: National School Public Relations Association, 1970.

Washington Research Project and the NAACP Legal Defense and Educational Fund, Inc. *Title I of ESEA: Is It Helping Poor Children?* Washington, D.C.: Washington Research Project, 1969.

Edward F. Carpenter sets forth the philosophy and program of Harlem Prep, an unusual secondary school located in Central Harlem in New York City. The school was created for "boys and girls between the ages of 16 and 21 who have dropped out of school and who, in the opinion of the administration, can be motivated to complete secondary education. . . ." Thus, the school was designed as a second chance, or an alternate school, for youth who, for a variety of reasons, had dropped out of the city's high schools. The aim was not only to provide a secondary school diploma but "to develop liaison with a number of colleges eager and willing to accept such graduates."

Harlem Prep, in its short existence, has already found answers to three questions it posed for itself at the outset. It has demonstrated that capable dropouts can re-enter and complete a high school program—providing the program is not the conventional one. It has shown that such students can perform successfully in a college preparatory program and that they can achieve at an academic level required for admissions to accredited colleges.

HARLEM PREP: AN ALTERNATE SYSTEM OF EDUCATION

Edward F. Carpenter

Carpenter describes the development of what he calls "a cycle-breaking system," temporary in duration, aimed at solving specific problems, flexible, and adaptable. Student, parent, and community are all involved in decision-making. The "courses" at Harlem Prep carry both traditional and non-traditional labels. It is an open school with a free and easy flow of activity.

The average student attends the Prep for only one year, although some stay as long as two years. Once having graduated from Harlem Prep and gone to college, the students continue their strong ties with the school, receiving support and counsel as needed.

The Prep is a private school, charging no tuition and receiving all its financial support from private sources—industry and foundations. It is planned as a five-year demonstration. Harlem Prep is well on the way to providing a model for an alternate system for the poor and politically powerless groups.

Edward Carpenter is the Headmaster of Harlem Prep.

HARLEM PREP: AN ALTERNATE SYSTEM OF EDUCATION

Edward F. Carpenter

The chief idols in the desecrated temple of mankind are none other than the triple gods of nationalism, racism, and communism, at whose altars governments and peoples, whether democratic or totalitarian, at peace or at war, of the East or of the West, Christian or Islamic, are in various forms and in different degrees now worshiping. Their high priests are the politicians and the worldly-wise, the so-called sages of the age; their sacrifice, the flesh and blood of slaughtered multitudes; their incantations, out-worn shibboleths and insidious and irrelevant formulas; their incense, the smoke of anguish that ascends from the lacerated hearts of the bereaved, the maimed, and the homeless.

The world has shrunk to the size of a plane ticket. What youth is taught, how they are taught, under what circumstances they are taught, and the directions we encourage them to take will determine the kind of international community that emerges. The purpose of man is to contribute to an ever advancing civilization. The educator's prime function today is to build up a regenerated humanity and to establish a functionally united world. To implement these goals, education is essential.

There are few options for "making it" in the ghetto. The line between success and failure is spidery thin. Success and education have not been seen as synonymous for youth in the ghetto. Indeed, for many black youths, if "education" has any synonyms, they are "pain," "rejection," "debasement," "alienation," and "failure." As Kenneth Clark (1965) has said:

"The dark ghetto's invisible walls have been erected by the white society, by those who have power, both to confine those who have no power and to perpetuate their powerlessness. The dark ghettos are social, political, educational, and—above all—economic colonies. Their inhabitants are subject peoples, victims of the greed, cruelty, insensitivity, guilt, and fear of their masters." (p. 11)

Harlem Prep was created to break this cycle.

Harlem Prep Is Born

Appalled by the increasing rate of dropouts of Harlem youths, the then executive director of the New York Urban League, Dr. Eugene Callender, met in the spring of 1967 with the administration of Manhattanville College to develop plans for an alternate system of education for these youths. Since there was no secondary school in Central Harlem, it was essential that the new school be located there. It was also in the late spring of 1967 that the writer and an assistant to the principal were employed. They were charged by the Board of Trustees to develop and implement an educational program that would reverse the old pattern of student disinterest. Further, they had the tasks of locating a temporary school plant, interviewing and contracting for staff, obtaining state accreditation, interviewing and enrolling students, purchasing supplies, developing a budget, and obtaining funds.

Harlem Prep received its first students (49) on October 2, 1967. The school was then located in the 369th Regiment Armory. Our facilities consisted of one auditorium, located in the basement, and two classrooms and office space on the second floor. We lived in the stolid, stark, and cavernous armory for one year. We moved to our permanent home, a renovated supermarket, in September, 1968. The lack of funds to purchase books and educational equipment, although frustrating, proved to be a boon. The faculty and students learned to consult with one another and developed a curriculum that was flexible and exciting. On July 28, 1967, the Board of Regents of the State of New York granted a three-year provisional charter to Harlem Preparatory School for the following purpose:

> To establish, conduct, operate and maintain a non-sectarian, private college preparatory school for boys and girls between the ages of 16 and 21 who have dropped out of school and who, in the opinion of the administration of the school, can be motivated to complete secondary education, to provide such education for such boys and girls and to develop liaison with a number of colleges eager and willing to accept such graduates.

Thus, another task of the school was to attempt to make institutional change in colleges and universities which had never accepted applicants with such spotty academic records.

As headmaster of the Prep, the writer was particularly concerned that the underlying philosophy of the school provide for the maximum intellectual, emotional, and social growth of student and teacher alike. Considering the deep social pathology of the community and of the world, the educator must be concerned with fostering concepts of world citizenship. He must point out the dangers of super-nationalism and over-concern with self, materialism, and racism. The philosophy of the Prep can be expressed by these three principles, from a talk by Abdu'l-Baha in 1920:

First: The whole-hearted service to the cause of education, the unfolding of the mysteries of nature, the extension of the boundaries of science, the elimination of the causes of ignorance and social evils, a standard universal system of instruction, and the diffusion of the lights of knowledge and reality.
Second: Service to the cause of morality, raising the moral tone of the students, inspiring them with the sublimest ethical ideals, teaching them altruism, inculcating in their lives the beauty of holiness and the excellency of virtue, and animating them with the graces and perfections of the religion of God.
Third: Service to the oneness of humanity; so that each student may consciously realize that he is a brother to all mankind, irrespective of religion or race. The thoughts of universal peace must be instilled in the minds of all the scholars, in order that they may become the armies of peace, the real servants of the body politic—the world. God is the Father of all. Mankind are His children. This globe is one home. Nations are members of one family. The mothers in their homes, the teachers in the schools, the professors in the colleges, the presidents in the universities, must teach these ideals to the young from the cradle to maturity.

The principles strongly determine the type of physical plant, organization structure, faculty selection, and curriculum. The Prep transformed a depersonalized supermarket into a school that is the extension of the aspirations of the community. No walls have been erected in the 10,000-square-foot area. Communication between students and between groups is stimulated. The rationale for this arrangement is based upon the theory that "ego organization must articulate ideas, objects and potential action—or, rather, their representations—into a coherent whole" (Cumming and Cumming, 1966). Then again, since many students from depressed areas are deprived of the experience of controlling their own life space, they must learn that flux is a normal state of human beings. The continual, smooth rapprochement between the individual and his environment is adaptation. We felt it highly desirable to stimulate the students by placing them in this situation. We believed that a healthful milieu would foster healthy individuals.

The school attempted to answer these questions:

Can capable dropouts re-enter and complete high school?
Can they perform successfully in a college preparatory program?

Can they achieve at such an academic level as to be admitted to college?

Individual interviews with these youth indicated that they had dropped out of traditional school systems for various reasons: they were lost among great numbers of students in classes in which teachers did not even know their names; the courses they studied were not related to their daily lives; they were powerless to make decisions affecting what was taught, who taught it, or how it was taught; they were forced continually to conform to the demands of the school system, a system which they felt was based upon values they did not hold. The writer felt that the most effective organization to serve students with these experiences was a cycle-breaking system.

Developing a Cycle-Breaking System

The cycle-breaking system, unlike the traditional one, does not seek to perpetuate itself. It is temporary in duration, directed toward solving specific problems, adaptable to internal and external stress, and capable of rendering service where needed. These features make it a non-bureaucratic system in which the needs of the individual are paramount. Furthermore, it can involve the student, parent, and community in the decision-making process and meet the needs which the traditional system has not met (Katz and Kahn, 1966).

Since the writer believes that the earth is but one country and all men are its citizens, he felt that the faculty of the Prep should reflect the spectrum of races and religions. Therefore, he recruited teachers with these diversities. At the Prep, Jew, Catholic, Protestant, Buddhist, Muslim, and Bahá'í faced the challenge of achieving unity from diversity.

Professional experience of the faculty ranged from twenty years' teaching experience to no experience at all. The teachers came from colleges, high schools, and the community, and their educational backgrounds ranged from the doctoral degree to undergraduate status. They were drawn together by the common belief that our students could achieve and contribute to the community and world. The prime requisite for a successful teacher at the Prep is the ability to be flexible in adapting subject matter and techniques of teaching to the changing interests and needs of the students. The teacher must possess the strength of personality to accept open criticism, incisive questions, and strong student challenge as part of the teaching-learning process.

The orientation of the curriculum was toward the development of skills and knowledge, stimulation of curiosity, development of individual research techniques, development of criteria for evaluation of self and others, and development of tolerance to accept the evaluation and criticism of others. Methodologically, an interdisciplinary approach was utilized in all subject areas. Traditional subjects were taught with a view toward bridging the gap between theory and its application to current social problems. Therefore, knowledge and skills learned were immediately used in solving problems within the subject area. This provided for individual assignments and individual research.

Courses at the Prep have traditional as well as non-traditional labels: in mathematics, integrated algebra and geometry, analytic geometry, trigonometry, and the calculus; in English, writing skills, comparative literature, literature of Africa, semantics, mass media, creative writing, and literature of the black man; in history, African studies, Egyptology, European studies, American studies, comparative economics, contemporary history, comparative economics, and the United Nations and world government; in science, integrated biology, chemistry, and physics; also logic, ethics, speech, and Swahili.

The Prep as a Prototype

Harlem Prep is a prototype of the school of the future. The concept of the "one-room school," quite an old one, organized to unite all elements of the learning-teaching process into an organic whole, works for the Prep. Wall-to-wall carpeting and the acoustical ceiling soften abrasive sounds to a gentle hum. Chairs and tables, scientifically designed to accommodate the growing youth, lessen fatigue. Concrete walls painted in warm bright hues add to the atmosphere of excitement.

The openness of the school inspires openness in student and teacher. Dialogue flows easily, unhampered by shyness or suspicion. The teacher and student are involved with the total activity of the school—not in the sense of distraction—but in the sense of belonging.

Still concerned with the spiritual development of our students, we never hesitate to discuss social, ethical, and moral problems. The principal of consultation is used: this is a method whereby strong anger or passion is minimized. Once a statement is made, it is no longer the private property of the spokesman. It is animated—fixed—for the group to deal with dispassionately and with detachment. Such a method develops skills in the group process for solving problems.

Students attending Harlem Prep are representative of the political, religious, ideological, and ethnic character of the city's ghettos. Two-thirds of the student body always come from the street academies scattered throughout the five boroughs. We have black, Spanish-speaking, and white students enrolled. They are Catholics, Protestants, Jews,

Muslims and Bahá'ís. Five-Percenters, Nationalists, Garveyites, and militants study together at the Prep. The student population is as diverse as the faculty. The important theme here is that with such rich diversity we have unity.

Most students remain at the Prep for one year. This is partially the result of their leaving high school in the eleventh year. For the first group of students, the average reading score upon entering the Prep was 9.0. Now their average reading level is 11.0. The age range is from 16 to 21, with the average age 18. There were two exceptions in the first group: one of our students was 26 and one a grandmother 50-years old.

Most of the questions concerning capable dropouts re-entering and completing high school can be answered "Yes." The question of their successful completion of college preparatory courses can be answered "Yes." "Can they achieve at such an academic level as to be admitted to college?" can be answered "Yes." In June 1968, 35 out of 70 students were graduated from the Prep and admitted to college. In June 1969, with a student enrollment of 180, 75 students were graduated, and all 75 were admitted to colleges.

It is important to indicate that students at Harlem Prep are not overly concerned with materialism. They view education as a vehicle for obtaining skills and knowledges which can be used to help poor people better their social and economic lot. To instill the desire to serve, the school developed a tutorial program whereby Prep students served as reading and mathematic tutors in the elementary schools of the area. The young ladies used their weekends to visit infants, the aged, and the infirm who were confined for long periods in the hospitals. They read stories to the infants and played checkers with the adults. Their sole purpose for performing such service was to let the "forgotten" know that we at the Prep cared.

The initial investment for launching a program like Harlem Prep might appear to be costly. The cost for educating a student is $2,000, a figure derived from combining capital and operating expenses and dividing this sum by the number of students enrolled. However, with the completion of renovation and permanent installations, the projected per capita cost will approximate $1500. At present Harlem Prep receives no funds from local, state, or federal government agencies. All financial support comes from private funds. We hope that industry will see the financial value of supporting projects like Harlem Prep. The Prep was created to be a temporary system, not to perpetuate itself. Five years are needed to determine the percentage of students who remain and then graduate from college. The goal that our students return to the depressed areas to serve must also be tested. There are many arguments for industry's participation in solving the urban crises. It costs $10,000 to maintain a youth in jail for four years, but, on the average, it costs $4,000 to educate a youth in college for four years.

The Prep and Its Parents

One persistent myth concerning inner-city parents is their alleged lack of interest and participation in public school programs. It was only recently that "baby-sitting" services were offered in some schools so that a mother with children could visit the schools.

All too many of the Prep's students alluded to poor family relations. The claim that parents did not understand them was frequent. Through a series of parent-student conferences, mutual problems were discussed and a redefining of parent-child relations resulted. However, there was a more meaningful outcome of this program. The parents asked and received consent to establish an Adult Evening School, with the purpose of preparing parents and other adults to receive the academic diploma. The parents displayed ability to interview and employ teachers, develop a budget, work with the professional staff in curriculum development, and evaluate their own efforts. The Adult Evening School offers courses in modern mathematics, modern algebra, general science, physics, communication, French, investment, and Swahili. Some two hundred adults participated in this program.

Another myth that deters effective cooperation between inner-city parents and school administrations is the alleged inability of the parents to work with committees, make decisions, and implement programs. There are 23 members on the Board of Trustees of Harlem Prep. They include bank and college presidents, five of our parents, and one student representative. They are involved with the decision-making process concerning school policy, funding, employing, and disbursing of funds.

The Prep as an Alternative

Traditionally, the vehicle for remedying inequities of poverty and political powerlessness was education. The same channel has not been available to the blacks and the poor. An alternate system must be made available to these people. Harlem Prep and its program could be a partial solution. Population mobility, underachievement, cultural differences, and irrelevant testing tools for the youngster from the ghetto will probably exist for some time. In no way should they be allowed to prevent the creation and implementation of programs designed to eradicate the causes.

The three key factors that seem to make for the success of the

Prep are its philosophy, program, and faculty. The philosophy provides the skeleton, the program the substance, and the faculty the thrust. If pressed to isolate the single major factor, the writer must select the philosophy. The Harlem Prep philosophy upholds the unity of God, recognizes the unity of his Prophets, and inculcates the principle of the oneness and wholeness of the entire human race. It is these factors that enable so diverse a school to achieve harmony and unity.

References

Clark, K. B. *Dark Ghetto: Dilemmas of Social Power.* New York: Harper and Row, 1965.

Cumming, J. and E. Cumming. *Ego and Milieu.* New York: Atherton Press, 1966.

Katz, D. and R. L. Kahn. *The Social Psychology of Organization.* New York: John Wiley and Sons, 1966.

Preston Wilcox discusses the significance of community control of schools as a social movement and its meaning for black development. Viewing the existing system as one of white domination and containment, Wilcox analyzes how the shift in control and decision-making can alter the system so that it will be more responsive to the needs of minority group children. The system, he feels, must be drastically altered, for it presently functions to produce educational genocide for minority group children. He draws on the experiences of the activists in the Harlem Intermediate School 201 struggle for community control.

Wilcox sets forth five requisites for change in the situation: (a) the stance of articulate spokesman rather than aggrieved complainant had to be taken; (b) the pursuit of the values and definitions of the white oppressors had to be rejected; (c) black and Puerto Rican youth had to be accepted and counted as important; (d) the ability to sustain and endure crises had to be cultivated; and (e) the concept of education and the function of the school had to be redefined. The issue of integration-segregation, as he sees it, is irrelevant, since both conditions are designed to insure that the white majority maintains power and control. Thus, the black community must build and pursue its own agenda.

SCHOOL COMMUNITY CONTROL AS A SOCIAL MOVEMENT

Preston Wilcox

The history of the black man's existence in America requires, as Wilcox sees it, that they "utilize their energies in confronting themselves *as a means to foster their own liberation." The school community control movement can only be understood as the most appropriate setting for this confrontation. The struggle itself, as it has grown and escalated, has become a significant educational force for minority groups. Minorities have learned that their interests are best served not simply by upward mobility but by bringing about meaningful social change.*

Wilcox describes several patterns which have emerged from the community control movement. One pattern involves the demise of the union movement within the black community and the growth of alliance with other black community groups. Even where there are multiracial organizations, black caucuses operate within them. A second pattern has been the increase of physically/fiscally and psychologically independent black educational institutions from preschool through college. A third pattern has moved toward control of other institutions and agencies—health centers, hospitals, anti-poverty programs, and urban renewal. Still another pattern involves the growth of black studies and humanization of the curricula. A fifth pattern is aimed at developing knowledge about education generally and black people specifically. The movement has aimed at creating more humane schools, defining new roles for students, staff, and citizens.

Efforts to involve parent and community leaders in the selection and evaluation of teachers and administrators (i.e., accountability to the community) have resulted in growth of militancy among teacher organizations. The entire system of credentialing—tests, admissions criteria, certification, etc.—has come under attack as minority groups have come to see it as a means for white control.

White resistance to community control is seen by Wilcox as a means of unifying previously diverse minority groups. Some whites have even seen their own salvation emerging from the struggle. Wilcox concludes that the most powerful lesson to be learned from the community control movement has general meaning for all education and for society in general—that individual lives are worth living and dying for. As he puts it, "Remember, everybody is somebody."

Preston Wilcox is President of Afram Associates, Inc.

SCHOOL COMMUNITY CONTROL AS A SOCIAL MOVEMENT*

Preston Wilcox

The two people whom I will always credit with having initiated the first move in the history of this country for community control of the schools were black females—E. Babette Edwards and Helen A. Testamark. My recollection is that they were the "green thumbs" who nurtured and engineered the initial thrust at Harlem's I.S. (Intermediate School) 201. They were, and they still remain, suspicious of professional expertise and competence; they both have steel-trap minds capable of dealing with any school official—from Board presidents to custodial staff; and they are deeply committed to the education of minority group children. As a kind of participant-theoretician at that stage of the struggle, I was convinced by their inability to be bought off or compromised of their commitment to build and sustain a movement. Despite the fact that Helen A. Testamark and E. Babette Edwards are now involved in different aspects of the struggle, they remain committed to this important social movement.

As I know and understand them, neither ever believed that the New York City Board of Education ever had any intention or capability to respond to minority group children as human beings. Neither ever believed that the vast majority of teachers are willing to risk themselves on behalf of their charges; nor do they believe it now. Both still refute the language of oppression, such as "culturally deprived," "disadvantaged," and all the code language used by the Establishment to prevent calling minorities "nigger." "Inner-city children," and "newcomers" are professional jargon for "niggers." They understood it all too well, and their ability to read this racist system as it really is gave them a decided advantage. They could not be

*This article is dedicated to Leonard "Pop" Covello, an Italian immigrant who became the first principal of East Harlem's Benjamin Franklin High School. As an early proponent of school community control, he earned the wrath of the New York City school system because he chose to involve the community in running the school. When he retired, he became an employee of the Commonwealth of Puerto Rico—and earned the wrath of the Italian community. He was an early proponent of English as a second language. He earned my respect because of the many ideas he shared with me. It was he who gave me the clues as to how an oppressed group could begin to manage its own destiny without identifying with their oppressors. He never did.

managed by a bureaucratic system whose continued existence depended heavily on blind compliance to its irrelevant rules and procedures.

Having been present at many of their encounters with the Board of Education, state officials, Negro Statesman, and other public officials, I observed their consummate skill in avoiding a response to such language of containment as the following:

"You cannot change an entire system by starting with one school."
"Don't you want a *qualified* principal instead of a black principal?"
"Even though you disagree with McGeorge Bundy, why don't you meet with him anyway?"
"We will support you *if* you agree to carry out steps (1) and (2) as outlined by us."
"Isn't that 'racism' in reverse?"
"If you get rid of Herman Ferguson, we will support you."
"Who do you represent?"

The question was not whether or not they wanted to become a part of the system. The question became: How could they alter the school system to make it work on behalf of minority group children? When that question was asked a righteous person, one who did not have a need to rationalize his own deprivation, there was but one alternative: to acquire the knowledge, skills, and insights to subvert the school system. Importantly, these two activists recognized several basic truths:

The materialistic "money on the mind" values of this society propel superordinates to expend their energies learning how to get subordinates to line up, how to "divide and conquer" them, and how to get them to adjust peacefully to an inhuman existence.
The reality of white institutional racism had rendered large numbers of white people incapable of making humane decisions about the lives of minorities.
Professionals had turned the school system into an employment playground; an arena for earning tenure for *not* doing the job they were being paid to perform.
Parents had been conditioned to delegate the responsibility for educating their children to a school system which systematically denied them a voice.
Large city boards of education have never been representative of the interests of the poor and of the minorities.
The inhumanness of a large school system is a prerequisite for its continued maintenance; it requires that its consumers subscribe to the same inhuman values.

The Requisites for Change

The requisites for change were based on avoiding becoming a participant in the integration-segregation argument, since both arguments were designed to maintain white control over minority group education and to build a minority group constituency for the white agenda. This was achieved by substituting the stance of an articulate spokesman for that of an aggrieved complainant. When the I.S. 201 activists began to maintain that one could be black or Puerto Rican *and successful,* it unsettled the minds of their oppressors. Such actions rendered white liberalism useless and the anti-blackness of the overt racists ineffective. White racists hate Blackness. The decision to perceive it as being beautiful was generated by Blacks.

A second requisite for change was to reject the pursuit of the values and the definitions of the oppressors. To have pursued them would have required that minorities utilize corporal punishment against their own kids and hate them as a way to win a response from the system. Recall that the services which are imported into minority group communities require a prior categorization of the ills and problems before appropriations are made. It is illegal to be black and human in this society. Helen and Babette chose to be labelled as being "illegal" by the N.Y.C. Board of Education. To be legitimized by that system is to be freed to produce drop-outs, drug addicts, criminals, and the like.

A third requisite for change was to begin to learn how to behave toward black and Puerto Rican youth as though they *counted* just because they existed. To become their advocates rather than their prosecutors was an important act in itself. To understand that their suffering was much more a factor of the system's negative definition of them than it was a factor of their own characters was also required. By any objective criteria, the system was stacked against them: it was organized to punish them, not reward them. This motive force has, perhaps, been the most propelling part of the movement. White America is slowly losing its ability to define minority group youth in a negative way in order to contain them. Such communities know now that they can survive. They are now opting for living or dying —in honor.

A fourth requisite for change was to incorporate an ability to sustain and endure crises. The uncertainty of life which had become a bane to the existence of oppressed minorities now became an asset. Establishment-types survive on order; oppressed peoples are masters at moving from crisis to crisis. A corollary to this phenomena was the development of a perception among minorities of themselves as being victims but not as being powerless. Those who define themselves as being powerless by definition, bestow power upon those in official positions. Those who define themselves as victims have an overwhelming need to manage their own de-victimization. In the same way that Nixon has become a victim of having achieved "the impossible dream," the victimized are learning how to succeed in guiding their own self-resurrections.

A fifth requisite for change was to redefine the function of the school and the concept of education. Professional and system control had been largely maintained by imposing their own definitions on the consumers. The consumers at I.S. 201 have sought to modify those definitions. The problem of police brutality, deteriorated housing, poor health, unemployment, inadequate welfare allowances, and drug addiction are increasingly being viewed as educational problems. Education is being perceived as a political act.

The white police system in such communities functions as "occupation troops" to protect outsiders from local residents. The brutalization of minority group residents is endemic to its functioning. The drug traffic is deliberately concentrated within such communities. It persists and expands because of police collusion. It has been said that one is either a part of the problem or a part of the solution and even that the solution is a part of the problem. That's the way it is with the drug problem. The high incidence of drug addiction is no accident. In several recent incidents, police informers utilized drugs as a means of framing the targets of their interests. Drug addiction is becoming a way to perpetuate genocide.

The inadequacy of the welfare allowance produces a nutritional problem of broad dimensions. Teachers as a group feel better about children who read; evidence suggests that they have little or no feeling about whether their children eat or not. It took the Black Panther Party to highlight the need for breakfast programs in this country. The Young Lords have picked it up. As their young charges eat, they are also having their heads put in the right place.

Housing conditions in such communities are both illegal and inhumane. Teachers don't visit homes largely because they will be confronted by their own lack of caring when they do so. If they really cared, the classroom system would become a social action system. The children would learn how to read the impersonality of this society as a requisite for *motivating themselves.*

The "Political" Aspects

The school community control movement cannot be fully understood unless put in the context of the totality of the black man's existence on white soil stolen from the Indians. The enslavement of black people, the systematic denial of their rights, and their history of oppression and subjugation have bestowed upon them a compelling need to utilize their energies in *confronting themselves* as a means to foster their own liberation. The Little Red School House was deliberately chosen as the site for the confrontation. The control of black minds by white America has been its foremost skill of oppression. Secondly, the school was an arena where the political, the economic, the physical, and the social could be combined into a single whole. Importantly, it lent itself to involvement of the family, and not just the student, as a part of a community. The school was actualized as the political instrument it has always been, except that now it would become a laboratory for black liberation, rather than black containment.

This movement has been defined and generated by minorities in this country. It is no accident in history that it began in the poorest section of the best known ghetto in the world. It is not an accident that an architectural palliative failed to anesthetize the subject community. It is no accident that the crisis has been sustained and the struggle escalated. The struggle has been the foremost educator.

Minorities have learned once and for all that their vested interests lie in meaningful social change—and not mere upward mobility. They have learned that their links to the Pan-African scene and to the Third World are deeply embedded in their abilities to refuse to acquire the skills and values that free them to oppress others. They have the most to gain by creating a pluralistic society. They have the most to gain from controlling and managing their own destinies. Their consummate skill in exercising power from a presumably powerless position is an additional asset.

Every black knows that white America does not believe that blacks will ever control their own schools. Whites feel so self-assured because they know that they have the biggest and most powerful weapons of destruction. It is a fact that whites have "guns on their mind," and blacks know it. What's more, whites have little compunction about turning their guns on their own. Witness Kent State and the "generals" who head up institutions of higher education. College presidents have become national guard "commanders" even as their students have tried to rid their campuses of the ROTC.

Blacks have learned that few whites have a vested interest in unloading the guns of other whites. They feel that they need to keep their guns in reserve in the same way that white liberals depend on white conservative support during crises and on the maintenance of white institutional racism during stable periods to maintain their status. The challenge for blacks, Chicanos, Indians, and Puerto Ricans has become that of liberating themselves without being forced to pick up a gun and precipitating its use by the white system. The school community control movement provided the first avenue for this approach.

Movement Patterns

The movement has exposed the "labor union" mentality of teacher associations in the up and in the down south. Any relationship between educational creativity and teacher organizations is strictly accidental. The position of the National Association for African-American Education is that black educators should give up membership within the AFT and the NEA and begin to act and behave as advocates for the students. This distaste for union membership is sure to deepen within minority group communities and to be replaced by *community unions,* designed to prevent fragmentation and to achieve operational unity. Parents, teachers, students, and community will organize to create a single viable political instrument. The increasing replacement of "interracial councils" in urban areas by Black Urban Coalitions is another case in point.

The demise of the union movement within the black community has been characterized by the growth in the number of all-black teacher organizations and their alliance with other community groups. This pattern has been escalated to the national level by a growing number of national black organizations and national black caucuses within multiracial national organizations.

A second pattern is the growth of independent black educational institutions from preschool through the college level. At least twenty such schools convened their first national meeting in Los Angeles in August 1970. These schools fall into two categories: *physically* independent and *psychologically* independent. Their common feature is their advocacy of minority group students. A similar move toward the establishment of independent educational institutions is alive in the white community. There is one difference: they are still toying with how to integrate. Their minority group counterparts are targeting in on how to educate for humanization.

A third pattern is the movement for control of police, of hospitals, of health centers, and of anesthetizing operations like Model Colonies, Negro Removal, and anti-depovertization programs. I suspect that the next major movement will be to control the prisons. Blacks are convinced that they can never be as cruel to their own as the white man has been. It's just that simple.

A fourth pattern has been that of escalating the movement to a national level. At least 47 cities in this country are engaged in finding new and more sophisticated ways of deceiving black students and communities. They are offering to "de-re-centralize" to mute the local struggles for community control. Afram's Action Library has a roster of 75 organizations—from coast to coast—which are actively advocating community control and/or decentralization. At least three states (New York, California, and Pennsylvania) have developed legislation leading to decentralization.

The Black Studies movement on college campuses is a direct response to the school community control movement. Recall that black students have not only demanded a humanization of the curricula, they have also sought autonomy, or a role in the selection of the staff and in the recruitment and admission of students. At Antioch College the students demanded black-controlled dormitories as legitimate educational instruments. The program was wiped out, not really because black students segregated themselves, but because they wanted to control the content and nature of their own separation. This movement, too, had its beginnings in the school community control movement.

A fifth pattern is the development of a new body of knowledge about education in general and black people in particular. Over one thousand articles have been published on the subject "community control/decentralization" since the movement began. A growing number of black scholars and white humanists are putting together bodies of knowledge which define the black condition in human terms. There are at least twelve centers of information about community control of schools which did not exist before the confrontation at I.S. 201.

The thrust toward learning how to create human institutions has also been propelled by this movement. New roles for principals, students, teachers, and parents are being articulated, transmitted, and carried out. The theme relates to an effort to rid schools of their oppressive, exploitative characteristics. Efforts are being undertaken to narrow the gap between the consumers and the producers and to assign specific powers and responsibilities to all of the actors. New techniques of conflict resolution are being developed and communities are developing the skills to solve their own problems without the intervention of outsiders. Recall that the black urban rebellions were cooled down by the blacks themselves, even though the guns of the National Guard were on the scene. Black people cared too much about each other to send each other to slaughter at the hands of the police.

The major dimension of the school community control movement is the problem it has provided for white people. White principals by the hundreds are being taught daily that they too have been miseducated. Most such principals now spend their time locked up in their offices trying to avoid being noticed. Ill-equipped teachers are trying to find new ways to explain their failures to teach. They can no longer complain of parental apathy when the school doors are being knocked down by the parents. They can no longer claim that black students do not want to learn when such students close down schools because teachers fail to teach them. They can no longer claim superior intelligence—despite Jensen and Shockley—when their so-called superior intelligences cannot be measured in terms of meaningful student achievement. Their "liberalisms" are going wanting for takers.

The growing militancy of teacher organizations can be said to be a direct consequence of the efforts at Ocean Hill–Brownsville and I.S. 201 to involve parent and community leaders in the selection and evaluation of teachers and administrators. The problem that bedevils minority group communities is their expanding recognition of their right to manage their own destinies.

Teachers are now more heavily involved in educational planning and community participation in the less-chance areas of the nation. It is both a requisite for survival and an educational imperative. Recall that it was the groups at I.S. 201, Two Bridges, and Ocean Hill–Brownsville who first considered that teachers be represented on policy-making boards.

Blacks are saying that the credentialing system, tenure as currently known, grades, IQ tests, admissions criteria, and the like are like "Mason-Dixon" lines in the minds of whites. Such "standards" are utilized to exclude, not include; to control, not liberate; to discipline, not develop self-reliance; to line up students, and not to help them not to need a line.

A raft of training programs have sprung up as a means to equip administrators and teachers to do their jobs. The thrust toward accountability in terms of performance, engineered by parent and community groups, has resulted in new learning opportunities for those who in the past insisted that it was the fault of the families and their children. Teacher training institutions will never be the same—if they survive.

White Resistance and Black Humanization

Interestingly enough, black communities need the resistance of the Establishment as a spur to get themselves together. The Establishment demonstrates daily that it does not believe in the constitution which it demands that minorities uphold. In addition, the thrust to control the schools with the black community is not perceived by blacks as an infringment upon white power. Rather, it is perceived as a non-negotiable expression of authentic black power. The control over institutions that serve one's community is a God-given right, as is the control over the internal relationships within one's community. Part of the confusion results from the differential perceptions of power and its uses. White communities struggle to gain the power to keep blacks out (neighborhood concept) and to be comfortably controlled by the system. Black communities are struggling *not* to be controlled by the system and to exclude no one. Part of the problem relates to the need of whites to control blacks as an end in itself, even if whites have to sacrifice their right to self-determination to do so.

Perhaps one of the most important learnings coming out of the movement is the recognition by a growing number of whites that their own salvation is inextricably tied to that of the oppressed masses. A *crisis coalition* that developed during the height of the Ocean Hill–Brownsville conflict involved white radical students, Black Panthers, the Peace and Freedom Party, the Freedom and Peace Party, CORE, SNCC, the Republic of New Africa, the Black Caucus within the UFT, a white coalition within the UFT, religious groups, the NAACP, the Progressive Labor Party, the Urban League, the Jewish Teachers for Community Control, and the like. Here was a group of organizations with divergent ideologies coming together around a single issue. Two groups were missing: the white liberal establishment and their overt racist bedfellows. The self-righteousness of the up south was exposed and later confirmed when Congress took action to balance the racism of the up south with that of the down south as it related to school desegregation.

This shift in white awareness exposed the unions as down south liberals and up south racists. It turned white liberalism into an up south luxury and white conservatism into an ally of black progress. The silent majority is the counterpart of the vocal black minority—now supplemented by white youth groups. The incipient violence of the hard hats and the chickenheartedness of white liberals have begun to teach this society what minorities have long understood: The scourge of this country is the violence of white people toward each other—not just toward blacks. Blacks now understand why white liberals have always cautioned them against the use of violence. White liberals understand fully the strength of white violence. It can kill you.

The most powerful lesson learned and the essential meaning of the movement is that minorities are saying something about all education and the society in their efforts to control their schools. They are saying that their lives are worth living and dying for. They are saying that they want to learn to be human. They are saying that they are not going to replicate the mistakes of whites and pass them on to their offspring. They are saying that they will learn despite the schools. They are saying that they know that they can achieve against great odds. They have survived nearly four hundred years of a systematic design to destroy them. The design failed—or else I would not be standing here today. My message: black communities so involved began to convince *themselves of their own worth.* They began to feel better about themselves and the capabilities. This turns out to be much more a confirmation of a concealed reality than it is a discovery of new information.

The major challenge of the community control movement is to develop the kind of changes in behavior, philosophy, attitudes, and perceptions that will persist over a period of time. In the final analysis, it is a movement to get individuals to confront their institutions first, to perceive themselves as being inseparable from their membership in a group, and to learn to function in humane ways. It has provided a growing number of theoreticians with the impetus to replace scientific colonialism with scientific humanism. It has provided opportunities to learn how to educate children without punishing them; to link the classroom to the real world; and to remove the invisible wall between school and community. Importantly, it has made the toughest job in America—that of being black—a compelling necessity to achieve the skills to accredit oneself and to be in control of one's own self-determination. Remember, everybody is somebody.

Bibliography on Community Control

Aronowitz, S. "The Dialectics of Community Control," *Social Policy* (May–June 1970), pp. 47–51.

Baraka, Imamu Ameer (Leroi Jones). "A Black Value System," *Black Scholar* (November 1969), pp. 54–60.

Berube, M. B. and M. Gittel. *Confrontation at Ocean Hill–Brownsville.* New York: Frederick A. Praeger, Inc., 1969.

Covello, L., S. Beagle, and L. Bock. "The Community School in a Great Metropolis" in *Education for Better Living: The Role of the School in Community Improvement.* Washington, D.C.: U.S. Government Printing Office, 1957. Pp. 193–212.

Gittel, M. and A. G. Hevesi. *The Politics of Urban Education.* New York: Frederick A. Prager, Inc. 1969.

Goldberg, G. S. "I.S. 201: An Educational Landmark" *IRCD Bulletin,* Vol. 2, No. 5 and Vol. 3, No. 1 (Winter, 1966–67), pp. 1–9.

Hall, R. *An Open Letter to Black Educators: White Teaching Can't Motivate Our Children.* New York: Afram Associates, Inc., Feb. 5, 1969. 2 pp.

Hare, N., A. Lynch, and P. Wilcox. *Black Power and Public Education.* New York: National Association for African American Education, 1970.

I Ain't Playin No More (A Film). Newton, Mass.: Educational Development Center, 1970. Also available through Afram Associates, Inc., 103 East 125th St., Harlem, N.Y. 10035.

Kent, D. B., Jr. *Proceedings of the First National Association of Afro-American Educators Conference.* New York: National Association for African American Education, August, 1968. 77 pp.

Levin, H. M. (ed.). *Community Control of Schools.* Washington, D.C.: The Brookings Institution, 1970.

Mamis, N. and P. Wilcox. *Toward a Policy Guide and Handbook for Community Control/Decentralization.* New York: Afram Associates, Inc., February 25, 1970. 5 pp. + Appendix.

Means, F. E. *Teachers Unions: Yes—Poor Children: No.* New York: Afram Associates, Inc., May, 1970. 9 pp.

Melrod, M. *A Bibliography on Decentralization.* Milwaukee: Institute of Governmental Affairs, University Extension, The University of Wisconsin, 1970.

Montgomery, M. L. (ed.). *New Perspectives: Findings of a Five Day Black University.* New York: National Association for African American Education, April 15, 1970.

Nyerere, J. K. *Education for Self-Reliance.* Washington, D.C.: Information Bulletin, Embassy of the United Republic of Tanzania, March, 1967.

Poverty, Participation, Protest, Power and Black Americans: A Selected Bibliography for Use in Social Work Education, compiled by Charlotte Dunmore. New York: Council of Social Work Education, 1970.

Riessman, F. and A. Gartner. *Community Control and Radical Social Policy.* May–June, 1970, pp. 52–55.

Rubinstein, A. T. *Schools Against Children: The Case for Community Control.* New York: Monthly View Press, 1970.

Seabrook, L. W. "A New Experiment in Black Education," *Social Policy* (May–June 1970), pp. 61–63.

Sizemore, B. A. "Separatism: A Reality Approach to Inclusion?" in *Racial Crisis in American Education,* ed. Robert L. Green. Chicago: Follett Educational Corporation, 1969. Pp. 249–279.

Spencer, D. and C. E. Wilson. *The Case for Community Control #1.* New York: I.S. 201 Complex, 1968. (mimeo)

———. *The Case for Community Control #2.* New York: I.S. 201 Complex, December 1, 1968. (mimeo)

Tricknology or Technology: White Teachers in the Black Community. New York: Afram Associates, Inc., June 8, 1970. 4 pp. (mimeo)

Walton, S. F., Jr. *The Black Curriculum: Developing a Program for Afro-American Studies.* East Palo Alto, Calif.: Black Liberation Publishers, 1969.

———. *Education for Humanization and Social Responsibility.* Sausalito, Calif.: Martin Luther King, Jr., School, 1970.

Wasserman, M. *The School Fix, N.Y.C., U.S.A.* New York: Outerbridge and Diensffrey, 1970.

Weinberg, M. (ed.). *W.E.B. DuBois: A Reader.* New York: Harper and Row, 1970.

What Is Community Control of Schools: A Citizen Fact Sheet. Pittsburgh: Training Center, Community Action Pittsburgh, Inc., 1968. (mimeo)

Wilcox, P. "The Community-Centered School," in *The Schoolhouse in the City.* New York: Frederick A. Praeger, Inc., 1968. Chap. IX.

———. "The Community-Centered School," in *Radical School Reform,* ed. Ronald and Beatrice Gross. New York: Simon and Schuster, 1969. Pp. 125–138.

———. *The Crisis Over Who Shall Control the Schools: A Bibliography.* New York: Afram Associates, Inc., December 27, 1968. (Vol. I, No. 1) (mimeo)

———. *Decentralization: A Listing of Some Ideas.* New York: Afram Associates, Inc., October 5, 1968. 8 pp. (mimeo)

———. "Integration or Separatism: K-12," *Integrated Education: Race and Schools,* 43, III:I (January–February 1970), 23–33.

———. "The Meaning of Community Control," in *Foresight,* 1, 3 (1969).

———. *On The Way to School-Community Control: Some Observations.* New York: Afram Associates, Inc., February 20, 1970. 4 pp.

———. "The Thrust Toward Community Control of the Schools in Black Communities," in *Racial Crisis in American Education,* ed. Robert L. Green. Chicago: Follett Educational Corporation, 1969. Pp. 300–318.

Wilson, C. E. *Guidelines and Expectations for Community Consultants.* New York: Afram Associates, Inc. Undated. 7 pp. (mimeo)

———. "Year One at I.S. 201," *Social Policy* (May–June 1970), pp. 10–17.

Wittes, G. and S. "A Study of Interracial Conflict: Researchers Study Factors Surrounding the Explosive Situation in Troubled High Schools," *American Education* (June 1970), pp. 7–10.

Max Wolff, known as one of the founding fathers of the concept of an educational park, discusses the potential value of such a clustering of facilities and resources for bringing equal quality education to all students in an area. Wolff explores the idea of a large school with a large student population on a centrally-located campus from several vantage points. To bring neighborhood schools up to the quality of the best school in the system would result, he feels, in a costly duplication of program, staff, facilities, and resources. Economies can be effected through better utilization of costly facilities such as labs, gyms, studios, and libraries. Individual students can prosper within a large pupil population by application of flexible design and organization. A central location can result in many children needing no transportation, and, where new systems of urban transport are needed, they can be used by and benefit the population as a whole.

THE CONCEPT OF AN EDUCATIONAL PARK

Max Wolff

The critical issues of quality and cost, of size, of travel, and of site are examined by Wolff. Setting forth standards for site selection, he indicates that racial, ethnic, and socioeconomic integration possibilities are probably the most critical considerations. Urban-suburban cooperation will be necessary if racial isolation is to be overcome. Wolff sees an educational park providing the kinds of flexibility in architectural design that enhance possibilities for innovative programs. By offering a greater variety of options, more individualized education can be provided in such a park. The scale and organization of a park can provide a richly varied educational environment in which individual specialization is possible. Staffing and resources can be made available as needed to a greater extent than in a smaller neighborhood school. Resources and programs can be provided for students with special problems as well as those with special handicaps. For Wolff, the very rich variety of students, representing the heterogeneous mix of society, is educative in itself.

The educational park has become a symbol of community participation in planning, in determining how the framework can suit the particular situation and how the program can meet communal needs. In addition to the possibilities of decentralization and community control, Wolff sees an educational park facilitating a variety of adult education possibilities—

educational, scientific, cultural, recreational, and commercial activities. The park can serve as the center of a broad-based community school for children, youth, and adults; it can and should be in active use during most hours of the day and night. Wolff would tie the educational center to a health center as well.

An educational park will, of course, cost a good deal of money. However, Wolff argues that each community must weigh the actual dollar costs against the benefits received, not only for the students but for every citizen and for the community as a whole. Such an evaluation, he feels, will indicate that cost-benefits are clearly in favor of the educational park. Taking the problems of the urban school as currently designed into account, the educational park provides a firm basis for innovative, quality education.

Max Wolff is Professor of Educational Sociology at Long Island University.

THE CONCEPT OF AN EDUCATIONAL PARK

Max Wolff

An educational park is a large clustering of educational facilities which brings together the school population of many small neighborhoods, thereby serving the children and all the citizens of a larger urban community. Within this fundamental notion, there can be tremendous variation, allowing each community to determine its own objectives and specific forms. There are, nevertheless, certain characteristics which are basic to all educational parks. Chief among these is the notion of a large school with a large student population drawn to a centrally-located campus from many smaller neighborhoods.

Can we bring equal quality education to all the students of the metropolitan areas simply by upgrading each neighborhood school to the quality of the best school in the system? Duplicating the best educational facilities, the best teacher staff, and the most enriched curriculum at numerous neighborhood schools is costly and wasteful and of doubtful practicality. Such upgrading of all neighborhood schools in a community will inevitably cost more than building one educational park.

With the creation of an educational park, substantial economies are effected through the full-time use of auditoriums, gymnasiums, libraries, science buildings, and art and music facilities. Where such facilities exist at all in neighborhood schools, they are idle a good part of the time. A cluster of 25 schools does not need 25 auditoriums and gymnasiums, but 25 fully equipped neighborhood schools do. Instead of the construction of school after school with identical and often inadequate facilities, the educational park can combine the buildings on a single site and place facilities such as administration, gyms, libraries, and health centers in a central location serving all the classroom units. But most important, considering costs versus benefits, the educational park can provide greater benefits to the students, the teachers, the parents, and the community at large.

The question is asked: How can the individual student prosper within a large, centrally-located school with a large student population? The answer is to be found in the organization of the individual schools within the park, for size is not a factor of numbers alone—many of us live in cities of millions, yet operate in very personal and individual ways—but rather a consequence of design and organization. A park is not one giant schoolroom; rather it can provide the flexible arena within which educators, architects, space designers, parents, and the community will organize and administer a system which will assure quality education of and for each child.

In many of the communities within our cities, a centrally-located site can insure that many children will need no transportation at all while others will have to make only short trips. And wherever new systems of urban transport are necessary to get all the students and personnel to the park each morning, such a facility can also serve the community at large, offering a much needed opportunity to replan and redesign obsolete systems of urban transportation.

The site of an educational park must be chosen not only for easy access from all neighborhoods, but also in terms of its present utilization. High-density housing or commercial areas would be immediately disqualified, since massive relocation would be required. But there are many large areas in the centers of our cities that are remarkably under-utilized: enormous railroad yards, for example, provide precisely the kind of currently wasted space over which a park could be constructed. The most thorough use of our valuable urban spaces would suggest building over other blighted and sparsely utilized urban wastelands (junkyards, parking lots, bus depots) in what urban planners call "air-rights."

Yet, it is obvious that an educational park cannot be built overnight. The schools we now have will have to continue to function. In many cases, they can provide the core facilities for future educational parks. By recognizing present schools, and building gradually around them as funds and philosophies evolve, a full-fledged park can emerge. And wherever such present-day schools are so inadequate or decayed or badly located as to be totally useless, buildings and land can be sold for their value as real estate or commercial properties.

These then are some of the critical issues which must be studied when considering the construction of a large, centrally-located educational facility serving the children and all citizens of an urban community: the capacities of the educational park as compared to the limitations of the neighborhood school; the organizational design of such a large facility; transportation; the selection of the most appropriate site and the use of present school buildings; and costs in terms of benefits to the entire population. Once these problems have been defined by a given community, the educational park can then provide the arena within which the graver issues of education and intergroup relations can be confronted.

Selecting a Site

The educational park serves the children and entire population of an entire urban community. Even before a site is selected, the community itself must be defined. A given school district should be designed to include an entire larger community made up of smaller neighborhoods which can feed into the park. This kind of student population was the original intent of the "common" school and is the first prerequisite of an educational park.

In many communities and cities, new boundaries must be drawn creating a larger school district which will then comprise a heterogeneous collection of neighborhoods and students from varied socioeconomic, racial, and ethnic backgrounds. The educational park site within that district must then be located so that all neighborhoods are equally served, not only for facility of transportation but to insure a neutral, common ground for a truly integrated school.

The following criteria must be fulfilled in choosing the site:

1. It is reasonably accessible to all of the district's neighborhoods without favoring one or another.
2. It is convenient to existing transportation facilities in a nearby downtown area which is already the focus of the city's commercial and recreational activities.
3. It is not now an important commercial or residential area, so that little relocation would be necessary, and, in fact, the development of an educational park would be a boon to the appearance and value of the surrounding area.

One final consideration when picking a site for your community: a recent report by the United States Civil Rights Commission entitled *Racial Isolation in the Public Schools* has suggested that true socioeconomic and ethnic integration may depend on connecting central city and suburban school districts.

It is fundamental to the basic notion of a park that its location provide a common ground for the broadest and most realistic spectrum of our many-faceted society, neither favoring nor penalizing any group, either by where it is constructed or by what its construction displaces.

Quality Education

The first and most important question about an educational park is: what kind of education will be offered to every child in the community? Ultimately, this question must be answered by each community. An educational park is, in fact, only a frame within which education can flourish. There is no one philosophy of education necessary to an educational park, no more than there is one kind of site location or physical layout or architectural design that is *the* educational park. On the contrary, the advantage of such a park is precisely that its flexibility can provide an arena within which each community can express its own needs and desires. Consequently, the education that can take place within each particular park must be designed by the community as it considers the myriad potentialities of this innovative facility. One of the advantages the construction of an educational park offers is the opportunity for a community to evaluate needs, set criteria and priorities, and execute a new program of quality education.

The size of the park and the variety of its pupil population will allow for more facilities used in more ways for more specialized groups of students. Practically, this means that the curriculum in an educational park can be more diverse, that more courses for particular needs can be offered to each individual. What these courses are will, of course, vary from community to community, but that fundamental difference remains: a park can offer more students a greater variety of choices suitable for their individual needs, and, hence, the potential for more "individualized" education.

The school, then, must teach not only *what* but *how* to learn. It must help children to learn from their own experiences, both internal and external, to make and test judgments, to experiment with and develop skills. And, potentially, an educational park can offer more such experiences than a single school can. A child can be allowed to go his own way at his own speed, experimenting and developing special skills under the guidance of teachers and counselors, spending some time with one group, some time with another, dealing with problems, cultivating interests—all within the enormous range of a park. But simultaneously, each student is being exposed to children from all over the entire urban community, children of widely divergent socioeconomic and ethnic backgrounds, with disparate values, academic needs, and interests. As a total community school, the park can and should include all children of all levels of intelligence and all states of emotional and physical health. Individual education, but realistic heterogeneous environment: the student can proceed at his own rate according to his own ability but within a psychologically realistic community of peers.

Other kinds of programs and innovations are possible in an educational park, according to whatever educational philosophies are put into effect. For example, all primary school students might have access to a special Motoric Room equipped with giant shoes, zippers, buttons, and the like, to teach basic motor tasks and psychophysical skills; a Visual and Perceptual Training Room equipped with a variety of light and sound equipment to develop and strengthen these areas of functioning and coordination; a Dark Room, with changeable textures, pressures, smells, and currents, to develop those kinesthetic perceptions; and so on. The younger children will also be able to use the zoo, planetarium, farmyard, and hothouse facilities, which are staffed by other middle and secondary school students and which also provide certain services to the community at large. All major core facilities can be used in this way—health centers, computers, transportational systems, radio, TV, movie and theatre centers, printing shops, banks, beauty salons, special exhibits. Whatever is planned for the educational park can simultaneously become a learning experience for some, a working apprentice-type experience for older students, and a necessary and valuable service to all members of the community.

In addition, an educational park can help solve one major problem of teaching today: specialization. Whereas in neighborhood schools one teacher is called upon to teach a variety of special subjects and one specialist must make time-consuming rounds from one school to the next, an educational park can provide an opportunity for each professional to cultivate special skills. All kinds of specialists can practice their particular educational craft with a continuing large group of students, avoiding wasteful travel time or unnecessary, dissipating generalization.

One way an educational park can help young, developing teachers is to bring teacher training back to the school itself by incorporating it into the regular program of the community's school. Under the supervision of "master" teachers—successful and experienced practitioners right on the job—young trainees can be instructed, and the best teachers can be retrained where they are most valuable to the children. Since the problem of teacher training is one of the most critical in education today, this kind of on-the-spot training by proud master professionals could be one of the most important programs made possible within the scale and flexibility of an educational park. The master professional, too, has a new incentive for staying in the school system. A new and varied career in teaching is opened up that will challenge the ambitious master teacher and will attract new young talent to the profession.

Depending on community desires, the educational park can be organized according to primary, middle, and secondary levels or with no actual grade divisions at all. Paraprofessionals may play an important role in the educational park; parents and other citizens of the community (who have the time and/or skill to work as classroom aides or service personnel) can readily be organized as an integral part of the park's functioning.

Building a Park

Why build so many buildings in one place? How can such an enormous facility be coherently designed? To begin with, what are some of the most basic advantages a park could provide? Neighborhood schools today may or may not have a gymnasium, science lab, auditorium, library, or machine shop. They may or may not be able to offer courses in advanced mathematics, foreign languages, computer programming, and commercial design. The reasons for this vary from school to school. In some cases local budgets may not be able to support the duplication of physical facilities; one school's gymnasium or auditorium may go unused for long periods of the day while a nearby school remains sorely in need of such facilities. Or there may not be sufficient pupils per school to justify the expense of adding special teachers and courses to the curriculum. Two or three pupils in every school—over forty in all throughout the city—may want *and need* to study quantum mechanics or perhaps the influence of socioeconomic factors on the American Civil War, but it is not feasible for each neighborhood school to provide such courses for small isolated groups of students.

Other kinds of classes are needed by many students with special problems: the blind, the deaf, the physically handicapped. Most of these students today must be isolated from their classmates and often from their families in order to attend distant special facilities.

In fact, all sorts of students need a great variety of educational facilities to insure that they can most completely fulfill themselves within the patterns of their unique identities. The limited facilities and curriculum of most neighborhood schools today are such that a child's individual needs are necessarily subservient to whatever his local facility is able to offer. It is the child who is forced to adjust to the school, not the school to the child.

An educational park, by its very size and complexity, can offer two opportunities to deal with this problem: it can bring together a rich variety of students representing a heterogeneous mix of our society, which is educational in itself, and can avoid any stifling isolation or exclusivity; and it can justify the inclusion of a highly diverse organization of teachers, facilities, and curriculum which would not be economically feasible within a neighborhood school. In other words, the needs of one hundred students would justify not only a general science lab but also an advanced physics lab; and two hundred students in one community needing special classes in braille or sign language would justify a special curriculum within the park itself. The actual number of the total community of children who could use programs in remedial reading, special teaching machines, advanced mechanical drawing, or training in a particular musical instrument would be such that a far greater number of special programs could be offered and fully utilized as an integral part of each student's particular education.

Size then is one of the principal advantages possible with an educational park which can have a profound effect upon the educational program and design: to provide the most flexible kind of individual education for each child, boy and girl, quick and slow, literary, dexterous, artistic, athletic, scientific, linguistic, visual, technical—each according to his very special requirements, each given the maximum possible assistance in becoming his maximum self.

Design

There is no one way an educational park should be constructed. Some communities, for a start, may find that urban density and available space only permit the construction of a high-rise park, with all the special design and organizational problems that that entails. Others may have sufficient space to spread out a little with low and medium buildings.

New concepts project new designs. In building any educational park, therefore, concepts must first be defined, then the structure that can be built to serve them within a given situation will evolve. While needs will differ from place to place, certain fundamentals will remain constant:

1. The design of the park must be consistent with its educational philosophy. The details of this philosophy will vary from community to community, but the basic notion of all parks is to provide the framework for maximum possible facility and innovation in each child's individual education. The physical plant, therefore, must be built so that home schools create small units in scale with the age and development of the child, while central facilities and resources are immediately available to all students.
2. The design of the park must provide equal access to all the neighborhoods along its border and at the same time blend in size and scale with the changing environments of each of these different neighborhoods.
3. The design must respond to the needs of its community in the nature and location of those many facilities in the park that will be used by all the people in the community.

4. The design must adjust to existing transportation systems and/or be able to accommodate new facilities. For the location and plane dimensions of the park will profoundly affect the nature of such innovative facilities.

A construction as ambitious and complex as an educational park cannot be "slapped together" overnight. Educational parks will probably be built over a period of many years, evolving first of all out of existing buildings and spaces to meet immediate needs, but then responding to new developments of a changing urban environment. Every park, therefore, must have a design which can accommodate new kinds of educational methods and facilities, innovations and improvements in the design and materials of urban architecture, and many other possible changes in the community which may affect the goals and makeup of the park.

The Community and the Educational Park

With the growing realization by parents that so many of the public schools were not educating their children came a groundswell of agitation for change. The reasons for this are complex. In some cases the inertia of local administrators has preserved a status quo long in need of reform. In other situations the movement for radical educational reform has become perhaps *the* critical arena of a larger movement for greater minority group equality and opportunity. In this sense, the field of public education has fallen heir to all the militancy and immediacy of the civil rights movement, with all the social, political, and cultural ramifications therein.

Another recent and highly significant development is the unrest and involvement of the students themselves. This cannot be dismissed as "youthful rebellion" for our children's criticism and resistance to school institutions is only a part—though certainly the most serious symptom—of the community's sense of being cheated by the schools and its determination to do something about it.

Increasingly, communities have realized that the quality of their schools not only determines what kind of education their children will receive but also plays a pivotal role in the evolving goals of our society. Students want a hand, a voice in the direction of these principles and philosophies and goals; they want the school to reflect the real character, needs, and aspirations of the community. In some communities where this new concern has been most strongly felt, the school has actually helped the community to define itself. In the best examples of this kind of happening, the school has ceased to function as an isolated institution providing inadequate education, and has become a kind of town meeting, social, and cultural center—a place where people of all ages can come together to work out their hopes and needs and to see how, with professional administration and techniques, they can best be realized.

Community Participation

The degree to which the citizens of each community want—or feel that they need—to participate in the daily life of their school varies. Consideration of a project as ambitious and far-reaching as an educational park is likely to involve many diverse interests, affecting not only parents, teachers, and students, but commercial, manufacturing and retail businessmen, zoning and real estate interests, transportation for the entire community, city government in regard to administration and problems of financing, private organizations, all taxpayers, the elderly, the children—in fact every citizen of the community. Representatives of these interests, therefore, will likely want to be involved at the earliest stages of planning. They will want a voice in determining where the park shall be built, what the nature of the design shall be, the facilities, the educational philosophy, how the whole thing can be financed, and what new kinds of transportation can or should be provided that may cross the whole city.

Decentralization, for example, is something very much on the minds of many urban communities which want to overcome the distance between citizens and unresponsive administrations. In most cases, decentralization is an honest wish to give the schools back to the people, to take the administration out of the hands of a distant and giant bureaucracy and break it down into more manageable and immediate local control. Many communities may discover, therefore, that an educational park can provide precisely the vehicle they need for real decentralization. Giant urban conglomerates like, for example, New York City, Philadelphia, Los Angeles, Washington, D.C., and Chicago, with hundreds of schools, have been controlled by one remote and isolated board of education. One educational park could easily serve the thousands of children in each subdistrict of such a city, thereby providing all the advantages of a park over existing neighborhood schools, while at the same time decentralizing the administrative control into independent local districts.

It is up to each community to determine how the framework of the park can suit its situation: In larger sprawling cities, many parks can be the instruments of decentralization and more localized control; in smaller urban areas where decentralization is not an issue, one or two parks can serve an entire community. In any case, not the size but rather the zoning and administrative design of an educational park will determine how it shall function and to what extent it will or will not be controlled by the community. And this must be determined by the people of the community themselves.

The questions and concerns about community control indicate that a growing number of communities want not only to have a hand in setting basic educational policies but also a system whereby they can be sure these policies are being implemented. This kind of involvement must be very carefully defined, since it necessarily involves the close cooperation of administrators, supervisors, teachers, and students themselves.

Community Services

The second major area of interaction between the educational park and the community is in the specific working services such a large assemblage can offer the community above and beyond the education of its children. The local neighborhood school may have an auditorium for an occasional adult concert or a gymnasium for some adult sporting events. But a park can offer facilities, activities, and opportunities for innovation: not just the usual PTA meetings or semi-pro basketball games—but new kinds of educational, scientific, cultural, and commercial activities made possible within the frame of the park and evolving from specific programs and needs of each community.

This means, to begin with, that the park should be in active use during most hours of the day and night; that not only predictable facilities like auditoriums be available, but that libraries, laboratories, workshops, and the like should be incorporated into programs for adult education, cultural events, and recreation. Often today, school authorities prohibit the use of such facilities after school hours or for non-school purposes during school hours. The expense and administrative complications are too great, they say. Perhaps within the budgetary and personnel limitations of neighborhood schools this is true, but an educational park—with its economy of centralized core resources plus a more diversified staff responding to particular group needs—can make maximum use of all facilities and programs at all possible times.

This kind of daily contact is important in the establishment of community rapport and involvement. Any citizen who makes regular use of the park or whose life is in some way bound up with the cultural, educational, or recreational life of this community center is going to be involved in its welfare. He is going to be committed to the park and consequently to quality public education, and to the successful operation of an ambitious community school.

Another broad area of park-community involvement can be the relationship between certain community activities and various specialized educational programs made possible within the flexibilities and resources of the park. For example, the specialized areas of accounting or banking, or even the practical use of computers in such commercial activities, can be serviced, because it is very likely that the park will have computers of its own. A handful of neighborhood schools across the country, if any, now have access to a computer. In an educational park, not only the conglomerate structure but the number of interested, qualified students will make the acquisition of computers necessary and justifiable as both a practical organizational and educational asset. These computers may be used for a variety of purposes, including to help run the park itself and to help train middle and secondary students and adults in computer operations and applications. An integral part of this training in application can be the use of the computer within the local community. Various programming, data storage, billing, bookkeeping, and accounting services can be provided as on-the-spot education for students as well as a valuable aid to local businessmen who might not otherwise be able to afford computers. Thus can a valuable educational resource be extended for practical use into the community at large, benefiting and involving all interested parties in an unprecedented way.

In each case, the park's facilities for innovation and flexibility in individualized education can provide new opportunities for the students and new services for the community. The child and young adult receive practical training; the citizen has access to valuable assistance and resources, thereby involving and committing him to the continuing welfare of his community school.

The Park as a Health Center

Another park-community facility which reveals how the structure of an educational park can benefit students and citizens alike is a health center. In a neighborhood school there is very likely a school nurse available at certain special hours throughout the week. In smaller, more isolated situations there may be medical facilities located at some distance. Consequently, regular preventive medicine, diagnostic medicine, and emergency care can be administrated haphazardly at best and are largely dependent on non-school facilities. In an educational park, however, the presence of such a large population of children and teachers and non-teaching personnel would necessitate the establishment of a more elaborate and permanent medical facility, one administering regular examinations, diagnoses, and routine health services like inoculation and recuperative follow-up, and an emergency clinic. The installation of such a necessarily complex health center can be of great educational value to the students, even serving as a training ground for those interested in health careers.

The establishment of such a health center in the park can also be of enormous significance to the surrounding community. Hospital planning consultants in both the United States and England now recommend that hospitals under the size of 400 beds be gradually phased out and that smaller "neighborhood clinics" replace them throughout the community to provide emergency treatment and comprehensive health services, including prenatal and infant care, under the auspices of a nearby general hospital. This kind of neighborhood clinic and the educational park's health center could become one and the same thing.

Transportation

The problem of transportation is the principal concern of many people when first challenged by the idea of an educational park in their community. The question is: How can we transport all the personnel of the complex—pupils of all ages, teachers, paraprofessionals, administrators, and maintenance workers—to the park quickly, efficiently, and safely? The answer must be given in terms of how each neighborhood's pupils and personnel are to be equitably transported to the park and how such transportation can fit into the overall architectural scheme of the park, what the educational experience of the transportation itself can be, and how whatever new system of transportation is constructed can become a valuable service to the entire community surrounding the park.

A community school cannot favor one neighborhood or another, but must be located at a point which is equally accessible to all. The site should also be selected with a careful eye to existing transportational facilities or possibilities.

In solving the problem of transportation, the first step is to determine exactly where the pupils live. Ideally, all students who are not able to walk to the park should take one form of rapid transit: either surface bus or rail. A bus conventionally holds about sixty persons, of whom thirty can be seated, a relatively low capacity. A bus also interferes and is interferred with by regular street traffic, which can seriously affect its schedule and efficiency. Rail transit, on the other hand, generally travels on its own right-of-way and is, therefore, unaffected by street traffic. Rail transit also has a larger capacity and can be speedier by far than other modes of urban transportation.

An ideal transportation system for some urban communities would be a single rapid transit rail line weaving its way through each neighborhood, like a system of canals or waterways, ultimately feeding into the educational park. This would provide a single mode of quick, safe transportation but would require a tremendous construction at great cost and inconvenience. Consequently, the ideal system is not really feasible, and some sort of efficient compromise must be found. If the park's site is located over an existing suburban railroad line that bisects the community, it would be feasible to construct a new kind of rapid transit system in the air rights over this line, thereby creating a new transit system running straight through the entire length of the community. Pupils from various neighborhoods could either walk to this rail line or, wherever necessary, take a surface bus which would feed into the system. This would create an Educational Park Transit System (EPTS) resembling a fish skeleton, wherein the high speed rail represents the spine and the lines of the feeder buses, the ribs of the skeleton.

Travel times would compare favorably with the average time and distances in most school districts. There is no question that the initial expense of setting up such a system (or capital cost) can be great. But this high initial cost appears less formidable when compared with the enormous benefit such a system brings not only to the educational park but to the entire community. The vastly superior standards of safety and convenience for the school's children is, of course, the primary advantage. But not only does this transit system provide quick and equitable service to all neighborhoods; it also serves as an internal circulation system within the park itself. For instance, students might use a "Skybus" to move from one end of a mile-long park to another along the five EPTS stations that fall within the campus itself. But, in addition, such an ambitious transit system can have far-reaching positive effects for all kinds of community activities.

These then are the significant factors which must be considered when confronting the problem of transportation to an educational park:

1. A site which is equidistant from all neighborhoods;
2. A system of transport which can supplement present facilities with whatever new construction is necessary in a manner that causes a minimum of interference with existing traffic or physical disruption and/or relocation;
3. Creating a new system—wherever necessary—that is safe, comfortable, efficient, and perhaps even educational in itself;
4. Working this new EPTS into the park itself as an organic part of the design, providing both external and internal transport.

Weighing the Cost

The expense of constructing an educational park is a problem that must be faced with candor, serious study, and—ultimately—democratic resolution. There is no avoiding the fact that such an ambitious, far-reaching undertaking is going to cost a lot of money. To avoid that issue is to deny the true definition and intention of any educational park. What each community must evaluate, however, is not simply what the total bill in dollars and cents will be, but rather what the costs will be *in relation to the benefits received,* not only for the students but for every citizen and for the community as a whole.

This kind of honest economic evaluation requires, therefore, a new, more sophisticated way of thinking about cost. First of all, present expenses must be weighed against benefits received and benefits desired. For example, how much is really being spent on education in the community today? Is the community really getting its money's worth? Are goals being achieved? Are real benefits being reaped for student and community? Or how far are these goals, these ideal benefits from being achieved? How much would it cost to reach them within the present system? How much would it cost to upgrade each and every neighborhood school to the level of the best local facility? And are there other services the community needs, benefits other than student education that the schools could provide presently? What are they, how could they be introduced in the existing neighborhood school system—and how much would that cost?

Turn now to the educational park and weigh the two alternatives. Be sure, however, that the comparison is correctly made, for any economic evaluation must be determined within clear and consistent definition of the benefits attributable to each of the alternatives as well as the costs each incurs. Assuming then, that, on the one hand, we can choose a neighborhood school system upgraded to its maximum potential quality, let us now evaluate the alternative educational park, first of all within the definitions of existing local goals, but also in terms of any other additional benefits.

The educational park uses complexity and large scale to achieve significant financial advantages. Basically, duplication of specialized facilities is avoided while such programs and personnel are utilized at greater levels of efficiency than could ever be achieved in a neighborhood school. In addition, such facilities and programs can be specialized for particular needs in a manner that would be impossible for smaller schools. In neighborhood systems such individual use of programs and facilities would result in reduced efficiency because there simply is not sufficient school population to make optimal use of all alternatives. In short, the kind of individualized education offered through an educational park is only economically feasible within the complexity and scale of such an undertaking. It is obvious, therefore, that matching such opportunities within present neighborhood systems would be far more costly and not economically feasible.

Going beyond this initial comparison now, the scale of the educational park can permit significant changes in the relationship of the school to the community. We have already discussed various ways in which the park and community can interact and particular services the educational program can offer all citizens. Taking just one as an example: every town needs certain basic health facilities, including a local clinic for various regular medical services. An educational park can provide such health facilities within its normal operation. Consequently, instead of building two such clinics (or perhaps having none at all!) the park offers the money-saving opportunity of combining such a necessity with its own complex health facilities. Many other such services and interactions are possible.

Longer-range economies should also be considered. The educational park will stabilize school attendance, eliminating the need to build new schools as residential fashions change. Most intra-city moves are within fairly short distances, yet children have to change their neighborhood school. The educational park, with its much larger attendance zone, is impervious to such moves.

In any event these are the factors to consider when making a serious economic evaluation of an educational park's construction in your community: see what you have; decide what you want; compare what it would cost to achieve these goals within the present system (if at all possible) with the expense of constructing an educational park; weigh the costs and benefits carefully. Discuss the results of this evaluation within your community, all of whose members should participate in the ultimate choice as part of the political process by which decisions are made.

Any economic evaluation, however, remains the same, regardless of where the money will eventually come from. And the fact clearly remains that the initial costs of an educational park may be greater than simply trying to upgrade a current system. These increased costs must be weighed against the needs and potentials of your community, which are unsatisfied within the current system and which the educational park concept can begin to meet.

FABLES AND FORECASTS IN URBAN EDUCATION

Robert A. Dentler

Robert A. Dentler discusses what he views as a number of fables in urban education, fables which must be understood as such if one is to forecast the nature of urban education for the next decade or so. He examines a number of issues which currently affect education in metropolitan areas and which will pivotally influence the future.

The first pivotal issue explored is an old one—the question of quality and content of instruction. As Dentler sees it, the "spectrum of options available to those who try to teach continues to widen excitingly and dangerously." The danger is that the changes which have come about in transforming content are as easily used to miseducate as to educate. Contrary to widely held impressions, Dentler suggests that schools in the past did not adequately serve as a grand melting pot, did not welcome immigrant children, and did not do a particularly good job of educating them. In fact, he observes, the immigrant child of the past may have been served less well than today's black or Puerto Rican child.

In the Metropolitan New York area, the question of quality of instruction has three aspects. One aspect has to do with the disillusionment of upper-middle-class and working-class people with the college preparatory function served by comprehensive public high schools. Parents are finding that the guidance function is being poorly served as well. Vocational offerings in city high schools are in chaotic state. Instructional performance, Dentler observes, is as dismal in rich suburbia as in the central city, with a consequent loss of confidence in public education. There has been an outpouring of rich and new materials, but the question of educating teachers to use these abundant resources adequately has not been resolved to date. Teachers remain uncertain of how to handle new materials which are available to them.

Dentler notes that "the cement that once bound individuals and families into niches in the social structure has begun to crumble." All of the educational arrangements of the past created to insure cementing processes no longer function. From tracking schemes to dress codes, old arrangements are being rejected. What he calls "chaos concerning stratification and identity" contributes to the dilemmas of cities, those leading to pluralism and social integration or to separatism and repression. The dilemmas lead to three quests for resolving intergroup conflicts—the quest for school integration, for increased community participation, and for metropolitanism. Each of these quests have encountered difficulties, and attainment of one may result in curtailment of another.

The question of community control is viewed by Dentler as an issue which predicates the shape of the future. Noting that the public schools were really designed to serve the interests of the elite and that the reason schools are vulnerable to a power struggle is that the WASP elite is no longer in control, Dentler suggests that all of the basic premises of urban education as a subsystem require radical reconsideration. Notions such as the neighborhood school, a school district, a local tax base to sustain a district, teacher tenure, personnel selection, credentialing, accountability, budget-making processes, and other generally accepted ideas about public education are being seriously questioned.

Unless instruction improves and the erosion of public legitimacy is halted, Dentler predicts that urban schools as we currently imagine they might be may well disappear.

Robert Dentler is Director of the Center for Urban Education and Professor of Sociology and Education at Teachers College, Columbia University.

FABLES AND FORECASTS IN URBAN EDUCATION

Robert A. Dentler

The high-school-age population will most likely increase by an additional 400 per cent between 1960 and 1975. The number of high school dropouts in the United States has remained relatively constant. From 1900 to 1930, it averaged about 500,000 each year, and from 1930 to 1950 the number averaged about 600,000 a year. At the end of the 1960's, it is still at the 650,000 a year level, but what is important and what is pulsing underneath this, is the tremendous increase in the number of school-age youths in the society as a whole. Each year the high school retention rate improves and each year the number of pupils coming through increases, so that the resulting number of educational withdrawals remains relatively constant. Thus, you may improve the school program and change the laws that obligate youths to remain in school and for all that such improvements accomplish, the population stream will still dictate the shape of the problem.

Turning away from example, I would like to deal with the issues that seem pivotal in making forecasts about the future of big city and big suburban, or metropolitan area, education. These pivotal issues must be viewed in terms of certain social origins. We are not talking about random events; we are talking about regularities, the outlines of which we can barely comprehend, but which do obtain nonetheless.

Instructional Content and Quality

The first pivotal issue for the future is as old as formal education in the United States, but it has been argued in the cities and big suburbs within the last ten years with a force that would lead some of us to the mistaken impression that it is the core issue in all educational change. This is the question of the quality and content of instruction.

We are in a time in this, the post-Sputnik period, when the spectrum of options available to those who try to teach continues to widen excitingly and dangerously. Just within the last decade, we have moved beyond the time when the only songs available to teach the third-grade child were the *Marine Hymn* and *Robin Red Breast.* There is a new abundance of materials penetrating formal instruction from pre-kindergarten through graduate classrooms. These are of astonishingly high quality compared to what was available only a decade ago. Faculties at all levels have begun to struggle to bring themselves abreast of some of these abundant and impressive new materials.

This spectrum of instructional options is dangerous, as well, because it is possible to cloak any ideology, any series of political or moral objectives, within these rich materials. It is possible, in the name of civic education, to teach repression rather than civil liberties and civil rights. Such trends are already apparent in some of the major cities. It is possible to produce mechanicalism in the course of teaching the new math and the new science, and it is possible to discourage discovery and inquiry. We face the dilemma that the kinds of changes that have come about in the radical transformation of the content of instruction can *miseducate* as effectively and consistently as they can educate.

Contrary to the impression conveyed by some commentators, institutions from kindergarten through graduate school have previously done a consistently poor, inadequate, unsatisfactory job of instructing and of adapting new materials. Contrary to some impressions about the immigrant era and the grand melting pot that was supposedly part of it, there was no golden age in our urban society when the immigrant child was welcomed into the big-city school system (public or parochial) and there equipped to face the requirements of adulthood. There is no college in our cities which at one time embraced liberal, let alone general education. In fact, the quality and content of instruction at all levels in our urban subsystem have *improved* relative to an historically dismal base.

If any commentator seeks to suggest that the child of the immigrant Russian Jew or the Sicilian was well served at the turn of the century in New York, Boston, or Philadelphia, and that today this good service has dropped away, there is abundant evidence to the contrary. The immigrant child was even less well served than today's black or Puerto Rican child! It simply made less difference in his adult family or work life than it makes in the lives of young black and Puerto Rican adults today.

Three Aspects of Quality

The quality of instruction in urban high schools has received profound public and professional scrutiny. In the New York metropolitan region, the quality question has three aspects. One of these has to do with the disillusionment that upper-middle-class, and now working-class, parents are experiencing with the college prep function of the comprehensive high school. As the competition for scarce slots in the colleges intensifies, parents are beginning to ask about the calibre of the offerings in the academic prep sequence. They are discovering that their children are shortchanged in various ways—that the prep sequence was designed historically to nudge along, to reinforce, and to shelter from disciplinary misconduct the fortunate few who were predestined to score in the 92nd percentile or above; and, that the school is not well equipped by virtue of this historic design to bring along other children who do not have this competitive potentiality. Parents are feeling the bind.

Parents are also discovering that the guidance counseling process leaves much to be desired. Apart from the quality of the clinical and helping process, it is increasingly obvious that guidance counselors have a certain power of licensure which, from the point of view of student protestors and parents, constitutes a stranglehold on a series of positions in our urban secondary schools. Guidance counselors are viewed as having created for themselves, by their licensing approach, a dear market, and in the process they have not improved their ability to transmit pertinent placement information. Yet, this placement information is more and more desperately needed by the youth they seek to serve.

In addition, city high school vocational offerings are in a chaotic state. The Center for Urban Education study of the vocational school systems of some cities, for example, found that vocational high school education was once neatly attuned to the industrial and commercial manpower requirements of each locality. But these requirements have changed so dramatically in the face of automation and the relocation of industry that vocational instruction has been left high, dry, and out-of-date. There has been an earnest and costly scramble inside the school establishment to revise this condition, but there has not been the ingenuity that would allow a readjustment. Furthermore, a radical reorganization would dislocate the faculty and staff in question; yet it is this staff that has been asked to carry out the reorganization.

At the elementary level, similar conditions in the economy and population have produced a public loss of confidence in public education that has reached its pitch in the case of New York City, but which may be found in other localities, far out in Suffolk County and up into the valleys of Connecticut as well. Here the problem is that the teacher appears to be incapable of fulfilling basic expectations. The Center for Urban Education has conducted public opinion polls among parents. Such polls indicate that the teachers are viewed as not accomplishing the task which is to bring about early basic literacy for 85 per cent of the incoming children. It is the civil rights movement which lifted the rock of performance on this literacy question and found failure underneath.

But those of us who have pursued this discovery beyond the ghetto have found it equally common in the well-heeled suburban districts. The instructional performance is as dismal in rich suburbia as in the inner city. It is simply that there are more children in suburbia who achieve early absolute literacy as a result of antecedent background advantages. The quality of instruction is not better. The teacher is equally unprepared to come abreast of the new science and the new math.

Abundant and rich as the new material offerings are, no one has faced the question of how to educate the teacher except by sending her to conferences and workshops and obliging her to go back to college—when colleges are themselves incapable of preparing their own faculties. So the teacher remains isolated and uncertain of how to take on instructional tasks in science and math, in spite of a dazzling array of new possibilities which children hunger for, parents are intrigued by, and teachers are fascinated with (if only they knew how to make use of them!). So, too, in the case of social studies. The rudiments of anthropology, economics, and political science, for example, have yet to penetrate most of our big-city high schools—again, in spite of increasingly rich materials.

Crises of Identification and Stratification

The binding dimensions of American urban social life have long been what the urban sociologist Scott Grier calls "the three binding rods" of ethnicity, occupation, and life style. We have only recently come out of a time during which having information on any one of these subjects allowed one to predict with some accuracy the circumstances of the individual on the other two. Today it is possible to be impoverished and to maintain life styles that are upper-upper-class. You can see this in our suburban schools and in our religious groupings that no longer follow the occupation or life styles peculiar to certain social strata.

As a result, the cement that once bound individuals and families into niches in the social structure has begun to crumble. We face a two-edged crisis of stratification chaos, on the one hand, and identity chaos, on the other. The important thing about the stratification chaos —that is, the fact that you cannot tell where somebody is in the pecking order any longer—is that Americans, following their profound allegiance to Adam Smith, still settle for an income indicator on this subject. You can drop away educational attainment, you can drop away occupation: cash or credit will do. So we are now stratified in our urban societies in terms of cash income or credit potential. The residues from past arrangements of occupation and education have crumbled, but the cash basis of the structure is flourishing and is of importance from day to day for individual families. This is the motif that pulses clearly through a crumbling organizational arrangement.

The identity crisis concerning the educational subsystem is one in which one or another of the binding rods—that is, ethnicity, life style, or occupation—is chosen and held on to for dear life by the individual youth. He decides that his personality consists of, or is going to be manifest in, his life style, or in his religious membership, or in his occupational aspiration. For example, "squares", to youths, are persons who are obsessed (as are "straights") with their occupational futures, their careers.

All of the arrangements of urban education which have been built up historically to reinforce the social niches created by these binding rods and to insure the cementing processes around them are now suffering severe loss of function. The grouping and tracking systems that professional educators still employ with elaborate psychological rationalizations are seen through by the children they are used on and are rejected as making no contribution to their development. Codes of manners and of dress and little day-to-day issues of mundane morality and conduct are rejected on similar grounds as immaterial to the acts of teaching and learning. Follow the absurd debates about the length of hair that may be worn to school, or the length of skirt, or whether you can wear shorts, but not shorts that were once long pants that have been cut off, and keep in mind that you are seeing the gulf between the professionals, who historically were conditioned to serve and reinforce these strata niches, and their clientele, who no longer behave in terms of these conditions.

A nihilistic solution to this identity chaos is not adequate. Some codes are required, but they can no longer refer to the ways in which people used to be stratified. In the absence of new guidelines, the city educators do not know what to do except to reassert their older notions. Perhaps we should admire the ingenuity that enables some city and suburban high school principals to somehow walk the resulting tightrope, to somehow explain away, day after day, the contradictions inherent in their outmoded codes and supervisory obligations. Their resilience is something to be studied and celebrated, not because it educates youth, but because it is in itself a study in occupational survival, and we are in a time when we should all learn more about this.

Dilemmas of the Cities and Three Quests

The chaos concerning stratification and identity brings us face to face with the persisting dilemmas of our cities: those that lead to pluralism and social integration or to separatism and social repression. The youth culture, even down to the sixth grade, is beginning to take pluralism seriously and to give it a vitality that those of us over forty can barely begin to comprehend. Some youths are, for example, struggling to make something very genuine out of their religious identities, and to live with one another at the same time in a socially-accepting and integrated fashion. When these serious impulses toward innovation are frustrated, the same youth absorb the hate that is directed toward them and choose, in place of pluralism, the separatism that is common to our generation.

Intergroup conflict is now so pervasive that only rather vast solutions can be suggested to even address the problem. There have been three great slogans for resolving intergroup conflict that have come up in the last two decades. The first we call *the quest for school integration.* In the New York metropolitan region, there are places where this quest miraculously persists, both in the white ghettos of our suburbs and in the black. Contrary to the impressions one might get from the media, there are still substantial proportions, shall we say 40 per cent, of the black and Puerto Rican adults in the eight burgeoning ghettos of New York City who would prefer racially and economically integrated schools. I say "miraculously," because studies of the rest of the United States, smaller cities and so on, suggest that this particular quest for school integration was forgotten pretty completely between 1965 and 1969. It is being forgotten in the New York region too. The Center for Urban Education has worked on school integration in several cities in the metropolitan New York region within the last four years where people have explained that they could not remember how this subject ever came up! They have gone blank about the origins of the subject, though they asked us in to plan for its advent. Now they say, "Couldn't we get on to something that matters educationally?" Nevertheless here are other kinds of quests persisting, not simply student transfer but quests for integration in curricular offerings, for respectful kinds of visitation. These should be cherished. The educator wonders whether any of them will survive the drift toward apartheid.

Decentralization is the next quest for resolution of the stratification and identity chaos. "Decentralization" should be translated as the *quest for increased community participation,* the progressive trend for the quest for community control. This quest has arisen not only in New York City but in dozens of large suburbs and in some cities from Boston down the Eastern seaboard and is now penetrating Ohio. It has come up and flourished in San Francisco, Los Angeles, and Portland.

Let us make plain that what is at risk here is the vitality of public confidence in education. What people want is a participatory role, irrespective of race or class. They are calling for it in order to make public education, and even higher education, believable again. I am ignoring the many other powers loading on this theme.

For many of our suburbs and most of the smaller cities in our 200 largest metropolitan areas, the issue of decentralization or increased community control will *not* take the form that it has taken in New York City. There are size and political differences, but the quest for increased citizen control at the local level will go on; it will show up in PTA circles and school board circles, for better or for worse. And, it will pervade alienated and hostile neighborhoods. As a student of decentralizaztion in New York City, I would comment that we can now see that decentralization is an extremely desirable, highly feasible solution to a variety of organizational and identity problems. It is a vehicle, as the Bundy Report asserted, for restoring connections between the alien agency of the neighborhood school and the citizens.

The third quest is just beginning to be pursued. This has more and more to do with the word *metropolitanism.* On the surface this trend seems contradictory. There seem to be contradictions between decentralization and regional metropolitanism of education. Yet for the planner, these are not logically mutually contradictory. It is possible to resolve citizen participation locally and to build local identification with services. It is possible at the same time to integrate socially and to fuse districts together into a regional scheme. That is the planner's vision; but the decision-maker's problem and the citizen's problem is something else. To get any one of these or any part of several of them together means that one may have to sacrifice some vital objectives in the process.

The Struggle for Control

The community control quest really brings us to the final pivotal issue which predicates the shape of the future. This is the one that endures throughout the history of American education; the struggle for control. Never mind community power; just think about the struggle over who controls what. This has been a latent struggle decade after decade since the early nineteenth century; now it is just more pitched and manifest in our city and suburban schools than ever before.

In contrast to what is taught in some history of education courses, public education was designed originally for, and controlled on behalf of, the white Anglo-Saxon Protestant elite in towns along the Northeastern seaboard. This elite was stimulated, not by the democratic dream of Horace Mann, but by what they believed to be the need to create an institution that would exclude the Irish and would bring a blessing from "little labor" (which became a big blessing later on from Big Labor as unionism among teachers matured). This is a harsh interpretation, but you have to go back and read who was teaching in our schools in what is the dark age of public education—the period after Horace Mann and before World War I—to see the way in which the institution was designed to serve the interest of this elite.

Locally, public education has operated on the "balanced-ticket premise." The board contained one of each ethnic or social status type characteristic of the district, and whichever group was more characteristic had more than one representative. In addition, the system has built up historically, in its preservation of control for the WASP elite, a civil service system, designed to prevent patronage to minority groups, which has its own merits and demerits. The uniform curriculum was designed to insure the easy mobility of children of the middle and upper middle classes into positions of control in their generation.

Currently, the schools are vulnerable to power struggles because the WASP elite is no longer in control and locally balanced tickets are no longer balanced. Historical lags in the balancing act produce a kind of vacuum into which struggling power advocates are bound to rush. You are familiar with this. But what may not be understood is the speed with which all the premises formerly characteristic of urban education as a subsystem have declined in their perceived validity.

For example, the classroom, as the WASP version of the final sanctuary, is now under radical reconsideration. The classroom can no longer prevail even if it conforms to the fantasies of the United Federation of Teachers. Notice in the Ocean Hill–Brownsville dispute the insistence on reassigning each "cave dweller" to her own "cave" once again. Team teaching, individualized instruction, and new materials have provided the ammunition for power struggles which have opened to question the notion that we should retain schools which are shaped like factories, within which there are a series of caves which guarantee, in turn, academic freedom based on administrative or public indifference.

Questioning Some Old Premises

The isolated school itself is subject to attack in the course of the struggles for new allocations of power. There are also neighborhood school advocates who have recently rediscovered the beauties of the neighborhood school. There are also those who have discovered the ugliness of the neighborhood school and unmasked its isolation. The Center has made some tests in two urban school districts and discovered that "isolation" is indeed the proper term. Teachers do not know the names of teachers in the school only two blocks away. They may have one meeting a year in common in some of our cities, but that is all. Districting itself, boundary-making, is now up for grabs. These are not merely issues that have been subject to contests in the quest for school integration; they are now subject to radical reconsideration in terms of community control, and they will be reexamined again in terms of the quest for regional control.

What is a school district? We cannot remember anymore. The only thing we know is that we should probably retain one; or that we should probably discard it and merge with another. And, either way, the criterion for setting the boundary has disappeared as the validity of the entire system has now become subject to examination.

What is the local tax base that should sustain a district? The report for the Newark Board of Education from Research for Better Schools, Inc., lists all the kinds of taxes that New Jerseyites *might* devise to assess themselves in order to finance public education in Newark. As you read down the list, you lose the ability to recall why there is no income tax in New Jersey to begin with. Then you cannot assess the merits of one source of new revenue against another, the debate is strung so wide. When we are without boundaries, suddenly we are subject to new power claims as somebody else wishes to redraw new boundaries.

Teacher tenure and replacement became subject to radical reconsideration long before the Ocean Hill–Brownsville dispute. Of course, the economics of teacher tenure are now under sustained attack and reexamination. Certification is subject to the onslaught of returning veterans by the thousands who are looking for jobs and who believe they have something to teach, and of Peace Corps and VISTA returnees and rejects as well.

Underneath is the more basic question which again has been raised by the civil rightists; namely, does one need paper credentials to take part in educating the young? What are those credentials, if they are needed? Why is it that some people who earn them seem to have a trained incapacity for rearing the young anyway? Or is it a native incapacity? And underneath these claims are all the groups that would like to introduce not merely uncertified personnel but personnel who are chosen exclusively by themselves. The basic challenge to certification is a reasonable one; it asks why we ever got into this certification routine in the first place. But we do not know how to answer the question we have raised.

"Accountability" is extremely fashionable in all of the big cities of the urban North. It is a word which was drawn over from industry and from McNamara, the wizard of the Defense Department. How do we know that a principal is doing a good job? How can we measure the output of teachers in city schools? Beneath these questions, again, is the quest for the power to hire, fire, transfer, replace, and assess the educational leadership.

Another premise which is open is budget-making. It is not true that the suburban schools of Larchmont and White Plains are in financial crisis. But as voters face what they see locally to be a limit on their revenue-raising capability, they ask, who is responsible for funding this institution which is in itself subject to radical reconsideration? What seem to be power struggles, then, are a series of points around which the conflicts referred to earlier as stratification problems have infused the education scene.

Forecasting the Future

In summary, I forecast the return of the urban college and university to their historical function, the building of scholarly disciplines. I forecast the continuing radical challenging of the legitimacy of the formal education system at the lower levels. I forecast continuing dissociation between the elements that once made up the binding rods of the urban community, to the point where increased student unrest and increased culture gaps between facilities and pupils are inevitable.

But by referring to instructional materials and to new curricular possibilities and by referring to the quest for integration, the quest for community participation, and the quest for regionalization or metropolitanism, I suggest that I am also assuming that schools are likely to survive these short-run conflicts. Contrary to the hopes of some critics, the school as such is likely to survive and flourish in our metropolitan area communities. It will most likely do so because the rate and quality of technological change requires a basic level of cognitive preparation, and because, embodied in the issues of participation and integration, are possibilities which will enable people to reorganize and reorder the place of schools in their midst.

In fact, when we ask adults, that is, parents, in Bedford-Stuyvesant and other ghettos to rate the priority of social problems in their midst, schools are *not* first on their lists. Underlying the open season of conflict in urban education is a residue of conviction that schools are honorable, warm, safe, and relatively quiet places in which to grow. This conviction is comparatively indestructable in the older generation, and I think it will give use the basis on which to endure the short-run conflict and survive in the future. But if instruction remains poor and public legitimacy erodes further, urban schools as we know them, or as we currently even *imagine* they might be, will disappear—and deservedly so.

Selected Bibliography on Urban Education

This bibliography is limited to publications issued since 1965. Readers are referred to two earlier selected bibliographies in *Education in Depressed Areas* (Teachers College Press, 1963) and *Developing Programs for the Educationally Disadvantaged* (Teachers College Press, 1968), both edited by A. Harry Passow. Information about unpublished materials and journal articles is available from the Educational Research and Information Center, Informational Retrieval Center on the Disadvantaged (ERIC-IRCD) at Teachers College, Columbia University, New York, New York 10027.

Allen, R. L., V. F. Allen and M. Shute. *English Sounds and Their Spellings.* New York: Thomas Y. Crowell Company, 1966.

Allen, R. and C. H. Adair. *Violence and Riots in Urban America.* Worthington, Ohio: Charles A. Jones Publishing Co., 1969.

Alloway, D. N. and F. Cordasco. *Minorities and the American City: A Sociological Primer for Educators.* New York: David McKay, 1970.

Almy, M., E. Chittenden, and P. Miller. *Young Children's Thinking: Studies of Some Aspects of Piaget's Thinking.* New York: Teachers College Press, 1966.

Anderson, D. and J. A. Niemi. *Adult Education and the Disadvantaged Adult.* Syracuse, N.Y.: ERIC Clearinghouse on Adult Education, 1969.

Ausubel, D. P. *The Psychology of Meaningful Verbal Learning.* New York: Grune & Stratton, 1963.

Baratz, J. and R. W. Shuy. *Teaching Black Children to Read.* Washington, D.C.: Center for Applied Linguistics, 1969.

Beck, J. M. and R. W. Saxe (eds.). *Teaching the Culturally Disadvantaged Pupil.* Springfield, Ill.: Charles C. Thomas, 1965.

Beggs, D. W. and A. S. Kern. *Integration and Education.* Chicago, Ill.: Rand McNally, 1969.

Bennett, W. S., Jr. and F. S. Falk. *New Careers and Urban Schools.* New York: Holt, Rinehart and Winston, Inc., 1970.

Benton, C. W., W. K. Howell, H. C. Oppenheimer and H. H. Urrows. *Television in Urban Education.* New York: Frederick A. Praeger, 1969.

Bereiter, C. and S. Engelmann. *Teaching Disadvantaged Children in the Preschool.* Englewood Cliffs, N.J.: Prentice-Hall, 1966.

Bernstein, A. *The Education of Urban Populations.* New York: Random House, 1967.

Berube, M. R. and M. Gittell (eds.). *Confrontation at Ocean Hill-Brownsville*. New York: Frederick A. Praeger, 1968.

Bibby, C. *Race Prejudice and Education*. New York: Frederick A. Praeger, 1960.

Birenbaum, W. M. *Overlive: Power, Poverty, and the University*. New York: Dell Publishing Co., 1969.

Blatt, B. and F. Garfunkel. *The Educability of Intelligence: Pre-School Intervention with Disadvantaged Children*. Washington, D. C.: Council for Exceptional Children, 1969.

Bloom, B. S. *Stability and Change in Human Characteristics*. New York: John Wiley and Sons, 1964.

———, A. Davis, and R. Hess. *Compensatory Education for Cultural Deprivation*. New York: Holt, Rinehart and Winston, 1965.

Booth, R. E. et al. *Culturally Disadvantaged: A Keyword-in-Context Index*. Detroit: Wayne State University Press, 1966.

Bottom, R. *The Education of Disadvantaged Children*. West Nyack, N. Y.: Parker Publishing Company, 1970.

Bouma, H. D. and J. Hoffman. *The Dynamics of School Intergration: Problems and Approaches in a Northern City*. Grand Rapids, Mich.: W. B. Eerdmans Publishing Co., 1968.

Bowers, C. A., I. Housego, and D. Dyke (eds.). *Education and Social Policy: Local Control of Education*. New York: Random House, 1970.

Bowman, G. W. and G. J. Klopf. *New Careers and Roles in the American School*. New York: Bank Street College of Education, 1969.

Brady, E. H. (ed.). *Seminar Selections on the Disadvantaged Child*. New York: Selected Academic Readings, no date.

Brandis, W. and D. Henderson. *Social Class, Language and Communication*. London: Routledge and Kegan Paul, 1970.

Brink, W. and L. Harris. *The Negro Revolution in America*. New York: Simon and Schuster, 1964.

Bullock, H. A. *A History of Negro Education in the South: From 1619 to the Present*. New York: Frederick A. Praeger, 1967.

Campbell, R. F.; L. A. Marx, and R. O. Nystrand (eds.). *Education and Urban Renaissance*. New York: John Wiley & Sons, Inc., 1969.

Carter, T. P. *Mexican Americans in School: A History of Educational Neglect*. New York: College Entrance Examination Board, 1970.

Cervantes, L. F. *The Dropout: Causes and Cures*. Ann Arbor: The University of Michigan Press, 1965.

Charnofsky, S. *Educating the Powerless*. Belmont, Calif.: Wadsworth Publishing Company, 1971.

Cheyney, A. B. *Teaching Culturally Disadvantaged in the Elementary School*. Columbus, Ohio: Charles E. Merrill Books, Inc., 1967.

Cicourel, A. V. and J. I. Kitsuse. *The Educational Decision Makers.* New York: Bobbs-Merrill Co., 1965.

Clark, K. B. *Dark Ghetto: Dilemmas of Social Power.* New York: Harper and Row, 1965.

——— and E. L. Gordon. *Racism and American Education.* New York: Harper and Row, 1970.

Clark, K. B. and L. Plotkin. *The Negro Student at Integrated Colleges.* New York: Natonal Scholarship Service and Fund for Negroes, 1963.

Coleman, J. S. *Equality of Educational Opportunity.* Washington, D.C.: U.S. Government Printing Office, 1966.

Committee for Economic Development. *Education for the Urban Disadvantaged from Preschool to Employment.* New York: CED, 1971.

Coons, J. E., W. H. Clune, and S. D. Sugarman. *Private Wealth and Public Education.* 1970.

Cordasco, F., M. Hillson, and H. A. Bullock. *The School in the Social Order: A Sociological Introduction to Educational Understanding.* Scranton, Pa.: International Textbook Company, 1970.

Council for American Unity. *Crisis in the Public Schools: Racial Segregation, Northern Style.* New York: The Council, 1965.

Countryman, V. *Discrimination and the Law.* Chicago: University of Chicago Press, 1965.

Cowles, M. (ed.). *Perspectives in the Education of Disadvantaged Children.* Cleveland: The World Publishing Company, 1967.

Crosby, M. *An Adventure in Human Relations.* Chicago: Follett Publishing Co., 1965.

Crow, L. D., W. I. Murray, and H. M. Smythe. *Educating the Culturally Disadvantaged Child: Principles and Programs.* New York: David McKay Company, 1966.

Cuban, L. *To Make a Difference: Teaching in the Inner City.* New York: The Free Press, 1970.

Dacanay, F. *Techniques and Procedures of Second Language Teaching.* Quexon City, Philippines: Phoenix Publishing Company, 1960.

Damerell, R. G. *Triumph in a White Suburb.* New York: William Morrow & Co., Inc., 1968.

Daniels, R. and H. H. L. Kitano. *American Racism: Exploration of the Nature of Prejudice.* Englewood Cliffs, N.J.: Prentice-Hall, Inc., 1970.

Dawson, H. *On the Outskirts of Hope.* New York: McGraw-Hill Book Co., 1968.

Dentler, R. A., B. Mackler, and M. E. Warshauer. *The Urban R's: Race Relations as the Problem in Urban Education.* New York: Frederick A. Praeger, 1967.

Dentler, R. A. and M. E. Warshauer. *Big City Dropouts and Illiterates.* New York: Frederick A. Praeger, 1968.

Deutsch, M.; I. Katz, and A. R. Jensen (eds.). *Social Class, Race, and Psychological Development.* New York: Holt, Rinehart and Winston, Inc., 1968.

Dodson, D. W. *Crisis in the Public Schools: Racial Segregation Northern Style.* New York: Council for American Unity, 1965.

Eddy, E. M. *Walk the White Line: A Profile of Urban Education.* New York: Doubleday Anchor Books, 1967.

Educational Policies Commission. *American Education and the Search for Equal Opportunity.* Washington, D.C.: National Education Association, 1965.

Edwards, T. B. and F. M. Wirt. *School Desegregation in the North: The Challenge and the Experience.* San Francisco: Chandler Publishing Co., 1967.

Elkins, D. *Reading Improvement in the Junior High School.* New York: Teachers College Press, 1963.

Englemann, S. *Preventing Failure in the Primary Grades.* Chicago: Science Research Associates, Inc., 1969.

Etzkowitz, H. and G. M. Schaflaner. *Ghetto Crisis: Riots or Reconciliation?* Boston: Little, Brown and Company, 1969.

Fagan, E. R. (ed.). *English and the Disadvantaged.* Scranton, Pa.: International Textbook Company, 1967.

Fantini, M., M. Gittell, and R. Magat. *Community Control and the Urban Schools.* New York: Frederick A. Praeger, 1970.

Fantini, M. D. and G. Weinstein. *Making Urban Schools Work: Social Realities and the Urban School.* New York: Holt, Rinehart and Winston, Inc., 1968.

———. *The Disadvantaged: Challenge to Education.* New York: Harper & Row, 1968.

Fantini, M. D. and M. A. Young. *Designing Education for Tomorrow's Cities.* New York: Holt, Rinehart and Winston, 1970.

Fasold, R. W. and R. W. Shuy (eds.). *Teaching Standard English in the Inner City.* Washington, D.C.: Center for Applied Linguistics, 1970.

Fedder, R. and J. Gabaldon. *No Longer Deprived: The Use of Minority Culture and Language in the Education of Disadvantaged Children and their Teachers.* New York: Teachers College Press, 1970.

Ferman, L.; J. L. Kornbluh, and A. Juber (eds.). *Poverty in America: A Book of Readings.* Ann Arbor: The University of Michigan Press, 1965.

Fitzgibbon, T. E. (ed.). *Evaluation in the Inner City.* New York: Harcourt, Brace and World, 1970.

Frost, J. L. and G. R. Hawkes (eds.). *The Disadvantaged Child: Issues and Innovations.* Boston: Houghton Mifflin Co., 1966.

Frost, J. L. and T. G. Rowland. *Compensatory Programming: The Acid Test of American Education.* Dubuque, Iowa: William C. Brown Co., 1971.

Fuchs, E. *Teachers Talk: Views from Inside City Schools.* New York: Doubleday Anchor Books, 1969.

———. *Pickets at the Gates.* New York: The Free Press, 1966.

Fusco, G. C. *School-Home Partnership in Depressed Urban Neighborhoods.* Washington, D.C.: U.S. Government Printing Office, 1964.

Gittell, M. *Participants and Participation: A Study of School Policy in New York City.* New York: Center for Urban Education, 1966.

——— (ed.). *Educating an Urban Population.* Beverly Hills, Calif.: Sage Publications, Inc., 1967.

Glazer, N. Y. and C. F. Creedon. *Children and Poverty: Some Sociological and Psychological Perspectives.* Chicago: Rand McNally and Co., 1970.

Gleason, H. A. *Linguistics and English Grammar.* New York: Holt, Rinehart and Winston, Inc., 1965.

Gold, M. *Delinquent Behavior in an American City.* Belmont, Calif.: Brooks Cole Publishing Co., 1970.

Goldstein, B. *Low Income Youth in Urban Areas: A Critical Review of the Literature.* New York: Holt, Rinehart and Winston, Inc., 1967.

Gordon, M. S. (ed.). *Poverty in America.* San Francisco: Chandler Publishing Co., 1965.

Gottlieb, D. and C. E. Ramsey. *Understanding Children of Poverty.* Chicago: Science Research Associates, 1967.

Gowan, J. C. and G. D. Demos (eds.). *The Disadvantaged and Potential Dropout: Compensatory Educational Programs, a Book of Readings.* Springfield, Ill.: Charles C Thomas, 1966.

Gray, S. W., R. A. Klaus, J. O. Miller, and B. J. Forrester. *Before First Grade: The Early Training Project for Culturally Disadvantaged Children.* New York: Teachers College Press, 1966.

Green, R. L. *Racial Crisis in American Education.* Follett Educational Corp., 1969.

Greene, M. F. and O. Ryan. *The School Children: Growing Up in the Slums.* New York: Pantheon, 1965.

Havighurst, R. J. *The Public Schools of Chicago.* Chicago: The Board of Education of the City of Chicago, 1964.

———. *Education in Metropolitan Areas.* Boston: Allyn and Bacon, 1966.

Hechinger, F. M. (ed.). *Pre-School Education Today.* Garden City, N.Y.: Doubleday and Co., 1966.

Heller, C. S. *Mexican American Youth: Forgotten Youth at the Crossroads.* New York: Random House, 1966.

Herman, M. and S. Sadofsky. *Youth-Work Programs: Problems of Planning and Operation.* New York: New York University Press, 1967.

Hickerson, N. *Education for Alienation.* Englewood Cliffs, N.J.: Prentice-Hall, 1966.

Hill, R. and M. Feely (eds.). *Affirmative School Integration: Efforts to Overcome De Facto Segregation in Urban Schools.* Beverly Hills, Calif.: Sage Publications, Inc., 1967.

Hillson, M.; F. Cordasco, and F. P. Purcell. *Education and the Urban Community: Schools and the Crisis of the Cities.* New York: American Book Co., 1969.

Horn, T. D. *Reading for Disadvantaged: Problems of Linguistically Different Learners.* New York: Harcourt, Brace and World, 1970.

Humphrey, H. *Beyond Civil Rights: A New Day of Equality.* New York: Random House, 1968.

———. (ed.). *Integration vs. Segregation.* New York: Thomas Y. Crowell Co., 1964.

Hunnicutt, C. W. (ed.). *Urban Education and Cultural Deprivation.* Syracuse, N.Y.: Syracuse University Press, 1964.

Hunt, J. McV. *The Challenge of Incompetence and Poverty: Papers on the Role of Early Education.* Urbana, Ill.: University of Illinois Press, 1969.

Janowitz, G. *Helping Hands: Volunteer Work in Education.* Chicago: University of Chicago Press, 1965.

Katz, I. and P. Gurin (ed.). *Race and the Social Sciences.* New York: Basic Books, Inc., 1969.

Keach, E. T., Jr.; R. Fulton, and W. E. Gardner (eds.). *Education and Social Crisis: Perspectives on Teaching Disadvantaged Youth.* New York: John Wiley and Sons, Inc., 1967.

Kendall, R. *White Teacher in a Black School.* New York: Devin-Adair, 1964.

Kensington, K. *The Uncommitted: Alienated Youth in American Society.* New York: Harcourt, Brace and World, 1965.

Kerber, A. and B. Bommarito (eds.). *The Schools and the Urban Crisis.* New York: Holt, Rinehart and Winston, Inc., 1965.

Klopf, G. and G. W. Bowman. *Teacher Education in a Social Context: A Study of the Preparation of School Personnel for Working with Disadvantaged Children and Youth.* New York: Mental Health Materials Center, 1966.

——— and I. Laster (eds.). *Integrating the Urban Schools.* New York: Teachers College Press, 1963.

Kramer, Ralph M. *Participation of the Poor.* Englewood Cliffs, N.J.: Prentice-Hall, 1969.

Kvaraceus, Wm. C. et al. *Negro Self-Concept: Implications for School and Citizenship.* New York: McGraw-Hill, 1965.

———, J. S. Gibson, and T. J. Curtin (eds.). *Poverty, Education, and Race Relations: Studies and Proposals.* Boston: Allyn and Bacon, Inc., 1967.

Lanning, F. W. and W. A. Many. *Basic Education for the Disadvantaged Adult: Theory and Practice.* Boston: Houghton Mifflin Co., 1966.

LeMelle, T. J. and W. J. LeMelle. *The Black College: A Strategy for Relevance.* New York: Frederick A. Praeger, 1969.

Levenson, W. B. *The Spiral Pendulum: The Urban School in Transition.* Chicago: Rand McNally & Co., 1968.

Levin, H. M. (ed.). *Community Control of Schools.* Washington, D.C.: The Brookings Institution, 1970.

Lin, S. C. *Pattern Practice in the Teaching of Standard English to Students with an Nonstandard Dialect.* New York: Teachers College Press, 1965.

Lohman, J. D. *Cultural Patterns in Urban Schools: A Manual for Teachers, Counselors, and Administrators.* Berkeley: University of California Press, 1967.

Loretan, J. O. and S. Umans. *Teaching the Disadvantaged.* New York: Teachers College Press, 1966.

Lurie, E. *How to Change the Schools.* New York: Random House, 1970.

Mack, R. W. (ed.). *Our Children's Burden: Studies of Desegregation in Nine American Communities.* New York: Vintage Books, 1968.

Manuel, H. T. *Spanish-Speaking Children of the South-West.* Austin: University of Texas Press, 1965.

Mark, G. T. *Protest and Prejudice: A Study of Belief in the Black Community.* New York: Harper & Row, 1969.

Mayerson, C. L. (ed.). *Two Blocks Apart: Juan Gonzales and Peter Quinn.* New York: Holt, Rinehart and Winston, Inc., 1965.

Mayor's Advisory Panel on Decentralization of the New York City Schools. *Reconnection for Learning.* New York: Frederick A. Praeger, 1969.

McDill, E. L., M. S. McDill, and J. T. Sprehe. *Strategies for Success in Compensatory Education: An Appraisal of Evaluation Research.* Baltimore: The Johns Hopkins Press, 1969.

McGeoch, D. et al. *Learning to Teach in Urban Schools.* New York: Teachers College Press, 1965.

McGrath, E. J. *The Predominantly Negro Colleges and Universities in Transition.* New York: Teachers College Press, 1965.

Mendelson, W. *Discrimination.* Englewood Cliffs, N.J.: Prentice-Hall, Inc., 1962.

Miller, E. W. (ed.). *The Negro in America: A Bibliography.* Cambridge, Mass.: Harvard University Press, 1966.

Miller, H. L. (ed.). *Education for the Disadvantaged: Current Issues and Research.* New York: The Free Press, 1967.

——— and M. B. Smiley. *Education in the Metropolis.* New York: The Free Press, 1967.

——— and R. R. Woock. *Social Foundations of Urban Education.* The Dryden Press, 1970.

Mink, O. and B. A. Kaplan. *America's Problem Youth: Education and Guidance of the Disadvantaged.* Scranton, Pa.: International Textbook Co., 1970.

Orem, R. C. (ed.). *Montessori for the Disadvantaged.* New York: Capricorn Books, 1968.

Moore, G. A., Jr. *Realities of the Urban Classroom: Observations in Elementary Schools.* Garden City, N.Y.: Doubleday and Co., 1967.

Moore, W. J. *Against the Odds.* San Francisco: Jossey-Bass, Inc., 1970.

Morine, H. and G. Morine. *A Primer for the Inner-City School.* New York: McGraw-Hill Book Co., 1970.

National Council of Teachers of English. *Language Programs for the Disadvantaged.* Champaign, Ill.: The Council, 1965.

Noar, G. *The Teacher and Integration.* Washington, D.C.: National Education Association, 1966.

Ornstein, A. C. (ed.). *Educating the Disadvantaged: School Year 1968–1969.* New York: AMS Press, 1970.

——— and P. D. Vairo. *How to Teach Disadvantaged Youth.* New York: David McKay Co., 1969.

Panel of Consultants on Vocational Education. *Education for a Changing World of Work.* Washington, D.C.: U.S. Government Printing Office, 1963.

Panel on Educational Research and Development, The President's Science Advisory Committee. *Innovation and Experiment in Education.* Washington, D.C.: U.S. Government Printing Office, 1964.

Parsons, T. and K. B. Clark. *The Negro American.* Boston: Houghton Mifflin Co., 1965, 1966.

Passow, A. H. (ed.). *Developing Programs for the Educationally Disadvantaged.* New York: Teachers College Press, 1968.

——— (ed.). *Reaching the Disadvantaged Learner.* New York: Teachers College Press, 1970.

——— (ed.). *Deprivation and Disadvantage: Nature and Manifestation.* Hamburg, Germany: Unesco Institute for Education, 1970.

———, M. Goldberg, and A. J. Tannenbaum. *Education of the Disadvantaged: A Book of Readings.* New York: Holt, Rinehart and Winston, Inc., 1967.

Pearl, A. and F. Riessman. *New Careers for the Poor: The Non-professional in Human Service.* New York: The Free Press, 1965.

Perel, W. M. and P. D. Vairo. *Urban Education: Problems and Prospects.* New York: David McKay Co., Inc., 1969.

Pettigrew, T. F. *A Profile of the Negro American.* Princeton, N.J.: D. Van Nostrand Co., Inc., 1964.

Rainwater, L. and W. L. Yancey (eds.). *The Moynihan Report and the Politics of Controversy.* Cambridge, Mass.: The M.I.T. Press, 1967.

Rees, H. E. *Deprivation and Compensatory Education.* Boston: Houghton Mifflin Co., 1968.

Reiss, A. J., Jr. *Schools in a Changing Society.* New York: The Free Press, 1965.

Riessman, F. *Helping the Disadvantaged Pupil to Learn More Easily.* Englewood Cliffs, N.J.: Prentice-Hall, 1966.

——— and H. I. Popper. *Up From Poverty: New Career Ladders for Nonprofessionals.* New York: Harper & Row, 1968.

Ribich, T. I. *Education and Poverty.* Washington, D.C.: The Brookings Institution, 1968.

Roberts, J. I. *Scene of the Battle: Group Behavior in Urban Classrooms.* New York: Doubleday and Co., 1970.

——— (ed.). *School Children in the Urban Slum: Readings in Social Science Research.* New York: The Free Press, 1967.

Rose, E. J. B. and Associates. *Colour & Citizenship: A Report on British Race Relations.* New York: Oxford University Press, 1969.

Ross, A. M. and H. Hill (eds.). *Employment, Race, and Poverty: A critical Study of the Disadvantaged Status of Negro Workers from 1865 to 1965.* New York: Harcourt, Brace and World, 1967.

Rudman, H. C. and R. L. Featherstone (eds.). *Urban Schooling.* New York: Harcourt, Brace and World, 1968.

Schlesinger, B. *Poverty in Canada and the United States: Overview and Annotated Bibliography.* Toronto: University of Toronto Press, 1966.

Schools Council. *'Cross'd with Adversity': The Education of Socially Disadvantaged Children in Secondary Schools.* London: Evans Methuen, 1970. 157 pp.

Schreiber, D. (ed.). *The School Dropout.* Washington, D.C.: National Education Association, 1964.

——— (ed.). *Profile of the School Dropout.* New York: Vintage Books, 1968.

——— and B. A. Kaplan. *Guidance and the School Drop-Out.* Washington, D.C.: American Personnel and Guidance Association, 1964.

Selakovich, D. *Social Studies for the Disadvantaged.* New York: Holt, Rinehart and Winston, Inc., 1970.

Sexton, P. C. *Spanish Harlem: Anatomy of Poverty.* New York: Harper and Row, 1965.

Sheldon, E. B. and R. A. Glazier. *Pupils and Schools in New York City: A Fact Book.* New York: Russell Sage Foundation, 1965.

Shuy, R. W. (ed.). *Social Dialects and Language Learning.* Champaign, Ill.: National Council of Teachers of English, 1964.

Silberman, C. E. *Crisis in Black and White.* New York: Random House, 1964.

Smilansky, S. *The Effects of Sociodramatic Play on Disadvantaged Preschool Children.* New York: John Wiley & Sons, Inc., 1968.

Smith, A. G. (ed.). *Communication and Culture: Readings in the Codes of Human Interaction.* New York: Holt, Rinehart and Winston, Inc., 1966.

Smith, B. O. et al. *Teachers for the Real World.* Washington, D.C.: American Association of Colleges for Teacher Education, 1969.

Smith, L. M. and Wm. Geoffrey. *The Complexities of an Urban Classroom: An Analysis Toward a General Theory of Teaching.* New York: Holt, Rinehart and Winston, Inc., 1968.

Stewart, Wm. A. (ed.). *Non-Standard Speech and the Teaching of English.* Washington, D.C.: Center for Applied Linguistics, 1964.

Stone, J. C. *Teachers for the Disadvantaged.* San Francisco: Jossey-Bass, Inc., 1969.

Storen, H. F. *The Disadvantaged Early Adolescent: More Effective Teaching.* New York: McGraw-Hill, Inc., 1968.

Strom, R. D. *Teaching the Slum Child.* Columbus, Ohio: Charles E. Merrill, 1965.

——— (ed.). *The Inner City Classroom: Teacher Behaviors.* Columbus, Ohio: Charles E. Merrill, 1966.

Sullivan, N. V.; T. L. Maynard, and C. L. Yellin. *Bound for Freedom: An Educators Adventures in Prince Edward County, Virginia.* Boston: Little, Brown and Co., 1965.

Suttles, G. D. *The Social Order of the Slum: Ethnicity and Territory in the Inner City.* Chicago: University of Chicago Press, 1968.

Swanson, B. E. *The Struggle for Equality.* New York: Hobbs, Dorman and Co., 1966.

Taba, H. and D. Elkins. *Teaching Strategies for the Culturally Disadvantaged.* Chicago: Rand McNally and Co., 1966.

Thomas, R. M. *Social Differences in the Classroom: Social-Class Ethnic and Religious Problems.* New York: David McKay Co., 1965.

Tiedt, S. W. (ed.). *Teaching the Disadvantaged Child.* New York: Oxford University Press, 1968.

Toffler, A. (ed.). *The Schoolhouse in the City.* New York: Frederick A. Praeger, 1968.

Torrance, E. P. and R. D. Strom (eds.). *Mental Health and Achievement: Increasing Potential and Reducing School Dropout.* New York: John Wiley and Sons, 1965.

Trubowitz, J. *Changing Racial Attitudes of Children.* New York: Frederick A. Praeger, 1969.

Trubowitz, S. *A Handbook for Teaching in the Ghetto School.* Chicago: Quadrangle Press, 1968.

Tucker, S. *Beyond the Burning: Life and Death of the Ghetto.* New York: Association Press, 1968.

Tuckman, B. W. and J. L. O'Brien (eds.) *Preparing to Teach the Disadvantaged: Approaches to Teacher Education.* New York: The Free Press, 1969.

Tussman, J. *Experiment at Berkeley.* New York: Oxford University Press, 1969.

U.S. Commission Civil Rights. *Racial Isolation in the Public Schools,* Vol. 1. Washington, D.C.: U.S. Government Printing Office, 1967.

U.S. Department of Labor, Manpower Administration. *Breakthrough for Disadvantaged Youth.* Washington, D.C.: U.S. Government Printing Office, 1969.

U.S. National Advisory Commission on Civil Disorders. *Report of the National Advisory Commission on Civil Disorders.* New York: Bantam Books, Inc., 1968.

U.S. Office of Education. *Programs for the Educationally Disadvantaged.* Bulletin 1963. No. 17. Washington, D.C.: U.S. Government Printing Office, 1963.

Usdan, M. and F. Bertolaet (eds.). *Teachers for the Disadvantaged.* Chicago: Follett Publishing Co., 1966.

Wanat, S. D. and M. R. Cohen (eds.). *Before the Fall.* Cornell University, 1969.

Warden, S. A. *The Leftouts: Disadvantaged Children in Heterogeneous Schools.* New York: Holt, Rinehart and Winston, Inc., 1968.

Washington, B. B. *Youth in Conflict: Helping Behavior Problem Youth in a School Setting.* Chicago: Science Research Associates, Inc., 1963.

Wattenberg, Wm. W. (ed.). *Social Deviancy Among Youth.* Sixty-Fifth Yearbook, Part I, of the National Society for the Study of Education. Chicago: University of Chicago Press, 1966.

Webster, S. W. (ed.). *The Disadvantaged Learner: Knowing, Understanding, Educating.* San Francisco: The Chandler Publishing Co., 1966.

Weinberg, M. *Integrated Education: A Reader.* Beverly Hills, Calif.: The Glencoe Press, 1968.

———. *Desegregation Research: An Apppraisal,* 2nd ed. Bloomington, Ind.: Phi Delta Kappa, 1970.

——— (ed.). *Learning Together: A Book on Integrated Education.* Chicago: Integrated Education Associates, 1964.

Weinstein, A. and F. O. Gatell. *The Segregation Era: 1863–1954, A Modern Reader.* New York: Oxford University Press, 1970.

Williams, F. (ed.). *Language and Poverty: Perspective on a Theme.* Chicago: Markham Publishing Company, 1970.

Wise, A. E. *Rich Schools Poor Schools: The Promise of Equal Educational Opportunity.* Chicago: University of Chicago Press, 1967.

Witty, P. A. (ed.). *The Educationally Retarded and Disadvantaged.* Sixty-

Sixth Yearbook, Part I of the National Society for the Study of Education. Chicago: University of Chicago Press, 1967.

Woock, R. *Education and the Urban Crisis.* Scranton, Pa.: International Textbook Co., 1970.

Yonemura, M. *Developing Language Problems for Young Disadvantaged Children.* New York: Teachers College Press, 1969.

INDEX